VIRGINIA WOOLF
AND THE REAL WORLD

D0865589

VIRGINIA WOOLF
AND THE REAL WORLD

ALEX ZWERDLING

University of California Press
Berkeley
Los Angeles
London

To Tony

University of California Press
Berkeley and Los Angeles, California

University of California Press, Ltd.
London, England

© 1986 by
The Regents of the University of California

Library of Congress Cataloging-in-Publication Data

Zwerdling, Alex.
  Virginia Woolf and the real world.

  Bibliography: p.
  Includes index.
  1. Woolf, Virginia, 1882–1941—Political and social
views. 2. Social problems in literature. I. Title.
PR6045.072Z99 1986   823'.912   85-24513
ISBN 0-520-05684-1 (alk. paper)

Printed in the United States of America

1 2 3 4 5 6 7 8 9

Contents

v

Acknowledgments

Of the many people who have read all or part of this book in manuscript and offered valuable suggestions for revision, I want to single out five who have helped me to reshape it significantly: Elizabeth Abel, Noel Annan, Florence Elon, Herbert Fingarette, and S. P. Rosenbaum. I am grateful also to Michael André Bernstein, John W. Bicknell, Catherine Gallagher, Martin Meisel, David A. Miller, Phyllis Rose, Brenda Silver, Peter Stansky, and Ruth B. Yeazell for more local, but equally insightful, comments. All of them have given me some perspective on what I was writing and shown me how it might be improved. At the same time, their interest and encouragement helped to make what might have been a burdensome task take on some of the qualities of a vital conversation with the kinds of readers I wanted to reach. I also want to thank Ann Banfield, Louise A. DeSalvo, Diane F. Gillespie, John Rae, Frances Spalding, and Barry Stroud for helping me to locate texts, manuscripts, or (in one case) people I needed to find.

Doris Kretschmer of the University of California Press has been a splendid editor to work with; her enthusiasm for the project as well as her patience and efficiency in seeing the manuscript through to publication helped to make my dealings with the press a pleasure. I am grateful also to Ellen Setteducati and Marilyn Schwartz for their expert copyediting; to Florence Myer for typing (and refining) more than one draft of the book; and to Mary Caraway for her care and good judgment in preparing the index.

Much of the material I use is (or was until very recently) available only in the manuscript holdings of various libraries. I am grateful first of all to the John Simon Guggenheim Me-

vii

morial Foundation for the award of a fellowship that gave me the leisure to explore the riches of some of these archives. The most valuable is of course the Henry W. and Albert A. Berg Collection, New York Public Library, Astor, Lenox and Tilden Foundations. Its unrivaled holdings of Woolf and Bloomsbury materials, and the knowledge and helpfulness of its curator, Lola Szladits, have made working there not merely indispensable labor but a delight. I am grateful also to the University of Sussex Library for permission to use the Monk's House and Leonard Woolf Papers and to Elizabeth Inglis of the Manuscripts Division for her expert guidance. I want to thank John Guido, Head of Manuscripts, Archives, and Special Collections at the Washington State University Libraries, Pullman, Washington, for letting me read through the Julia Stephen Papers and Leila Luedeking for her help with them; R. Russell Maylone, Curator of the Special Collections Department of the Northwestern University Library, Evanston, Illinois, for access to the J. M. Keynes letters in the Garnett Collection; and the Librarian of King's College, Cambridge, for the opportunity to use the manuscripts in the E. M. Forster and Charleston Papers.

For permission to quote from these materials, I am grateful to the following executors or agents of the various literary estates: Quentin Bell (Virginia Woolf, Vanessa Bell, Julia Stephen, Leslie Stephen); Trekkie Parsons (Leonard Woolf); Henrietta Garnett (Duncan Grant); the Hon. Mrs. Mabel Smith (Elizabeth Robins); The Society of Authors as Agents for the Strachey Trust (Lytton Strachey letters, © 1986); the Society of Authors as Agents for the E. M. Forster Estate (E. M. Forster letters, © 1986); The Provost and Scholars of King's College, Cambridge (J. M. Keynes letters, © 1986).

Finally, I want to thank the editors of *ELH, Novel: A Forum on Fiction, PMLA, Representations,* and the *Sewanee Review* for permission to reprint the portions of this book that originally appeared in those journals.

Abbreviations

Parenthetical citations use the abbreviations below and refer to the following works:

AROO   *A Room of One's Own* (London: Hogarth, 1967)

BA   *Between the Acts* (London: Hogarth, 1969)

Berg Diary   Manuscript of Woolf's early diaries, 1897–1909, Berg Collection, New York Public Library

BP   *Books and Portraits: Some Further Selections from the Literary and Biographical Writings of Virginia Woolf*, ed. Mary Lyon (London: Hogarth, 1977)

CE   *Collected Essays*, ed. Leonard Woolf, 4 vols. (London: Hogarth, 1966, 1967)

CW   *Contemporary Writers*, ed. Jean Guiguet (London: Hogarth, 1965)

D   *The Diary of Virginia Woolf*, ed. Anne Olivier Bell with Andrew McNeillie, 5 vols. (London: Hogarth, 1977–1984)

F   *Flush: A Biography* (London: Hogarth, 1968)

HH   *A Haunted House and Other Short Stories*, ed. Leonard Woolf (London: Hogarth, 1973)

JR   *Jacob's Room* (London: Hogarth, 1971)

L   *The Letters of Virginia Woolf*, ed. Nigel Nicolson with Joanne Trautmann, 6 vols. (London: Hogarth, 1975–80)

MB   *Moments of Being: Unpublished Autobiographical Writings*, ed. Jeanne Schulkind (Sussex: The University Press, 1976)

MD   *Mrs. Dalloway* (London: Hogarth, 1968)

MDP   *Mrs Dalloway's Party: A Short Story Sequence*, ed. Stella McNichol (London: Hogarth, 1973)

ND   *Night and Day* (London: Hogarth, 1971)

O   *Orlando: A Biography* (London: Hogarth, 1970)

P   *The Pargiters: The Novel-Essay Portion of "The Years,"* ed. Mitchell A. Leaska (New York: New York Public Library, 1977)

QB   Quentin Bell, *Virginia Woolf: A Biography*, 2 vols. (London: Hogarth, 1972)

RF   *Roger Fry: A Biography* (London: Hogarth, 1940)

TG   *Three Guineas* (London: Hogarth, 1968)

TL   *To the Lighthouse* (London: Hogarth, 1967)

VO   *The Voyage Out* (London: Hogarth, 1971)

W   *The Waves* (London: Hogarth, 1972)

Y   *The Years* (London: Hogarth, 1972)

Introduction

There was a time, not so very long ago, when books on Virginia Woolf could legitimately aim to provide a comprehensive account of her career. She seemed firmly placed: an interesting but lesser modern writer whose innovative fictional techniques were clearly important. No description of the modernist movement could afford to ignore her work. Nevertheless, her range was thought too narrow to put her in a class with the "major" writers of her time. She was not one of the *Eight Modern Authors* J. I. M. Stewart chose to canonize in his volume of that name in the Oxford History of English Literature (1963), although Kipling and Shaw were. In 1953 one of Woolf's admirers could write, quite accurately, that "E. M. Forster stands, in the general estimation, on a much higher pedestal than Virginia Woolf."[1] The order of names in the subtitle of J. K. Johnstone's book on the Bloomsbury group is significant: *A Study of E. M. Forster, Lytton Strachey, Virginia Woolf, and Their Circle.* Her work was indispensable to an understanding of stream of consciousness technique; she wrote shrewd and engaging essays for what she called "the common reader"; and she was a member of Bloomsbury. But all of this did not seem to add up to a major career, and so it was thought that a single book dealing with all aspects of her work could easily do her justice.

What changed this view was the appearance in 1972 of Quentin Bell's biography, not so much because of its interpretation of Woolf's life as because it revealed that there existed an enormous body of unpublished material of the highest quality—diaries, memoirs, letters—and suggested that these writings, once they had found their way into print, would substantially alter our sense of her achievement. In the dozen years that followed the appearance of Bell's book, almost all of this material was published. The diary and memoirs are now generally recognized as masterpieces of their kinds; the letters have given us a sense of the breadth of Woolf's interests and the variety of her engagements. During this time, many of her uncollected critical essays were also printed in book form. The changed sense of her achievement is both quantitative and qualitative. She is no longer simply the author of a handful of "experimental" novels and of some lively criticism. In fact her collected works fill a long library shelf and rival in bulk those of her energetic Victorian predecessors. But more important, the publication of these private and fugitive writings has changed our understanding of the more familiar works on which her original reputation was based. It seemed increasingly clear that the visible writings rested on a previously unknown foundation.

As a result, Woolf's life and work are now seen to have a denseness and complexity that were not apparent earlier even to her most sympathetic readers. The sheer variety of her talent and its deployment in so many different forms revealed a multifaceted writer of great range and extraordinary powers of transformation. The attempt to grasp her whole enterprise in a single book seemed doomed, as it does with any major writer. Even the biographers were forced to specialize. Quentin Bell made the astonishing decision to exclude any extended discussion of her works from his book. Phyllis Rose's biography concentrates on Woolf's feminism and shows how it shapes her literary and personal choices. Lyndall Gordon's life of Woolf focuses on what Gordon calls "the dark side" of her personality.[2] Similarly, critical studies of her work have inevitably become more pointed and selective. The pretense that all the important forces that engaged her attention could be accounted for in a single book has been quietly abandoned. Some of the best recent commentary has focused on one element in Woolf's writing—for example, her fascination with death, her treatment of mental process, her use of the literary tradition. Although there is obviously some loss in such specialization, there is also the chance that one of the many shapes this Proteus assumed can at last be seen rather than merely glimpsed in passing.

My own focus in this book is on Woolf's social vision—her complex sense of how historical forces and societal institutions influence the behavior of the people she describes in her fictional and nonfictional works. "Invisible presences" was the term Woolf coined in her memoirs for such influences. She catalogues their effects on our lives in this way: "The consciousness of other groups impinging upon ourselves; public opinion; what other people say and think; all those magnets which attract us this way to be like that, or repel us the other and make us different from that" (*MB*, 80). Her description is based on an antithesis between external and internal and suggests the likelihood of conflict between the two. She is tracing forces in the world around us that shape the life of any responsive human being; and the language she uses to describe them ("impinging," "attract," "repel") suggests a power outside ourselves that can coerce us into unwilled actions and responses. But as we will see, this way of understanding the relation between public and private simplifies the dynamics of the encounter as Woolf depicts it. Significantly, even if the passage I have quoted from the memoirs, one of the influences she is talking about is the remembered voice of her mother, which has become a part of herself. Furthermore, Woolf understood and welcomed the fact that people, working either alone or in groups, can have a powerful impact on their society—that pressure is sometimes exerted in the opposite direction. She came from a family that had been deeply engaged in such reform. Her grandfather had drafted the bill that abolished slavery in the British Empire; and she herself became involved in some of the major progressive movements of her time.

It is Woolf's account of this complex relationship between the interior life and the life of society that I want to examine in this book. By the "interior life" I mean the thoughts, feelings, needs, and fantasies that constitute the core of the self, whether or not they find expression in action or speech. By the "life of society" I mean the whole range of external forces that may be said to influence our behavior: familial ideals, societal expectations, institutional demands, significant historical events or movements that affect our lives. In my title I have chosen to call this societal life "the real world," not because it is more real than the interior life but because the term as it is commonly used conveys the sense of an ineluctable impediment to some of our deepest desires. It is real because we cannot wish it away, because its force must inevitably be taken into account. The phrase "the real world" is often used ironically, both to suggest some hostility to its rules and to record an awareness that our attempts to ignore them are futile. Woolf's vision of the "invisible presences" that influence our lives seems to register all these responses.

The word "real" is of course ambiguous and indirectly evaluative. As E. M. Forster put it in one of his essays, " 'Real' is at the service of all schools of thought."[3] Woolf's steady interest in the forces of society certainly did not mean that she considered them more fundamentally real than those that dominate our mental and emotional life. She has long been recognized as one of the great explorers of the psyche, and her novels in particular have given us a vividly realistic sense of how our minds and feelings work.[4] In addition, from early childhood Woolf lived in a world of books. She was an avid reader and a highly self-conscious artist for whom esthetic and philosophical issues were as essential and absolute as any forces emanating from "the real world." But here again, this fact has been long recognized and much explored. Finally, there is an important mystical or meditative element in Woolf's life and work that is only now beginning to be understood. Woolf's psychological, esthetic, philosophical, and quasi-religious concerns were of the deepest interest to her, and although they were associated in her mind with solitude rather than with society, she considered them as real—authentic, urgent, and significant—as the forces of public life.

Much less familiar, but I believe equally important, is her intense interest in the life of society and its effect on the individual. It is a rich subject that has not, I think, been adequately addressed. Yet in almost everything she wrote, Woolf demonstrated her concern with the ways in which private and public life are linked. In both her fiction and her discursive prose, she describes this encounter in all its complexity and variety. Her sense of the subject is deepened by her understanding of the interrelationship of the social forces at work—familial, institutional, ideological, historical—and by her awareness of the range of individual human response—internalization, compliance, rebellion, withdrawal, and all the combinations and contradictions such different reactions can produce. One of the important connections between Woolf's fictional and nonfictional writing is her persistent interest in how people—real and imagined—have negotiated the conflict between what they want and what is expected of them. Her characters are not free agents but must respond to the demands of the world around them. So Lily Briscoe, in *To the Lighthouse*, becomes conscious of Mr. Ramsay's voracious need for women's pity: "He sighed profoundly. He sighed significantly. All Lily wished was that this enormous flood of grief, this insatiable hunger for sympathy, this demand that she should surrender herself up to him entirely . . . should leave her, should be diverted" (*TL*, 235). The compulsion here is ideological: the behavior expected of women. In other contexts such external pressure is historical. In her essay "The Leaning Tower" Woolf describes the constraints affecting writers in that highly politicized decade, the 1930s: "They feel compelled to preach, if not by their living, at least by their writing, the creation of a society in which everyone is equal and everyone is free. . . . They must teach; they must preach. Everything is a duty—even love" (*CE*, II, 175). What links these passages and connects them with hundreds of others in Woolf's work is her interest in how people respond to external pressures that embody the wishes of society. The important words are "demand," "compelled," "must."

This way of conceptualizing the relationship between the self and the world is at the heart of Woolf's social vision. It is a power relationship and as such constantly subject to shifts reflecting the relative strengths of the opponents. These can change over time, in a person's life and in the life of society. Historical eras differ in the nature and intensity of the demands they make upon the individual. And a comparable change can often be seen in the course of a single lifetime: Lily Briscoe, for example, becomes more resistant, less compliant in middle age. The opportunity to record such shifts in fiction and biography is one of the reasons Woolf was so drawn to these kinds of writing. What I hope to show in this book is that the subject fascinated her from first to last; that it took many forms; and that she was as interested in the forces of "the real world" as in the responses of people whose lives were deeply affected by those forces.

The dialogue between public and private voices was carried on in Woolf's mind and in her works from the earliest stages of her career to the end of her life. The consciousness of "what other people say and think" was often represented by a monitory voice, like that of her mother. Before she wrote *To the Lighthouse*, Woolf says, "my mother obsessed me. I could hear her voice, see her, imagine what she would do or say as I went about my day's doings." Only after Woolf wrote the novel that is in some sense a reply to her mother could she say "I no longer hear her voice" (*MB*, 80–81). But she did not always emerge triumphant from such encounters: in her own life too the balance of power often shifted. "I am always hearing voices," she writes in her last, desperate letter to her sister, when she fears the return of madness (*L*, VI, 485). I have tried in this book to give a sense of what such monitory voices were saying to Woolf and to her characters and of how they were or might be answered.

PART ONE

1

The Enormous Eye

There she weaves by night and day
A magic web with colors gay.
She has heard a whisper say,
A curse is on her if she stay
    To look down to Camelot.
She knows not what the curse may be,
And so she weaveth steadily,
And little other care hath she,
              The Lady of Shalott.

It has taken us a long time to dissociate Virginia Woolf from Tennyson's portrait of the artist isolated from her kind. For much of Woolf's career, and in the decades that followed her death in 1941, the dominant image in the minds of her readers and commentators seemed to be modeled on "The Lady of Shalott." The delicate face suggested refinement, esthetic withdrawal, a commitment to the contemplative rather than the active life. The difficult novels revealed an intense scrutiny of individual psychic life and an obsession with new techniques for describing it in fiction. The mannered prose had clearly been worked—and reworked—with intense concentration. Add to this the vision of Bloomsbury as a literary fortress and the awareness of Woolf's madness and suicide, and all the pieces of the jigsaw puzzle seemed to fit together. "Her gift was for the pursuit of shadows, for the ghostly whispers of the mind and for Pythian incomprehensibility," Quentin Bell writes in the biography of his aunt (QB, II, 186). His words evoke the immured priestess in the temple of art—dedicated, solitary, out of touch with the life of her time. It is only in the past decade that Woolf's readers have come to see this portrait as at best a caricature of the author.

Like all good caricatures, it highlights and exaggerates real features. It is not inaccurate to think of Woolf as a poetic novelist interested in states of reverie and vision, in mapping the intricate labyrinth of consciousness. She herself defended the legitimacy of such fiction in her essay "The Narrow Bridge of Art" (1927), in which she predicted that the novel would take over some of the functions formerly assigned to verse: "It will resemble poetry in this that it will give not only or mainly people's relations to each other and their activities together, as the novel has hitherto done, but it will give the relation of the mind to general ideas and its soliloquy in solitude" (*CE*, II, 225). And in her first novel, *The Voyage Out*, one of her characters sets himself a similar task: "'I want to write a novel about Silence,' he said; 'the things people don't say. But the difficulty is immense'" (*VO*, 262). Thought is more important than speech in Woolf's fiction, unsorted impressions more important than systematic thinking. The new task of the psychological novelist, she writes in a well-known passage from her essay "Modern Fiction" (1919), is to transcribe the apparent chaos of individual mental life: "Let us record the atoms as they fall upon the mind in the order in which they fall, let us trace the pattern, however disconnected and incoherent in appearance, which each sight or incident scores upon the consciousness" (*CE*, II, 107).

The most complete embodiment of this vision is Woolf's novel *The Waves*. It is a book almost entirely written in soliloquies recording the thoughts and impressions of its six major characters. Conversation, observable action, setting, circumstantial reality of every kind have been virtually eliminated. What matters is the interior monologue of the isolated character. It is a novel about Silence—the things people don't say but think and feel. *The Waves* seems to me not only an attempt to record "the atoms as they fall upon the mind in the order in which they fall" but also a vision of human solitude. It is based on the feeling that even our most intimate relationships are flawed by our limited access to other minds. In *Night and Day* Woolf's heroine looks with incomprehension at the young man to whom she is engaged: "The conviction that he was thus strange to her filled her with despondency, and illustrated quite beyond doubt the infinite loneliness of human beings" (*ND*, 299). This sense of human isolation is given its definitive treatment in *The Waves*. If people are permanent strangers to one another, why should their conversation matter? It could only be a parody of "communication." Why should their families, their work, their identifying characteristics be described? They are mere facades—the illusory appearance the world sees, masking the true and very different reality of individual mental life. And so Woolf consciously ignores or obliterates ordinary fictional detail—the outer lives of her six characters. By the end of the novel we know a great deal about the mental worlds of Jinny, Susan, Rhoda, Bernard, Louis, and Neville; but we do not know what they looked like, whom they married, exactly when and where they lived, how they filled their days; we do not even know their surnames. "I shall do away with exact place & time," Woolf wrote in her diary as she was planning her book, and she protested against "this appalling narrative business of the realist: getting on from lunch to dinner: it is false, unreal, merely conventional. Why admit any thing to literature that is not poetry—by which I mean saturated?" (*D*, III, 230, 209–10).

The Waves is Woolf's boldest attempt to transform the language of fiction and so has often been treated as the logical culmination of all her formal experiments. It is an easy step from this position to the conclusion that the novel is her masterpiece. E. M. Forster hailed it as "an extraordinary achievement . . . her greatest book," though he went on to confess almost apologetically that *To the Lighthouse* was his favorite.[1] And Woolf records her husband's first reaction in her diary: "'It is a masterpiece,' said L[eonard] coming out to my lodge this morning. 'And the best of your books'" (*D*, IV, 36). There has been a persistent assumption that *The Waves* is Woolf's quintessential work, the novel—in Jean Guiguet's words—"that most faithfully conveys its author's conception of the world, and in which she includes the most completely what she thinks, feels and is."[2]

This was not, however, how Woolf herself felt about the book. She knew that it was both experimental and selective, that like all of her other works it expressed no more than a part of what she saw. And she was highly conscious of and uneasy about what she was leaving out: "Is there some falsity, of method, somewhere? Something tricky?—so that the interesting things aren't firmly based? I am in an odd state; feel a cleavage; here's my interesting thing; & there's no quite solid table on which to put it" (*D*, III, 264). Firmness, solidity, a realistic base: these are what she was forced to sacrifice in order to achieve her effect in *The Waves*. The relentlessly elevated discourse of the book denied entry to the prosaic, the comic, the particular. It was an experiment she was not tempted to repeat. And it is a striking fact that the work of her final decade is almost entirely constructed of elements *The Waves* intentionally excludes: the parodic spirit in *Flush*; historical specificity in *The Years*; intense political commitment in *Three Guineas*; the detailed factual record of an individual life in *Roger Fry*; the deliberate interlarding of the exalted with the sordid in *Between the Acts*. If *The Waves* was a culminating achievement (as in a sense it was), Woolf felt no temptation to press beyond it in the same direction. Her pinnacle was also a dead end; to go on she would have to go back.

For *The Waves* had expressed only part of her rich nature and had forced her to ignore the rest. "The world seen without a self," as Bernard describes it in that book (*W*, 204), too easily turned into an insubstantial self without a world. Yet Woolf had always been intensely interested in what her eye could see when she looked out rather than in. From her earliest years she had specialized in the art of noticing. Commanded by her socially ambitious half-brother to attend the fashionable parties she detested, she took her revenge by sitting out the dances and turning the occasion into a spectator sport. She finds herself content to adopt the role of observer, she notes in her diary.[3] To venture into the world from the secure shelter of home, to gaze and gaze upon the city's life, was a daily necessity for her, as she confesses in her essay "Street Haunting" (1930): "The shell-like covering which our souls have excreted to house themselves, to make for themselves a shape distinct from others, is broken, and there is left of all these wrinkles and roughnesses a central oyster of perceptiveness, an enormous eye" (*CE*, IV, 156). Despite the echo effect, "eye" in this passage is I think meant to be read as the antithesis of "I." For the self could be a prison; and the contemplative life lived exclusively on the heights would produce only an arid and private vision, fatal to a writer. Woolf's summary judgment of Goldsworthy Lowes Dickinson, the Cambridge don who counted Forster, Leonard Woolf, and Roger Fry among his intimate friends, calculates the price of such withdrawal from the world: "Always alone on a mountain top asking himself how to live, theorising about life; never living . . . always Shelley & Goethe, & then he loses his hot water bottle; & never notices a face, or a cat or a dog or a flower, except in the glow of the universal. This explains why his high-minded books are unreadable" (*D*, IV, 360). Even the lyric poet impoverishes his art, Woolf says, when he writes exclusively about "a self that sits alone in the room at night with the blinds drawn." She demands in her "Letter to a Young Poet" (1932) that poetry "once more open its eyes, look out of the window and write about other people," as it did in the time of Shakespeare, Crabbe, and Byron (*CE*, II, 189–90). And in one of her last diary entries, she reminds herself to "mark Henry James's sentence: Observe perpetually" (*D*, V, 357).

This interest in external reality—in the object as well as the subject—was not merely the product of Woolf's alert senses, which, as Forster puts it, "were always bringing her first-hand news of the outside world."[4] It was an expression of her conviction that "the self" was to a great extent the product of forces over which it had no control. In *Night and Day, Jacob's Room, Mrs. Dalloway, To the Lighthouse, The Years*, and *Between the Acts*, and of course in her two feminist books, *A Room of One's Own* and *Three Guineas*, Woolf is deeply engaged by the question of how people are shaped (or deformed) by their social environment, by how historical forces impinge on an individual life and shift its course, by how class, money, and gender help to determine a person's fate. The legend of the isolated invalid immured in the ivory tower of Bloomsbury has little basis in fact, as Leonard Woolf insists: "She was intensely interested in things, people, and events, and . . . highly sensitive to the atmosphere which surrounded her, whether it was personal, social, or historical."[5] Even the familiar plea in "Modern Fiction" that the novelist "record the atoms as they fall upon the mind" is based on Woolf's conception of the mind not as a free agent but rather as the helpless target of a relentless bombarding force: "The mind receives a myriad impressions—trivial, fantastic, evanescent, or engraved with the sharpness of steel. *From all sides they come, an incessant shower of innumerable atoms . . . . Let us record the atoms as they fall upon the mind* in the order in which they fall, let us trace the pattern, however disconnected and incoherent in appearance, *which each sight or incident scores upon the consciousness*" (*CE*, II, 106–7, emphasis added). The "sights" and "incidents" are not mental events but external stimuli; and Woolf's metaphors stress their compelling power.

Her critical essays make it clear that she was as sympathetic to writers who emphasized the shaping force of the environment or of circumstance as to those who explored the psyche. She sees two distinct literary traditions and honors them both. Montaigne and Sir Thomas Browne are for her the first ruminative explorers of the self, that "greatest monster and miracle in the world" ("Montaigne," *CE*, III, 26). Browne "paved the way for all psychological novelists, autobiographers, confession-mongers, and dealers in the curious shades of our private life. He it was who first turned from the contacts of men with men to their lonely life within" ("The Elizabethan Lumber Room," *CE*, I, 51). The line leads eventually to Dostoevsky, Proust, Joyce, and—many critics have said—to Woolf herself. But her interest in the opposing tradition was also quite strong. The essays on Defoe, Austen, and George Eliot in *The Common Reader* are all warmly appreciative, and all emphasize the power of circumstance in their fictions. In

Defoe, money—rather than character—is destiny: "Even the sordid subject of money, which plays so large a part in their histories, becomes not sordid but tragic when it stands not for ease and consequence but for honour, honesty, and life itself" (*CE*, I, 68). Austen's realistic portrayal of the narrow provincial world that limits the choices of her characters, her profound insight into the significance of the seeming "trivialities of day-to-day existence," is honored for its accuracy and truth: "Of all this prosiness, of all this littleness, she evades nothing, and nothing is slurred over" (*CE*, I, 151, 149). And Eliot is praised for "dwelling upon the homespun of ordinary joys and sorrows" while largely ignoring "that romantic intensity which is connected with a sense of one's own individuality, unsated and unsubdued, cutting its shape sharply upon the background of the world" (*CE*, I, 199–200).

Why has Woolf's strong interest in realism, history, and the social matrix been largely ignored? Why has it taken us so long to understand the importance of these elements in her work? The answers to these questions are complicated and will, I hope, emerge in the course of this book. But one cause can be singled out immediately—the smokescreen Woolf herself created in her classic essay "Mr. Bennett and Mrs. Brown" (1924). In this brilliant polemical piece Woolf invents a radical disjunction between "the Edwardians" (Arnold Bennett, H. G. Wells, John Galsworthy) and "the Georgians" (Joyce, Forster, Lawrence, Eliot, Strachey, and of course herself) as a stratagem for rejecting the antiquated fictional methods of the older group. The Edwardians are described both here and in the closely related essay "Modern Fiction" as "materialists"—obsessive observers who cannot keep their eyes off the object and who thus manage to ignore the perceiving subject. In their work, Woolf claims, the inner life is forgotten or effaced in the steady focus of the writer's attention on material reality: "They have laid an enormous stress upon the fabric of things. They have given us a house in the hope that we may be able to deduce the human beings who live there" (*CE*, I, 332).

The chief culprit in this group is Arnold Bennett, whose detailed descriptions of his characters' environments—their houses, their neighborhoods, their class identities, the historical moment in which they live—succeed only in trivializing the human beings who are supposed to be at the center.[6] Woolf's devastating attack on the long descriptive prolegomenon to the introduction of Hilda Lessways, in Bennett's novel of that name, seems to question the utility of such circumstantial realism as a way of illuminating character, particularly in passages like this:

> The bailiwick of Turnhill lay behind her; and all the murky district of the Five Towns, of which Turnhill is the northern outpost, lay to the south. At the foot of Chatterley Wood the canal wound in large curves on its way towards the undefiled plains of Cheshire and the sea. On the canal-side, exactly opposite to Hilda's window, was a flour-mill, that sometimes made nearly as much smoke as the kilns and the chimneys closing the prospect on either hand. From the flour-mill a bricked path, which separated a considerable row of new cottages from their appurtenant gardens, led straight into Lessways Street, in front of Mrs. Lessways' house. By this path Mr. Skellorn should have arrived, for he inhabited the farthest of the cottages.

Woolf's dismissive comment on this passage is illuminating: "One line of insight would have done more than all those lines of description; but let them pass as the necessary drudgery of the novelist" (*CE*, I, 328–29).

"Insight"—the ability to see into the inner nature of things—is here contrasted with "description"—the art of translating appearances into words. The antithesis is apparently between internal and external and places Woolf firmly on the side of writers who look within. Yet her characterization of the passage as "the necessary drudgery of the novelist" suggests the problem is more complicated. It treats description as indispensable fictional labor and makes it clear that Woolf's quarrel with Bennett is as much concerned with economy as with the choice of inner over outer reality. "All those lines of description" is a protest against Bennett's laboriousness, his need to spell out in such exhaustive detail every material fact of Hilda's world. His vision is unselective; his eye lingers and never darts; it seems to count each brick in the path.

Bennett was, I think, trying to create an image of Hilda trapped within the narrow and rigid confines of her little world, an aim that Woolf for complex reasons chose to ignore. Her own descriptive methods are very different, for example in this passage from *Mrs. Dalloway* recording Peter Walsh's "stream of visual impressions" as he walks to Clarissa's party:

Was everybody dining out, then? Doors were being opened here by a footman to let issue a high-stepping old dame, in buckled shoes, with three purple ostrich feathers in her hair. Doors were being opened for ladies wrapped like mummies in shawls with bright flowers on them, ladies with bare heads. And in respectable quarters with stucco pillars through small front gardens, lightly swathed, with combs in their hair (having run up to see the children), women came; men waited for them, with their coats blowing open, and the motor started. Everybody was going out. What with these doors being opened, and the descent and the start, it seemed as if the whole of London were embarking in little boats moored to the bank, tossing on the waters, as if the whole place were floating off in carnival. And Whitehall was skated over, silver beaten as it was, skated over by spiders, and there was a sense of midges round the arc lamps; it was so hot that people stood about talking. And here in Westminster was a retired Judge, presumably, sitting four square at his house door dressed all in white. An Anglo-Indian presumably.

And here a shindy of brawling women, drunken women; here only a policeman and looming houses, high houses, domed houses, churches, parliaments, and the hoot of a steamer on the river, a hollow misty cry. But it was her street, this, Clarissa's; cabs were rushing round the corner, like water round the piers of a bridge, drawn together, it seemed to him, because they bore people going to her party, Clarissa's party.

(*MD*, 180–81)

Clearly the difference between this passage and the one from *Hilda Lessways* is not that Bennett concentrates on the outer world while Woolf focuses on the life within. Both seem to describe external reality; but Woolf's method is neither exhaustive nor laborious. She moves swiftly from one sight to the next, constantly changing the focus from close-up to panorama, concentrating momentarily, unpredictably, on an old lady, a retired judge, then moving back or up to survey a street, the river, the city itself. The movement is not steady and inevitable, as in Bennett, but erratic and highly selective; it uses the particular to stand for the general, and it erases or slurs identifying detail. Furthermore, the eyes through which we see are not detached and objective, as Bennett's supposedly are in the passage from *Hilda Lessways*—the eyes of a surveyor with no emotional investment in what he inspects. They are the eyes of Peter Walsh, back in London for the first time after five years of colonial exile, on his way to see Clarissa Dalloway, whose presence after all these years still fills him with "terror," with "ecstasy," with "extraordinary excitement" (*MD*, 213). His vision expresses his enchantment and expectation, and the prosaic city takes on a magical quality that finds expression in the breathless tone, the highly charged metaphorical and rhythmical style: Whitehall "silver beaten," London "floating off in carnival," the cabs near Clarissa's house "rushing round the corner, like water round the piers of a bridge."

Woolf had found a way of transforming what she had called "the necessary drudgery of the novelist" into a different kind of imaginative labor both by learning to move more rapidly and by making external description illuminate psychic process. These goals were equally important to her. She found most of her precursors in the art of fiction longwinded. The age of the three-decker novel was over, not a moment too soon, and she was determined to replace it with something more compact. In this she was responding not only to a century whose rhythms and movements had accelerated but to something restless and impatient in her own nature. "Is that not my grudge against novelists," she asks herself in her diary, "that they select nothing?" (*D*, III, 210). And in the highly self-conscious short story "An Unwritten Novel," she deliberately stops herself from inventing an elaborate descriptive setting for the character she is trying to imagine: "Skip, skip," she exhorts herself, especially when tempted to detail "ornaments, curtains, trefoil china plate" (*HH*, 17). She was eager to free the new novel from what she called "the beast-of-burden work . . . of carrying loads of details, bushels of

fact" ("The Narrow Bridge of Art," *CE*, II, 228). Her fictional
project was comparable to her friend Lytton Strachey's transformation of Victorian biography. The tome became a slim
volume; prose was put on a diet; what emerged from the bulk
was a sharply featured face, a lean body. "In the first twenty
years of the new century," Woolf writes, "biographies must have
lost half their weight" ("The New Biography," *CE*, IV, 231).

Her own narrative methods reveal a conscious pursuit of
the goal of economy. She perfected a shorthand that gives a
fictional page the dense, allusive quality of poetry without
sacrificing prosaic naturalness. She prided herself on being
able to provide "in a very few strokes the essentials of a person's character" (*D*, III, 300). Her model was not a novelist at
all but Shakespeare, whose words "rush and leap out with a
whole character packed in a little phrase. When Sir Andrew
says 'I was adored once', we feel that we hold him in the hollow of our hands; a novelist would have taken three volumes
to bring us to that pitch of intimacy" ("*Twelfth Night* at the
Old Vic," *CE*, I, 28). By the time she came to write *Between
the Acts*, she felt "a little triumphant" that she had learned
how to compress: "I think its more quintessential than the
others" (*D*, V, 340). But she had been practicing the art of verbal thrift from the time of her early experimental works, "Kew
Gardens," "The Mark on the Wall," and especially *Jacob's
Room* (1922).

Consider the following passage from that novel. It is the
only recorded conversation in the book between Jacob's wid-
owed mother, Betty Flanders, and Captain Barfoot, married
to an invalid but clearly on intimate terms with Mrs. Flanders
("calls every Wednesday as regular as clockwork, and never
brings his wife"—*JR*, 13). This is the scene in its entirety:

> "Oh, Captain," said Mrs. Flanders, bursting into the draw-
> ing-room, "I had to run after Barker's man . . . I hope Re-
> becca . . . I hope Jacob . . ."
> She was very much out of breath, yet not at all upset, and as
> she put down the hearth-brush which she had bought of the
> oil-man, she said it was hot, flung the window further open,
> straightened a cover, picked up a book, as if she were very

confident, very fond of the Captain, and a great many years younger than he was. Indeed, in her blue apron she did not look more than thirty-five. He was well over fifty.

She moved her hands about the table; the Captain moved his head from side to side, and made little sounds, as Betty went on chattering, completely at his ease—after twenty years.

"Well," he said at length, "I've heard from Mr. Polegate."

He had heard from Mr. Polegate that he could advise nothing better than to send a boy to one of the universities.

"Mr. Floyd was at Cambridge . . . no, at Oxford . . . well, at one or the other," said Mrs. Flanders.

She looked out of the window. Little windows, and the lilac and green of the garden were reflected in her eyes.

"Archer [her older son] is doing very well," she said. "I have a very nice report from Captain Maxwell."

"I will leave you the letter to show Jacob," said the Captain, putting it clumsily back in its envelope.

"Jacob is after his butterflies as usual," said Mrs. Flanders irritably, but was surprised by a sudden afterthought, "Cricket begins this week, of course."

"Edward Jenkinson has handed in his resignation," said Captain Barfoot.

"Then you will stand for the Council?" Mrs. Flanders exclaimed, looking the Captain full in the face.

"Well, about that," Captain Barfoot began, settling himself rather deeper in his chair.

Jacob Flanders, therefore, went up to Cambridge in October, 1906.

(JR, 26–27)

The passage suggests a great deal without spelling anything out and without excluding the inconsequential "accidents" of a real conversation. The whole flavor of this proper-improper relationship is given in a few lines—Betty Flanders's middle-aged flirtatiousness, her girlish dependence on the Captain when making significant decisions (in this case about her son's future); the Captain's pride in his own competence, his political ambitions, his need to talk them over with Betty Flanders rather than with his own wife; the easy intimacy that grows out of long attachment, a continuing romantic attraction that has never been consummated, the pleasure each takes in the role the other plays. All these elements could (and would) have been illustrated at length in a nineteenth-century novel, in many such scenes rather than in one. We might have learned about the whole history of this idiosyncratic lifelong courtship, the nature of the Captain's interest in municipal politics and his success in the forthcoming contest, his relationship with his wife and with Mrs. Flanders's sons.

What Woolf has done instead is to make the part stand for the whole and leave the rest to the reader's imagination. The slices of life she chooses to give are very thin but include an entire cross section. The representative vignette becomes the unit of her fiction, rather like a Joycean "epiphany," which Richard Ellmann has described in terms that also illuminate Woolf's technique. The epiphany, Ellmann writes, "claims importance by claiming nothing; it seeks a presentation so sharp that comment by the author would be an interference. It leaves off the veneer of gracious intimacy with the reader, of concern that he should be taken into the author's confidence, and instead makes the reader feel uneasy and culpable if he misses the intended but always unstated meaning." [7] Behind the new technique is a new relationship to the audience—a hope that the quick-witted reader will rapidly fill in the details. Gertrude Stein claimed that the nineteenth century had invented explanation. The twentieth-century writer learned to do without, even at the risk of baffling or alienating the reader, feeling that to explain everything was to become a drudge. The focus in many modern novels (including *Jacob's Room*) often remained on the external world or on the relation between characters. But what had once taken whole chapters to describe was now given in a brief scene that epitomized the whole. When Forster wrote to congratulate Woolf on her achievement in *Jacob's Room*, he saw her success as a surgical excision of the clogged detail of her previous novel: "You have clean cut away the difficulties that so bother me and that I feared in *Night & Day* were gaining on you—all those Blue Books of the interior and exterior life of the various characters—their spiritual development, income, social positions, etc. etc." [8] She had mastered the technique of descriptive economy.

Woolf's other important innovation in the art of describing was to challenge the familiar distinction between objective and subjective observation. The tissue separating inner from outer becomes wholly permeable, so that the most ordinary sights and sounds can suddenly be flooded with intense emotional meaning. A passage from *To the Lighthouse*, in which the awkward and arrogant Charles Tansley accompanies Mrs. Ramsay on one of her philanthropic visits to the homes of the poor, provides a good example:

> There he stood in the parlour of the poky little house where she had taken him, waiting for her, while she went upstairs a moment to see a woman. He heard her quick step above; heard her voice cheerful, then low; looked at the mats, tea-caddies, glass shades; waited quite impatiently; looked forward eagerly to the walk home, determined to carry her bag; then heard her come out; shut a door; say they must keep the windows open and the doors shut, ask at the house for anything they wanted (she must be talking to a child), when, suddenly, in she came, stood for a moment silent (as if she had been pretending up there, and for a moment let herself be now), stood quite motionless for a moment against a picture of Queen Victoria wearing the blue ribbon of the Garter; and all at once he realised that it was this: it was this:—she was the most beautiful person he had ever seen.
>
> With stars in her eyes and veils in her hair, with cyclamen and wild violets—what nonsense was he thinking? She was fifty at least; she had eight children. Stepping through fields of flowers and taking to her breast buds that had broken and lambs that had fallen; with the stars in her eyes and the wind in her hair—He took her bag.
>
> (*TL*, 27)

The first sentences of this passage could be taken from a screenplay rather than a novel, so precise are the notations of sight, sound, and action. It would be difficult to distinguish the scene from the kind of interior described in Arnold Bennett's fiction. But quite abruptly, in the middle of this detailed, apparently objective delineation, the language changes completely. Mrs. Ramsay is no longer the philanthropic lady with a bag but a goddess, a figure of pastoral. Charles Tansley is a generation younger than she is. He is not in love with her.

What can account for this sudden emotional explosion? The answer, I think, is that the whole scene triggers his intense feelings about his own childhood and class identity. Born into poverty, ambitious, self-educated, determined to enter the leisured and affluent world of the Ramsays by force if necessary, he sees Mrs. Ramsay as a kind of *dea ex machina* who brings the balm of her own generous nature to heal the wounded creatures struggling below. Her charity and concern suggest that her house is as open to him as to the family she visits. Her beauty is a beauty of spirit—nurturing, enfolding; and in worshiping it he can momentarily forget his aggressive struggle to reach the top. The whole vision may be dismissed as sentimental, but the sentimentality is not Woolf's, it is Tansley's. What she has shown us is how even the most meticulously objective act of attention can suddenly be transformed into poetic rapture by the heart's need. And in using psychological significance as a principle of selection, she has simultaneously reduced the number of scenes that need to be described.

This fusion of external and internal observation, along with her pursuit of descriptive economy, were expressions of Woolf's impatience with "the Edwardians." But they were not the only important differences in her quarrel with Bennett and his colleagues. Behind her dissatisfaction with the methods and assumptions of her immediate predecessors lay a disagreement about the nature of realism. The term itself has become virtually useless in literary criticism, as Roman Jakobson has argued, because of the extraordinary variety of contradictory or even antithetical ways in which it has been used, as if realism "were a bottomless sack into which everything and anything could be conveniently hidden away."[9] Essays like "Mr. Bennett and Mrs. Brown" have contributed to this terminological chaos, in part deliberately. When Woolf started writing, the realistic tradition in fiction was much easier to define than now, and writers like Bennett, Galsworthy, and Wells were thought to embody it, with their emphasis on material fact, circumstantial detail, and recognizable social setting. But "realism" had become an honorific as well as a descriptive term, and Woolf was determined to transform and appropriate it. Bennett, she writes sarcastically, "says that it is only if the characters are real that the novel has any chance of surviving. Otherwise, die it must. But, I ask myself, what is reality? And who are the judges of reality? A character may be real to Mr. Bennett and quite unreal to me." The kind of realism that interests her has little connection with a photographic fidelity to appearance or with an objective rendering of a character's milieu. It takes two forms: on the one hand, a detailed representation of mental life that tries to mirror its apparently chaotic or random nature; on the other, a sense of individuals as embodying or reflecting forces beyond themselves. A major character in a novel like *War and Peace*, *Vanity Fair*, *Tristram Shandy*, or *Madame Bovary*, Woolf argues in the essay, is so real "that it has the power to make you think not merely of it itself, but of all sorts of things through its eyes— of religion, of love, of war, of peace, of family life, of balls in country towns, of sunsets, moonrises, the immortality of the soul" (*CE*, I, 325).

Woolf was trying to expand the theory and practice of realism. She wanted to bring the mimetic techniques of the genre to the recording of psychic process, and this has often been recognized.[10] At the same time, she tried to show that psychic life was far more responsive to external forces than has generally been assumed. This became clear when one looked at war and peace, or religion, or family life, not as the province of history or sociology but as institutions shaping private experience. This second aim was more difficult to achieve than the first, in part because the antithesis between public and private was so firmly entrenched. When Woolf saw the task as too difficult, she accepted the traditional compartmentalization of inner and outer life, or "fact" and "vision," as she frequently called them. In such moments she saw herself specializing temporarily in one or the other. So *Night and Day* and *The Years* were novels of fact: she couples them in one of her diary entries about the later book, contrasting them with "the tug of vision" embodied in *The Waves* (*D*, IV, 129).[11] But the antithesis did not satisfy her, because she was really interested in finding a seamless fictional language that constantly revealed the relationship between the two. Like Mr. Ramsay in *To the Lighthouse*, she explored "subject and object and the nature of reality" (*TL*, 40). Her heroine in *Night and Day* is appalled by the "perpetual disparity between the thought and the action, between the life of solitude and the life of society," and she wonders whether it is even "possible to step from one to the other, erect, and without essential change" (*ND*, 358–59). It was a question that also deeply troubled her creator.

To be able to move freely in her fiction between the life of solitude and the life of society was one of Woolf's major goals. Many of her works are rooted in a realistically rendered social setting and in a precise historical time. Her attention was focused as sharply on society as on individual consciousness; and she was fascinated by how these two elements—one supposedly the province of the psychological novelist, the other of the sociological—interpenetrated. "Consider what immense forces society brings to play upon each of us," she writes in her autobiographical memoir "A Sketch of the Past," "how that society changes from decade to decade; and also from class to class; well, if we cannot analyse these invisible presences, we know very little of the subject of the memoir" (*MB*, 80). By the time she came to write *Three Guineas* (1938), she had become entirely convinced "that the public and the private worlds are inseparably connected; that the tyrannies and servilities of the one are the tyrannies and servilities of the other" (*TG*, 258). By that point in her career, the stream of history, the stream of consciousness, and the flow of her artistic imagination had become a single current. The noun in the title of her last work, *Between the Acts*, refers simultaneously to the two world wars, to the acts of love in a marriage, and to the parts of a village pageant. But the realization that public and private are really inseparable was not a sudden revelation; it was an insight Woolf gradually won over the course of her career.

As I hope to show, most of the works of that career are illuminated by an understanding of the "invisible presences," the "immense forces society brings to play upon each of us."

For Woolf herself the most important of these were class and money, the transformation of family life, the women's move-ment, and peace and war. All were issues of major impor-tance in her time, and a reading of her essays, letters, and diaries as well as her fiction makes it clear that she thought about them constantly. It is in part because these fugitive or private writings have now been published that we have come to understand the inadequacy of a purely esthetic approach to Woolf's work. The critical obsession with her important ex-periments in narration, symbolism, and style has left a whole area of her achievement largely unexplored. She was acutely aware of the ways in which her society was changing and used her pen both to record the effects of those changes on the lives of her characters and to bring about change. In order to understand the influence of these "invisible presences," we will have to reconstruct the social and intellectual matrix in which her works took shape. Her voice has survived; many of the other voices to which it was responding have not. In at-tempting to recapture the whole chorus to which she listened and replied, we are likely to gain a new kind of access to the harmonies and deliberate discords of her prose. For Woolf was both an attentive observer and a voracious reader. Her reading, though discriminating, was extraordinarily hetero-geneous. It was by no means narrowly literary: she consumed biography, history, philosophy, the newspapers as greedily as fiction, poetry, and drama. "Reading at Random" was the title she originally intended to use for the critical book she left unfinished at her death. It captures the freedom and expan-siveness of her intellectual life, her willingness to follow her own curiosity wherever it led.

This wide-ranging curiosity was greatly strengthened by Woolf's association with the Bloomsbury group. Bloomsbury has been attacked from the first as elitist and narrowing, and of course it was a coterie in all the senses of that word. But for a young woman born and raised by the rules in Victorian En-gland and denied a university education, the group offered an extraordinary opportunity for mental expansion. This was not because Woolf was less well read than her male peers but because this community of intimate friends was so unspecialized in its intellectual interests. If we count both the inner circle of Bloomsbury and its satellites, we can see that Woolf's private university included not only writers but painters, art critics, political theorists and practical politicians, economists, feminist reformers, philosophers, and psychoanalysts. Far from narrowing her vision, her association with the group opened her eyes to different ways of seeing and saved her from the intellectual parochialism and shoptalk of an exclusively literary clique. It fed her natural curiosity about the world and strengthened her conviction that only a wider understanding of society and human history would illuminate some of the darker stretches of personal experience.

It is ironic that Woolf's membership in Bloomsbury has contributed to the image of her artistic isolation. In the violent attacks on the group published first in the 1930s and continuing to this day, the exclusiveness of the set is taken as a sign of its pernicious influence. Coterie culture is simply assumed to be detrimental in its effects, producing only a hot-house art—unnatural, unreal. Bloomsbury has been called a mutual admiration society that compounded the sin of intellectual snobbery by its comfortable reliance on unearned income. When the attacks by the Leavises, Wyndham Lewis, and others began in the 1930s, they were based on the idea that a little circle of the elect could produce only an intellectually complacent and trivial culture: "Articulateness and unreality cultivated together; callowness disguised from itself as articulateness; conceit casing itself safely in a confirmed sense of high sophistication; the uncertainty as to whether one is serious or not taking itself for ironic poise"—so runs the devastating summary of the Bloomsbury ethos in one of F. R. Leavis's essays.[12] And in R. H. Tawney's group portrait, the very idea of a civilized elite is treated as a contradiction in terms: "Culture may be fastidious, but fastidiousness is not culture. . . . A cloistered and secluded refinement, intolerant of the heat and dust of creative effort, is the note, not of civilization, but of the epochs which have despaired of it."[13] Unreal, cloistered, secluded: the words recall the image of the

Lady of Shalott; and the charges, insofar as they were applied to Woolf and have stuck, confirmed the sense of her isolated pursuit of shadows.

No doubt she paid a price for her close association with the more lightweight members of the group—Lytton Strachey, Desmond MacCarthy, and Clive Bell. Some of her works seem to me to embody the shallower aspects of Bloomsbury "sophistication"—*Freshwater, Flush*, even *Orlando*. She herself treated these works as busman's holidays, taken up in a spirit of play, and very different in tone from her serious books. She says of *Orlando*, for instance, that "I never got down to my depths & made shapes square up, as I did in The Lighthouse" (*D*, III, 203). The ironic dedicatory preface to *Orlando* thanks virtually every member of Bloomsbury, including her eighteen-year-old nephew "Mr. Quentin Bell (an old and valued collaborator in fiction)" (*O*, 12). But it is a mistake to think of such books as typical of Woolf's achievement or even as representing the influence of Bloomsbury. The more serious members of the group could be and were quite searching, even devastating, in their criticism of one another's work. "A mutual admiration society," as Woolf puts it, "would have expelled Roger Fry at the first meeting" (*RF*, 293). In addition, both Virginia and Leonard Woolf developed a private network of intellectual peers and associates who were not "Bloomsbury" but whose varied interests helped to strengthen their links with the wider culture. Paradoxically, the influence of their circle of friends made Woolf's works not more hermetic but more generally available. The coterie reader was a version of "the common reader" she hoped to reach—intellectually alert, interested in the world outside his immediate experience, but not *du métier*.

In any case, Woolf was never really in danger of being overwhelmed by the ethos of a group. She had a very independent mind—critical, detached—and she often used it to question the assumptions of any intellectual dispensation, as we will see when we look at her transformation of the feminist and pacifist traditions she appropriated or her skeptical examination of certain received ideas concerning class and money, marriage and family life. But though she could judge for herself, she would also listen carefully. And there is no doubt that the more political and historical interests of people like John Maynard Keynes, Beatrice and Sidney Webb, Margaret Llewelyn Davies, Ray Strachey, Ethel Smyth, and, most important, her husband greatly expanded the range of her vision. Their methods were not hers; she was not a social reformer. Yet a writer who teaches for several years at an evening college for working-class men and women, who marries a Fabian socialist and attends Labour Party conferences, who spends time working for the Adult Suffrage movement, who presides at meetings of the Women's Co-operative Guild held in her own house, and who writes significant texts for the feminist and pacifist cause can hardly be accused of political indifference. Woolf was the first to acknowledge that she was "not a politician: obviously." She goes on to say that she "can only rethink politics very slowly into my own tongue" (*D*, V, 114); this work of translation marks both her continuing involvement and her need to see public issues in her own highly individual terms.

One example must suffice for the moment. Septimus Smith's mental breakdown and suicide in *Mrs. Dalloway* is described by Dr. Bradshaw in that book as an example of "the deferred effects of shell shock" (*MD*, 201). The novel is set in 1923, five years after the end of World War I, so it may seem peculiar that Woolf should make Septimus's belated crisis so central to the book. Yet in doing so she was showing her awareness of an issue that had assumed major importance at the time and expressing her revulsion from the way it had been interpreted. It was not at all unusual for veterans of the war to show the first symptoms of mental disorder long after they had returned to civilian life. "In numerous cases," Robert Graves and Alan Hodge write in their history of Britain between the wars, "men who had managed to avoid a nervous breakdown during the war collapsed badly in 1921 or 1922." [14] The issue became significant enough to warrant the creation of a War Office Committee of Enquiry into "Shell-Shock," which submitted its 215-page report to Parliament in 1922.

The report is an extraordinary document. It shows very little sympathy for such victims of the war, insists that often "shell-shock" is indistinguishable from cowardice or insubordination, and argues that these breakdowns are usually the product of a "congenital or acquired predisposition to pathological reaction in the individual concerned."[15] The recommendations for treatment are a blend of persuasion and coercion. The medical officer "brings into play all the moral suasion he can, appealing to the patient's social self-esteem to make him co-operate and put forth a real effort of will. If moral suasion fails, then recourse may be had to more forcible methods, and according to certain witnesses even threats were justified in certain cases." Force is defended on the grounds that it can do no damage: "It should be noted that very little harm could be done at this stage even by misapplied forceful persuasion to a non-responsive case. . . . The most forceful methods of persuasion or suggestion are negligible as regards their capacity for producing any deleterious results."[16]

Whether or not Woolf read excerpts or summaries of this report in the newspapers when it was published, she clearly understood the habits of mind that produced it. The two physicians "treating" Septimus Smith in *Mrs. Dalloway* seem to be working with similar assumptions. When Septimus throws himself out the window to escape from one of them, Dr. Holmes's first reaction is "The coward!" (*MD*, 164). He cannot admit that he himself has been responsible "for producing any deleterious results." His has been the language of moral suasion: " 'So you're in a funk,' he said agreeably, sitting down by his patient's side. He had actually talked of killing himself to his wife, quite a girl, a foreigner, wasn't she? Didn't that give her a very odd idea of English husbands? Didn't one owe perhaps a duty to one's wife? Wouldn't it be better to do something instead of lying in bed?" (*MD*, 102). By contrast, Dr. Bradshaw's is the language of threat and coercion. If suasion failed, Dr. Bradshaw "had to support him police and the good of society, which, he remarked very quietly, would take care, down in Surrey, that these unsocial impulses, bred more than anything by the lack of good blood, were held in control. . . . He swooped; he devoured. He shut people up" (*MD*, 113). Woolf's language in such passages suggests her own revulsion both from the allegedly therapeutic methods used and from the moral arrogance, the failure of imaginative sympathy, behind them. She is clearly on the side of the victim, and Septimus's hostile summary of his physicians ("Holmes and Bradshaw are on you. . . . The rack and the thumbscrew are applied"—*MD*, 108) is confirmed by Clarissa Dalloway's sense of Dr. Bradshaw, whom she sees as "obscurely evil . . . capable of some indescribable outrage—forcing your soul" (*MD*, 203).

This is typical of the way in which Woolf rethinks politics slowly into her own tongue. She takes up a public issue under discussion in her society, translates its dry abstract language into a particular human situation, finds her way to the heart of the conflict, and gives it intense dramatic life. At the same time, she invests herself in the action rather than treating it from a detached sociological point of view. In this instance she calls upon the memories of her own mental breakdowns and treatment to describe Septimus Smith's case. And her personal experience and involvement give her the authority to question the accepted wisdom on the subject. In such a fashion social, historical, and political issues enter the world of Woolf's fiction—not as "issues" but as forces that stamp the fabric of mental and emotional life. The inner and outer world carry on a continuing conversation; historical events become episodes in the psychic history of individuals and affect their destinies profoundly. Public life and private life are inextricably intertwined.

Only in very recent commentary on Woolf's work has this sense of her as an original and important social observer emerged. The earlier view that she fostered what one critic called "the development of a cult of sensibility, inadequately based on the realities of the social situation"[17] has been long adying. The impetus for change has come from the contemporary women's movement, and particularly from its rereading of *A Room of One's Own* and *Three Guineas*. A closer scrutiny of these works than the Leavises and their disciples had given them revealed that Woolf was very much in touch with the historical forces of her time; it also showed that she looked with highly critical eyes on "the realities of the social situation." As she reads through the daily paper in *A Room of One's Own*, she detects the domination of a self-serving male establishment in every significant sphere of activity: "The most transient visitor to this planet, I thought, who picked up this paper could not fail to be aware, even from this scattered testimony, that England is under the rule of a patriarchy" (*AROO*, 50). This summarizing insight, elaborated at greater length and with greater force in the later *Three Guineas*, is at the heart of Woolf's social criticism and of the revaluation of her work by feminist readers. In an important essay by Berenice Carroll, for instance, Woolf is seen as a writer "with a comprehensive and penetrating grasp of the social and political fabric of the society we inhabit"; her writings "evidence a consistent and intense concern with the political foundations of the social order, even while scorning the political parties." Carroll shows that this concern extended to "all the interlocking institutions of society," and she notes that Woolf understood— fifty years before the idea became familiar in present-day feminism—that "personal relations are the mirror of the social system, and its crucible."[18] This insight has been the basis for a number of significant feminist reinterpretations of Woolf's work, including many of the essays in two recent anthologies edited by Jane Marcus.[19]

It would be difficult to overemphasize the importance of Woolf's own feminism to an understanding of her career. I agree with Phyllis Rose that it was "the crux of her emotional as well as her intellectual life."[20] Nevertheless, the appropriation of her works by some contemporary feminist critics has, I believe, produced serious problems of interpretation. Too often the ideological assumptions and imperatives of the late twentieth-century (chiefly American) women's movement have been superimposed on Woolf's own in order to minimize the distinctions between the two eras and cultures. In "thinking back through our mothers"—as Woolf said women do—

the mother's recalcitrant identity has all too easily been erased or made over. Woolf has been turned into the matron saint of contemporary feminism. Margaret Drabble writes: "I feel that could she see us now, as we struggle through the noise and smoke and exhaustion of our social upheavals, our new freedoms, she would wish us well and wave with cheerful encouragement."[21] And Jane Marcus sees Woolf as voicing ideas and attitudes that have only now acquired substance: "She seems hardly to have lived among her contemporaries but to speak directly to the future, to our generation." For Marcus, Woolf is a "consistent socialist, pacifist, and feminist" who "presented ideas that survive unscathed and undated."[22]

Such ahistorical thinking seems to me to disregard the particular contribution of Woolf's work to the various social and political movements it engages. It takes her out of her own time and place, ignores the revisionist strain in her interpretation of those movements, and makes of her complex and often contradictory sensibility a reliable witness for the cause. In seeing Woolf as an infallible precursor, it plays down the importance of her divided motives and turns her into a more consistently militant, self-righteous polemical writer than she was. It reads the whole career through the lenses of *Three Guineas*—a book Woolf could not have written before her midfifties, and one that does not represent her earlier attitudes. And it appropriates that text not so much because it illuminates Woolf's work but because it is useful to contemporary feminism. *Three Guineas* is, in Marcus's words, "a primer for protest and an encouragement for women to struggle."[23]

Perhaps such political utilization of Woolf's writings and the hagiographic impulse behind some of the recent portraits are helpful to the cause. Unwittingly, however, they simplify and distort her achievement. If we read everything she wrote rather than focusing only on the works and passages that seem to confirm our own ideological imperatives, we soon discover a chameleon writer—unpredictable, unreliable, capable of growth and change: a feminist who disliked the label and frequently wrote for an audience of men; a pacifist who despaired of the movement; an uneasy woman of property who alternately denied and defended her establishment status; a hostile critic of the patriarchal family who nevertheless felt a powerful attraction to that institution. All of these contradictions are expressed in her work and help to account for its appeal to many different kinds of readers and its survival through several major shifts of thought.

Her writings are complex, ironic, ambiguous, indeterminate in meaning. Such a catalogue deliberately invokes the critical terminology of praise that has been in fashion since her own time. I use the words descriptively rather than evaluatively, however. It seems quite unlikely that such esthetic standards are any more permanent than the various criteria for literary greatness they have displaced. They are the virtues appropriate to an age of skepticism and would probably be discarded if our culture ever again moved toward an era of belief. They can, however, be used to characterize Woolf's work because she herself was skeptical by nature and training and had a deep distrust of ideological purity. Reverence and discipleship were not among her mental habits. Though she read widely and with obvious delight, she had no masters; nor did she wish to become one herself.

She was conscious of the seductive pleasure of finding a consistent program in an author's work, yet she counseled resistance to the impulse. "Nothing is easier, especially with a writer of marked idiosyncrasy," as Woolf puts it in her essay on Thomas Hardy, "than to fasten on opinions, convict him of a creed, tether him to a consistent point of view. Nor was Hardy any exception to the rule that the mind which is most capable of receiving impressions is very often the least capable of drawing conclusions" (*CE*, I, 263). Woolf is impatient with Hardy's most "conclusive" novels—*Jude the Obscure*, for instance—in which the bare bones of his pessimistic message show through the finely modeled flesh of his fictional creations. The ideal reader, in her view, ignores the summarizing statements and listens for the quieter sounds of the life actually being depicted. Nor should we try to impose our own values on a writer and make the book we are reading confirm what we already believe: "Do not dictate to your author,"

Woolf admonishes us; "try to become him" ("How Should One Read a Book?" *CE*, II, 2).

It is difficult advice to follow. The writers who matter to us, whom we read with passionate engagement rather than out of duty or the wish to be entertained, seem to confirm what we most need to hear. We find in them a more perfect expression of our own inchoate desires and resentments, a magic mirror that gives us back an ideal image of ourselves. They become powerful allies in our continuing project of finding support from others for the more angular, less easily acceptable parts of ourselves. In a highly politicized intellectual climate such as ours has become, we tend to read in a partisan spirit, with an exaggerated concern for ideological correctness. In such an atmosphere, the texts we appropriate are treated as models, even as scripture, while the less reassuring passages in them and the more alien aspects of the author are largely ignored.

Too much of what has been written about Woolf and about the Bloomsbury group has been highly partisan in spirit, at first hostile, more recently reverent. The negative and positive labels attached to her work in the process—"elitist," "cloistered," "socialist," "anti-patriarchal"—do not accurately identify the incongruous mix of ingredients that make up her rich recipes. She wanted to be understood rather than praised or blamed. Her response to the massive correspondence generated by the publication of *Three Guineas* is instructive: "Letters fret me," she complains in her diary. "Never one thats disinterested" (*D*, V, 164). The postures of attack and defense that have dominated Woolf criticism for decades have become serious impediments to a more impartial and historically informed understanding of her work.

Such a project involves an attempt to grasp the disparate forces that helped to shape Woolf's fiction and discursive prose: her complex feelings about the literary canon and traditional narrative methods; her alternating confidence and diffidence in questioning entrenched positions; her wavering sense of audience; her absorption of nonliterary materials and her responsiveness to some of the major social and historical movements of her time; her attempt to make the novel bear witness to the effect of such forces without abandoning the central position of the human psyche. To offer a minimally adequate account of Woolf's social vision demands first of all that her work be seen in the context that produced it, the network of assumptions and traditions she inherited or absorbed. Only against this background do her own innovations take on their unique shape. And so, in Part II of this book, I have alternated chapters describing some of the received ideas that engaged Woolf's attention—about class and money, family life, feminism, pacifism—with detailed analyses of her own most complex treatments of those themes. In this way, I hope to show that her works were carrying on a kind of dialogue with other voices in her culture and that an awareness of this fact enriches our sense of her achievement.

A continuing dialogue implies consent, the ability to listen and respond. A writer whose attitude toward society is more implacably hostile than I think Woolf's was will not agree to carry on such a conversation. The truly alienated spirit is likely to use more confrontational tactics or to retreat into exile and private discourse. If we compare Woolf with some of the more powerfully antagonistic spirits of her generation— Lawrence, Joyce, Pound, Stein, for example—her more conciliatory methods and decisions are highlighted. She did not go into exile but stayed on in the society into which she had been born. Her use of scorn was strictly rationed and seldom put on public display. She tried to write as often for the common reader as for the fit audience though few that had become the norm in avant-garde literary discourse. These choices offer further evidence that Woolf thought of herself as neither sheltered nor withdrawn and that she expected her voice to be attended to, as she attended to the voices of others.

All this is paradoxical because Woolf so often described herself as an "outsider," a critical spirit who challenged the male-dominated institutions and traditions of her society. Her criticism was real and urgent and might well have produced a more consistently adversarial form of writing than it did. But to adopt a more hostile language would have meant ending the dialogue and cutting herself off from a tradition to which, when all is said and done, she had the strongest ties. Before we look at the particular elements of Woolf's social vision—the ways in which her attitudes harmonized or clashed with those that had found favor in her culture—we should try to understand the conflict in her own nature between these opposing impulses. For most of her career she managed to hold on both to her outsider status and to her establishment credentials. As we will see, the "enormous eye" with which she examined her society was naturally satiric. What it noticed, however, could not always be revealed in print. This fact created acute problems of *method* that I want to describe in the next two chapters before going on to analyze the *content* of her satiric vision. Her self-censorship made her published work more refined and etiolated and helped to establish the image of her esthetic withdrawal. Fortunately, what could not be published during her lifetime has been preserved. The diary, the voluminous correspondence, the memoirs, the manuscripts that have now found their way into print reveal that the words she kept from the public were often as striking as those familiar to an earlier generation of readers. They could never have been written in the tower of Shalott.

2

The Reluctant Satirist

Virginia Woolf's satiric demolition work began in the nursery. "We were not very old," her sister Vanessa Bell later recalled, "when speech became the deadliest weapon as used by her. When Thoby and I were angry with each other or with her, we used good straightforward abuse, or perhaps told tales if we felt particularly vindictive. How did she know that to label me 'The Saint' was far more effective, quickly reducing me to the misery of sarcasm from the grown-ups as well as the nursery world?"[1] Irony and sarcastic wit seemed to come to her instinctively and precociously. Her tongue was not easily tied, and when loosed it could wound. Her satiric talent was a mark at once of her extraordinary intellectual assurance and of her sense of powerlessness. She took revenge on her elders and supposed betters by annihilating them in her diary, her intimate letters, her private conversation. By the time she was fifteen, she could sarcastically dismiss the poems of her adult cousin Dorothea Stephen as effusive and insubstantial (Berg Diary, 4 July 1897), a remarkably cool assessment for someone not yet out of childhood. In her maturity her greatest satiric gift had become a hypersensitive ear, capable of reporting the follies of other people's talk with deadly accuracy—a tape recorder that switched on whenever a powerful, complacent monologist began to discourse. The transcripts are presented (no doubt after careful editing) for the entertainment of the right audience. Here, for example, is a putatively verbatim report of her mother-in-law's opinions on Radclyffe Hall's lesbian novel, *The Well of Loneliness*, recorded in a letter to Vanessa:

> It is a dreadful pity I think that such a book should have been published. I do not mean for the ordinary reasons. What I

mean is there are many unmarried women living alone. And now it is very hard on them that such a book should have been written. That is what I think. And you may think me very foolish—I am seventy six—but until I read this book I did not know that such things went on at all. I do not think they do. I have never heard of such things. When I was at school there was nothing like that. I was at boarding school for two years and I never heard of such a thing. Once a girl was dispelled; but I never knew what she was dispelled for. It may have been for something unpleasant; but it may have been for nothing of the kind.

(L, III, 525)

The letter, which goes on for four closely printed pages, epitomizes Woolf's satiric impulse. The immediate target is her mother-in-law's moral complacency and willed stupidity, which is reflected not only in her opinions but in her inflexible sentence structure, with its primitive vocabulary and syntax and its mindless repetition. Such opinions (and the whole style of thinking that produced them) were representative rather than idiosyncratic, which is why Woolf took the trouble to mock them. The monologue often seemed like a chorus chanted in unison by the society, its aim to drown out the voices of the deviant, the experimental, the worried. Like Dickens's Mr. Podsnap, the chorus greeted everything unfamiliar with the refrain "I don't want to know about it; I don't choose to discuss it; I don't admit it!"[2] But unlike Dickens's account of Podsnap, Woolf's deadliest satiric descriptions did not appear in print during the author's lifetime. She was an inhibited, a reluctant satirist with a very strong sense of the power of the opposition.

Such satire is a form of impiety, a refusal to worship at the traditional shrines. It was a Bloomsbury group technique, honed to an edge by the young men and women who felt themselves oppressed by the weight of the conventions they had inherited and were trained to accept. As Quentin Bell suggests, "irreverence is the great weapon of minorities: it is an engine for teasing the powerful."[3] The members of Bloomsbury felt themselves to be an impotent minority despite their impeccable establishment credentials. There was a time lag between their original sense of themselves and the powerful figures they became in maturity. But the persistence of such youthful self-definitions past the point of their appropriateness is common, and it helps to account for Bloomsbury's reluctance to think of itself as established and victorious long after it had become both. As Leonard Woolf was to explain in his eighties, "People of a younger generation who from birth have enjoyed the results of [our] struggle for social and intellectual emancipation cannot realize the stuffy intellectual and moral suffocation which a young man felt weighing down upon him in Church and State, in the 'rules and conventions' of the last days of Victorian civilization." He considered it his lifelong duty "to question the truth of everything and the authority of everyone, to regard nothing as sacred and to hold nothing in religious respect."[4]

This lack of reverence appalled one of Bloomsbury's sharpest critics, D. H. Lawrence: "There is never for one second any outgoing of feeling, and no reverence, not a crum or grain of reverence."[5] But while his description is in some ways accurate, his summary dismissal shows no curiosity about what might account for such an attitude. Bloomsbury's irreverence was a necessity of intellectual independence and survival. They had been taught to revere, not simply to accept. Their answer was to ridicule, not simply to reject. Again and again we discover that the root cause was their sense of being dwarfed by powerful opponents. So Virginia Woolf recalls her childhood feelings in a late memoir: "The cruel thing was that while we could see the future, we were completely in the power of the past" (*MB*, 126). In her own eyes she would always remain the powerless child in the nursery, forced to use the weapons of the weak.

It is common to treat Woolf's satiric gift as relatively unimportant. Jean Guiguet, for example, calls her "caustic turn of mind . . . secondary" and believes that it provided "no positive elements capable of fertilizing her art."[6] It is often dismissed as mere "bitchiness," a word that suggests both triviality and the impropriety of any critical stance for women. But Woolf's satiric impulse has increasingly come to seem both pervasive and principled; it asks to be looked at with more sympathetic understanding than it has received. She says of one of her first fictional characters that he "had a mind like a torpedo . . . aimed at falsehood" (*VO*, 361), but the words could describe herself equally well. She explains to Vita Sackville-West that in her youth "honesty was so important that all my spies had to be forever watching what came in with a view to imposters" (*L*, III, 219). In challenging late-nineteenth-century conventions and proprieties, Bloomsbury in general and Woolf in particular released their inhibited energy. Lytton Strachey wrote her that the Victorians seemed to him simply "a set of mouthing bungling hypocrites."[7] Woolf saw herself as a rebel fighting the outmoded values and habits of mind to which the society still paid lip service: "By nature both Vanessa and I were explorers, revolutionists, reformers" (*MB*, 126–27).

"Explorers, revolutionists, reformers": the identification of these quite different terms is revealing. For Woolf was never able to decide whether her criticism of certain conventions was designed to liberate herself and her coterie or to transform the larger social world. Explorers, reformers, and revolutionists each speak a different language, and, as we shall see, her satiric methods often reveal a considerable uneasiness about which style to adopt. One of her models was Jane Austen, about whose satire she writes: "She wishes neither to reform nor to annihilate; she is silent. . . . For even if the pangs of outraged vanity, or the heat of moral wrath, urged us to improve away a world so full of spite, pettiness, and folly, the task is beyond our powers. People are like that—the girl of fifteen knew it; the mature woman proves it" (*CE*, I, 149–50). In this passage, pessimism about the possibility of change is connected with authorial silence. Such fiction is written for the quick-witted reader who needs nothing explained because of an instinctive understanding of and sympathy with the author's point of view. Beyond the charmed circle stretches the vast army of the benighted, with no capacity for insight or self-criticism. The Podsnaps of the world would not be improved by seeing their own follies described or attacked in print.

Woolf's dislike of what she called "preaching" in fiction is pervasive and has many causes. She tends to reject writers who express their moral imperatives directly and to favor those who work by more subterranean means. Meredith's "teaching seems now too strident and too optimistic and too shallow" (*CE*, I, 230). Lawrence is "like a person delivering judgment when only half the facts are there" (*D*, IV, 126). Her own literary models were not Meredith and Lawrence but acute social observers like Austen and Chekhov and Chaucer. As she put it in *The Common Reader*, "It is safe to say that not a single law has been framed or one stone set upon another because of anything that Chaucer said or wrote; and yet, as we read him, we are absorbing morality at every pore" (*CE*, III, 13).

For Woolf, an author's insistent presence in a work of art was too reminiscent of the methods of her predecessors; her contempt for the style is an aspect of her programmatic anti-Victorianism. She detested the moral complacency of Victorian biographers who simply assumed "that the truth was revealed about the year 1850 to the fortunate natives of the British Isles" (*CE*, III, 100). The trouble with Victorian morality, according to Bloomsbury, was that it worked deductively from general principles rather than inductively from individual cases: it was not casuistical enough. Keynes described Bloomsbury's alternative moral assumptions with a retrospective sense of the group's brashness: "We entirely repudiated a personal liability on us to obey general rules. We claimed the right to judge every individual case on its merits, and the wisdom, experience and self-control to do so successfully." [8] By contrast, the Victorian sage used individual instances illustratively, as John Holloway concludes in his study of such writers. Their works "abound with real or invented examples that illustrate and indeed largely replace general propositions." [9]

Woolf rejected these methods because they undercut both the writer's unconscious impulses and the complexity of his characters. Her reaction is based not only on her anti-Victorianism but on her theory of composition. In propagandistic writing, the artist's most important faculties lie dormant.[10] Ideas in fiction rapidly become coercive and "hold up the creative, subconscious faculty," she says in her diary (*D*, IV, 281). And even in semipropagandistic works like *Three Guineas* she stresses the need for the imaginative writer to free himself from such pressures: "If we use art to propagate political opinions, we must force the artist to clip and cabin his gift to do us a cheap and passing service" (*TG*, 302). It is the reader's obligation, then, "to know when to put aside the writer's conscious intention in favour of some deeper intention of which perhaps he may be unconscious" (*CE*, I, 263). As these quotations show, Woolf is working with the expressive theory of creation the Romantic movement had popularized. She reaches back beyond Arnold's insistence that "the elements with which the creative power works are ideas" to Shelley's that imaginative literature has "no necessary connection with the consciousness or will."[11]

The persistent presence of the author's voice in a novel was also a direct threat to the vitality and complexity of his characters. In Woolf's conception of how the novelist works, there is a kind of power struggle between author and character. This theory is at the heart of "Mr. Bennett and Mrs. Brown." Bennett, Galsworthy, and Wells, she argues, are manipulative and domineering and use their fictional characters illustratively to prove a point. In the process, the character herself—the mythical Mrs. Brown—is radically simplified. Woolf insists that this hierarchical relationship be reversed, the author deliberately inhibiting himself and straining to listen to his characters. The people created in such works will be closer to the chaos of contradictions we sense in ourselves: "You have gone to bed at night bewildered by the complexity of your feelings. In one day thousands of ideas have coursed through your brains; thousands of emotions have met, collided, and disappeared in astonishing disorder" (*CE*, I, 336).

To recapture this sense of molten, shifting, unreliable impressions is essential to the novelist's art and clearly conflicts with the wish to use characters illustratively. Woolf's goal was to expunge herself and let her characters take over. As she put it in her diary, "I think writing, my writing, is a species of mediumship. I become the person" (*D*, V, 101). It is an art of projection rooted in humility and self-denial, a test that many writers fail. Elizabeth Barrett Browning, Woolf writes in her essay on *Aurora Leigh*, "could no more conceal herself than she could control herself, a sign no doubt of imperfection in an artist" (*CE*, I, 212). And even Henry James, who experimented constantly with seeing the world through the eyes of his characters, had not sufficiently mastered the art of self-abnegation. In reading *What Maisie Knew*, James's strenuous exercise in point of view, Woolf still senses "the author's hands on the characters all the time. Smooth hammered phrases that keep one a little from him—the suave shewman. Seldom allows direct speech." [12] The ventriloquist's art was a demanding discipline.

In idealizing the kind of fiction in which the author becomes invisible, or at least unobtrusive, Woolf was expressing an idea that is now seen as one of the premises of modernism. Most of the influential novelists of her time adopted the principle of authorial reticence. The familiar passage in Joyce's *Portrait* about the artist who "remains within or behind or beyond or above his handiwork, invisible, refined out of existence, indifferent, paring his fingernails" was paradigmatic. Flaubert may be said to have originated the method, but James translated it for an English audience, as his first serious critic, Percy Lubbock, observed: in James's later novels "the intervention of a seeing eye and a recording hand, between the reader and the subject, is practically avoided altogether." [13] Conrad noted that in writing *Under Western Eyes* his "greatest anxiety was in being able to strike and sustain the note of scrupulous impartiality." [14] And Ford Madox Ford became the chief apologist in England for what he called the Flaubertian "novel of Aloofness." Its first principle, he writes in his book on Conrad, is that the author "must not, as author, utter any views." In projecting himself fully into the novel's characters and actions, "the first lesson that an author has to learn is that of humility." [15]

Woolf's adoption of authorial aloofness as a fictional method was gradual, and as we shall see she was never entirely comfortable with it. It was only in her third novel, *Jacob's Room*, that she decided to withhold herself in any deliberate way; the result was a highly experimental book that has intrigued and confused readers from the first, for reasons I hope to clarify in the next chapter. From that point on, she never really went back to the use of an evaluative narrator in her fiction. Joan Bennett has noted that Woolf increasingly "eliminates herself from her books."[16] As the narrator withdraws, the characters expand, until the novel becomes a vehicle for the recording of internal contradictions. And yet the authorial voice is never entirely suppressed and is sometimes used to explain the very method itself. Here, for example, is Woolf's analysis (rather than direct rendering) of what is happening in Lily Briscoe's mind as she tries to sort out her feelings about Mr. Ramsay and Mr. Bankes:

> Impressions poured in upon her of those two men, and to follow her thought was like following a voice which speaks too quickly to be taken down by one's pencil, and the voice was her own voice saying without prompting undeniable, everlasting, contradictory things . . . until her thought which had spun quicker and quicker exploded of its own intensity.
>
> (*TL*, 43)

Such passages show that Woolf was reluctant to accept the ideal of the disappearing author. She soon saw that there was a fundamental conflict between the imperatives of psychological fiction and the needs of the satirist. A character into whose consciousness we enter fully and without intermediaries cannot be a satirical target: *tout comprendre c'est tout pardonner*. Despite her unremitting hostility to Victorian moralism, she very much wanted to move the reader in certain directions, and she tried to find a way of writing fiction that would allow her to be present without seeming to be. Her most ambitious attempt to solve this problem was *The Years*, on which she worked with increasing desperation from 1932 until the end of 1936—a much longer period than she had given to any of her other mature works. She later called the novel a failure, a summary judgment that suggests her frustration in trying to solve the methodological problem of satiric narration. Her diary entries concerning *The Years* offer the most illuminating comments we have about her attempts to write her particular kind of satire. The essential difficulty, as she realizes early on, is that her antididacticism makes it extremely hard for her to express or embody ideas: "There are to be millions of ideas but no preaching—history, politics, feminism, art, literature—in short a summing up of all I know, feel, laugh at, despise, like, admire, hate and so on." This moralistic impulse is however at war with her commitment to the narrator's reticence, and the result is a kind of impasse: "I must somehow comment; Lord knows how" (*D*, IV, 152).

Her first attempt to solve the problem proved abortive: she would write an "essay-novel" in which chapters of objective narration would alternate with chapters of explanatory and didactic comment. The result was *The Pargiters*, the first draft version of *The Years*, in which the narrative's meaning is spelled out in discursive prose. When Woolf first thought of this solution, she was elated. Here was an opportunity to criticize the whole Victorian family system directly while still allowing the narrative to retain its independent status. The interlarded essays in this draft did indeed permit Woolf to comment on such issues as women's restricted education, patriarchal power, the class system, and so on. This is how she describes the inhibiting effects of sexual typecasting on one of the female characters in the novel: "Kitty took it for granted that the laws of conduct were fixed. A woman behaved in one way and a man in another. Ever since she could remember, she had been trained as a woman" (*P*, 151).

But before long such explanatory comments began to weary her. A few months after beginning this version, she abandoned it with the confession that "I'm afraid of the didactic; perhaps it was only that spurious passion that made me rattle away before Christmas" (*D*, IV, 145). She suddenly decides to leave out the interchapters entirely and conceives the idea of using them in a subsequent, directly propagandistic book on women's lives to be called *On Being Despised*. This work eventually turned into *Three Guineas* and did indeed use some of the more general passages from the interchapters. But she kept herself from writing it until *The Years* was finished on the grounds that "one cant propagate at the same time as write fiction" (*D*, IV, 300). She forced herself to write the novel first, deliberately inhibiting her wish to expose the whole system of family life it describes until she had finished her narrative account. But when a reviewer of the later book commented on its relationship to the earlier, Woolf wrote in her diary: "Thats the end of six years floundering, striving, much agony, some ecstasy: lumping the Years & 3 Gs together as one book—as indeed they are" (*D*, V, 148).

Despite the sense of achievement in this passage, Woolf's solution to the problem of satiric narration—to segregate illustration and explanation into separate texts—did not really satisfy her or many of her readers. "No one has yet seen the point—*my* point," she laments in reading the first reviews of *The Years* (*D*, V, 70). As might have been predicted, the leftover narrative portions of the book were neither self-explanatory nor entirely coherent. Woolf sensed this early, and her long, agonized attempt to revise *The Years* was a search for a solution to the problem. It finally proved intractable; her acknowledgment that the book is "a failure, & that its failure is deliberate" (*D*, V, 65) probably reflects her sense that the whole project, though an important experiment, was nevertheless doomed from the start. She was not at all sure the novel hung together, and she came close to burning the proofs and entirely suppressing the book before publication (see *D*, V, 29), an unprecedented reaction. The failure until quite recently of most reviewers and critics to understand Woolf's purposes in *The Years* suggests that her fears were well grounded.[17]

At the same time, it is not difficult to understand why she gave up the project of writing an "essay-novel." The didactic portions of *The Pargiters* quickly became unwieldy and would surely have made a monster out of a narrative that tried to follow a large family's fortunes through three generations. She also came to dislike the manipulation of the reader the method involved. We are left unfree to respond naturally, personally, idiosyncratically, and while some novelists would have welcomed such management of the reader's reactions, Woolf was not among them. Furthermore, the essays treated the fictional portions illustratively and made it appear that all details were consciously chosen in order to make a historical or ideological point. Yet that really was not the way Woolf worked, either here or in her other novels. As she puts it in the original speech "Professions for Women" that was the germ of *The Years*, the female novelist often deliberately works in the dark: "She was not thinking; she was not reasoning; she was not constructing a plot; she was letting her imagination down into the depths of her consciousness while she sat above holding on by a thin ⟨but quite necessary⟩ thread of reason" (*P*, xxxvii–xxxviii). Woolf must have begun to feel that her method was short-circuiting the very current she needed to make her work come to life.

Conceived and written in the 1930s, that highly politicized decade, *The Pargiters*, *The Years*, and *Three Guineas* were in effect responses to the new pressure to write propagandistically, in a style that violated Woolf's natural instincts. Jointly, they represent a temporary loss of confidence in the more indirect satiric methods she had perfected over the previous decade. For in fact her earlier (and later) works never entirely withhold comment. Woolf is no Thackerayan puppeteer, but the observant reader does not remain oblivious to her presence. She had already found a number of solutions to the problem that troubled her in the 1930s: how to shape our response without guiding our every step.

She perfected her method only gradually. In her first two novels, *The Voyage Out* and *Night and Day*, the explanatory and evaluative narrator is often conspicuously present. Here, for example, she explains the defects of Rachel Vinrace's education in a passage that foreshadows the much later attacks on female education in *Three Guineas*: "She had been educated as the majority of well-to-do girls in the last part of the nineteenth century were educated. . . . There was no subject in the world which she knew accurately. . . . She would believe practically anything she was told, invent reasons for anything she said" (*VO*, 31). This is telling rather than showing, and though the method allows Woolf to attack her satiric target directly, it does so at a price: the intimacy of our relation with the character. The narrator's (and by contagion the reader's) patronage tends to undercut Rachel's significance, even though she is the central character in *The Voyage Out*. In *Night and Day*, the sense of Woolf's evaluative presence is even stronger, especially in her treatment of minor personages. Mrs. Hilbery, for instance, is summed up with barely benevolent satire: "She was beautifully adapted for life in another planet. But the natural genius she had for conducting affairs there was of no real use to her here. Her watch, for example, was a constant source of surprise to her" (*ND*, 39). In such passages, Woolf's character is quickly turned into a "character," and despite Mrs. Hilbery's significance in the novel's resolution, it is impossible to take her quite seriously.

What changes in Woolf's later fiction are not her satiric targets but her methods of dealing with them. Occasionally, she will go back to the didactic satiric style, as in her scathing portrait of Sir William Bradshaw in *Mrs. Dalloway*—the closest thing to a villain in Woolf's work—or in some passages of the more light-hearted *Orlando*. But even in *Orlando* she mocks her moralistic tendency as often as she indulges it: "Life is a dream. 'Tis waking that kills us. He who robs us of our dreams robs us of our life—(and so on for six pages if you will, but the style is tedious and may well be dropped)" (*O*, 185). In place of this "tedious" style she perfected an art of ironic mimicry that made it possible to comment more indirectly. In *Jacob's Room*, for instance, she describes her hero's missionary attempt to rescue the Elizabethan writers from the bowdlerizing butchery of nineteenth-century editors: "One must do the thing oneself. Useless to trust to the Victorians, who disembowel, or to the living, who are mere publicists. The flesh and blood of the future depends entirely upon six young men. And as Jacob was one of them, no doubt he looked a little regal and pompous as he turned his page" (*JR*, 106). The rapid shift in perspective here is striking. We begin with two sentences that might be a direct quotation from

Jacob, modulate to one that seems to summarize his theories of the cultural elect, and end with the narrator's ironic defense of his grandiloquent tendencies. In *Jacob's Room* character and narrator are given equal time, but the narrator often has the (dry) last word.

By the time she came to write the works of her maturity, *Mrs. Dalloway, To the Lighthouse*, and *The Waves*, more of this power had shifted to the characters, and the reader is asked to follow the course of their ruminations with minimal authorial intrusion. The method culminates in the soliloquies of the six characters in *The Waves*, though here also the voices of the characters are not sufficiently individualized to make us forget the authorial presence behind them. But even in the two earlier novels Woolf's particular handling of internal monologue still leaves her considerable room for the subtle incursion of her own voice. Take, for example, the description in *Mrs. Dalloway* of Lady Bruton's militantly patriotic thoughts on the decay of the British Empire:

> But what a tragedy it was—the state of India! . . . for really it prevented her from sleeping at night, the folly of it, the wickedness she might say, being a soldier's daughter. . . . For she never spoke of England, but this isle of men, this dear, dear land, was in her blood (without reading Shakespeare), and if ever a woman could have worn the helmet and shot the arrow, could have led troops to attack, ruled with indomitable justice barbarian hordes and lain under a shield noseless in a church, or made a green grass mound on some primeval hillside, that woman was Millicent Bruton. Debarred by her sex, and some truancy, too, of the logical faculty (she found it impossible to write a letter to the *Times*), she had the thought of Empire always at hand, and had acquired from her association with that armoured goddess her ramrod bearing, her robustness of demeanour, so that one could not figure her even in death parted from the earth or roaming territories over which, in some spiritual shape, the Union Jack had ceased to fly. To be not English even among the dead—no, no! Impossible!
>
> (*MD*, 198)

The satiric shaping of such passages is quite subtle. At first the narrator adopts the pose of a mere court reporter rather than a judge, transcribing the thoughts and words of the character and apparently changing only the pronouns from first to third person. Yet from this neutral beginning the passage soon shifts into mock-heroic panegyric, with its ringing phrases and piled-up clauses, culminating in the wild imaginative flight of the last sentences. This shift is accomplished without entirely surrendering the strategy of seeming simply to follow Lady Bruton's thoughts. The satiric demolition work is brilliantly accomplished but directed toward readers for whom the British Raj does not bring to mind "barbarian hordes" treated with "indomitable justice." It is entirely possible that a real-life version of Lady Bruton could have read such a passage without recognizing its satiric intent. Woolf's method is not only an indirect way of presenting her own values to a sympathetic audience but a form of self-protection. If challenged, her alibi might have been the quotation Strachey uses in the preface to *Eminent Victorians*: "Je n'impose rien; je ne propose rien; j'expose."

It should be clear, then, that for all Woolf's dislike of hortatory novelists, she had managed to find her own way of "preaching"—at least to the converted. Her particular shaping of internal monologue did not entirely surrender authority to the characters, though it often seemed to do so. As a number of critics have noted, she is simultaneously inside and outside their minds. In James Hafley's words, "Although the reader has often a momentary illusion of entering a character's consciousness, he never 'actually does so.'" [18] The *style indirect libre* Woolf frequently adopts masquerades as the narrator's self-effacement while permitting the author to manage the alert reader's response.[19] It was essential for Woolf to keep herself and her readers raised a little above her characters, no matter how sympathetic she found them. Her fastidious ironic poise is ultimately a form of control.

Rather than surrender such control, Woolf is willing to move in the opposite direction, to turn her carefully modulated art of innuendo into unmistakable sarcasm, particularly in some of her essays. There the inhibitions she felt obligated to practice in her fiction could be relaxed; the portraits could be more obviously caricatures. And yet her pose as a mere scribe is maintained even there, as in this passage from *The Common Reader* on the politically complacent Archbishop Thomson:

> He was fond of watching the rolling of armour plate, and constantly addressed meetings of working men. 'Now what are these Nihilisms, and Socialisms, and Communisms, and Fenianisms, and Secret Societies—what do they all mean?' he asked. 'Selfishness,' he replied, and 'assertion of one class against the rest is at the bottom of them all.' There was a law of nature, he said, by which wages went up and wages went down.
>
> (CE, IV, 118)

As usual, her satirical target is the establishment monologist hypnotized by his own rhetoric and incapable of conceding that the opposition has a case. Woolf's verbs—"he asked," "he replied," "he said"—suggest the uninterruptible relentlessness of the Archbishop's voice. For her such people were the enemy, and she was determined to use her satiric gifts to show that their pedestals were merely another kind of soapbox.

Such satiric mimicry is a constant technique of her novels and discursive works. She lets the monologist go on and on, sometimes recording the speech directly, sometimes shifting to the free indirect style, but always suggesting that such people have no internal censor. Woolf expects her reader to provide the skeptical consciousness these characters lack, and her confidence that this critical audience exists allows her to relinquish more of the words on the page to the benighted soliloquist. When, for example, Mrs. Hilbery in *Night and Day* carries on about poetry as a refuge, Woolf trusts us to see through rather than with the character and so can remain silent:

> "Lovely, lovely Ophelia!" she exclaimed. "What a wonderful power it is—poetry! I wake up in the morning all bedraggled; there's a yellow fog outside; little Emily turns on the electric light when she brings me my tea, and says, 'Oh, ma'am, the water's frozen in the cistern, and cook's cut her finger to the

bone.' And then I open a little green book, and the birds are singing, the stars shining, the flowers twinkling—"

(*ND*, 369)

Like the real-life characters in Strachey's *Eminent Victorians*, such people condemn themselves. The satirist need only record their speech and aim the spotlight. Strachey worked largely with the record of his targets' actual words, "taken from their books, their letters, their diaries, and their recorded conversation." [20] Woolf worked with her powers of observation, her perfect pitch, her ability to magnify absurdity.

This was her way of dealing with the more patently ridiculous, essentially minor characters in her fiction. For the protagonists she perfected a different technique, a form of indirect criticism that was also based on her need to efface herself. Rather than having the narrator expose the major characters, she relied on them to expose one another. The point of view is deliberately shifted with great frequency, and no character (with the single exception of the modest Bernard at the end of *The Waves*) is allowed to go on without interruption for long stretches of the narrative. This distinguishes her use of stream of consciousness from Dorothy Richardson's or Joyce's or Faulkner's. The great danger of internal monologue as a fictional technique, in Woolf's eyes, is that it undercuts the reader's satiric and critical distance. Even the most absurd monologist can begin to seem haunted, driven, sympathetic if permitted to continue long enough. In order to keep us aware of each character's deficiencies (and of the thematic concerns of the book), Woolf displaces one voice with another at regular intervals. Even *The Waves*, which began as a monologue by a single, undefined central consciousness—"I am very anxious that she should have no name," Woolf says—soon resolved itself "into a series of dramatic soliloquies" (*D*, III, 229, 312).

The major characters are often acutely critical of one another and record such feelings in their own thoughts. The method is used consistently in *Mrs. Dalloway*, *To the Lighthouse*, and *The Waves*, and often in *Between the Acts*. The uninterrupted record of a single consciousness, for example

Dorothy Richardson's surrender to her heroine's mind in *Pilgrimage*, was not suitable for Woolf's purposes. It would have made it impossible for her characters to be evaluated, as they are for example in the following passages:

> The obvious thing to say of her was that she was worldly; cared too much for rank and society and getting on in the world.
> (Peter Walsh on Clarissa Dalloway,
> *Mrs. Dalloway*, 85)

> "Bernard's stories amuse me," said Neville, "at the start. But when they tail off absurdly and he gapes, twiddling a bit of string, I feel my own solitude. He sees everyone with blurred edges. . . ."
> (*The Waves*, 37)

> How imperceptive her religion made her! The fumes of that incense obscured the human heart.
> (Bart Oliver on Mrs. Swithin,
> *Between the Acts*, 237)

Such examples could be multiplied many times over. They constitute Woolf's way of placing *all* her characters, even the most important and sympathetic, in a judgmental frame. They serve to remind us that she sees people as flawed and limited, even if not equally so, and that she uses the conflict of personalities as a way of revealing those limitations. No character in Woolf's fiction can be treated simply as a reliable commentator on the others, as a disguised omniscient narrator, not even Lily Briscoe, not even Bernard. For as Lily says about Mrs. Ramsay, "One wanted fifty pairs of eyes to see with. . . . Fifty pairs of eyes were not enough to get round that one woman with" (*TL*, 303). And "getting round" the character rather than being satisfied with a view from a single angle is vital to judgment.

Irony, mimicry, and shifting perspective were not Woolf's only satiric methods; she also used metaphor. Her fictional style is heavily imagistic, and in many cases the figurative language functions as another indirect way of criticizing her characters. One of her consistent targets is male aggression and domination—qualities she permits herself to attack directly in *A Room of One's Own* and *Three Guineas*. In her fiction the critique is expressed by a set of overlapping images:

> He seemed to come from the humming oily centre of the machine where the polished rods are sliding, and the pistons thumping.
>
> (Richard Dalloway in
The Voyage Out, 48)

> Standing between her knees, very stiff, James felt all her strength flaring up to be drunk and quenched by the beak of brass, the arid scimitar of the male, which smote mercilessly, again and again, demanding sympathy.
>
> (James Ramsay in *To the Lighthouse*
on his mother's response to his
father, 63)

> There, couched in the grass, curled in an olive green ring, was a snake. Dead? No, choked with a toad in its mouth. . . . So, raising his foot, he stamped on them. The mass crushed and slithered.
>
> (Giles Oliver in *Between the*
Acts, 119)

These images, metaphors, and symbolic actions have a common purpose: to present the male pursuit of power in a fundamentally unfavorable light by associating it with repulsive or destructive things and with the phallic drive. They owe their force to Woolf's willingness to rely on what she called "the creative, subconscious faculty" rather than rational argument. But they are also a subterranean method of attack: the depth charge rather than the visible weapon.

It should be clear that for all Woolf's genuine sense of moral complexity and her self-effacing strategies, her art was deeply judgmental. She was a satirist by impulse and on principle. Yet she had both a need and a wish not to define herself strictly in these terms: she consistently backed away from savage indignation as a form of speech. There were many reasons for this reluctance to use direct attack, but the most important was probably the familial and societal training that encouraged women to suppress their own feelings and to please men. The intellectual and emotional concessiveness that such training encouraged is so significant for an understanding of Woolf's life and work that it will be discussed at length in a later chapter. Her stance was that of the critical, quietly mocking observer of a world in which she felt she had no power. She describes the attitude best in her autobiographical essay "A Sketch of the Past," in which she analyzes her relation in girlhood to her highly conventional half-brother, George Duckworth: "I must obey, because he had force, of age, of wealth, of tradition, behind him. But even while I obeyed I asked, 'How could anyone believe what he believed?' There was a spectator in me who, while I squirmed at his criticism and deferred to it, yet remained cool, critical, observant" (*MB*, 132–33).

This mixture of fear and independence helped to shape Woolf's particular satiric methods and also at times made her deny the seriousness of her criticism. It encouraged her to work a vein of self-mockery that might compensate for some of the hostility she allowed herself, however indirectly, to express. Her satiric style became a whole system of checks and balances struggling to achieve a sense of ironic poise. To mock her own beliefs as a compensation for satirizing society's became almost a form of good manners. And so she devised the method of embedding some of her most deeply held convictions in deliberately light-hearted works that seemed to say, "Forgive me. I didn't really mean it."

The self-mockery is most obvious in *Orlando*, in which such serious Woolfian themes as androgyny, the passage of time, and artistic dedication are rather archly guyed. Her purpose in writing it, she says in her diary, is "to give things their caricature value," and she compares the book unfavorably to the more deeply felt *To the Lighthouse* (*D*, III, 203). The contrast with one of her most intense novels is instructive, and indeed there are many parallels between *Orlando* and her darker fiction. For example, there is a passage in *Orlando* on ideological coercion: "No passion is stronger in the breast of man than the desire to make others believe as he believes" (*O*, 136). It reminds us of Woolf's attack on Sir William Bradshaw's worship of the goddess Conversion in *Mrs. Dalloway* and of her persistent criticism of preaching writers. Yet in *Orlando* the subject is lightly dismissed in the concluding sentence of the passage: "Each seeks peace of mind and subserviency rather than the triumph of truth and the exaltation of virtue— But these moralities belong, and should be left to the historian, since they are as dull as ditch water" (*O*, 137).

Such self-mockery is a kind of treaty with the opposition and represents an impulse in Woolf's work that makes her draw back from a full affirmation of her own values and feelings. She suggests that she doesn't *really* care about such issues and certainly doesn't want to convince anyone else that they matter. The mode is self-protective, as though she is assuring herself of a safe retreat in case she is challenged by more aggressive, less sophisticated moralists on the other side—by the masters. This impulse to write in a lighter vein, in works like *Orlando, Flush*, or the coterie play *Freshwater*, seems to come upon her at regular intervals, and particularly after she has been immersed in her more serious fiction. *Orlando* followed *To the Lighthouse, Flush* followed *The Waves*. She explains the impulse by saying that "there are offices to be discharged by talent for the relief of genius" (*D*, III, 203), but it is also a way of pretending to deny or take back the bitter, sarcastic words of her more critical books. She would have understood the entry in Katherine Mansfield's journal that reads "I am so frightened of writing mockery for satire that my pen hovers and won't settle."[21]

It was not only Woolf's sense of the relative powerlessness of women that inhibited her satire, however. We can see a similar tendency in the writings of the males in Bloomsbury, especially in Forster, Strachey, and Roger Fry, and this contained rebelliousness is one of their major links. The targets of their satire were many of the received social and political doctrines of the class from which they sprang: its celebration of the marriage tie and the submissive wife, its sexual puritanism, its sense of the inevitability of class hierarchy, its belief that "dulce et decorum est pro patria mori," its faith in Britain's imperial mission. One can see their work as a major influence in redirecting public thinking on such issues and in creating the climate of opinion that made possible (or at any rate less devastating) the loss of empire, the decline of the Victorian family and the emergence of the "new woman," and the coming of the welfare state.

Nevertheless, it is obviously inaccurate to think of the Bloomsbury group as a set of militant rebels locked in mortal combat with their society. Rather, they quickly became "established" and soon proved vulnerable—despite their unconventional ideas—to attacks from the left. For their social criticism was regularly inhibited by a need or wish to exonerate the system they attacked; their satire was always kept at less than full force or else moved from assertion to denial of its most destructive tendencies. Lytton Strachey, for example, turns from the mordant sarcasm of *Eminent Victorians* to the nostalgic, almost celebratory picture of the same age in *Queen Victoria*. As Leonard Woolf saw, Strachey "was an iconoclast who loved traditions, so that, for instance, on a subject like the French Revolution he could feel with Burke and think with Tom Paine."[22]

Their group concessiveness requires an explanation. Why does Virginia Woolf take the fully satirized Clarissa Dalloway of her first novel, *The Voyage Out*, and treat her with such loving charity in the later *Mrs. Dalloway*? Why does Forster let the Wilcox family off so lightly in *Howards End*? The class conflict that threatens to explode in such books is somehow finally mitigated or contained. "Only connect," the epigraph of *Howards End*, could serve equally well for *A Passage to India* and a number of other Bloomsbury works. Behind this attitude is a deep reluctance to reject a social system that—for all its gross inequities and moral blindness—had nurtured each of these writers and was still sustaining them. Forster defines Bloomsbury itself in class terms: "Essentially *gentlefolks*. . . . Academic background, independent income."[23] He was acutely aware that his own emotional loyalty to his highly conventional mother, with whom he lived until her death at the age of ninety, "froze the depths" in him.[24] Her disapproval of his use of the illegitimate child in *Howards End*, to say nothing of his own aberrant sexual life, must have contributed more than a little to his deliberately inhibited satire and to his long silence as a novelist.

Their "independent income" only underlined their dependence. For what were the sources of the wealth that guaranteed their freedom to devote themselves to writing? In every case it was family money that came from people who would not have taken a favorable view of some of their progeny's moral experiments or satiric impulses. While Strachey wrote *Eminent Victorians*, that book in which, as his biographer says, "he did not openly attack his own family, but his family's friends and associates," he was in fact living in part on money from his mother, Lady Strachey.[25] Forster realized that his inheritance of £8,000 from his great-aunt Marianne Thornton had been "the financial salvation of [his] life,"[26] giving him the leisure to travel and to write. The major source of Virginia Woolf's money, on which she says in *A Room of One's Own* "intellectual freedom depends" (*AROO*, 162), was the inheritance from that eminent Victorian Sir Leslie Stephen. If he had lived into his nineties, she speculates in her diary, "What would have happened? No writing, no books;—inconceivable" (*D*, III, 208). And Roger Fry accepted his father's financial support long into adulthood, though he knew his family disapproved of his choice of vocation, associates, and wife.

Such financial dependence creates a psychological loyalty. As Forster's Margaret Schlegel says in *Howards End*, "More and more do I refuse to draw my income and sneer at those who guarantee it."[27] The complex relationship to one's family and class that such divided feelings engender was once analyzed by George Orwell as typical of the middle-class English intellectual, whose culture "has educated him in scepticism while anchoring him almost immovably in the privileged class. He has been in the position of a young man living on an allowance from a father whom he hates. The result is a deep feeling of guilt and resentment, not combined with any genuine desire to escape."[28] The compromised rebellion of such writers seems peculiarly English, as Noel Annan has suggested in his essay on the influential families from which Bloomsbury was descended:[29]

> The influence of these families may partly explain a paradox which has puzzled European and American observers of English life: the paradox of an intelligentsia which appears to conform rather than rebel against the rest of society. The proclivity to criticize, of course, exists. . . . But the pro-consular tradition and the English habit of working through established institutions and modifying them to meet social needs only when such needs are proven are traits strongly exhibited by the intelligentsia of this country.[29]

Woolf painted a picture of such a family in *Night and Day*, which traces her heroine's attempt to escape the stranglehold of her illustrious predecessors. Katharine Hilbery falls in love with an obscure, brilliant outsider and decides to marry him against her father's wishes because she needs to escape from the crushing sense of propriety and obligation that has dominated her youth. For a moment in the novel, the stage is set for a real insurrection as Mr. Hilbery and the young lovers clash. But the conflict is soon resolved. The world of the Hilberys and the culture they represent will be continued rather than shattered by this marriage. The intellectual aristocracy they represent, though it consists of a few families, is adaptive rather than rigidly exclusive and will make room for a really able interloper like Ralph Denham, Katharine's penniless suitor; in this way it either knowingly or unwittingly assures its own survival *as* an aristocracy.

How the reader feels about Bloomsbury's contained social criticism has more to do with his or her own political convictions than with esthetic standards. One of the reasons the group remains so controversial is that the question of how to deal with the faults of one's society produces little agreement. Revolutionists, reformers, and private explorers are often more critical of one another's strategies than of the flaws they jointly see in the world around them. But if one wants to understand Woolf and the other Bloomsbury writers, it is essential to look at their choices with some imaginative sympathy. Whatever the advantages and disadvantages that flow from Woolf's impacted satiric impulse, that she felt it and that it affected the matter and manner of her work seem indisputable. Understanding this fact can help us grasp what she was doing and illuminate some of her more elusive works, as I hope to show in the next chapter.

3

Jacob's Room: Woolf's Satiric Elegy

Jacob's Room appeared in 1922, the *annus mirabilis* of modern literature that also produced *Ulysses* and *The Waste Land*. Perhaps because it was associated with these works, and because the novel was the first of Woolf's longer fictions to break with conventional narrative technique, it is often interpreted as a quintessential modernist text rather than as a unique work. Its peculiarities are treated as illustrative of the revolution in twentieth-century literature, though in fact some of them are idiosyncratic. The book was certainly Woolf's first consciously experimental novel, and it has remained her most baffling one. Its narrative techniques are so innovative that they call attention to themselves; its central character, Jacob Flanders, seems to be a classic instance of psychological inscrutability in fiction; and its rapidly shifting tone, now somber, now mocking, deprives Woolf's audience of a stable sense of her own attitude toward the world she describes. These problems of narrative method, characterization, and tone are interrelated, but they can be illuminated only by attempting to understand Woolf's fundamental aims in writing the particular novel *Jacob's Room*, rather than by assuming she was interested in fictional innovation for its own sake.

Jacob's Room is often taken to be simply a technical exercise. David Daiches, for example, suggests that it was written, "one might say, for the sake of style."[1] And indeed Woolf's first thoughts about the book in her diary are concerned with method rather than matter: "Suppose one thing should open out of another—as in An Unwritten Novel—only not for 10 pages but 200 or so—doesn't that give the looseness & lightness I want: doesnt that get closer & yet keep form & speed, & enclose everything, everything?" (*D*, II, 13). Her diary entries as she works on the book continue to deal more with narrative strategy than with defining the "everything, everything" the novel is designed to present. Essentially, Woolf was trying to work free of the conventions of realism she attacked with such devastating wit in "Mr. Bennett and Mrs. Brown," that style of fiction in which the character is kept waiting in the wings until his entire environment and life history have been exhaustively described.

The style of *Jacob's Room* is that of the sketchbook artist rather than the academic painter. Scenes are swiftly and allusively outlined, not filled in, the essential relationships between characters intimated in brief but typical vignettes chosen seemingly at random from their daily lives: a don's luncheon party at Cambridge, a day spent reading in the British Museum, a walk with a friend. No incident is decisive or fully developed. Nothing is explained or given special significance. The narrative unit is generally two or three pages long and not obviously connected to the one before or after. The effect is extremely economical and suggestive but at the same time frustrating for an audience trained to read in larger units and to look for meaning and coherence. All of this was clearly innovative, as Woolf's first readers saw. Lytton Strachey writes her: "The technique of the narrative is astonishing—how you manage to leave out everything that's dreary, and yet retain enough string for your pearls I can hardly understand."[2] And E. M. Forster is similarly baffled; he wonders how Woolf keeps the reader interested in Jacob when almost everything that would have defined his character has been eliminated. "I don't yet understand how, with your method, you managed it," he writes, but he is certain that this is the book's greatest achievement.[3]

Not all of Woolf's readers have been convinced that the narrative technique, interesting as it is, *was* successful, however. The book is often attacked on the grounds that it has no unity and that Jacob himself remains unknowable. Joan Bennett, for example, insists that the novel's vividly realized episodes "build up no whole that can be held in the mind" and that "Jacob remains a nebulous young man, indeed almost any

young man." [4] J. K. Johnstone complains that the very vividness of the incidents "detracts from the unity of the novel,"
while "the character who might unite all its various scenes,
is—not there; his effects upon others are there; but he himself
is absent." [5] Such dismissive judgments seem to me based on
an unwillingness to think about Woolf's technique in relation
to purpose. Both the obvious fragmentation of the novel and
the inscrutability of its central character are, I think, deliberate. But in order to understand why Woolf chose to write a
novel that can be characterized in these ways, one has to move
beyond speculation about narrative technique as such to an
understanding of why she needed these particular techniques
in the particular book she was writing. For despite her obvious interest in technical experiment, she always thought of
narrative style as purposive—a means to an end. Since the
ends of her individual novels were never the same, her technical choices ought to be looked at not as attempts to "revo-
lutionize modern fiction" but as individual solutions to the
problem at hand. And the problem at hand cannot be intel-
ligently discussed without considering the book's subject
matter. [6]

Jacob's Room is about a young man who is killed in the First
World War. By naming her hero Jacob Flanders, Woolf immediately predicts his fate. As her first readers in 1922 would certainly have known, Flanders was a synonym for death in
battle. The words of John McCrae's "In Flanders Fields"—"the
most popular poem of the war" [7]—were common property:

> In Flanders fields, the poppies blow
> Between the crosses, row on row. . . .
> We are the Dead. Short days ago
> We lived, felt dawn, saw sunset glow,
>   Loved and were loved, and now we lie
>   In Flanders fields. [8]

According to official sources, nearly a third of the million British soldiers killed in World War I lost their lives in the Flanders mud. And the heaviest losses were among the young
officers of Jacob's class. In the words of A. J. P. Taylor, "The roll

of honour in every school and college bore witness to the talents which had perished—the men of promise born during the eighteen-nineties whose promise was not fulfilled." [9]

Although *Jacob's Room* is not in any direct sense a war novel, references to the coming conflict are carefully embedded in the narrative and would have constantly reminded Woolf's first readers of the imminent catastrophe. Jacob goes up to Cambridge in 1906. His growth from adolescence to young manhood takes place against the relentless ticking of a time bomb. We may be reading about his intellectual and amorous adventures, but we are also witnessing the preparation of cannon fodder. Woolf keeps us aware of Jacob's impending fate by moving back and forth in time: for example, when she rounds off the story of a young couple in Jacob's social set with the words "And now Jimmy feeds crows in Flanders and Helen visits hospitals" (95–96). Her novel alludes to certain well-known public events of the years just before the war— the Irish Home Rule Bill (97), the transformation of the House of Lords (129)—in a way that indirectly would have reminded her original audience of dates—1911, 1912, 1913. [10] Toward the end of the book the preparations for war become direct. The ministers in Whitehall lift their pens and alter the course of history (172); and the young men die. Woolf's only description of the fighting is remarkable for its contained rage, its parody of reportorial detachment: "Like blocks of tin soldiers the army covers the cornfield, moves up the hillside, stops, reels slightly this way and that, and falls flat, save that, through field-glasses, it can be seen that one or two pieces still agitate up and down like fragments of broken match-stick" (155).

Many readers have seen that such references to the war are significant and that *Jacob's Room* is a response to that event even though it records the years before it begins. Winifred Holtby, in the first book-length study of Virginia Woolf, suggested that Woolf was less interested in trench warfare (about which she knew nothing) than in the group identity of its victims: "When such a young man was killed, she seems to ask, what was lost then? What lost by him? What was lost by his friends? What exactly was it that had disappeared?" [11] These still seem to me the essential questions to ask in reading *Jacob's Room*. I hope to show that they also illuminate the book's technical innovations and its experiments in portraiture, as well as Woolf's puzzling shifts in tone.

The question of what might have become of the Jacobs is asked by Woolf herself in a review of a book on Rupert Brooke, that classic example of the gifted young man killed before his time: "One turns from the thought of him not with a sense of completeness and finality, but rather to wonder and to question still: what would he have been, what would he have done?" (*BP*, 89). As her questions suggest, the truncated lives of such men provoke doubt rather than certainty. "Promising" they surely were. But their early deaths only magnified the absence of achieved identity and accomplishment. As she says of a different young casualty in another review, "What the finished work, the final aim, would have been we can only guess" (*BP*, 96). Such questions are unanswerable, and Woolf does not really deal with them in *Jacob's Room*. Rather, she writes the book largely to give us a sense of what this particular stage in a young man's life—the promising stage— is like.

The major obstacle in her way was the almost universal impulse to sentimentalize the subject. Obituaries for the war dead are not noted for their realism; Woolf, however, was determined to write an honest account rather than a heroic one. She does not avoid the likelihood that such young men, for all their native gifts and youthful promise, were confused and immature. Her novel emphasizes the image of Jacob *adrift*, moving rapidly but lightly from one social set to another, from one romantic attachment to another, without either the intention or the ability to "settle." In his own rather despairing words, "One must apply oneself to something or other— God knows what" (71).

Woolf's fragmented narrative creates a kaleidoscopic picture of the range of Jacob's opportunities. Particularly in the London chapters, she gives us the sense that the world is all before him. His family connections, his education, and his good looks provide him with an entry into many different social circles—bohemian, professional, aristocratic. And his romantic experiments suggest a similar smorgasbord: the amiable, promiscuous Florinda, the emotionally unstable Fanny Elmer, the steady but frozen young heiress Clara Durrant, the "sophisticated" older married woman Sandra Wentworth Williams. These opportunities and experiences are deliberately presented in an incoherent way because for Jacob they do not add up; they cannot be thought of as sequential steps leading to his definition as an adult human being. Unlike the classic *Bildungsroman*, *Jacob's Room* lacks a teleology. Woolf's hero remains an essentially molten personality interrupted by death at the stage of experimenting upon himself, a young man by turns brashly self-confident and utterly confused. The novel treats this situation as an inevitable but early stage of growing up. Woolf's perspective is that of an older person who can describe "the obstinate irrepressible conviction which makes youth so intolerably disagreeable—'I am what I am, and intend to be it,' for which there will be no form in the world unless Jacob makes one for himself" (34). But as the last part of her sentence suggests, it is by no means certain that such attempts to define oneself will be successful, no matter how long we are given. There is always the possibility, perhaps even the likelihood, that our rebellious adolescence will give way not to strong adult individuality but to a stale, despairing conformity.

No one has written about this stage of life better than Erik Erikson, and though Woolf could not, of course, have read him, certain passages in his work illuminate Jacob's situation because both writers focus on the same phenomenon. In *Childhood and Society* (1950) and more fully in *Identity: Youth and Crisis* (1968), Erikson defines a stage of deliberately prolonged adolescence which he calls a *"psychosocial moratorium,"* a period in which "the young adult through free role experimentation may find a niche in some section of his society, a niche which is firmly defined and yet seems to be uniquely made for him." Before he is expected to take on any of his life commitments—in love, in work—the young man is offered a legitimate period of delay "often characterized by a combination of prolonged immaturity and provoked precocity."[12] His reluctance to bind himself vocationally or to choose a mate is honored or at least tolerated for a period of years because his society accepts his need for self-exploration and social mobility before demanding that the ultimate choices be made.

By its very nature, such a stage cannot be a record of triumphs, and those who are going through it often seem simply confused and self-indulgent to their elders, particularly those with short memories. Furthermore, a person in this position remains in some sense a blank—undefinable, unknowable—and therefore not an easy subject for fiction. We expect a novel to give us characters who have an identity or whose progressive change we can follow sequentially, as in the *Bildungsroman*. In *Jacob's Room*, however, Woolf was faced with the problem that this fictional convention does not hold good for all human beings at all stages of life. She had tried to deal with a similarly inchoate personality in her first novel, *The Voyage Out*, and would do so again in *The Waves*. All three of these characters (Rachel, Jacob, Percival) die young, before they have been fully defined. But it is notable that in trying to depict such people, Woolf's technique becomes more and more stylized, until in Percival she creates a mythical rather than a realistically conceived character.

Why did she move in this direction? Why did she deliberately avoid the technique of interior monologue that might have given her readers a vivid sense of the inner turmoil in which such people find themselves? In certain obvious ways, the record of a fictional character's thoughts is ideally suited to depicting identity confusion, yet in *Jacob's Room* (and even more in *The Waves*) the characters who might have been illuminated by it are never presented in this way. The inner lives of Jacob and Percival remain a mystery. In *The Waves* this is clearly a deliberate choice, since the six major characters surrounding Percival all soliloquize at length, whereas Percival himself has no voice. It is sometimes assumed that Woolf depicts Jacob without recording his inner life in detail because when she was writing *Jacob's Room* she had not yet perfected the techniques of rendering consciousness she learned to use so brilliantly in her later fiction. But the explanation is unconvincing, since in the first place the thoughts of many minor characters in the novel *are* consistently recorded, even if not in the elaborate form found in *Mrs. Dalloway* or *To the Lighthouse*. Woolf deliberately minimized the reader's access to Jacob's thoughts. This is evident if one reads the holograph draft of the novel alongside the revised, final version. Again and again Woolf eliminates the vestiges of Jacob's inner life. For example, in the potentially romantic scene in which he helps Clara pick grapes while the younger children scamper about, Woolf excises the hints of Jacob's attachment from the first version:

> "Little demons!" she cried.
> ~~"I haven't said it"~~ Jacob thought to himself.
> ~~I want to say it. I cant say it. Clara! Clara! Clara!"~~
> They're throwing the onions," said Jacob.
>
> > (holograph version, with Woolf's deletions)[13]

> "Little demons!" she cried. "What have they got?" she asked Jacob.
> "Onions, I think," said Jacob. He looked at them without moving.
>
> > (published version, 61)

As a result of such excisions, we never know exactly what Jacob feels about Clara, nor about most of the other people whose lives touch his.

There is something obviously artificial and deliberate in such narrative reticence. Any attempt to account for it must be speculative, but two reasons suggest themselves for Woolf's peculiar strategy. It is possible that she wants to give us the sense of a character still so unformed that even the relatively chaotic record of interior monologue seems too defining. The flux of feelings must be recorded in words, and words give shape. Even Jacob's conflicted "I want to say it. I cant say it. Clara! Clara! Clara!" clearly suggests romantic attachment, when it is possible that what he feels about her is less easily describable. By their very nature, words articulate confusion too neatly to be true to the extremes of the state. This is why Jacob's letters home communicate so little: "Jacob had nothing to hide from his mother. It was only that he could make no sense himself of his extraordinary excitement, and as for writing it down—" (130). It is possible that Woolf refused to record Jacob's deepest feelings because such a transcript comes too close to presenting a finished product rather than a consciousness in process. She wanted to give the sense of someone who remains a permanently unknown quantity. And so she concentrates on the conflicting impressions of Jacob among all the people he meets, and our point of view shifts abruptly every few pages as we move from one unreliable observer to another, none of them managing to fathom this young man because, as Woolf concludes, "nobody sees any one as he is. . . . They see a whole—they see all sorts of things—they see themselves" (28–29).

But to pose the problem in this epistemological way does not fully explain the absence of anything resembling stream of consciousness. Mrs. Ramsay is similarly unknowable, Lily Briscoe tells us in *To the Lighthouse* ("One wanted fifty pairs of eyes to see with, she reflected. Fifty pairs of eyes were not enough to get round that one woman with, she thought" [*TL*, 303]), and yet this fact does not prevent Woolf from recording her character's inner life in detail. For a better explanation, we must go back to the problematic tone of *Jacob's Room*. Uninterrupted stream of consciousness tends to create sympathy and to work against satiric intent in fiction. And there are many indications in *Jacob's Room* that Woolf wanted to maintain an ironic distance between her reader and her main character. Her tone in describing him and his friends is often patronizing. For example, when Jacob first becomes involved with the brainless Florinda, Woolf describes his feelings with obvious mockery:

> Jacob took her word for it that she was chaste. She prattled, sitting by the fireside, of famous painters. The tomb of her father was mentioned. Wild and frail and beautiful she looked, and thus the women of the Greeks were, Jacob thought; and this was life; and himself a man and Florinda chaste.
> She left with one of Shelley's poems beneath her arm. Mrs. Stuart, she said, often talked of him.
> Marvellous are the innocent.
>
> (77)

Such ironic detachment is evident not only in the narrator's attitude toward Jacob but in her treatment of most of the young characters in the book. The narrative voice is that of an older, more experienced, highly skeptical consciousness, determined to puncture youthful illusion and undercut intense feeling of any kind. This satiric narrator often steps in to correct romantic excess—for example, when describing Richard Bonamy's passion for Jacob:

> "Urbane" on the lips of Jacob had mysteriously all the shapeliness of a character which Bonamy thought daily more sublime, devastating, terrific than ever, though he was still, and perhaps would be for ever, barbaric, obscure.
>
> What superlatives! What adjectives! How acquit Bonamy of sentimentality of the grossest sort; of being tossed like a cork on the waves; of having no steady insight into character; of being unsupported by reason, and of drawing no comfort whatever from the works of the classics?
>
> (164)

The cumulative effect of such passages is to make it impossible for the reader to sympathize fully with the character. We are, in effect, told to keep our distance. And in one way or another, the narrative techniques of the novel reinforce this sense of a wide gap. Woolf frequently pretends ignorance: she imagines herself so far from the action that she can't hear the words of the characters. In one of the Cambridge scenes, for instance, the perspective suddenly lengthens, like an aerial shot in film:

> The laughter died in the air. The sound of it could scarcely have reached any one standing by the Chapel, which stretched along the opposite side of the court. The laughter died out, and only gestures of arms, movements of bodies, could be seen shaping something in the room. Was it an argument? A bet on the boat races? Was it nothing of the sort? What was shaped by the arms and bodies moving in the twilight room?
>
> (42–43)

In such passages the omniscient narrator suddenly and rather disturbingly pleads ignorance, becomes at best "semiscient." There are also many instances in the book in which our involvement with and understanding of the characters is made more difficult because our view is filtered through an alien consciousness—for example, that of Richard Bonamy's charwoman, who gives us an obviously garbled version of what she overhears the young friends saying in the next room as she washes up in the scullery: "'Objective something,' said Bonamy; and 'common ground' and something else—all very long words, she noted. 'Book learning does it,' she thought to herself" (101). The effect is to deflate the intellectual pretensions of these budding philosophers and bring them down to earth.

Is this any way to treat a young man whose life is about to be snuffed out? Why does Woolf challenge the ancient wisdom that dictates "de mortuis nil nisi bonum"? Is there some meanness of spirit evident in the games she plays with her characters? Such irreverence might well have seemed offensive to a generation of readers trained to think about the dead soldiers by the literature World War I produced. These works, written during and immediately after the conflict, convey a sense of high idealism or heroic indignation or romantic intensity. One has only to recall some of the classic passages:[14]

> If I should die, think only this of me:
>   That there's some corner of a foreign field
> That is for ever England.
>   (Rupert Brooke, "The Soldier")

> What passing-bells for these who die as cattle?
>   Only the monstrous anger of the guns.
>   Only the stuttering rifles' rapid rattle
> Can patter out their hasty orisons.
> (Wilfred Owen, "Anthem for Doomed Youth")

> *Have you forgotten yet?* . . .
> *Look down, and swear by the slain of the War that*
>   *you'll never forget.*
>   (Siegfried Sassoon, "Aftermath")

> *Massacres of boys! That indeed is the essence of modern war. The killing off of the young. It is the destruction of the human inheritance, it is the spending of all the life and material of the future upon present-day hate and greed.*
>
>   (H. G. Wells, *Mr. Britling*
>   *Sees It Through*)

Whether the sentiment is patriotic or bitterly disillusioned, such passages treat the war dead with absolute seriousness, in a style that is characteristically intense and even reverent and that works at a high level of generalization.

By contrast, Woolf's elegiac novel is persistently small-scaled, mischievous, and ironic.[15] As we have seen, she had an instinctive distrust for reverence of any kind, treating it as a fundamentally dishonest mental habit that made symbols out of flesh-and-blood human beings. She was no more interested in a cult of war heroes than she had been in a religion of eminent Victorians. For one thing, such attitudes indirectly glorified war, even if the writer was, like Wilfred Owen, consciously working against the martial myth. Woolf's elegy for the young men who died in the war is revisionist: there is nothing grand about Jacob; the sacrifice of his life seems perfectly pointless, not even a cautionary tale. *Jacob's Room* is a covert critique of the romantic posturing so common in the anthems for doomed youth. Its author's attitude anticipates Dylan Thomas's World War II poem, "A Refusal to Mourn the Death, by Fire, of a Child in London":

> I shall not murder
> The mankind of her going with a grave truth
> Nor blaspheme down the stations of the breath
> With any further
> Elegy of innocence and youth.[16]

Woolf's bedrock pacifism, then, helps to account for her ironic distance from Jacob and his contemporaries. But she would probably have felt much the same about the milieu that produced him if he had never fought in the war at all, since there was something about his whole life pattern that she disliked intensely. Jacob Flanders is a paradigmatic young man of his class. Handsome, clever, and well-connected if not rich, his credentials are impeccable and his future course apparently secure. Rugby; Trinity College, Cambridge; a London flat; a couple of mistresses; the Grand Tour: everything in his life is a traditional step on the road to establishment success. The class was Woolf's own, but the sex was not, and between the training and expectations of its young men and of its young women there was a great gulf. Woolf's satiric detachment is in part attributable to her feeling that Jacob's world was created by men for men and essentially excluded her. She reacted with a characteristic mixture of condescension and apprehension. As she says in describing her own attitude toward him, "Granted ten years' seniority and a difference of sex, fear of him comes first" (93).

The fear is not so much of Jacob himself as of the "patriarchal machinery" that guaranteed him a powerful position in his society. Woolf describes the rites of passage for such young men in an illuminating autobiographical essay written shortly before her death. She considers the career of her illustrious cousin, H. A. L. Fisher: "What, I asked myself the other day, would Herbert Fisher have been without Winchester, New College, and the Cabinet? What would have been his shape had he not been stamped and moulded by the patriarchal machinery? Every one of our male relations was shot into that machine and came out at the other end, at the age of sixty or so, a Headmaster, an Admiral, a Cabinet Minister, a Judge" (*MB*, 132). Jacob too appears to be on such a trajectory. Woolf's feelings about her exclusion from this world are quite complex. She envies the men their guaranteed success (assuming they follow the rules) while pitying them their lack of freedom. The whole exploratory stage of life through which Jacob is passing is subtly undermined by the preordained, mechanical program he is acting out; and the machinery that would have assured him a place in *Who's Who* sends him off to war instead. In *Jacob's Room* Woolf describes a "dozen young men in the prime of life" whose battleship has been hit; they "descend with composed faces into the depths of the sea; and there impassively (though with perfect mastery of machinery) suffocate uncomplainingly together" (155).

The public schools and ancient universities were the training grounds for such complaisant attitudes, and Woolf's feelings about these institutions differed sharply from those of the Bloomsbury males. When people like Lytton Strachey and Leonard Woolf looked back on their undergraduate years, they saw paradise lost. Strachey writes Leonard an ecstatic letter about a visit to Cambridge: "Good God! The Great Court is the most thrilling place in the world, it's no good trying to get over it; whenever I come in through the great gate my heart thumps, and I fall into a million visions." [17] Virginia Woolf's picture of the university in *Jacob's Room* is much more ambiguous. On the one hand, she understands its magical spell, as in the passage that describes Cambridge as a city of light, "the light of all these languages, Chinese and Russian, Persian and Arabic, of symbols and figures, of history, of things that are known and things that are about to be known" (40). On the other, she constantly emphasizes the disparity between the university's high ideals and the pettiness and complacency of its distinguished scholars. Jacob's Cambridge bears the stamp of pretension and provinciality: "It is not simple, or pure, or wholly splendid, the lamp of learning. . . . How like a suburb where you go to see a view and eat a special cake! 'We are the sole purveyors of this cake'" (38).

Her critical distance was a response to feeling shut out, a reaction she would examine at length in the first of her feminist books, *A Room of One's Own*. The Cambridge suburb admitted women only on sufferance, and it taught its male products to patronize them. So Jacob fails to understand why women are allowed to attend service at King's College Chapel: "No one would think of bringing a dog into church," he reflects, "a dog destroys the service completely. So do these women" (31). It is interesting that Woolf's first draft version of the novel included a chapter about a young woman student at Cambridge which in some ways parallels the Jacob portions of the narrative; the chapter was excised from the final version, however, probably to underline the fact that the university was still a young man's world, despite the presence of a few female interlopers. [18]

From Woolf's point of view Jacob fits all too easily into this world. His rebellious gestures are relatively superficial, and the picture of him at Cambridge stresses his confident appropriation of his position: "He looked satisfied; indeed masterly; which expression changed slightly as he stood there, the sound of the clock conveying to him (it may be) a sense of old buildings and time; and himself the inheritor; and then to-morrow; and friends; at the thought of whom, in sheer confidence and pleasure, it seemed, he yawned and stretched himself" (43). His Cambridge training reinforces the sense of membership in an elite, and there is more than a hint of arrogance in his makeup. The attitude provokes Woolf's sarcasm, though the tone remains good-humored: "The flesh and blood of the future depends entirely upon six young men. And as Jacob was one of them, no doubt he looked a little regal and pompous as he turned his page" (106).

There are many indications that Jacob is far from extraordinary, despite his membership in this exclusive fraternity. The novel records the classic events in the life of a presentable young man. Jacob's thoughts and experiences are treated as typical rather than unique, and his individual identity is made to merge with that of a group. Woolf's descriptions of him at Cambridge, in London, and on the continent often seem to efface his defining characteristics and turn him into a representative figure, as in this passage:

> But Jacob moved. He murmured good-night. He went out into the court. He buttoned his jacket across his chest. He went back to his rooms, and being the only man who walked at that moment back to his rooms, his footsteps rang out, his figure loomed large. Back from the Chapel, back from the Hall, back from the Library, came the sound of his footsteps, as if the old stone echoed with magisterial authority: "The young man—the young man—the young man—back to his rooms."
> (45)

They move in packs, these young men, and their most antisocial ideas are quickly ratified by their fellows. For Jacob's friend Richard Bonamy, life is "damnably difficult" because he feels the world neglects its gifted youth; "but"—the narrator comments—"not so difficult if on the next staircase, in the large room, there are two, three, five young men all convinced of this—of brutality, that is, and the clear division between right and wrong" (42).

In such ways the unexamined idea of the promising young man is challenged by Woolf's vision of incipient convention-

ality. It is instructive to contrast Jacob's rather banal and predictable effusions on Greece with Woolf's own first vision of
that country. His thoughts are not individualized but reflect
the familiar romantic Hellenism of his society and set: "He
could live on bread and wine—the wine in straw bottles—for
after doing Greece he was going to knock off Rome. The
Roman civilization was a very inferior affair, no doubt. But
Bonamy talked a lot of rot, all the same. 'You ought to have
been in Athens,' he would say to Bonamy when he got back"
(134). Contrast this with a passage from a diary Woolf kept on
her first trip to Greece in 1906, when she was, like Jacob, in
her mid-twenties. Her description of the Acropolis is clearly
the product of a keen observer who does not rely on potted
history or Baedeker's sense of the sublime:

> No place seems more lusty and alive than this platform of an-
> cient dead stone. The fat Maidens who bear the weight of the
> Erectheum on their heads, stand smiling tranquil ease, for
> their border is just meet for their strength. They glory in it; one
> foot just advanced, their hands, one conceives, loosely curled
> at their sides. And the warm blue sky flows into all the crevices
> of the marble; yet they detach themselves, and spring into the
> air, with edges unblunted, and still virile and young.
>   (Berg Diary, 14 Sept. [1906]–
>   25 April 1909, 9)

A description like this, though it has a self-conscious air and
is clearly an attempt at fine writing, stands out as genuinely
"promising" because it suggests freshness of observation and
expression. It shows us how far Jacob still was from finding
his own voice.

What would have happened to such young men had they
been permitted to live out their term? It is a question the novel
constantly raises but can never, of course, answer. Woolf's attempts at prediction are cut short by her sense of their group
fate, which makes her hastily withdraw the question: "Behind
the grey walls sat so many young men, some undoubtedly
reading, magazines, shilling shockers, no doubt; legs, perhaps, over the arms of chairs; smoking; sprawling over tables,
and writing while their heads went round in a circle as the

pen moved—simple young men, these, who would—but there is no need to think of them grown old" (41). There are, however, a few passages in the novel in which Woolf allows herself to imagine a future life for Jacob and some of his companions, and the picture is seldom radiant with hope. Respectability, responsibility, establishment success: that is the image in the crystal ball. As Jacob rails against women in youthful fervor, the narrator comments dryly in a parenthesis: "This violent disillusionment is generally to be expected in young men in the prime of life, sound of wind and limb, who will soon become fathers of families and directors of banks" (150). And after giving us a sense of his "desperate" infatuation with Sandra Wentworth Williams, Woolf notes that Jacob "had in him the seeds of extreme disillusionment, which would come to him from women in middle life" (158).

Such passages make it clear that *Jacob's Room* is a novel much more about a stage of life than about a particular person. The fate that lies ahead for her young man is extinction in the war. But the fate from which he is saved is not presented as much more attractive: middle age, in the novel, is a kind of slow death or betrayal of youthful promise. The book is filled with poignant images of the brevity of youth: "And for ever the beauty of young men seems to be set in smoke, however lustily they chase footballs, or drive cricket balls, dance, run, or stride along roads. Possibly they are soon to lose it" (116). The very intensity of the experimental stage is too violent to be sustained, as Woolf suggests in a vivid metaphor: "Why, from the very windows, even in the dusk, you see a swelling run through the street, an aspiration, as with arms outstretched, eyes desiring, mouth agape. And then we peaceably subside. For if the exaltation lasted we should be blown like foam into the air" (119). And even those who do not agree to fit themselves into the comfortable niches society has prepared for them when the season of youth is over are not presented as heroic rebels. In one of her predictive passages, Woolf draws a bleak picture of what lies ahead for a young bohemian painter whose work so excites Jacob in Paris:

And as for Cruttendon and Jinny, he thought them the most remarkable people he had ever met—being of course unable to foresee how it fell out in the course of time that Cruttendon took to painting orchards; had therefore to live in Kent; and must, one would think, see through apple blossom by this time, since his wife, for whose sake he did it, eloped with a novelist; but no; Cruttendon still paints orchards, savagely, in solitude.

(130)

An elegy is a work of consolation as well as desolation. If anything in Jacob's early death can be thought of as consoling, it is the fact that he is spared the disillusionment that awaits him. Never to be defined means never to be bounded. Middle age in Woolf's work is regularly seen as a diminution. In *The Waves*, the novel in which she follows her characters through all their life stages from childhood to old age, one of them sums up the difference between youth and "maturity" in this bleak way: "Change is no longer possible. We are committed. Before, when we met in a restaurant in London with Percival, all simmered and shook; we could have been anything. We have chosen now, or sometimes it seems the choice was made for us—a pair of tongs pinched us between the shoulders" (*W*, 151). Jacob's life does not reach the treadmill stage, and he seems fixed forever at the moment of infinite possibility, before the seeds of conventionality Woolf notices in him have sprouted. In her preliminary notes for the novel, there is this cryptic notation: "Intensity of life compared with immobility." [19] It is possible that her terms define the two life stages her book consistently contrasts: the experimental intensity of youth and the fixity of what follows. Jacob dies young, but he never dwindles into the banal life he sees ahead of him, that of "settling down in a lawyer's office, and wearing spats" (49).

Woolf's sharp sense of the brevity of life, of the inevitability of death, puts Jacob's "tragic" fate in longer perspective. To die young, to die later: the book seems to say that the distinction borders on the trivial. From the first page of her novel, we hear the note of mortality. Mrs. Flanders weeps for her husband, long since dead. Though Seabrook Flanders was no war victim, he too died young, before the world knew what to call him. And Woolf comments: "Had he, then, been nothing? An unanswerable question, since even if it weren't the habit of the undertaker to close the eyes, the light so soon goes out of them" (14). The book's focus on the present moment constantly blurs to give us a sense of time past and time future. For Julia Eliot, walking down Piccadilly, "the tumult of the present seems like an elegy for past youth and past summers, and there rose in her mind a curious sadness, as if time and eternity showed through skirts and waistcoats, and she saw people passing tragically to destruction" (168). This elegiac note is not connected exclusively to the carnage of the war but seems rather a response to the inescapable fact of mortality. It is, Woolf says, a sorrow "brewed by the earth itself. . . . We start transparent, and then the cloud thickens. All history backs our pane of glass. To escape is vain" (47). The sense of death broods over the novel, and Woolf's images constantly reinforce it: Jacob finding the sheep's skull on the beach; the momentary illumination of faces on Guy Fawkes night, before the fire is extinguished "and all the faces went out" (73); a mason's van passing "with newly lettered tombstones recording how some one loved some one who is buried at Putney" (111); Mrs. Jarvis walking through the cemetery or telling her friend, "I never pity the dead" (130).

This atemporal awareness of mortality Woolf carried with her always. She asks herself in her diary as she works on *Jacob's Room*, "Why is life so tragic; so like a little strip of pavement over an abyss. I look down; I feel giddy; I wonder how I am ever to walk to the end" (*D*, II, 72). Though she says later in the same entry that this tragic sense is pervasive "for us in our generation," her novel's repeated stretching of time and space suggests a fundamentally religious perception of the issue, though without a religious consolation. Her vision recalls the "Ithaca" chapter in *Ulysses*, in which Joyce's sense of cosmic time nearly obliterates his characters. He sees the "so-called fixed stars, in reality evermoving from immeasurably remote eons to infinitely remote futures in comparison with which the years, threescore and ten, of allotted human life formed a parenthesis of infinitesimal brevity."[20] Similarly, in *Jacob's Room*, one of the guests at the Durrants' evening party examines the constellations through the telescope only to find herself suddenly deserted by all her companions: "'Where are you all?' she asked, taking her eye away from the telescope. 'How dark it is!'" (59).

This sense of the universal darkness surrounding us both elevates and trivializes Jacob's death. From the aspect of eternity individual death is meaningless, and even the annihilation of a million young men in battle is a fact that history will swallow without special effort. But, at the same time, the extinction of any life inevitably recalls the fate that awaits us all and is invested with that resonance. This is why the lament for Jacob becomes, for all the novel's irony, so moving: "Ja-cob! Ja-cob!" his brother calls in the novel's first scene, and the narrator comments: "The voice had an extraordinary sadness. Pure from all body, pure from all passion, going out into the world, solitary, unanswered, breaking against rocks—so it sounded" (7). "Jacob! Jacob!" It is a refrain that will be heard again and again in the book, from Mrs. Flanders, from Clara Durrant, from Richard Bonamy, from all those fellow mortals who make the mistake of attaching their deepest feelings to someone who precedes them into the earth. For all Woolf's ironic distance and critical awareness of Jacob's limitations, she knows that such composure dissolves when our emotions are engaged. Her complex attitude is conveyed in an important reflective passage in the book:

> In any case life is but a procession of shadows, and God knows why it is that we embrace them so eagerly, and see them depart with such anguish, being shadows. And why, if this and much more than this is true, why are we yet surprised in the window corner by a sudden vision that the young man in the chair is of all things in the world the most real, the most solid, the best known to us—why indeed? For the moment after we know nothing about him.
>
> Such is the manner of our seeing. Such the conditions of our love.
>
> (70–71)

This double awareness of the sharpness of grief and its absurdity gives Woolf's satiric elegy its special edge and accounts for the novel's rapid shifts in tone. She worked hard to avoid sentimentalizing her subject and casting her book in the romantic mold. As Strachey writes her after reading *Jacob's Room*, romanticism is "*the* danger for your genre," and she agrees that he has put his "infallible finger upon the spot."[21] But Strachey was hardly the standard of feeling in such matters, as some of his own letters attest. When Thoby Stephen, Virginia's brother and Strachey's intimate friend, died of typhoid fever at the age of twenty-six, Strachey's letter to Leonard Woolf exemplifies the uninhibited and unreflecting expression of grief Virginia Woolf came to distrust: "I don't understand what crowning pleasure there can be for us without him, and our lives seem deadly blank. There is nothing left remarkable beneath the visiting moon. It is idle to talk; but it is only to you that I can say anything, that he was the best, the noblest, the best—oh god! I am tired out with too much anguish. Oh god!"[22]

Such threnodies, Woolf came to feel, were finally self-serving and insincere, a rhetorical exercise in pulling out all the stops. The literary allusions, the exaggerated sense of Thoby's qualities, the indulgence of intense emotion would have struck her as more like a public performance than a private expression of loss. Her own very different style of lament deliberately understates or withholds such sentiment. In the book's last scene Bonamy can say no more than "Jacob! Jacob!" and Mrs. Flanders unpredictably focuses on a pair of her son's old shoes, as though their emptiness conveyed everything: "What am I to do with these, Mr. Bonamy?" (176). The significance of the scene is clarified by an anecdote about Woolf told by one of her friends: "The only other remark I remember from that afternoon was when she was talking about the mystery of 'missing' someone. When Leonard went away, she said, she didn't miss him *at all*. Then suddenly she caught sight of a pair of his empty shoes, which had kept the position and shape of his feet—and was ready to dissolve into tears instantly."[23]

"Such is the manner of our seeing. Such the conditions of our love." Jacob's death, like his life, has no intrinsic significance. He is not clearly "the best, the noblest, the best." Rather, he is an engaging young man, in many ways typical of his class and training, who has unintentionally managed to secure the love of a few human beings. His absence, like his presence, is not likely to alter the world significantly. His youthful promise might well have been betrayed, his eager ambition have turned into the ordinary life choices. Only on the small canvas appropriate to such a view, rather than on the grand frescoes of the heroic imagination, could Woolf allow herself to sketch—in a deliberately halting and fragmented style and a conspicuously impure tone—her vision of a permanently inscrutable young man.

The hesitation of her style and the impurity of her tone are manifestations of the impacted satiric impulse expressed in *Jacob's Room* and in many of Woolf's other works. It should be clear that this experimental novel is not merely a technical exercise but a book that raises issues to which she would return again and again: class identity, the conflict between the sexes, the cost of war. As we will see, Woolf brooded about these and related problems in all of her works. Her concern with them helped to direct her reading and is clearly expressed in her discursive prose. As we look at the component parts of Woolf's social vision, we will see that what she writes is often a response to the treatment of such issues in the culture of her time. But it is a mistake to think of that response as direct and straightforward: she was neither a social theorist nor a polemicist. Rather, her imagination absorbed and processed the discussion of "issues" until what emerged in her imaginative writing became a very different, often elusive product. As I hope to show, the public discourse on social issues is indispensable to an understanding of some of Woolf's greatest works; but its terms and assumptions are only the raw material she used to shape structures that were finally very much her own.

PART TWO

4

Class and Money

The familiar image of Virginia Woolf as a social and intellectual snob, complacently exercising the rights of her station, presiding with confident authority over the Bloomsbury clique, has been deliberately distorted by the unsympathetic reader. Perhaps it was inevitable, in a century in which words like "bourgeois," "highbrow," "elite," and "coterie" have become terms of abuse, that Woolf's complex feelings about her class identity should have been simplified in this way. At times she even saw herself in a similarly unflattering light, as in the ironic essay she called "Am I a Snob?" (*MB*, 182–98) and read to the Memoir Club, the inner circle of Bloomsbury. Yes, she confesses, the charges are true: she is a social and intellectual snob. She has a weakness for titles, for elegant social occasions; she is indifferent to public sentiment, cares only for the good opinion of her set. The rest don't matter.

If this self-parodying essay were an accurate account of her deepest feelings, Woolf would have been both a more contented person and a less interesting writer. In fact her sense of these issues was far less secure. The class into which she had been born seemed at times a refuge, at times a prison. The aristocracy above was both dazzling and tinselly. The working class below was simultaneously remote and threatening, worthy and contemptible. Her response to the speeches she heard at a meeting of the Working Women's Guild reveals a volatile mixture of class feelings—impatience, sympathy, resentment, enthusiasm: "All these questions . . . which matter so intensely to the people here, questions of sanitation and education and wages, this demand for an extra shilling, for another year at school, for eight hours instead of nine behind a counter or in a mill, leave me, in my own blood and bones, untouched. If every reform they demand was granted this very instant it would not touch one hair of my comfortable capitalistic head. Hence my interest is merely altruistic. It is thin spread and moon-coloured. There is no life-blood of urgency about it. . . . I sit here hypocritically clapping and stamping, an outcast from the flock."[1] These are not the words of a complacent or indifferent observer. They suggest both condescension and self-criticism, anger and relief in being excluded from this sorority, and above all an inability to get past the barrier of social rank. For Woolf knew that her own leisure-class identity was ineradicable. It defined her, for better or for worse. She had an acute sense of exactly how much class and money contributed to the shaping of the individual. And this insight became one of the major subjects of her work.

She wrote about class and money with exceptional frankness at a time when these subjects were increasingly felt to be indecent. The democratic pressures of her culture encouraged many writers to suppress or minimize the signs of privilege in their own backgrounds. Others—less democratically minded—idealized an older, essentially hierarchical culture in which the links between artist and aristocratic patron were still strong. The realistic acceptance of one's actual social identity was rare; Woolf's work is remarkable for the forthrightness with which she discusses these issues. In *Three Guineas*, for example, she addresses the gentleman who requested her help in preventing war by first establishing their common class credentials: "When we meet in the flesh we speak with the same accent; use knives and forks in the same way; expect maids to cook dinner and wash up after dinner" (*TG*, 9). And in *A Room of One's Own* she identifies her ideal audience in even narrower terms: "There must be at this moment some two thousand women capable of earning over five hundred a year in one way or another" (*AROO*, 170).

In both passages, Woolf insists on setting down facts and figures virtually certain to give offense to a larger, less fortunate audience—those with the wrong accents and manners, no servants, and considerably less than £500 a year at their disposal. And yet I think there is no flaunting of privilege here, but rather a sense that these differences are real and not to be ignored, though for some they had become dirty little secrets. This, presumably, is what E. M. Forster meant when he called Woolf's snobbery "honest" and even "courageous": "She was a lady, by birth and upbringing, and it was no use being cowardly about it, and pretending that her mother had turned a mangle, or that Sir Leslie had been a plasterer's mate. . . . Her snobbery—for she was a snob—has more courage in it than arrogance. It is connected with her insatiable honesty."[2]

It is connected, also, with Woolf's conviction that a detailed and nuanced sense of class identity is an indispensable tool of the novelist. As Quentin Bell notes, she was unusual in her time for "her frank and unequivocal acceptance of the importance of the class structure in literature" (QB, II, 219). In her essay "Women and Fiction" she predicts that in the future the characters in novels written by women "will not be observed wholly in relation to each other emotionally, but as they cohere and clash in groups and classes and races" (*CE*, II, 147). This vision of the future extrapolates from Woolf's sense of the peculiar tradition of English fiction, in which the barriers between classes, their differing traditions, manners, and language, had always been of primary concern. She saw this as the central tradition in which she was working—for "English fiction is so steeped in the ups and downs of social rank that without them it would be unrecognizable" ("The Niece of an Earl," *CE*, I, 219).

It was a tradition Woolf's own work was to continue, even to highlight. As a new kind of puritanism made class and money increasingly difficult to discuss straightforwardly, she determined to focus the reader's attention on them. Virtually every character in her novels is "placed" socially with unusual exactness. This is true not only of more realistic novels like *Night and Day*, in which the difference between two middle-class London residential districts (Chelsea and Highgate) becomes a major issue and in which the heroine's neighbors are identified as families "whose incomes must be between a thousand and fifteen-hundred a year . . . and [who] kept, perhaps, three servants" (*ND*, 330). It also helps to define characters in more poetic novels like *The Waves*, in which Louis says to himself again and again, "My father is a banker in Brisbane and I speak with an Australian accent" (*W*, 14), or *Between the Acts*, in which William Dodge's class identity is immediately established by the trained eye: "He was of course a gentleman; witness socks and trousers" (*BA*, 48).

Woolf was writing about a society in which such seemingly absurd distinctions dictated one's fate. The individual's freedom was strictly circumscribed by the accident of birth, so that the range of his opportunities could be imagined if one had a realistic sense of his starting point. This idea is at the back of the almost clinical scrutiny—as pitiless in tone as a medical report not designed for the patient's eye—with which Woolf regards some of her major characters, such as Septimus Smith in *Mrs. Dalloway*:

> To look at, he might have been a clerk, but of the better sort; for he wore brown boots; his hands were educated; so, too, his profile—his angular, big-nosed, intelligent, sensitive profile; but not his lips altogether, for they were loose; and his eyes (as eyes tend to be), eyes merely; hazel, large; so that he was, on the whole, a border case, neither one thing nor the other; might end with a house at Purley and a motor car, or continue renting apartments in back streets all his life; one of those half-educated, self-educated men whose education is all learnt from books borrowed from public libraries, read in the evening after the day's work, on the advice of well-known authors consulted by letter.
>
> (*MD*, 93)

The passage is bound to give offense to anyone with strong egalitarian sympathies. Its detached hauteur is unmistakable and marks it as the perspective of someone whose better opportunities permit her to look down even on the motor car and house at Purley, the upper limit of Septimus's possibilities. There is neither anger nor warmth here, but there is a sense of the waste of a system that restricts the range of individual human achievement by raising the insurmountable barrier of class. That Septimus is both the conscience of his society and its silent, helpless victim is the result of his being at best "a border case," incapable of making his force felt among the confident, powerful people who surround him. A more sentimental writer would simply have made him the hero of the novel and ignored the limitations his class identity imposes. But Woolf knew that in the world she was describing his kind of individual authority was more often than not obliterated by the pressures of money and rank.

Class, then, is a pervasive concern of Woolf's work. But to stress her abiding interest in the subject reveals nothing about where her sympathies lay. Her presentation of upper-, middle-, and lower-class characters suggests that her own firm social identity did not make her an entirely reliable witness for her own class. She came from what Noel Annan has called "the intellectual aristocracy," that stratum of the middle class associated with higher education and professional life. Their talents were intellectual and administrative, and by the beginning of the twentieth century they had fully mastered the arts that brought men to the top of their professions and institutions. The universities and great public schools, the government services and the courts, the publishing houses and respected journals of opinion—all were dominated by this relatively new meritocracy.

Such a group, it might seem, required no apology for its privileges: it had earned them by ability and hard work. The principle on which it was based—that of the career open to talent—minimized social guilt even in a democratic century by translating equality into equality of opportunity. As the sociologist Karl Mannheim argued, "The key to the new epoch of learning lies in the fact that *the educated no longer constitute a caste or a compact rank, but an open stratum* to which persons from an increasing variety of stations gain access."[3] A closer look, however, soon revealed that what began as a heterogeneous collection of talented individuals soon hardened into a hereditary caste. Annan showed that in practice "certain families gain position and influence through persistent endogamy," gradually "spread over the breadth of intellectual and official life," and eventually "form a new class in society."[4] It was a form of inbreeding designed to produce superior brains and to ensure the continuity of characteristics that had brought them into prominence in the first place. Like any other powerful class, it soon developed a private network of communication and influence, of nepotism, of early training for success in the competitive sweepstakes, that effectively excluded all but the most exceptional interlopers.

At this stage the emerging class did require a new apology. It may be said to have found it in the work of the influential Italian political theorist Gaetano Mosca, who defended the transformation of an aristocracy of talent into one of birth by insisting that the growth of its necessary intellectual and moral qualities required "that the same families should hold fairly high social positions for a number of generations."[5] In England such hereditary privilege was vigorously defended by T. S. Eliot. He argued in his *Notes Towards the Definition of Culture* that the family, considered as an institution spanning many generations, was indispensable for the transmission of culture. Its function was to maintain the traditions of high intellectual achievement by protecting and fostering it. To make sure such fragile distinction survives, "there must be groups of families persisting, from generation to generation, each in the same way of life."[6]

Woolf would have encountered such ideas not only in her own family, which had certainly worked by these rules, but almost everywhere in Bloomsbury. Leonard Woolf wrote in his autobiography that the Stephen and Strachey families were the British equivalent of "the French eighteenth century noblesse de robe" and that the Stracheys represented "that comparatively small ruling middle class which for the last 100 years had been the principal makers of British history."[7] Virginia Woolf's brother-in-law Clive Bell argued in his book *Civilization* for the importance of what he called "a civilized nucleus" freed from material cares.[8] And John Maynard Keynes, as his first biographer tells us, was strongly imbued with "the idea that the government of Britain was and would continue to be in the hands of an intellectual aristocracy" and that essential decisions would be "reached by a small group of intelligent people."[9]

These, then, were the accepted ideas of Woolf's milieu: that culture, financial independence, and power were closely allied; that those at the top had earned their high station; that the network of family tradition best safeguarded the continuity of civilization. Since she was a direct beneficiary of this legacy, we might expect that she would defend it with vigor. But she did not. We have seen her ironic treatment of Jacob Flanders's conviction that "the future depends entirely upon six young men" (*JR*, 106). Her attitude toward establishment success is scarcely celebratory. In *Night and Day* she paints a group portrait of the Hilberys, a thoroughly representative family of intellectual aristocrats: "One finds them at the tops of professions with letters after their names; they sit in luxurious public offices, with private secretaries attached to them; they write solid books in dark covers, issued by the presses of the two great universities, and when one of them dies the chances are that another of them writes his biography" (*ND*, 30–31). She depicts their world as a secure fortress designed to protect them from "the vast mass of humanity which is forced to wait and struggle, and pay for entrance with common coin at the door" (*ND*, 387). The tone of Woolf's description is characteristically ironic, the perspective that of the outsider, the petitioner at the gates unlikely to gain entry.

Even within the gates all is not well. Katharine Hilbery is unable to take the privileges of her station for granted. Her illustrious family is for her an oppressive force, its traditions restricting her freedom. She reluctantly agrees to collaborate with her mother on a biography of her famous grandfather, though neither of them is cut out for the task. But the customary rituals of such families ("when one of them dies the chances are that another of them writes his biography") must be observed, even if they go against the grain of individual talent. Katherine, as it happens, is interested in mathematics but must pursue her vocation furtively while devoting herself to the obligatory labor. Her underlying motive is guilt: "If they could not between them get this one book accomplished they had no right to their privileged position. Their increment became yearly more and more unearned" (*ND*, 35).

"Oppression" is a word that has been legitimately appropriated by the dispossessed. But Woolf showed that in its psychological rather than economic sense it could also be accurately applied to people who had no material cares. The competitive ethic that had brought the intellectual aristocracy into prominence exacted a heavy price. In *To the Lighthouse* Mr. Ramsay cannot stop worrying about his exact place in the pecking order of his profession. His restless ambition makes him miserable; it is like a machine that cannot be switched off. He and his young disciple Charles Tansley spend their summer holiday "walking up and down, up and down . . . saying who had won this, who had won that, who was a 'first-rate man' at Latin verses, who was 'brilliant but I think fundamentally unsound', who was undoubtedly the 'ablest fellow in Balliol'" (*TL*, 17). They are constitutionally incapable of enjoying the fruits of their labor.

Woolf's highly critical picture of the professions in *Three Guineas* suggests that such insatiable ambition is endemic in them, for they "make the people who practise them possessive, jealous of any infringement on their rights, and highly combative if anyone dares dispute them." Most professions seem to her "as bloodthirsty as the profession of arms itself" (*TG*, 121, 116). To belong to the upper middle class, then, is to be afflicted with a lifelong disease—pushing, striving, living up to the high expectations imposed from birth *by* birth. In her feminist books Woolf tries to locate these anxieties in the male sex. Since men dominated professional life, she clearly had a point. But the pattern of her own career—her restless literary experiments and perfectionism as well as her highly competitive attitude toward contemporaries ("a rival the less" is her first reaction to the news of Katherine Mansfield's death—*D*, II, 226) suggests that she could also describe the disease from personal experience. Her "unearned income" had to be earned after all, by an achievement matching or surpassing those of her ancestors and of the petitioners at the gates.

It was the absence of such competitive restlessness in *titled* aristocrats that made them attractive to Woolf. They seemed to have fewer sharp edges; the images she uses to describe them emphasize ease, sleekness, an unruffled exterior. This is what one of her middle-class characters sees in the aristocratic company assembled at Lady Lasswade's house in *The Years*: "They all looked as if they had been rubbed with wash leather, like precious stones; yet the bloom seemed ingrained; it went through the stone. And the stone was clear-cut; there was no blur, no indecision" (*Y*, 274). They exuded an air of confidence far removed from the ethic of striving. Of Orlando, Woolf writes, "There was a serenity about him always which had the look of innocence" (*O*, 25). Unhurried, unanxious, perfectly content simply to be: that is the mark of the class. A youthful, more energetic version of such qualities attracted her to Vita Sackville-West, whom she describes as "very free & easy, supple jointed as the aristocrat is" (*D*, II, 306). Here was a world in which confident people did exactly as they liked and apologized to no one. Their privileges had existed so long in the family that they no longer had to be earned; they could at last be taken for granted.

But such easy assurance, attractive as it was, necessarily abandoned the more strenuous virtues. Woolf's interest in the aristocracy (and even in Vita Sackville-West, who represented the class at its most vital) was finally only a flirtation. Their style of life and habits of mind were incompatible with the kind of excellence she valued. Effort, effort—the dissatisfaction with what comes easily, the determination to push oneself to the limit of one's capacity, the mood expressed in Yeats's line "Myself must I remake"—only this self-punishing standard would produce work that she respected. On closer inspection most of the titled people she had known proved to be intellectually vapid: "coarse & usual & dull" is how she describes the two society hostesses, Lady Cunard and Lady Colefax, who had taken her up (*D*, III, 202). And even Vita Sackville-West, who had brightened her life and inspired *Orlando*, eventually succumbed to the intellectual complacency of her class: "very much the indolent county lady, run to seed, incurious now about books; has written no poetry; only kindles about dogs, flowers, & new buildings" (*D*, IV, 287). Despite Woolf's snobbish interest in titles and delight in aristocratic manners, she was never seriously attracted to this world. Her highly irreverent picture in the essay "Lady Dorothy Nevill" presents it as a gilded prison. She imagines Lady Dorothy "hopping from perch to perch . . . in a large, airy, magnificently equipped bird-cage" (*CE*, IV, 114). Again and again in her descriptions of class, Woolf uses such images of confinement.

The middle class Woolf knew intimately and could criticize from within. The aristocracy she had observed closely, with a mixture of envy and intellectual condescension. She was familiar enough with both classes to write about them convincingly. But how could she get at "the lower orders," as the working class and the servants were still called in her youth? Her fiction is characterized by a refusal or inability to describe anyone below the rank of the middle class in persuasive detail. The apparent exceptions (Charles Tansley, Septimus Smith) are really aspirants to middle-class status, like Forster's Leonard Bast in *Howards End*. The chapter in Forster's novel that describes Leonard begins, "We are not concerned with the very poor. They are unthinkable, and only to be approached by the statistician or the poet," a comforting aphorism for a middle-class novelist, and one that Woolf might have echoed. Though she taught courses to working-class men and women, married a socialist, and held meetings of the Women's Co-operative Guild at her own house, the "lower orders" in her fiction are conspicuous by their absence. When they do appear, they are often given a generic identity, their individual characteristics expunged, as in this description of a slum in *The Years*:

> The shabby street on the south side of the river was very noisy. Now and again a voice detached itself from the general clamour. A woman shouted to her neighbour; a child cried. A man trundling a barrow opened his mouth and bawled up at the windows as he passed. There were bedsteads, grates, pokers and odd pieces of twisted iron on his barrow. But whether he

was selling old iron or buying old iron it was impossible to say;
the rhythm persisted; but the words were almost rubbed out.

(*Y*, 174–75)

This impressionist erasure of detail is characteristic of
Woolf's depiction of lower-class life. The observation point is
very distant; individual words cannot be made out; the sense
conveyed is of group life. As Bernard says in *The Waves*, "I am
not part of the street—no, I observe the street" (*W*, 82). It is as
though the people spoke a foreign tongue that the middle-
class observer barely understands. There are a number of passages in Woolf's fiction that render the language of the poor as
nonsense: the song of the beggar woman in *Mrs. Dalloway* that
is transcribed as "ee um fah um so / foo swee too eem oo"
(*MD*, 90); the incomprehensible words of the cockney children at the end of *The Years* as they sing "Etho passo tanno
hai, / Fai donk to tu do" (*Y*, 463).[10]

A whole section of society is thus treated as *terra incognita*.
English novelists have often written as if workers and servants
had no place in fiction. The tradition stretches from Jane
Austen to Henry James and is based on the assumption that
the literary imagination need not sink below the level of the
impoverished governess. What differentiates Woolf from the
earlier practitioners of the novel of manners is that she is distinctly uneasy about the limits of her knowledge. In *The Voyage Out* St. John Hirst concludes the story of the suicide of his
mother's maid by wondering "Why had she done it? . . . Why
do the lower orders do any of the things they do do? Nobody
knows" (*VO*, 375). The "nobody" in this sentence must be
read as "nobody who is anybody." And though Elizabeth Barrett's maid, Lily Wilson, is a character of some importance in
Woolf's *Flush* so long as her mistress is alive, her old age is
unimaginable because she has left no written record and thus
has joined "the great army of her kind—the inscrutable, the
all-but-silent, the all-but-invisible servant maids of history"
(*F*, 160).

There is a good deal of special pleading in such passages,
as though the class relations of an earlier time are being made

to account for an altered set of circumstances in the present day. Woolf certainly knew that some of her fellow novelists treated lower-class characters in a very different fashion. Even if she ignored the rival tradition of French naturalism or the complex example of Dickens, there was her exact contemporary, James Joyce, a mandarin capable of recording the words and thoughts both of intellectuals and of "the lower orders" (for example, in "Counterparts" and "Clay," two stories from *Dubliners*) with equal authority. Woolf's notorious comments on *Ulysses*, which she called an "underbred" book (*D*, II, 199), betray a distinct class uneasiness. Joyce was much the better ventriloquist, and he had observed people very different from himself not from the perspective of the remote spectator but with a full and close attention. Why had it proved too difficult for Woolf to see and hear a class below her own with equal accuracy?

The answer, I think, lies in her middle-class guilt. She had inherited enough capital to permit her to live on income from investments, and she could afford to hire the help that allowed her to devote the day to writing. But unlike many of her predecessors who had found themselves in such a position, she did not feel comfortable in it. The contrast between her attitude toward servants and that of her own mother is striking; in one generation the situation had changed completely. Julia Stephen wrote an essay on "the servant question" in which she defended the institution of the live-in servant with all the hierarchical confidence of an earlier epoch, insisting that there was nothing degrading in domestic service, that the mistress was responsible for the welfare of her servants, and that she must therefore keep a constant watch over them. For her there was a "strong bond between server and served"[11] that she did not wish to see broken. Julia Stephen's daughter could no longer rely on this sense of legitimacy. Woolf's extremely uneasy relationship with her own servants, Nelly Boxall and Lottie Hope, has been described by Quentin Bell (QB, II, 57–58). She saw the issue not as a conflict of individual personalities but as a fault of the class system: "It is an absurdity, how much time L[eonard] & I have wasted in talking about servants. And it can never be done with because the fault lies in the system. How can an uneducated woman let herself in, alone, into our lives?—what happens is that she becomes a mongrel; & has no roots any where. . . . Here is a fine rubbish heap left by our parents to be swept" (*D*, III, 220).

But the Woolfs were not to be among the sweepers, despite their left-wing sympathies. Servants were absolutely indispensable to the life they invented for themselves. Though Virginia Woolf had nothing resembling a "job," she kept to a working schedule as rigid as that of most professionals. The servants made it possible for her to produce the long shelf of books that now represents her achievement. Her problem was that she could not justify the system that was liberating her. Her solution was to widen the distance between herself and "the lower orders," both the servants that released her from household drudgery and the working class that indirectly provided a return on her capital. Like many other middle-class people of her generation, she had acquired a guilty conscience. It was no longer easy to build a social faith on the assumptions that class hierarchy was inevitable and that "the poor always ye have with you." There is a distinct nostalgia in her description of the nineteenth-century writer's belief in permanent class demarcations, "like a landscape cut up into separate fields. In each field was gathered a different group of people. . . . And the nineteenth century writer did not seek to change those divisions; he accepted them" ("The Leaning Tower," *CE*, II, 165–66).

The previous century had found a way of minimizing social guilt—the tradition of Victorian philanthropy, that special province of middle-class women. It was part of their duty to smooth out class antagonisms by "befriending" the poor, visiting their homes regularly, offering advice, charity, help in crises. Henrietta Barnett, a social reformer who worked with the poor in the East End of London in the 1880s, describes her work as "the friendship between the member of one class and another, the care of one woman whose heart is sorry because of the pain of another woman, the strength-giving link between two human beings." [12] In the important work of Octavia

Hill, this benevolent impulse merges with modern capitalist management. Hill's influential book, *Homes of the London Poor* (1875), describes her highly successful methods of improving slum housing by a policy that a modern skeptic might call concerned surveillance. It also provided a reliable 5-percent return on the landlord's capital. But it too was described by Hill as a form of friendship: "I have long been wanting to gather near us my friends among the poor, in some house arranged for their health and convenience, in fact a small private model lodging-house, where I may know everyone, and do something towards making their lives healthier and happier." [13]

By the twentieth century this form of middle-class benevolence had begun to appear both ineffectual and bogus. Woolf hoped to find a servant who would treat her "as an employer, not friend" (*D*, III, 220). And she recorded the frustration of women still trying to play the game by the old rules. Mrs. Ramsay in *To the Lighthouse* tries unsuccessfully to turn herself into a modern professional social worker, noting down facts and figures about the lives of the poor "in the hope that thus she would cease to be a private woman whose charity was half a sop to her own indignation, half a relief to her own curiosity" (*TL*, 20). Eleanor Pargiter in *The Years* spends one day a week visiting the poor in the cottages she has had built for them, but we see her, as she returns to her own comfortable family home, through the eyes of a sarcastic observer: "a well-known type; with a bag; philanthropic; well nourished; a spinster; a virgin; like all the women of her class, cold" (*Y*, 108). Even Woolf's close friend Violet Dickinson seemed to her a faintly absurd relic: "One of the lay sisters who go about doing good, & talking gossip, almost improved out of existence nowadays I suppose; a survival of the 19th Century era of individual goodness" (*D*, II, 96).

The theory that individual goodness might significantly alleviate social suffering could not survive the impact of a concerted attack on the basis of class society. The influence of Marx and Engels and of other socialist and egalitarian thinkers undermined the foundations of private philanthropy.

Perhaps the class structure was neither permanent nor inevitable; perhaps individual charity merely masked the fundamental injustice of the system. A classless society seemed to many a real possibility, and it might only come about by provoking, rather than avoiding, class war. These radical ideas put all privileged classes on the defensive by treating them as impediments to desirable social change.

One did not have to be a Marxist to hold such views. Thorstein Veblen in his *Theory of the Leisure Class* (1899) mounted a devastating attack on the privileged group that did no work. He unmasked their "culture" as an indirect way of demonstrating power, attacked their patronage of the arts as self-serving, and generally deprived them of their traditional justifications for existence by translating their high ideals back into economic realities. For him, the life of leisure "is closely allied in kind with the life of exploit." [14] A more directly influential work in the Woolfs' circle was R. H. Tawney's *Equality* (1929). Tawney was a Fabian socialist. He dedicated his book to Leonard's close friends Sidney and Beatrice Webb, and his ideas eventually entered the mainstream of English left-wing thought. His egalitarianism was uncompromising, providing no excuse for traditional differentiations in class, income, or education. He attacked even the idea of the meritocracy and censured any form of privileged education because it helped "to perpetuate the division of the nation into classes of which one is almost unintelligible to the other." [15] His words recall the incomprehensible cockneys of Virginia Woolf's fiction.

Such egalitarian ideals generated both fear and a new defensiveness in the class under attack. They produced a philosophical justification of elites that had never before been considered necessary. Both Vilfredo Pareto and Gaetano Mosca attempted to demonstrate the inevitability of class divisions and the need for a ruling elite in a healthy society. Although Pareto argued that "aristocracies do not last," that "history is a graveyard of aristocracies," he saw no evidence that they were being replaced by egalitarian societies. [16] Rather, history demonstrated the displacement of decadent elites by healthier successors and argued for the usefulness of a Darwinian competition for places in any elite to ensure its continuing vitality. Pareto's defense of elites is a form of *Realpolitik*, though it is fueled by an underlying success-worship. Mosca's version of the argument is more high-minded. He too sees the distinction between "a class that rules and a class that is ruled" as permanent and inevitable; he too speculates on how an elite can remain vital rather than rigidifying into a decadent caste. But his defense of hereditary privilege and leisure is principled: "We are obliged to admit that science and social morality originated in aristocracies," that is, in classes with the means to exempt some of their more gifted members "from the material cares of life and from the worries that go with defending one's social position from day to day." And he directly attacks as "utterly fantastic" the Marxist vision "of an era of universal equality and justice": "We shall not stop to refute that utopia once again. This whole work is a refutation of it." [17]

This need to combat what was sometimes called "the virus of Marxism" was also felt in England, particularly after the Russian Revolution had made the abolition of bourgeois privileges more than a theory. Bloomsbury contained both Fabian socialists and defenders of elites. Clive Bell's *Civilization* (1928), which begins with a dedicatory letter to Virginia Woolf, tries to justify the continued existence of an elite whose primary function is to preserve high art by cultivating taste among its members. The book probably did more to create the image of Bloomsbury as an exclusive cultural mafia than any other work. It is directly attacked in Tawney's *Equality*, and even Woolf herself criticized it for confusing civilization with "a lunch party at no. 50 Gordon Square" (QB, II, 137). For all its apparent complacency, *Civilization* is really a symptom of leisure-class anxiety and hostility in the wake of the General Strike and the democratization of British society since the war. Bell sees the civilizing nucleus shrinking: "The few grow less. The spirit of the age is against them." [18] This fear for the survival of the intellectual aristocracy also found expression in Keynes's work. As an economist, he provided a conceptual alternative to what he took to be the hopeless muddle of

Marx's economic theory. His work challenges the Marxist dogma that capitalism is doomed and attempts to rescue the system by controlling and modifying its more destructive tendencies. Behind Keynes's project lies an unshakable loyalty to his own class. As he asks rhetorically in "A Short View of Russia," an essay originally published by the Woolfs in their Hogarth Pamphlets, "How can I adopt a creed which, preferring the mud to the fish, exalts the boorish proletariat above the bourgeois and the intelligentsia who, with whatever faults, are the quality in life and surely carry the seeds of all human advancement?" [19]

Such anxiety about the impending triumph of "the boorish proletariat" was widely felt among intellectuals. Ortega y Gasset's *The Revolt of the Masses* (1930) depicts a mass culture that "crushes beneath it everything that is different, everything that is excellent, individual, qualified and select." The new mass man is hostile not to any particular culture, but to culture itself. Ortega pictures him as a barbarian, "a primitive who has slipped through the wings on to the age-old stage of civilization." [20] Karl Mannheim also saw the elite as an endangered species. The process he calls "negative democratization" or "negative selection"—a kind of reverse Darwinism—"gives a position of pre-eminence to those who were unable to live up to the standards of modern culture." [21] Cultural leveling was seen as the result of more democratic forms of education, and so even "equality of opportunity," the credo that had helped to produce the nineteenth-century intellectual aristocracy, eventually came under assault. In the words of T. S. Eliot, "In our headlong rush to educate everybody, we are . . . destroying our ancient edifices to make ready the ground upon which the barbarian nomads of the future will encamp in their mechanised caravans." [22] The heightened rhetoric of such attacks suggests panic. The terms are those of melodrama: civilization is threatened; the savages are at the border; only the strengthening of traditional elites holds out the hope of rescue.

Two diametrically opposed middle-class responses can thus be seen in Woolf's milieu—a sense of guilt about their own privileges, and a determination to justify and defend them. That Woolf felt both emotions, and felt them strongly, helps to account for the complexities and contradictions of her own social attitudes. Her guilt is recorded in the reactions of her fictional characters as well as in more directly self-revealing works. In the novels, those who have complacently accepted the comforts of their station are often shocked into awareness of the world beyond their borders. When the innocent Rachel Vinrace, in *The Voyage Out*, fantasizes about the life of leisure and freedom she and Terence will have, he reminds her that this idyll depends on their unearned income, and that others are forced to live in squalor. Rachel asks him, appalled, "Is it true, Terence . . . that women die with bugs crawling across their faces?" (*VO*, 369). In *Flush* the pampered invalid Elizabeth Barrett is forced to make an excursion from the elegant world of Wimpole Street to the worst slums of London in search of her dog. The journey is a revelation: "They were in a world that Miss Barrett had never seen, had never guessed at. They were in a world where cows are herded under bedroom floors, where whole families sleep in rooms with broken windows; in a world where water is turned on only twice a week, in a world where vice and poverty breed vice and poverty." The contrast generates guilt: "Here lived women like herself; while she lay on her sofa, reading, writing, they lived thus" (*F*, 89, 91). And in *The Years* Peggy Pargiter confesses "I've a sense of guilt always" and can never escape an awareness "of people toiling, grinding, in the heart of darkness, in the depths of night" (*Y*, 427, 418).

These feelings were not unknown to her creator. In the wake of the Russian Revolution, Bloomsbury was full of talk about giving up capital and abandoning the middle class. In her diary for 1918 Woolf records a number of such conversations as well as her own uneasiness: "I'm one of those who are hampered by the psychological hindrance of owning capital" (*D*, I, 101). This feeling was not really urgent—otherwise it would have led to action—but it was persistent. Particularly in the 1930s, when millions of her countrymen were unemployed, when the hunger marchers passed her door, it came back with renewed force. She records the incident of a young girl—out of work, no prospects, no friends, no money—who stops at her house and asks for water. She gives her food and some money but is appalled by the girl's situation: "Never saw unhappiness, poverty so tangible. And felt its our fault. And she apologised. And what could we do. . . . What a system" (*D*, V, 19). Woolf's combination of sympathy, guilt, and helplessness is characteristic. As in her response to the "system" of live-in servants ("Here is a fine rubbish heap left by our parents to be swept") she feels both a need for reform and a sense of impotence.

She knew that many younger middle-class writers had by this time seen a way out of this impasse. They were rejecting their bourgeois heritage and "actively working for a social revolution." Marx and Engels had predicted in *The Communist Manifesto* that the vanguard of the middle class would cut itself adrift and join the proletariat. In England writers like Auden, Day Lewis, Spender, MacNeice, Isherwood, and Woolf's own nephew Julian Bell were sometimes seen in this light. She was conscious of the challenge to her own life choices this alternative presented, and she defended her point of view in an important essay, "The Leaning Tower." She attacked those who pretend to join the ranks of the working class without surrendering their middle-class retreat rights. Woolf felt that most of these writers were guilty of false consciousness. They continued to benefit from the privileges of their education and family background while pretending they had burned their bridges. Woolf saw their middle-class slumming as self-indulgence, designed essentially to provide relief for a guilty conscience. In her view "the playboys and playgirls of the educated class who adopt the working-class cause without sacrificing middle-class capital, or sharing working-class experience" (*TG*, 312) had not passed the test of seriousness.

That test would be the surrender of everything an unearned income and family sponsorship could provide—leisure, freedom, superior education, domestic help, travel. Here was the impediment to a genuine left-wing commitment among people of her class, and Woolf could not see her way around it. She knew how essential her capital had been in making it possible to follow her artistic vocation. The Woolfs had no real taste for luxury; they used their money to buy time to write. Leonard's detailed financial records of Virginia's earnings from her fiction are instructive. Though her first three novels had been very well received and were published in both England and America, her royalties from them averaged out to £38 a year. She was in her late forties by the time she could have supported herself from her fiction. And Leonard concludes that if she had had to earn her own living in her twenties and thirties "it is highly improbable that she would ever have written a novel." [23] This is of course an overstatement; many writers managed to write novels without an independent income. They wrote in the evenings and on weekends; they wrote for a more popular audience; they produced journalism; some were lucky enough to find a patron. What Leonard means is that Virginia's independent income made it possible for her to devote her primary energy to the writing of fiction without constantly worrying about public taste and the pressures of the marketplace. It allowed her to write painstakingly rather than fluently, to invent alternatives to traditional narrative forms rather than follow the literary fashions.

This is surely what Woolf had in mind when she announced, in "The Leaning Tower," that "it is death for a writer to throw away his capital" (*CE*, II, 172). An independent income was a means to intellectual independence. "I'm the only woman in England free to write what I like," Woolf noted in her diary; "the others must be thinking of series & editors" (*D*, III, 43). This need encouraged her and Leonard to found the Hogarth Press, which was to bring out all of Woolf's books in England after her first two novels. These had been published by Duckworth, the firm owned by her half-brother Gerald. Although he never censored her work, she felt his intellectually complacent habits of mind exerting a sort of pressure on her as she wrote. Leonard Woolf recalls her relief when she realized that the Hogarth Press might free her forever: "The idea, which came to us in 1920, that we might publish ourselves the book which she had just begun to write, *Jacob's Room*, filled her with delight, for she would thus avoid the misery of submitting this highly experimental novel to the criticism of Gerald Duckworth and Edward Garnett [Duckworth's reader]."[24] And Woolf herself felt that this new arrangement had freed her to write in a style more clearly her own: "It is I think true, soberly & not artificially for the public, that I shall go on unconcernedly whatever people say. At last, I like reading my own writing. It seems to me to fit me closer than it did before" (*D*, II, 205). It was the Hogarth Press that published the works of her maturity—*Mrs. Dalloway*, *To the Lighthouse*, *The Waves*, and the rest—novels that many a commercial publisher would have been eager to handle. "When the publishers told me to write what they liked," she recalls, "I said No. I'll publish myself and write what I like" (*L*, IV, 348). It was a decision she never regretted: her independent income guaranteed the integrity of her work.

She was highly conscious of the perils of writing for money. The pen for hire was not an instrument of truth. In many of her literary essays she connects financial necessity with literary prostitution. Her picture of Laetitia Pilkington, a friend of Swift's but not his equal, gives a vivid account of such a state: "Ever since she could form her letters, indeed, she had written, with incredible speed and considerable grace, odes, addresses, apostrophes to Miss Hoadley, to the Recorder of Dublin, to Dr. Delville's place in the country. 'Hail, happy Delville, blissful seat!' 'Is there a man whose fixed and steady gaze—' the verses flowed without the slightest difficulty on the slightest occasion" (*CE*, IV, 131). And Woolf's description, in *Three Guineas*, of the prolific Mrs. Oliphant treats the same situation with a greater sense of tragedy, as she deplores "the fact that Mrs. Oliphant sold her brain, her very admirable brain, prostituted her culture and enslaved her intellectual liberty in order that she might earn her living and educate her children" (*TG*, 166).

She was also conscious of how the money trap was baited nearer home. Financial need had forced Roger Fry into essay writing and public lecturing and prevented him from concentrating on his own paintings, which did not sell. He thus abandoned "that absorption in art, that isolation and concentration which, as he was often to remark, the great artists, like Cézanne, have found essential" (*RF*, 88). The sentence recalls Woolf's own strenuous work habits as Leonard Woolf has described them: "I have never known anyone work with more intense, more indefatigable concentration than Virginia. This was particularly the case when she was writing a novel. The novel became part of her and she herself was absorbed into the novel. . . . It was this intense absorption which made writing so exhausting mentally for her." [25] Like Cézanne she used her freedom from financial cares to legitimize a total commitment to her work, with no serious concern about whether it sold or not. "The great desirable," Woolf concludes in her diary, "is not to have to earn money by writing" (*D*, V, 91).

For her generation of writers the real temptation was journalism. Fleet Street had become the new Grub Street. There were dozens of highly intelligent writers in London who squandered their talents in coining incessantly the small change of the profession—reviews of new books, topical pieces, "middles," whatever the editors were willing to buy. For the beginner such opportunities seemed to offer a version of the intellectual life that actually provided a living wage. When Woolf started writing journalism at the age of twenty-two, she was excited by the instant rewards of her new trade— the checks that arrived so promptly, her own words in print only days after she had written them. But her excitement soon gave way to concern as she grasped the long-term mental cost of such labor. At the lowest levels the work was simply a form of manufacture. But even those writing for the respectable weeklies like the *Times Literary Supplement* (as Woolf herself did) had surrendered their freedom of thought. When the editor of the *TLS* asks her to remove the word "lewd" in one of her reviews, she realizes that his conventional taste cramps her style: "One writes stiffly, without spontaneity" (*D*, II, 152). Furthermore, the task of reviewing current works makes it impossible to maintain genuine intellectual standards. With rare exceptions, the books under review are not worth reading attentively in the first place. Gradually Woolf came to understand that steady reviewing had nothing to do with serious literary commentary. Her analytic talents went into her critical books and into longer pieces of her own choosing. The rest was trivia, a real threat to her more ambitious work.

She was free to make such conditions because she was not dependent on journalism for her livelihood. And she understood the gravity of the threat not only from her own experience but from the careers of others she had known well. The first of these was her own father, who felt he had given up serious writing for various forms of hackwork. Leslie Stephen was appalled to hear himself described as a "notorious penny a liner" because he felt there was a "horrible plausibility" in the description.[26] Woolf would also have seen the cost of treating writing as a trade in some of the most promising members of her own circle. There was Desmond MacCarthy, who frittered away his gifts in occasional pieces and never produced the great book his friends thought him capable of writing. And there was her husband, who felt intellectually compromised by his regular work as a reviewer and editor. Leonard Woolf's considered opinion on the dangers of a journalistic career for a serious writer could hardly be more negative. He insists that "journalism is the opiate of the artist" and that "habitual or professional journalism destroys any ability to write literature."[27] Inevitably it turned the free spirit into a member of the intellectual proletariat.

Woolf was determined to avoid steady journalism not only because it took her away from her most serious work but because it was an aspect of the mass culture she and other modern artists had come to despise. Bloomsbury elitism has important links with the fear of democratic institutions that flourished in the early twentieth century. Yeats, Pound, Eliot, Lawrence, and Joyce responded with hostility to the urge to translate high culture into something a newly literate readership could easily assimilate. The Bloomsbury writers were more conciliatory and were never drawn to the authoritarian politics that attracted so many modern authors. Yet their distrust of popular appeal was not dissimilar. As the *possible* audience of literature widened, artists more often than not retreated to a much narrower sense of their ideal audience than their nineteenth-century precursors had imagined. "You will never sell more than five hundred copies," Ezra Pound warned Marianne Moore, "as your work demands mental attention." He was convinced that it takes only "about 600 people to make a civilization."[28] And when Woolf starts to write her first really experimental works, she records the feeling "that I write for half a dozen instead of 1500" (*D*, II, 107).

Although she eventually found a different, more accessible voice for what she called "the common reader," Woolf's fear of the large public audience persisted. She described her own age as "deafened with boom and blatancy" ("The Humane Art," *CE*, I, 105), a time of *loud*speakers and *broad*casting in which the subtle voice was drowned. She hated any form of publicity not only because it invaded her privacy but because it transformed the strenuous art of reading into the easily digestible pap of "interviews with the author," reviews *of*, lectures *on*—everything but the thing itself. She felt that serious reading was gradually becoming extinct, to be replaced by forms of communication designed by a new class of cultural middlemen who had insinuated themselves between writer and reader. She thinks of the writer in the glare of publicity as "like a trouser mender in Oxford Street, with a horde of reviewers pressing their noses to the glass and commenting to a curious crowd upon each stitch" ("Reviewing," *CE*, II, 213).

The mixture of fear and contempt in such passages is striking: Woolf loses her customary ironic detachment and composure. It is as though she feels herself a member of an endangered species fighting for survival. The class of creatures to which she belonged had become fair game, as the title of Leonard Woolf's 1927 essay, "Hunting the Highbrow," suggests. They had learned their lesson as early as 1910, in the hysterical fury that greeted Roger Fry's first Post-Impressionist Exhibition. The event was a turning point in the lives of the Bloomsbury group, as they first grasped the force of British philistinism. Woolf's description of the reactions to the Exhibition in her biography of Fry stresses both public outrage and the failure of the professional reviewers to observe with more sympathetic eyes (*RF*, 155). And Leonard Woolf's account of the second Post-Impressionist Exhibition, in 1912, suggests how implacably hostile and deliberately uncomprehending the great British public could be to the masterpieces of modern painting even after an earlier exposure: "Large numbers of people came to the exhibition, and nine out of ten of them either roared with laughter at the pictures or were enraged by them."[29]

Was it any wonder that serious artists exposed to such reactions might retreat to the relative safety of the like-minded? There, at least, one could count on the initial sympathy of people with a comparable vocational commitment. The coterie was essentially an enabling force, providing group support for controversial methods and conclusions. Its members constituted a sympathetic yet tough-minded group of peers who encouraged each other's best work because they understood the importance of intellectual or artistic vocation and the many ways it could be compromised. It was Forster's praise for her difficult novel *The Waves* that mattered to Woolf, not the reviewers' applause for *Orlando*, a book she considered facile. The private audience was more reliable than the public one because it was composed of fellow artists and writers rather than casual readers or harried journalists.

Nevertheless, Woolf saw there was a penalty in defining one's ideal audience so narrowly. She knew something about the history of coterie culture and wrote about it with a sense of the vital elements it excluded as well as of those it confirmed. In her essay on Madame de Sévigné she describes the charmed circle that also included La Rochefoucauld, Racine, and Madame de La Fayette "growing together in harmony, each contributing something that the other lacks," making and mastering "the private language of their set." Yet the last sentences of her essay suggest that this harmony is monophonic rather than polyphonic: "The voices mingle; they are all talking together in the garden in 1678. But what was happening outside?" (*CE*, III, 70). And in her essay on Henry

James's last phase, she suggests that his growing contempt for the larger audience of his early work exacted a heavy price: "Is not genius itself restricted, or at least influenced in its very essence by the consciousness that its gifts are to the few, and its revelation apparent only to scattered enthusiasts . . . ? The seclusion is so deliberate; the exclusion so complete" (*CE*, I, 282).

E. M. Forster's quite critical definition of Bloomsbury as a coterie stresses its narrow base: "Essentially *gentlefolks* [who] have acquired a culture in harmony with their social position. . . . Academic background, independent income."[30] A literary culture in harmony with the social position of the leisure class ignored problems of survival, excluded rival groups from serious consideration, and displayed a style that presupposed familiarity with the habits and specialized knowledge of that class. Woolf's limitations as a novelist have often been attributed to her acceptance of those terms as final. Raymond Mortimer complains that unlike Balzac or Tolstoy, who seem to have known "what any coarse, money-minded or brutal human being was like," Woolf could not "put herself into the shoes of people very different from herself."[31]

Perhaps this was so, but it was not for want of trying or from a comfortable conviction that it was unnecessary to go farther. Woolf often tried to break out of the set into which she had been born and recorded her frustrated sense of how little she knew about people different from herself. She was a restless and indefatigable city walker, as she recounts in her essay "Street Haunting," and she thought of these excursions as a way to "shed the self our friends know us by and become part of that vast republican army of anonymous trampers" (*CE*, IV, 155). In her diary she describes seeing a beggar woman singing on a street (perhaps the original of the one in *Mrs. Dalloway*) and then bursts out, "How she came to be there, what scenes she can go through, I can't imagine. O damn it all, I say, why cant I know all that too?" (*D*, II, 47).

She tried to acquire such knowledge by a sort of relentless interrogation of possible informants even if she could not get it by direct experience. "In whatever company I am I always try to know what it is like—being a conductor, being a woman with ten children and thirty-five shillings a week, being a stockbroker, being an admiral, being a bank clerk, being a dressmaker, being a duchess, being a miner, being a cook, being a prostitute," she writes in one of her essays ("Middlebrow," *CE*, II, 197). Many of her friends mention her habit of cross-examining those with access to worlds different from her own. Elizabeth Bowen recalls, "She wanted to know all the details of people's lives." Barbara Bagenal writes, "One of her characteristics was to ask innumerable questions. She was intensely interested in what other people were thinking and why." [32] It was a kind of eager research to make up in some measure for the narrowness of her own experience.

She envied writers who had somehow managed to get beyond the limits of their station. The vitality of *Sons and Lovers*, for example, she attributed to Lawrence's crossing over from working to middle class (*CE*, I, 354). And Mrs. Gaskell, though "she was hampered by a refined upbringing and traditions of culture," had nevertheless been able to find out "how the poor enjoy themselves; how they visit and gossip and fry bacon and lend each other bits of finery and show off their sores" (*BP*, 139). Compared with this heterogeneous mix, the "aristocratic world" of a George Meredith—"strictly bounded, thinly populated, a little hard-hearted" (*CE*, I, 236)—lacked vitality.

Woolf thus came to see her own upbringing, with its refinement, its exclusions, its special language, as closing her in. She felt that the class snobbishness in which she had been trained, and which she had mastered, had impoverished her both as a writer and as a human being. In her diary she records seeing two working-class girls on a country walk:

Two resolute, sunburnt, dusty girls, in jerseys & short skirts, with packs on their backs, city clerks, or secretaries, tramping along the road in the hot sunshine at Ripe. My instinct at once throws up a screen, which condemns them: I think them in every way angular, awkward & self assertive. But all this is a great mistake. These screens shut me out. Have no screens, for screens are made out of our own integument; & get at the thing itself, which has nothing whatever in common with a screen. The screen making habit, though, is so universal, that probably it preserves our sanity. If we had not this device for shutting people off from our sympathies, we might, perhaps, dissolve utterly. Separateness would be impossible. But the screens are in the excess; not the sympathy.

(*D*, III, 104)

The passage is highly self-critical. Though it offers excuses related to Woolf's particular situation—her perilous sanity, her need for isolation—she finally sees them as inadequate. The screens were another form of enclosure invented to protect the privileged that only cut them off from the sources of vitality.

She felt trapped in her own class enclave. We have already seen that she refused to pretend to working-class sympathies while holding on to the capital that guaranteed her freedom as a writer. Even more important, perhaps, had been her sheltered upbringing. Like her first heroine, Rachel Vinrace, "she had scarcely walked through a poor street, and always under the escort of father, maid, or aunts" (*VO*, 70). Young ladies of her station seldom got away from the confines of their family or its approved acquaintances. Unlike their brothers, they were not sent away to school or university and encouraged to travel. Rather, in the words of Quentin Bell, "they would, in a decorous way, become accomplished and then marry" (*QB*, I, 21). The accomplishments had nothing to do with serious vocational training, and the marriage was expected to be to a suitable member of the same set.

Given all these pressures, it is important to understand that Woolf did move quite a distance from her moorings, despite her own dissatisfaction with how far she had managed to travel. She turned her back on many of the conventions of her set and sex; some of her most important life decisions reflect a conscious rejection of traditional limits. The move from Kensington to Bloomsbury was a move from an upper-middle-class preserve to a semiderelict world of "offices, lodgings, nursing homes and small artisans' workshops," as Duncan Grant described it.[33] Woolf's decision to live there went against her class's obsession with the desirable location and proper address. Her contempt for finery—fashionable clothes, jewelry, dressing for dinner, stylish furnishings—was so extreme that it amounted to a declaration of independence. The sexual frankness that became one of the hallmarks of Bloomsbury talk also helped to move her out of the sheltered harbor of her girlhood by making no distinction between what was fit for men and women to hear and say. She had entered the fringes of bohemia, "that section of Society which lives out of Society," as one Victorian observer pithily defined it.[34] Though she herself was not really bohemian, her sister, Duncan Grant, and many of their friends certainly were. And the outsider status that bohemianism conferred seemed to her a treasure.

"Outsider" is a word Woolf regularly uses to describe herself. Even in a diary entry written when she was twenty-one and still under her family's tutelage, she saw herself and Vanessa as outsiders, alienated from the close-knit social group to which they officially belonged (Berg Diary, Hyde Park Gate, June 30–Oct. 1, 1903, 10). She was not certain at that point whether her marginal identity was imposed or chosen. In her maturity she came to see it as a badge of honor and associated it with being a woman. In *Three Guineas* she proposed that women refuse to join a pacifist organization dominated by men but form their own, to be called "the Outsiders' Society" (*TG*, 193). And in her diary she connected professionally successful men with an "insider" identity she was glad not to share: "I like outsiders better. Insiders write a colourless English. They are turned out by the University machine" (*D*, V, 333). The connection between Woolf's feminism and her class identity is so complex that it will be discussed at length in a later chapter. But it is worth emphasizing that she was not entirely unhappy to be excluded from the male-dominated institutions of her class. Her exclusion gave her what she called in another context "the outsiders privilege of irresponsible mockery."[35]

But perhaps the most important of Woolf's rejections of her class training was her decision to marry "a penniless Jew," as she repeatedly calls Leonard at the time of her engagement (*L*, I, 500, 501). He would hardly have been considered a suitable match in the world from which she came even though he had been educated at St. Paul's and Trinity College, Cambridge, and had made a promising start in a respectable profession. He was not quite penniless, but when he married Virginia he had practically no capital and had given up his position in the Ceylon civil service in order to stay in England. He had no immediate prospects and wanted, like Virginia, to write.

Furthermore, the fact that Leonard was a Jew was no minor consideration, given the reflex antisemitism of Woolf's set—a prejudice she herself occasionally voiced and had not entirely put behind her when she accepted him. A letter from Keynes to Vanessa Bell written five years after the Woolfs' marriage gives some sense of the unapologetic contempt for Jews still in vogue. On his last visit to the Woolfs, Keynes writes, he was relieved to find Virginia "but no Jew; nor did he appear at all, which gives a great pleasure." And in a later letter he refers casually to "Virginia and the Jew," as though Leonard had no name.[36] In addition, this particular Jew was a socialist and an active member of the Labour Party. Virginia went with him to Party conferences, met dozens of people involved in left-wing politics, listened to and participated in highly critical conversations about British imperialism and social injustice that would have been quite offensive to many members of the Kensington circle in which she had been reared. Her unconventional marriage moved her far outside the boundaries that had originally been drawn for her.

And yet, despite all these departures from expectation—her move to Bloomsbury, her easy concourse with bohemia, her feminism, her "unsuitable" marriage—Woolf continued to feel that *as a writer* she was trapped in the class into which she had been born. Perhaps if she had not been a psychological novelist, interested in knowing people from the inside rather than concentrating on their circumstances, she would have felt this less intensely. But since this was her gift, she could hardly fail to notice that her opportunities for observing people across class barriers were exactly that—a form of observation rather than of lived experience. As she puts it in her introduction to *Life as We Have Known It*, "The imagination is largely the child of the flesh. One could not be Mrs. Giles of Durham because one's body had never stood at the wash-tub; one's hands had never wrung and scrubbed and chopped up whatever the meat may be that makes a miner's supper."[37]

Though she had haunted the London streets, kept her eyes open and asked countless questions, what she had managed to find out did not satisfy her. It was inevitably superficial and second-hand. She often writes about observing strangers, inventing a life history for them, and then realizing that it was all merely the product of her own fantasy. The mysterious Mrs. Brown in "Mr. Bennett and Mrs. Brown" remains unknown to us, though she is scrupulously observed, for the important thing is not to describe what she looks like or to record what she says but "to realize her character, to steep oneself in her atmosphere" (*CE*, I, 324), and this Woolf knows she cannot do through close observation alone. Variants of this anecdote appear in Woolf's story "An Unwritten Novel" and her narrative essay "Three Pictures." In all the versions she stresses the experiential basis of the literary imagination and insists that its limits are determined by class identity: "If my father was a blacksmith and yours was a peer of the realm, we must needs be pictures to each other" ("Three Pictures," *CE*, IV, 151). This class estrangement was exacerbated, as we have seen, by the protective cocoon the British upper middle class secreted to protect its young women.

Woolf is arguing for what one might call a theory of class doom in British society. Despite the pressures of modern democracy, despite the rhetoric of community, England had been, and was fated to remain, a highly stratified world in which class was inescapable. Woolf clearly thought this situation unfortunate. She describes it in her essay "The Niece of an Earl" as the peculiar "disability" from which the English novelist suffers: "He is fated to know intimately, and so to describe with understanding, only those who are of his own social rank. He cannot escape from the box in which he has been bred" (*CE*, I, 221). Once again, the image is of enclosure.

Woolf knew that there were exceptions to this rule, and that Chaucer and Shakespeare (who were not of course novelists) did not suffer from this disability. She was also exaggerating the hopelessness of the problem because she had failed to solve it and needed to point to comparable failures. Nevertheless, there is clearly a good deal of truth in what she says, particularly if we exclude the writers who had managed to rise in the world (like Dickens or Lawrence) and were not required to sink in order to expand the range of their sympathies.

In the privileged world from which Woolf came, the impediments to the imaginative understanding of other classes were formidable. Karl Mannheim has argued in his essay "The Problem of the Intelligentsia" that this situation is virtually inescapable for members of that class:

> The obvious assets of a leisure-class existence are balanced by its temptations, and practically all intellectual leisure classes face the same dilemma. Surely, a certain spare time is a necessary basis of cultivation, and the precondition of attention to affairs which do not wholly concern the daily satisfaction of wants. But a leisure-class existence is in itself a source of estrangement from reality, for it conceals the frictions and tensions of life and invites a sublimated and internalized perception of things.[38]

In certain obvious ways Mannheim's analysis can be used to describe the limitations of Woolf's work. But it defines "reality" too narrowly, assuming that the daily struggle for existence is more real than the lives of those who are exempt from it. This is of course one of the received ideas of our time, but that does not make it any more convincing. Zola's world is no more, and no less, real than Proust's. The "frictions and tensions of life" are not limited to those who have to earn a living, and an "internalized perception of things"—as Woolf and other modern novelists have shown—can have extraordinary interest and vitality. Nevertheless, the fact of leisure-class estrangement from the life of other classes, the existence of a gulf that is nearly impassable, can scarcely be denied. Woolf, as we have seen, both acknowledged and lamented its existence: "There is no animosity, perhaps, but there is no communication. We are enclosed, and separate, and cut off" ("The Niece of an Earl," *CE*, I, 219). If she had really been the complacent snob of legend, she would have remained essentially indifferent to this situation. In fact, she was both obsessed by the existence of such social gulfs and anxious to write about them. The image of one's class as a prison—gilded or otherwise—is one of the central metaphors of her work. As we have seen, it recurs in one form or another in practically everything she wrote. But its greatest embodiment is in the separate worlds she created in *Mrs. Dalloway*, her most searching account of the class isolation of her society.

5

Mrs. Dalloway and the Social System

"I want to criticise the social system, & to show it at work, at its most intense" (*D*, II, 248). Woolf's provocative statement about her intentions in writing *Mrs. Dalloway* has regularly been ignored. It denies the traditional view of her work as apolitical and indifferent to social issues, the view that allowed Forster to say with confidence that "improving the world she would not consider" or Jean Guiguet to insist that "the mechanical relations between individuals, such as are imposed by the social structure, dominated by concepts of class and wealth . . . are not her problem."[1] *Mrs. Dalloway* reveals that such generalizations do not hold up under scrutiny. The novel is in large measure an examination of a single class and its control over English society—the "governing class" (86), as Peter Walsh calls it. Woolf's picture of Clarissa Dalloway's world is sharply critical, but as we will see it cannot be called an indictment, because it deliberately looks at its object from the inside.

Woolf examines the governing class of England at a particular moment in history. Unlike *The Waves*, *Mrs. Dalloway* has a precise historical setting, which it is important to understand. It takes place on a day in June 1923, five years after the end of the First World War. Peter Walsh, who has been out of England since the war, notes the transformation of society in that period: "Those five years—1918 to 1923—had been, he suspected, somehow very important. People looked different. Newspapers seemed different," and morals and manners had changed (80). There are a number of other topical references in the novel that its first readers would certainly have understood. The early 1920s brought to an end the Conservative-Liberal coalition in British politics; the elections of 1922 and

1923 marked the eclipse of the Liberals and the rise of Labour. For the first time the Labour Party became the official government opposition. It was only a matter of time before this "socialist" power, with its putative threat to the governing class examined in the novel, would be in office. Indeed, Conservative M.P.'s like Richard Dalloway are already making plans for that event. He will write a history of Lady Bruton's family when he is out of Parliament, and she assures him that the documents are ready for him at her estate "whenever the time came; the Labour Government, she meant" (122). The Conservative prime minister who appears at Clarissa's party at the end of the book remained in office only until January 1924, when he was succeeded by the first Labour prime minister, Ramsay MacDonald. And though the new government lasted less than a year, the Labour Party has remained the ruling or opposition party ever since. *Mrs. Dalloway* was published in 1925; Woolf's first readers would certainly have been aware of these crucial events.

The historical references suggest that the class under examination in the novel is living on borrowed time. Its values—"the public-spirited, British Empire, tariff-reform, governing-class spirit" (85–86), in Peter's words—were very much under attack. Characters like Lady Bruton, Miss Parry, and Peter himself are identified with Britain's imperial mission, but the empire was crumbling fast. In 1922 the Irish Free State was proclaimed and the last English troops left Dublin. When Lady Bruton cries in dismay, "Ah, the news from India!" (122), she probably has in mind the beginnings of the agitation for independence in that country. The *Times* in June 1923 was full of "news from India" sure to disturb someone with her values: imperial police "overwhelmed and brutally tortured by the villagers" (2 June); "Extremists Fomenting Trouble" (23 June); "Punjab Discontent" (29 June). Peter Walsh goes to Clarissa's party not only to see her again but also "to ask Richard what they were doing in India—the conservative duffers" (177).

As a class and as a force, then, the world to which the Dalloways belong is decadent rather than crescent. The party at the end of the novel, for all its brilliance, is a kind of wake. It reveals the form of power without its substance. When the prime minister finally arrives, he is described as looking "so ordinary. You might have stood him behind a counter and bought biscuits—poor chap, all rigged up in gold lace" (189). And the imagery of the last section suggests rigidity, calcification, the exhumation of relics: "Doors were being opened for ladies wrapped like mummies in shawls with bright flowers on them" (180). Clarissa's ancient aunt, whom Peter had mistakenly thought dead, appears at the party: "For Miss Helena Parry was not dead: Miss Parry was alive. She was past eighty. She ascended staircases slowly with a stick. She was placed in a chair. . . . People who had known Burma in the 'seventies were always led up to her" (195–96). Even the young people of the class, in Clarissa's words, "could not talk. . . . The enormous resources of the English language, the power it bestows, after all, of communicating feelings . . . was not for them. They would solidify young" (195).

Solidity, rigidity, stasis, the inability to communicate feelings—these are central concepts in *Mrs. Dalloway*. As they apply to the governing class in the novel, they point to something inflexible, unresponsive, or evasive in their nature that makes them incapable of reacting appropriately to the critical events of their time or of their own lives. The great contemporary event of European history had of course been the First World War, and it is no exaggeration to say with one critic that "deferred war-shock" is the major theme of *Mrs. Dalloway*.[2] Though the war had transformed the lives of millions of people, only one character in the novel—Septimus Smith— seems to have counted its cost, both to the victims of the slaughter and to the survivors. He does not, of course, belong to the governing class, whose way of responding to the war is crucially different. Woolf suggests that they are engaged in a conspiracy to deny its pain or its significance. Their ideal is stoicism, even if the price they pay is petrifaction. Clarissa consistently idealizes the behavior of Lady Bexborough, "who opened a bazaar, they said, with the telegram in her hand, John, her favourite, killed." The sentence comes from one of several passages in which the war is mentioned, a section in which Clarissa complacently muses, "For it was the middle of June. The War was over . . . thank Heaven—over. It was June. The King and Queen were at the palace" (6–7). The easy assumption that the war is a thing of the past and need no longer be a subject of concern is also voiced in Richard Dalloway's momentary thought for the "thousands of poor chaps, with all their lives before them, shovelled together, already half forgotten" (127), and in the words of "little Mr. Bowley, who had rooms in the Albany and was sealed with wax over the deeper sources of life": "poor women, nice little children, orphans, widows, the War—tut-tut" (23).

Neither Virginia Woolf nor any of her Bloomsbury associates could have brought themselves to say "the War—tut-tut." "Curse this war; God damn this war!" the man in her story "The Mark on the Wall" cries out (*HH*, 48). For all of them, the war was an unmitigated catastrophe that forced them to examine their consciences and make major ethical decisions—whether to declare themselves conscientious objectors, whether to participate in any form. If the war had any justification, it could be only as a liberating force likely to transform society and human relations. Perhaps the brave new world it might help to bring to birth could make one believe in its necessity. In *The Years*, this hope for the regeneration of humanity is expressed in the crucial air raid scene that takes place in 1917. Eleanor asks, with the ardor and desperation of a character in Chekhov, "When will this new world come? When shall we be free? When shall we live adventurously, wholly, not like cripples in a cave?" (*Y*, 320). But in *The Years*, as in *Mrs. Dalloway*, the hopes for a new society are betrayed by the return of the old. The sacrifice has been meaningless. As Clarissa Dalloway says in the short story out of which the novel grew, "Thousands of young men had died that things might go on" (MDP, 28).

The sense of living in the past, of being unable to take in or respond to the transformations of the present, makes the governing class in *Mrs. Dalloway* seem hopelessly out of step with its time. Peter turns Miss Parry's glass eye into a symbol: "It seemed so fitting—one of nature's masterpieces—that old Miss Parry should turn to glass. She would die like some bird in a frost gripping her perch. She belonged to a different age" (178–79). Woolf gives us a picture of a class impervious to change in a society that desperately needs or demands it, a class that worships tradition and settled order but cannot accommodate the new and disturbing. Lady Bradshaw is described, in an extraordinary phrase, as feeling "wedged on a calm ocean" (105). But the calm is only on the surface; there is turbulence beneath. The class, in fact, uses its influence to exclude and sequester alien or threatening forces—the Septimus Smiths, the Doris Kilmans—and to protect itself from any sort of intense feeling. It may well be this calculated emotional obtuseness that has kept it in power, since Woolf makes it clear (in the sky-writing scene) that many others in the society long for a restoration of the status quo ante. The political activities of the novel—Richard's committees, Lady Bruton's emigration project, Hugh Whitbread's letters to the *Times*, the ritual appearance of the prime minister—are all essentially routine in nature and suggest that it is only by ignoring the more devastating facts and deep scars of recent history that the "social system" has managed to keep functioning.[3] Perhaps Woolf saw a necessary connection in unstable times between traditional political power and the absence of empathy and moral imagination.

Certainly the governing class in the novel demonstrates these qualities. It worships Proportion, by which it really means atrophy of the heart, repression of instinct and emotion. A. D. Moody has pointed to the impulse in the class "to turn away from the disturbing depths of feeling, and towards a conventional pleasantness or sentimentality or frivolousness."[4] Richard Dalloway, for example, finds it impossible to tell his wife that he loves her or even, for that matter, to say the word "I": "The time comes when it can't be said; one's too shy to say it. . . . Here he was walking across London to say to Clarissa in so many words that he loved her. Which one never does say, he thought. Partly one's lazy; partly one's shy" (127). When the desperate Septimus stammers "I—I—" in

Dr. Bradshaw's consulting room, Sir William cautions, "Try to think as little about yourself as possible" (109).[5] That this repression of feeling is very much the product of upper-class training is suggested not only in *Mrs. Dalloway* but in a crystallizing minor incident in *The Years*: "Here a footman's white-gloved hand removing dishes knocked over a glass of wine. A red splash trickled onto the lady's dress. But she did not move a muscle; she went on talking. Then she straightened the clean napkin that had been brought her, nonchalantly, over the stain" (*Y*, 274).

Such unruffled self-control has everything to do with the ability to retain power and to stay sane. The characters in *Mrs. Dalloway* who cannot learn to restrain their intense emotions (Septimus, Miss Kilman, even Peter Walsh) are all in serious trouble. They are the outsiders in a society dedicated to covering up the stains and ignoring the major and minor tremors that threaten its existence. When such people become too distressing, they are dealt with by the "authorities," agents of the governing class like the psychiatrist Sir William Bradshaw who act to make sure that "these unsocial impulses . . . [are] held in control" (113). For the anesthesia of the governing class must not be permitted to wear off. And so Sir William "made England prosper, secluded her lunatics, forbade childbirth, penalised despair, made it impossible for the unfit to propagate their views" (110). This whole section of the novel makes us realize that the complacency of the governing class is not a natural state but must be constantly defended by the strenuous activity of people like Sir William. There is a conspiracy to keep any kind of vividness, any intense life, at a safe distance. The doctor's gray car is furnished in monotone, with gray furs and silver gray rugs "to match its sober suavity" (104).

This sense of living in a cocoon that protects the class from disturbing facts and feelings is reiterated in the treatment of its relations with its servants. Lady Bruton, for example, floats gently on "the grey tide of service which washed round [her] day in, day out, collecting, intercepting, enveloping her in a fine tissue which broke concussions, mitigated inter-

ruptions, and spread round the house in Brook Street a fine
net where things lodged and were picked out accurately,
instantly" (119). Service is assumed to be part of the natural order by the governing class, dependable in its regular
rhythms, creating an environment of basic security by main-
taining a predictable daily routine. The fact that the entire
system is based on the power and wealth of one class and the
drudgery of another is ignored by master and servant alike in
an unending ritual of deception and self-deception, as Woolf
sarcastically suggests:

> And so there began a soundless and exquisite passing to and
> fro through swing doors of aproned, white-capped maids,
> handmaidens not of necessity, but adepts in a mystery or
> grand deception practised by hostesses in Mayfair from one-
> thirty to two, when, with a wave of the hand, the traffic ceases,
> and there rises instead this profound illusion in the first place
> about the food—how it is not paid for; and then that the table
> spreads itself voluntarily with glass and silver, little mats,
> saucers of red fruit; films of brown cream mark turbot; in cas-
> seroles severed chickens swim; coloured, undomestic, the fire
> burns; and with the wine and the coffee (not paid for) rise
> jocund visions before musing eyes; gently speculative eyes;
> eyes to whom life appears musical, mysterious.
>
> (115–16)

It is a way of life that seems part of some eternal order,
functioning without apparent friction or even choice. But
Woolf makes us see the connection between the elegance and
composure of the governing class and the ceaseless activity of
the lower. Clarissa Dalloway, in a little hymn of praise to her
servants, mentally thanks them "for helping her to be . . .
gentle, generous-hearted" (44). She sends her "love" to the
cook, Mrs. Walker, in the middle of one of her parties; but we
are given a vivid glimpse of the pandemonium below stairs
not visible to the guests pleasantly floating on "the grey tide
of service":

> Did it matter, did it matter in the least, one Prime Minister
> more or less? It made no difference at this hour of the night to
> Mrs. Walker among the plates, saucepans, cullenders, frying-
> pans, chicken in aspic, ice-cream freezers, pared crusts of

bread, lemons, soup tureens, and pudding basins which, however hard they washed up in the scullery, seemed to be all on top of her, on the kitchen table, on chairs, while the fire blared and roared, the electric lights glared, and still supper had to be laid.

(181–82)

The relationship between master and servant in *Mrs. Dalloway* is typical of the gulf between all classes in the novel. Clarissa's party is strictly class-demarcated. No Septimus, no Rezia, no Doris Kilman could conceivably set foot in it. Miss Kilman, indeed, bitterly notes that "people don't ask me to parties" (145). Even impoverished gentlefolk, like Clarissa's cousin Ellie Henderson, are invited only under pressure and out of habit. Clarissa defends her parties as an expression of her ideal of unity, the wish to bring together "so-and-so in South Kensington; some one up in Bayswater; and somebody else, say, in Mayfair" (134), and critics have often stressed her ability to merge different worlds and create a feeling of integration.[6] But the London neighborhoods she mentions are upper-middle-class preserves, the residential areas where the members of the Dalloway set are likely to live (though Bayswater might require an amusing explanation). Clarissa's integration is horizontal, not vertical.

The Dalloways shut out not only the Septimus Smiths and the Doris Kilmans but the artists as well. The novel makes it clear that their world is consistently and uneasily philistine. Though a token poet makes an appearance at Clarissa's party, her set has a deep distrust of writers, precisely because they might disturb its complacency. Richard opines that "no decent man ought to read Shakespeare's sonnets because it was like listening at keyholes (besides, the relationship was not one that he approved)" (84). Sally says of Hugh Whitbread that "he's read nothing, thought nothing, felt nothing" (81); Dr. Bradshaw "never had time for reading" (108); and Lady Bruton, though Lovelace or Herrick once frequented her family estate, "never read a word of poetry herself" (116). This indifference or hostility to literature is symptomatic of the class's lack of curiosity about life outside its precincts. In the novel an obsession with Shakespeare (as in the thoughts of Septimus and Clarissa) is a kind of shorthand indication that the soul has survived, that some kind of sympathetic imagination is still functioning.

Clarissa's instant empathy with Septimus when his suicide is mentioned at her party is in marked contrast to the way her set usually deals with outsiders. His death shatters her composure and touches her in a profoundly personal way. This is not at all the manner in which the rest of the governing class treats the threatening presences by which it is surrounded. Their method is rather to turn the individual into a "case," as Bradshaw does in mentioning Septimus in the first place: "They were talking about this Bill. Some case Sir William was mentioning, lowering his voice. It had its bearing upon what he was saying about the deferred effects of shell shock. There must be some provision in the Bill" (201). In this way of treating alien experience, the living Septimus becomes a category, his life an "it" to be considered by government committees drafting legislation. The ability to translate individual human beings into manageable social categories is one of the marks of the governing-class mentality Woolf examines in the novel. They have learned to think and talk in officialese. Richard "championed the downtrodden . . . in the House of Commons" (127). A young woman he passes in the park ("impudent, loose-lipped, humorous") immediately becomes an example of "the female vagrant" in a passage that perfectly suggests his need to keep people at a distance: "Bearing his flowers like a weapon, Richard Dalloway approached her; intent he passed her; still there was time for a spark between them—she laughed at the sight of him, he smiled good-humouredly, considering the problem of the female vagrant; not that they would ever speak" (128–29). Lady Bruton's emigration project is designed for "young people of both sexes born of respectable parents" (120). Sir William sees Septimus as merely another of "these prophetic Christs and Christesses" (110). These examples suggest that the governing class has remained unruffled by viewing all social problems as involving distinct categories of people different from themselves. Like all good administrators, they compartmentalize in order to control and make things manageable.

These managerial skills are used to keep the society stable and to retain power. Emigration is a way of handling the massive unemployment of the period;[7] benefits in cases of delayed shell shock will separate the lunatics who insist on flaunting their rage or guilt about the war from those who are trying to forget it; Richard's work on committees for "his Armenians, his Albanians" (132) might defuse another explosive international situation. All the governing-class types in the novel think of themselves as progressive reformers, even the unctuous Hugh Whitbread, whose "name at the end of letters to the *Times*, asking for funds, appealing to the public to protect, to preserve, to clear up litter, to abate smoke, and stamp out immorality in parks, commanded respect" (114). But behind the public concern and tradition of social service is the need to dominate, the habit of power. It is here that one can see the social system "at work, at its most intense." Its symbol is the figure of Dr. Bradshaw, preaching Proportion but worshiping Conversion, a goddess who "feasts on the wills of the weakly, loving to impress, to impose, adoring her own features stamped on the face of the populace," a deity at work not only in Sir William's consulting room but also "in the heat and sands of India, the mud and swamp of Africa, the purlieus of London, wherever, in short, the climate or the devil tempts men to fall from the true belief which is her own" (110–11). The passage clearly connects the "case" of Septimus Smith with British imperialism and social repression and reveals the iron hand in a velvet glove. It is entirely appropriate that this psychiatrist-policeman and the Prime Minister should be invited to the same party.

The passages concerning Dr. Bradshaw are markedly different in tone from the rest of the book, but this is not simply because Woolf is writing out of her own painful experience of how mental derangement is handled by some professional therapists. Such "treatment" is itself a symptom of a disease in the social system—the easy assumption of the habit of command. It connects with Woolf's angry criticism of the patriarchy in *A Room of One's Own* and *Three Guineas* as well as with her satiric picture of the imperial policeman in *Between the Acts*, her symbol of Victorian England, who tells the audience:

> Go to Church on Sunday; on Monday, nine sharp, catch the City Bus. On Tuesday it may be, attend a meeting at the Mansion House for the redemption of the sinner; at dinner on Wednesday attend another— turtle soup. Some bother it may be in Ireland; Famine. Fenians. What not. On Thursday it's the natives of Peru require protection and correction; we give 'em what's due. But mark you, our rule don't end there. It's a Christian country, our Empire; under the White Queen Victoria. Over thought and religion; drink; dress; manners; marriage too, I wield my truncheon.
>
> (*BA*, 190)

In *Mrs. Dalloway* too the representatives of power wield their truncheons. "What right has Bradshaw to say 'must' to me?" Septimus demands (162). Behind philanthropy and reform, industriousness, morality, and religion there is the same impulse—telling others how to live, "forcing your soul," as Clarissa puts it (203). In a diary entry about Victorian philanthropists, Woolf reveals how repugnant the easy assumption of power in this class was to her: "More & more I come to loathe any dominion of one over another; any leadership, any imposition of the will" (*D*, I, 256).

The fundamental conflict in *Mrs. Dalloway* is between those who identify with Establishment "dominion" and "leadership" and those who resist or are repelled by it. The characters in the novel can be seen as ranged on a sort of continuum with Bradshaw at one end and Septimus at the other. Thus far I have concentrated on the characters at the Establishment end of the scale: Sir William, Hugh Whitbread, Lady Bruton, Miss Parry, and Richard Dalloway. Among the rebels (present or former) we must count Septimus Smith, Doris Kilman, Sally Seton, and Peter Walsh, though there are important distinctions among them. And in the center of this conflict—its pivot, so to speak—stands Clarissa Dalloway.

Septimus Smith is instantly seen as a threat to governing-class values not only because he insists on remembering the war when everyone else is trying to forget it but also because his feverish intensity of feeling is an implicit criticism of the ideal of stoic impassivity. In Woolf's preliminary notes for the novel, she treats this as the essence of Septimus's character: "He must somehow see through human nature—see its hypocrisy, & insincerity, its power to recover from every wound, incapable of taking any final impression. His sense that this is not worth having."[8] Septimus comes through the war unscathed—"The last shells missed him" (96)—but afterward discovers a psychic wound from which he has no wish to recover because it is a badge of honor in a society that identifies composure with mental health. The mark of his sensibility is perpetual turbulence, as in this passage: "The excitement of the elm trees rising and falling, rising and falling with all their leaves alight and the colour thinning and thickening from blue to the green of a hollow wave. . . . Leaves were alive; trees were alive" (26). It is as if Septimus were a repository for the suppressed feelings of the rigidly controlled people around him, those like Mr. Bowley "sealed with wax over the deeper sources of life." Far from being sealed, Septimus is a seething cauldron of emotions constantly threatening to overflow, a sacrificial victim or scapegoat who takes upon himself the sins of omission rather than commission. Woolf planned that he "should pass through all extremes of feeling."[9] Like Leontes in *The Winter's Tale*, Septimus is "a feather for each wind that blows," but his emotional instability is a compensation for his society's repression and can be understood and judged only in relation to it.

For Septimus has not always been a rebel. He begins, indeed, like the classic ambitious working-class boy entering the Establishment: moving to the city from the provinces, "improving himself" by taking evening classes, impressing his superiors at work and in the army by his ability and detachment. He volunteers early in the war, and when his friend Evans is killed, he congratulates himself "upon feeling very little and very reasonably. The War had taught him. It was sublime. He had gone through the whole show, friendship, European War, death, had won promotion, was still under thirty and was bound to survive" (96). But this mood of self-congratulation is suddenly displaced by the "appalling fear . . . that he could not feel" (98). His stoic fortitude in the face of slaughter sends him into a panic incomprehensible to a society that idealizes Proportion. For his fear of emotional aridity is finally greater than his dread of insanity. And so he surrenders to the force of feeling in all its variety and intensity—guilt, ecstasy, loathing, rage, bliss. His emotions are chaotic because they are entirely self-generated and self-sustained; he becomes a pariah. That Septimus should have no contact with the Dalloway set is absolutely essential to Woolf's design, though it has often been criticized as a structural flaw of the novel.[10] And among the people in his own world, Rezia has no idea what goes on in his mind; Dr. Holmes recommends bromides, golf, and the music hall; Sir William orders seclusion and bed rest. His only companion is the dead Evans, whom he must resurrect in fantasy. He is alone.

It is no wonder that the resultant vision of the world is as distorted as the governing-class view. Where Richard complacently sees his times as "a great age in which to have lived" (129), Septimus is conscious only of "the brute with the red nostrils" all around him (103). In Shakespeare, in Dante, in Aeschylus, he can find only one message: "loathing, hatred, despair." His wife's innocent wish for a child is seen as an example of the "filth" of copulation, and the ordinary run of humanity at his office is "leering, sneering, obscene . . . oozing thick drops of vice" (98–100). All this is an obvious projection of his own guilt, which he feels simultaneously: "He had not cared when Evans was killed; that was worst; . . . and was so pocked and marked with vice that women shuddered when they saw him in the street" (101). These black feelings are unendurable and consistently alternate with their opposites, with pastoral visions of a world of eternal beauty and harmony. In his fantasy, Evans is brought back to life and the sparrows sing "how there is no crime . . . how there is no death" (28). Though Septimus is intended to serve as an antithesis to the governing-class spirit, he is in no sense a preferable alternative to it. And he, too, is finally forced to pretend that the war's cost was not real, that death is an illusion. He is a victim not only of the war but of the peace, with its insistence that all could be forgotten and the old order reestablished. The pressure to do so is eventually too much for him, and he succumbs.

Like Septimus, Doris Kilman is a war victim. Dismissed from her teaching position because "she would not pretend that the Germans were all villains" (136), she must earn her living by occasional tutorial instruction. The degrading poverty and isolation her dismissal brings about embitters her profoundly, making her despise herself and her society in alternate flashes of emotion. Like Septimus, she cannot control "the hot and turbulent feelings which boiled and surged in her" (137). And also like him, she finds release in a quasi-mystical experience that momentarily assuages her distress. But her religious calm is temporary; her passionate nature continues to vent itself in unpredictable and uncontrollable surges—her murderous hatred of Mrs. Dalloway; her agonized love for Elizabeth: "If she could grasp her, if she could clasp her, if she could make her hers absolutely and for ever and then die; that was all she wanted" (145). But what hope is there that the discreditable feelings Doris Kilman harbors—her lesbian attachment to Elizabeth, her class rage, her contempt for British jingoism during the war—could ever see the light of day? The lid of convention is heavily and firmly in place in the world around her, and so her intense emotional life must be lived entirely in her own mind, where it takes on a nightmare quality comparable to that of Septimus. She, too, is alone.

Between the extremes of Dr. Bradshaw and Hugh Whitbread on the one hand and Septimus and Doris Kilman on the other, Woolf invents three characters who cannot be placed so easily: Sally Seton, Peter Walsh, and Clarissa. Though all belong to the upper middle class, all have gone through a passionate rebellious phase, rejecting what their world stood for—the worship of convention, the inevitability of the class structure, the repression of feeling. As young women, Sally and Clarissa planned "to found a society to abolish private property"; they read the utopian socialists and talked about "how they were to reform the world" (38). Sally once radiated "a sort of abandonment, as if she could say anything, do anything" (37), that made Clarissa fall passionately in love with her. The girlhood attachment was as intense as Miss Kilman's feeling for Elizabeth. Clarissa too had longed for a *Liebestod*: " 'If it were now to die 'twere now to be most happy.' That was her feeling—Othello's feeling, and she felt it, she was convinced, as strongly as Shakespeare meant Othello to feel it, all because she was coming down to dinner in a white frock to meet Sally Seton!" (39). Sally's unconventional behavior and readiness to take risks strike Clarissa as wonderful and dangerous, bound "to end in some awful tragedy; her death; her martyrdom." The extravagant terms suggest Septimus's fate, but Sally's future course is anything but tragic: she marries "a bald man with a large buttonhole who owned, it was said, cotton mills at Manchester" and surfaces at Clarissa's party as the prosperous Lady Rosseter, the mother of five boys, her voice "wrung of its old ravishing richness" (199–200). Her rebellion is merely a youthful stage in the process that transforms "the wild, the daring, the romantic Sally" (81) into a marginally acceptable adult member of her class.

Peter's rebellion is longer lived but no more dependable. He too revolts against convention in youth, becomes a socialist, defines himself as an outsider:

> He was not old, or set, or dried in the least. As for caring what they said of him—the Dalloways, the Whitbreads, and their set, he cared not a straw—not a straw (though it was true he would have, some time or other, to see whether Richard couldn't help him to some job). Striding, staring, he glared at the statue of the Duke of Cambridge. He had been sent down from Oxford—true. He had been a Socialist, in some sense a failure—true. Still the future of civilization lies, he thought, in the hands of young men like that; of young men such as he was, thirty years ago; with their love of abstract principles; getting books sent out to them all the way from London to a peak in the Himalayas; reading science; reading philosophy. The future lies in the hands of young men like that, he thought.
>
> (56–57)

The passage is a good example of Woolf's satiric exposure of her character's illusions. We come to know Peter better than he knows himself, can see through his heroic posturing ("striding, staring"), his rhetoric ("the future of civilization"), his verbal formulas and clichés ("he cared not a straw"). His whole personality in middle age is a flimsy construct designed to reassure himself that the passion and radicalism of his youth are not dead. At various moments in the novel he fantasizes himself a romantic buccaneer (60), a solitary traveler (63), and "as young as ever" (178). He continues to patronize the conservatism of people like Richard Dalloway and the social conventions crystallized in Clarissa's role of hostess.

Nevertheless, he is as firmly a part of the Establishment by this time as Lady Rosseter. Though no great success, he is not a failure either, has "done just respectably, filled the usual posts adequately" (171) as a colonial administrator, and expects to use the influence of the people he patronizes—Richard's, Hugh's—to find a position in England. The old school tie is fully exploited. The class conditioning he rejects so violently in youth returns in middle age almost against his will, makes him feel "moments of pride in England; in butlers; chow dogs; girls in their security" (62) and see the ambulance coming for Septimus as a symbol of British efficiency, "one of the triumphs of civilisation" (166). This compromised rebellion or permanently inhibited aggression is epitomized in the pocket knife Peter carries and is forever opening and closing, a weapon that becomes a toy in his hands.

Yet a part of his youth has survived intact—his passion for Clarissa; the emotional anesthesia of his set has not managed to kill off the deepest attachment he has ever felt. He recalls every incident of their painful courtship in precise detail and can summon up the intense emotions of that time in all their power: "He had spoken for hours, it seemed, with the tears running down his cheeks" (72). His susceptibility to sudden gusts of feeling "had been his undoing in Anglo-Indian society" (167), Peter thinks, and it is true that he is in some sense an emotional exhibitionist. But in a world that penalizes despair and idealizes Lady Bexborough's ramrod bearing, the passions have no legitimate channel and will flow unpredictably. Peter's tears and moments of joy are paler variants of Septimus's rages and rapturous visions. What one sees throughout *Mrs. Dalloway* is a single disease that takes different forms. Peter's or Septimus's or Doris Kilman's emotional compulsiveness and display, their gaudiness or profligacy, are the antithesis of the denial of feeling in the governing class. But both are failures to maintain a natural flow of response commensurate with the occasion or situation, a failure that expresses itself variously as the inhibition or exhibition of emotion. Perhaps Woolf's complex attitude is paradoxically also rooted in an ideal of Proportion, though in a form very different from the goddess Dr. Bradshaw worships. In *Macbeth* Macduff breaks down on hearing that his wife and children have been brutally murdered. When he is encouraged to "dispute it like a man," he replies, with great dignity, "I shall do so; / But I must also feel it as a man" (IV, iii, 219–20). It is precisely this dual commitment to self-control and to emotional expression that the characters in *Mrs. Dalloway* lack.

In the Establishment rebels the failure is related to the passage of time. Peter notes that the "governing-class spirit" had grown on Clarissa, "as it tends to do" (86), but the same could be said about Sally or about Peter himself. Woolf was interested in the process through which an independent, responsive, emotionally supple young man or woman is gradually transformed into a conventional member of his or her class. Her interest in this change of human beings through time underlay what she called "my prime discovery so far" in writing *Mrs. Dalloway*: "my tunnelling process, by which I tell the past by instalments, as I have need of it" (*D*, II, 272). As J. Hillis Miller has shown, *Mrs. Dalloway* "is a novel of the resurrection of the past into the actual present of the characters' lives"[11] (though for some of these characters the past can no longer be resuscitated: Lady Bradshaw, for example, had "gone under" fifteen years before [111]). Even Septimus is out of touch with his former self; his youthful passions for Shakespeare, for England, for Miss Isabel Pole are now utterly alien to him, dismissed by the narrator as "such a fire as burns only once in a lifetime" (94).

In Sally, Peter, and Clarissa, Woolf traces the process of socialization from the extended moment in which each was intensely alive—young, brash, open, taking emotional risks—to the stage of conventionality. The class to which these characters belong, it is made clear, is not at all hospitable to such intense feelings. Gradually it blunts, denies, trivializes, or absorbs them, transforming the young rebels into wooden creatures whose public lives no longer express their buried selves. The result is a failure of imaginative sympathy and emotional resonance, an absence of "something central which permeated," as Clarissa puts it in a highly critical summary of her own failings, "something warm which broke up surfaces and rippled the cold contact of man and woman, or of women together" (36).

But Clarissa is harder on herself than her creator is. For *Mrs. Dalloway* finally presents a sympathetic picture of someone who has surrendered to the force of conventional life and permitted her emotions to go underground. Woolf's decision to record Clarissa's thoughts and feelings as well as her words and actions is crucial and represents a deliberate change in her own attitude toward such people. The Dalloways had made an extended appearance in her first novel, *The Voyage Out* (1915), where they were treated with unremitting satiric contempt and where their inner lives were kept dark. We can trace Woolf's conception of Clarissa Dalloway through several stages, from her first appearance in *The Voyage Out*, to her resurrection in the short story "Mrs. Dalloway in Bond Street" (1923), to her flowering in the novel that grew out of that story. In *The Voyage Out* the Dalloways are simply caricatures of their class—worldly, jingoistic, snobbish, smug, philistine, and utterly devoid of inwardness. They exist in a self-contained satiric pocket of the novel and make no connection with the characters the author takes seriously. When Woolf decided to write about them again in the next decade, she must have felt that she had done them an injustice. But even in "Mrs.

Dalloway in Bond Street," in which something approximating stream of consciousness is first used to reveal Clarissa's inner life, the character who emerges remains a satiric object. She is utterly loyal to her country, her class, and its leaders. As she passes Buckingham Palace, she treats the monarch's ceremonial functions as an example of British "character": "something inborn in the race; what Indians respected. The Queen went to hospitals, opened bazaars—the Queen of England, thought Clarissa, looking at the Palace" (*MDP*, 21).

In the course of revising "Mrs. Dalloway in Bond Street" to make it into the first section of the novel, Woolf modifies most of the cruder manifestations of Clarissa's snobbishness and complacency. For example, in the story she thinks, "It would be intolerable if dowdy women came to her party! Would one have liked Keats if he had worn red socks?" (*MDP*, 26). But in the novel a dowdy woman (Ellie Henderson) is invited to her party, though reluctantly, and the young poet Jim Hutton appears wearing red socks, "his black being at the laundry" (194). In the course of the book Clarissa becomes less a typical member of her class and more an individual. This impression is reinforced by some of the titles Woolf apparently considered using—"The Life of a Lady," "A Lady of Fashion"— before she settled on *Mrs. Dalloway*.[12] She was convinced that the book would be an advance on her previous work because "the human soul will be treated more seriously."[13] Clarissa Dalloway became the first character in Woolf's fiction whose inner life is completely known to us.

Clarissa has troubled readers from the first. Woolf noted in her diary that Lytton Strachey complained of "some discrepancy in Clarissa herself; he thinks she is disagreeable & limited, but that I alternately laugh at her, & cover her, very remarkably, with myself." And she recalls nearly abandoning the novel because she found the main character "in some way tinselly. Then I invented her memories. But I think some distaste for her persisted" (*D*, III, 32). This ambiguity of response is reflected in nearly all subsequent commentary on the novel, the attacks on or defenses of Clarissa determined in part by the critic's attitude toward convention and governing-class values. In one of the most interesting treatments of the novel, A. D. Moody insists that Clarissa is not an individualized character at all but merely an embodiment of society's code, an "animated mirror" of the shallow world she reflects.[14] But other commentators have stressed Clarissa's progress to "the freedom of full maturity"[15] or her determination "never to bow to the laws of limitation set up in society, but instead to carry a sense of freedom and love into her world."[16]

What seems to me to account for such discrepancies is that Clarissa's is essentially a laminated personality, made up of distinct layers that do not interpenetrate. Like Peter and Sally she has both a conformist and a rebellious side, a public and a private self. But though it is true that the governing-class spirit has increasingly come to dominate her life, the stream of her thoughts and feelings shows us that the various strata of her personality are all intact and that the movement from rebellion to conformity is not necessarily inexorable or irreversible. Certainly convention dominates her words and actions. She has indeed become "the perfect hostess," as Peter predicted she would, with all the suppression of self that this ideal demands. She is proud that she is descended from courtiers and sees herself continuing a great tradition: "She, too, was going that very night to kindle and illuminate; to give her party" (7). And like the other Establishment characters in the novel, she worships the stoical ideal and connects it with the war: "This late age of the world's experience had bred in them all, all men and women, a well of tears. Tears and sorrows; courage and endurance; a perfectly upright and stoical bearing. Think, for example, of the woman she admired most, Lady Bexborough, opening the bazaar" (12). The passage suggests an apparently inevitable sequence in Clarissa's mind from misery to endurance to rigidity. This ideal of conduct is manifested in her original decision to reject Peter Walsh, with all his emotional violence, and marry the stolid and reliable Richard Dalloway. When she tells Peter their affair is over, he recalls "She was like iron, like flint, rigid up the backbone" (72).

But though the decision to give up Peter and Sally and

identify herself with the governing-class spirit is never reversed, it is also never final, because Clarissa continually goes over the reasons for her choice thirty years later. This accounts for her obsession with the past, for her continued attraction to Peter and vulnerability to his criticism, decades after the issue was supposedly settled. At one point Peter thought he could write her obituary: "It was her manner that annoyed him; timid; hard; arrogant; prudish. 'The death of the soul.' He had said that instinctively, ticketing the moment as he used to do—the death of her soul" (66). But Clarissa's soul is not dead; it has only gone underground. She has moments in which she feels herself "invisible; unseen; unknown," a mood she connects with her married state and public identity, "this being Mrs. Dalloway; not even Clarissa any more; this being Mrs. Richard Dalloway" (13). In her world the soul has no public function and can only survive in solitude. But even her marriage to Richard is not really a betrayal of self so much as a compact between two people to live together yet allow the soul a little breathing space: "And there is a dignity in people; a solitude; even between husband and wife a gulf; and that one must respect, thought Clarissa . . . for one would not part with it oneself, or take it, against his will, from one's husband, without losing one's independence, one's self-respect— something, after all, priceless" (132).

In feeling this need for solitude, Clarissa is expressing one of Woolf's own cherished beliefs. In her essay on E. M. Forster she describes a technique of his fiction that applies equally to her own: "He is always constrained to build the cage—society in all its intricacy and triviality—before he can free the prisoner" (*CE*, I, 344). Even Mrs. Ramsay in *To the Lighthouse*, one of Woolf's most social characters, can allow herself to think: "To be silent; to be alone. All the being and the doing, expansive, glittering, vocal, evaporated; and one shrunk, with a sense of solemnity, to being oneself, a wedge-shaped core of darkness, something invisible to others" (*TL*, 99). In her essay on Elizabethan drama Woolf suggests that a modern audience has an absolute need for some exploration of the private as against the public self. Immersed as we are in the "extravagant laughter, poetry, and splendour" of an Elizabethan play, we gradually become aware that there is something we are being denied: "It is solitude. There is no privacy here. Always the door opens and someone comes in. . . . Meanwhile, as if tired with company, the mind steals off to muse in solitude; to think, not to act; to comment, not to share; to explore its own darkness, not the bright-lit-up surfaces of others" (*CE*, I, 61).

There is an exact parallel here to Clarissa's withdrawal from the party at the climax of *Mrs. Dalloway* in order to reflect on Septimus's suicide. The little room is a solitary retreat where "the party's splendour fell to the floor, so strange it was to come in alone in her finery" (202). And in this solitude Clarissa allows herself to think about Septimus's death with full imaginative sympathy, understanding his feelings and situation instinctively with some part of her self that scarcely functions in the public world she normally inhabits. She realizes that Septimus had managed to rescue in death an inner freedom that her own life is constantly forcing her to barter away: "A thing there was that mattered; a thing, wreathed about with chatter, defaced, obscured in her own life, let drop every day in corruption, lies, chatter. This he had preserved" (202). Septimus is Clarissa's conscience, is indeed the conscience of the governing class, though only she is willing to acknowledge him. In doing so, she sees her acceptance of the governing-class code in a highly critical light: "She had schemed; she had pilfered. She was never wholly admirable. She had wanted success, Lady Bexborough and the rest of it. And once she had walked on the terrace at Bourton" (203). This juxtaposition of present and past stresses the loss of the intense feeling of her youth, for it was on the terrace at Bourton that she had known "the most exquisite moment of her whole life," when Sally kissed her on the lips and released the torrent of Clarissa's first romantic passion (40).

In feeling a sense of kinship with Septimus, Clarissa is crossing class lines in her imagination, for certainly he is beyond the pale of her set. Woolf moves in this passage from the traditional social satire of the English novelist of manners to what she called "The Russian Point of View" in one of her essays. Unlike the class-obsessed English writer, Dostoevsky is indifferent to class barriers and social identity: "It is all the same to him whether you are noble or simple, a tramp or a great lady. Whoever you are, you are the vessel of this perplexed liquid, this cloudy, yeasty, precious stuff, the soul" (*CE*, I, 244). Though they have never exchanged a word, on the deepest level Septimus and Clarissa are kin. And so, for all their mutual hatred, are Clarissa and Miss Kilman. Just before she withdraws to the little room, Clarissa has a moment of contempt for her social triumphs, which she feels "had a hollowness; at arm's length they were, not in the heart." At the same instant she recalls "Kilman her enemy. That was satisfying; that was real. Ah, how she hated her—hot, hypocritical, corrupt; with all that power; Elizabeth's seducer. . . . She hated her: she loved her. It was enemies one wanted, not friends" (192). These reactions to Septimus and Doris Kilman (with their characteristic mixture of exalted and base feelings) together suggest that Clarissa's soul is far from dead, that she can resurrect the intense emotions of youth despite the pressure of a society determined to deny them quarter.

In such passages Woolf gives Clarissa her pivotal role, balancing the anesthesia of the governing class against the fervor of a Septimus Smith or a Doris Kilman. At the same time, Peter Walsh is asking himself, "What is this terror? what is this ecstasy? . . . What is it that fills me with extraordinary excitement?" And replying, "It is Clarissa" (213). These ardent feelings will probably never be translated into action, or even speech. It seems improbable that the outer life of Peter or Clarissa will change, for "the social system" Woolf describes in *Mrs. Dalloway* is not likely to be transformed soon enough to allow either of them to build their lives on the flow as well as the containment of emotion, especially since both must also be regarded as accomplices to if not agents of repression. Woolf was too convinced of the fundamental inertia in human nature and institutions to imagine a rapid transformation of either. But she was conscious of change, too, in both societal and individual values, even if it sometimes appeared to be taking place in geological rather than human time. *Mrs. Dallo-*

way captures a moment in which the domination of the ideal of rigid self-control began to seem oppressive rather than admirable. In illuminating the price the characters in her novel have had to pay to live under the sway of this ideal, Woolf is not only fulfilling her ambition "to criticise the social system, and to show it at work, at its most intense," but also contributing indirectly to its replacement by one less hostile to the buried life of feeling in every human being. She knew that even the most fundamental institutions and forms of behavior could be altered. As we will see, her sense of continual transformation also affected her vision of what looked like mankind's most enduring social arrangement—the family.

6

The Bonds of Family Life

I

The first, and usually the last, eyes that gaze on us with interest belong to members of our family: mother, father, brother, sister; later, husband, wife, child. This experience is so close to universal that exceptions are often treated like aberrations rather than plausible alternatives. The very commonness of the condition has encouraged us to think of the family as immutable and as the source of our deepest loyalties. In mid-Victorian England especially, the worship of the domestic hearth took on some of the qualities of idolatry. G. M. Young notes that there were only two things an Englishman of the period could be relied upon to believe in—Representative Institutions and the Family.[1] And Walter Houghton interprets this domestic religion as a form of displaced transcendental faith. When Christianity lost its hold, "the living church more and more became the 'temple of the hearth.'"[2] The greatest apologist for this new faith was probably John Ruskin, whose influential *Sesame and Lilies* (1865) apotheosized the home as a safe haven from the storms of the surrounding world: "This is the true nature of home—it is the place of Peace; the shelter, not only from all injury, but from all terror, doubt, and division."[3] And in this shrine was to be found the spiritual being Coventry Patmore called the Angel in the House, in his popular poem of that name (1854–56), the submissive wife, whose maternity was a Mission and who was worshiped by husband and children alike.

Virginia Woolf would have been exposed to such domestic idolatry from her earliest years. Her father frequently preached the same gospel and might be said to have turned it into the first commandment of his own faith. In his major philosophical work, *The Science of Ethics* (1882), Leslie Stephen describes the family as a sort of First Cause, the basis of all human attachments and the key to contentment; it is "beyond all comparison the most vitally connected with the happiness of the individual, and the condition of which most immediately affects the gratification of all his strongest instincts."[4] A faith in Home becomes the standard by which he judges every moral system: "The degree in which any ethical theory recognises and reveals the essential importance of the family relation is, I think, the best test of its approximation to the truth."[5] It is difficult to imagine a more zealous defense of a particular human institution. Stephen uses absolute terms and sees the family as ahistorical. Like all First Causes it is not subject to change through time.

This assumption, more than any other, would make the Victorian religion of the family unacceptable to later generations, especially Woolf's own. Born in 1882, she was destined to witness and participate in an extraordinary transformation of the ideals of marriage and family life. In the last years of Victoria's reign and the first decades of the twentieth century, the institution of the family was subjected to a remorseless skeptical scrutiny that would radically alter the ways in which people lived together. And at the root of the transformation was the historicist assumption that no human institution is immutable, that the current forms of marital and familial life are merely the products of a long evolutionary process and that they would continue to change.

So Woolf would write in 1924, with her characteristic mixture of playfulness, self-mockery, and seriousness, that "in or about December, 1910, human character changed." The date, she says, is arbitrary but must be post-Victorian. The change occurred not so much in human individuals as in the relations between them. Woolf is describing a fundamental shift in power, authority, and sympathy:

> Read the *Agamemnon*, and see whether, in process of time, your sympathies are not almost entirely with Clytemnestra. Or consider the married life of the Carlyles and bewail the waste, the futility, for him and for her, of the horrible domestic tradition

> which made it seemly for a woman of genius to spend her time
> chasing beetles, scouring saucepans, instead of writing books.
> All human relations have shifted—those between masters and
> servants, husbands and wives, parents and children.
>
> ("Mr. Bennett and Mrs. Brown,"
> *CE*, I, 320–21)

Her examples are taken from domestic life and suggest a
redistribution or redefinition of power, in which earlier hierarchical orderings are no longer taken to be inevitable. The
formerly impotent seem suddenly invested with authority,
the formerly masterful now despotic and contemptible.

To look at family life in this way is to see a particular social
institution as mutable—responsive to the reforming pressure
of the generations. The familial traditions Leslie Stephen took
to be quintessential and eternal his children treated as accidental and in drastic need of revision. Societal imperatives
lost some of their power when it became evident that they
were subject to fashion. We have seen that Woolf was conscious not only of the "immense forces society brings to play
upon each of us" but also of "how that society changes from
decade to decade" (*MB*, 80). The later nineteenth century saw
the beginning of such a time-based inquiry into familial structures. Engels's *Origin of the Family, Private Property and the State*
(1884) describes with withering scorn the complacent mid-
nineteenth-century assumption that domestic life had not
changed since the time of the Pentateuch, "so that the family
had really experienced no historical development at all."[6]
From the 1870s through the 1920s, historians, comparative
sociologists, and anthropologists published a series of influential books that revealed the essentially arbitrary and
fortuitous nature of any particular set of marital and familial
customs. Works like Morgan's *Systems of Consanguinity and Af-
finity of the Human Family* (1871), Westermarck's monumental
History of Human Marriage (1891; revised and expanded, 1921),
Malinowski's books on sexual life in savage societies (1913 ff.),
Briffault's *The Mothers* (1927), and Margaret Mead's *Coming of
Age in Samoa* (1928) had the effect of making the nineteenth-
century code of respectable family life look less than inevi-

table and of confirming the impression that it was ripe—rotten-ripe—for change. In the words of the historian George Dangerfield, "by 1910 the ideal of personal security through respectability had become putrid."[7]

What in mid-Victorian times had simply been called "The Family" or "The Home"—often capitalized—was now referred to by the rebels and reformers as "the family system." This interesting locution is pervasive in the writings of those hostile to Victorian mores. Samuel Butler, in his classic fictional exposé of the Victorian family, *The Way of All Flesh* (1903), concludes that "the question of the day now is marriage and the family system."[8] And Bernard Shaw, in the preface to *Misalliance* (1910), gives us a sense of what the phrase means: "Our family system does unquestionably take the natural bond between members of the same family, which, like all natural bonds, is not too tight to be borne, and superimposes on it a painful burden of forced, inculcated, suggested, and altogether unnecessary affection and responsibility which we should do well to get rid of by making relatives as independent of one another as possible."[9] Something systemic is pervasive, inescapable; Shaw's point is that the Victorian family transformed the necessary but temporary dependence of childhood into a life-long sentence: the stage of independence recedes perpetually into the distance. The individual unit in a complex system can function only when the other parts are working simultaneously, like a machine in which all the gears must engage to produce motion.

Woolf's frequent use of the phrase "the family system" probably has its roots in her reading of *The Way of All Flesh*, a book that influenced her deeply. She talks about "the startling freshness" of Butler's work (*CW*, 29) and credits him with calling into question the Victorian emphasis on duty, solemnity, and sentiment, especially as they converge in family life. Her own use of the term "family system" also emphasizes the idea of an artificial and enforced connection that inhibits individual growth. One of the powerful links between the young lovers in *Night and Day* is their shared sense of the family as a threat: "Surely you must have found with your own family,"

Katharine says to Ralph, "that it's impossible to discuss what matters to you most because you're all herded together, because you're in a conspiracy, because the position is false." And Ralph, Woolf notes, "agreed with her as to the destructiveness of the family system" (*ND*, 356).

This coercive familial atmosphere, in which individual human beings are treated as functional units in a system over which they have no control, was for Woolf part of the Victorian legacy that could hardly be abandoned soon enough. Its dissipation is an aspect of the change she saw in "human character" around 1910. But that it managed to survive longer in pockets is evident from her diary description of a visit to the Booth family in 1920: "Chill superficial seemliness; but thin as a March glaze of ice on a pool. . . . I took against the family system. Old Mrs Booth enthroned on a sort of commode in widows dress: flanked by devoted daughters; with grandchildren somehow symbolical cherubs. Such neat dull little boys & girls. There we all sat in our furs & white gloves" (*D*, II, 24–25). In this satiric picture the system is no longer vital; and yet the individual human beings still trapped in it are real enough. Beneath their frostbitten dullness and propriety the blood flows. It was in order to rescue such helpless creatures from the spell under which they languished that Woolf worked to discredit nineteenth-century domestic traditions.

She was not without allies. The mood of the times was insurrectionary and the impulse toward reform very widespread. When H. G. Wells's Ann Veronica, in the novel that bears her name (1909), breaks with her family and comes unchaperoned to live in London, she becomes sensitive to "a big diffused impulse toward change, to a great discontent with and criticism of life as it is lived, to a clamorous confusion of ideas for reconstruction." The people around her, their talk, their gestures, even their clothing seem "charged with the suggestion of the urgency of this pervasive project of alteration." [10] Wells was one of the "protagonists of revolt" to whom Leonard Woolf paid homage in his autobiography, in a passage that eloquently records the smoldering disaffection of the young in the last days of Victoria's reign:

When in the grim, grey, rainy January days of 1901 Queen Victoria lay dying, we already felt that we were living in an era of incipient revolt and that we ourselves were mortally involved in this revolt against a social system and code of conduct and morality which, for convenience sake, may be referred to as bourgeois Victorianism. We did not initiate this revolt. When we went up to Cambridge, its protagonists were Swinburne, Bernard Shaw, Samuel Butler in *The Way of All Flesh*, and to some extent Hardy and Wells. We were passionately on the side of these champions of freedom of speech and freedom of thought, of common-sense and reason. We felt that, with them as our leaders, we were struggling against a religious and moral code of cant and hypocrisy.

To this list of English rebels Leonard Woolf adds the name of Ibsen, in whose plays "the cobwebs and veils, the pretences and hypocrisies which suppressed the truth, buttressed cruelty, injustice, and stupidity, and suffocated society in the nineteenth century, were broken through, exposed, swept away." [11]

The rhetoric of the disaffected was one of uncompromising rejection. Leonard Woolf's language of heroes and villains, imprisonment and liberation, is echoed by most of the Bloomsbury writers. For Lytton Strachey the Victorians were "a set of mouthing bungling hypocrites." [12] And even Virginia Woolf, usually more circumspect and ironic in her choice of words, can denounce "the inanity, the pettiness, the spite, the tyranny, the hypocrisy, the immorality" that Victorian family life engendered (*TG*, 143). Such melodramatic terms, such radical simplifications, have the flavor of wartime propaganda. They make no allowance for the possibility that the warring sides may after all have something in common, that they were in this case quite literally members of the same family, and that there is such a thing as generational continuity. Like his future son-in-law Leonard Woolf, Leslie Stephen also admired Thomas Hardy and was in fact responsible for the publication of some of his earliest fiction. Noel Annan writes that Stephen "bequeathed the deprecating glance to his children in Bloomsbury." [13] Those eminently respectable Victorians Sir Richard and Lady Strachey sponsored a family performance of Ibsen's *John Gabriel Borkman* in 1896, when their son Lytton, who took one of the roles, was only six-teen.[14] Such generational echoes seem to mock the uncompromising revolutionary ardor of the children, their myth of a complete break with the nineteenth century. Why was it necessary for them to see things in this way?

Some of the peculiar characteristics of Victorian family life may help to explain the anomaly. The normal gap between generations was stretched to the limit in these families, and the youth of the parents was, for one reason or another, unimaginable to the children. Sometimes the parents' early death deprived their children of a real sense of them in adulthood: Leonard Woolf's father died when he was eleven, Virginia Woolf's mother when she was thirteen. On the other hand, the common assumption that a man married only when he was successfully established and then proceeded to have a very large family meant that the younger children in such families knew their fathers long after the season of youth. Leslie Stephen was fifty when Virginia was born and an old man by the time she came of age. Sir Richard Strachey was sixty-three in the year of Lytton's birth and seventy when his youngest child was born. It is no wonder that the generations were estranged and appeared to have nothing in common. Virginia Woolf had an acute sense of the wide gap between the world of Leslie Stephen and that of his younger children: "Two different ages confronted each other in the drawing room at Hyde Park Gate: the Victorian age; and the Edwardian age. We were not his children, but his grandchildren" (*MB*, 126). Over the whole era brooded the figure of Queen Victoria, who by 1900 had been on the throne for sixty-three years and must have begun to seem immortal. Was it possible she had ever been a young girl? The reverence for old age that her long reign was supposed to inspire filtered down to affect the familial relationships of her subjects and increased the silent estrangement of the young.

Virginia Woolf's novels are filled with such ancient figures still invested with power, but her attitude is decidedly not reverent. One has a sense of a geriatric *ancien régime* hanging on to life by a thread, as in Martin Pargiter's clinically observed picture in *The Years* of old Lady Warburton leaving her niece's dinner party:

> She was robing herself. Now she was accepting her cloak with a violet slash in it; now her furs. A bag dangled from her wrist. She was hung about with chains; her fingers were knobbed with rings. Her sharp stone-coloured face, riddled with lines and wrinkled into creases, looked out from its soft nest of fur and laces. The eyes were still bright.
>
> The nineteenth century going to bed, Martin said to himself as he watched her hobble down the steps on the arm of her footman.
>
> (*Y*, 287)

In a far more sinister passage in *Jacob's Room*, probably inspired by the common post–Great War contempt for "the old men" who were thought to have engineered the conflict, Woolf shows the ancient ministers deciding the course of history in a room in Whitehall with the marble statues of Pitt, Chatham, Burke, and Gladstone looking over their shoulders. The heads of the ministers are "bald, red-veined, hollow-looking. . . . Moreover, some were troubled with dyspepsia; one had at that very moment cracked the glass of his spectacles; another spoke in Glasgow tomorrow; altogether they looked too red, fat, pale, or lean, to be dealing, as the marble heads had dealt, with the course of history" (*JR*, 172). Victorian veneration gave way to modern debunking, irreverence, and demystification. It seemed the only antidote to the poison. Every individual or institution that had formerly been elevated must not merely be brought down to earth but sent to outer darkness. The heroine of Shaw's *Misalliance* exclaims: "Oh home! home! parents! family! duty! how I loathe them! How I'd like to see them all blown to bits!" And in his *Getting Married* (1908) domestic life is "exposed as an Augean stable, so filthy that it would seem more hopeful to burn it down than to attempt to sweep it out."[15] The style of such attacks on Victorian values is that of paradox, which rapidly established itself as the language of fresh thought around the turn of the century. In Butler, Oscar Wilde, W. S. Gilbert, and Shaw one need only stand a received idea on its head to set it right. So Butler could write in his notebooks, "Those who have never had a father can at any rate never know the sweets of losing one," and his hero in *The Way of All Flesh* longs to end his familial connection forever: "'There are orphanages,' he exclaimed to himself, 'for children who have lost their parents—oh! why, why, why, are there no harbours of refuge for grown men who have not yet lost them?'" [16] This paradoxical style is essentially formed on the model of conventional thought. Its topsy-turvydom uses the traditional pieties to generate its own countertruths. Butler called himself an "enfant terrible," and there is justice in this self-estimate; but he did not consider that even an "enfant terrible" remains an "enfant" and is permanently dependent on the continued outrageousness of his terrible parent. The stance can create neither mature nor highly original work.

In Bloomsbury the art of debunking produced such anti-establishment gestures as the *Dreadnought* Hoax of 1910, in which Adrian and Virginia Stephen, along with some of their friends, disguised themselves as the emperor of Abyssinia and his entourage and received an official tour of the British Navy's prize vessel, the *Dreadnought*. Most of their elders were duly outraged by this send-up of His Majesty's forces. But it is worth noting that the escapade was the product of the most careful strategic planning by a group whose average age was closer to thirty than twenty. And this irreverent spirit was still alive as late as 1935, when Bloomsbury put on a performance of Virginia Woolf's private theatrical entertainment, *Freshwater*. The play caricatures such eminent Victorians as Tennyson, G. F. Watts, Julia Margaret Cameron, and the queen herself, who enters with the line "We have arrived";[17] all the roles were played by members of the Bloomsbury family and set, presumably in the style of high farce. Even in middle age the participants must have felt that such pranks expressed a necessary rebellion. The "enfant terrible" seemed to have a permanent life in each of these grown-up men and women. For reasons that I hope to make clear, their break with the past remained incomplete.

Characteristically, the rebellious spirit in most of the anti-

Victorians took the form of a conflict between "rights" and "duties," and these terms were constantly used in writings about family life throughout the nineteenth and early twentieth centuries. The new spirit of skepticism and insubordination is apparent in some of the titles given to works about marriage published around the turn of the century: Edward Carpenter's *Love's Coming-of-Age* (1896), Mona Caird's *The Morality of Marriage* (1897), Cicely Hamilton's *Marriage as a Trade* (1912). The reader is immediately warned to expect something very different from what was promised by such politically quietist nineteenth-century titles as John Maynard's *Matrimony: Or, What Marriage Is, and How to Make the Best of It* (1864) or Mary Taylor's *The First Duty of Women* (1870). Gradually the word "duty" and all it connoted began to seem oppressive and morally bankrupt. By 1903 the new point of view had found its authoritative text, at least for the members of the Bloomsbury group, in G. E. Moore's *Principia Ethica*—the quiet Magna Charta of that generation—which included an important reconsideration of the ethos of duty.

For Moore an action is justified only if it can be demonstrated that it increases the amount of good in the universe. He uses the principle to question the whole idea of a rule-bound morality or "list of duties" by suggesting how difficult it is to establish that any contemplated action is right. The skeptical language of the passage in the *Principia* suggests that an ethical choice is so complicated that it becomes virtually impossible to make:

> In order to shew that any action is a duty, it is necessary to know both what are the other conditions, which will, conjointly with it, determine its effects; to know exactly what will be the effects of these conditions; and to know all the events which will be in any way affected by our action throughout an infinite future. We must have all this causal knowledge, and further we must know accurately the degree of value both of the action itself and of all these effects; and must be able to determine how, in conjunction with the other things in the Universe, they will affect its value as an organic whole. And not only this: we must also possess all this knowledge with regard to the effects of every possible alternative; and must then

> be able to see by comparison that the total value due to the existence of the action in question will be greater than that which would be produced by any of these alternatives.

As he contemplates this hopelessly difficult task, Moore is forced to conclude "that our causal knowledge alone is far too incomplete for us ever to assure ourselves of this result. *Accordingly it follows that we never have any reason to suppose that an action is our duty.*" [18] Having thus disposed of the first principle of Victorian conduct, Moore can proceed to build up a much more tentative and flexible ethical system, one that denies the authority of all established codes and supposedly self-evident moral laws. Some of his Bloomsbury disciples took this liberation a step further and dismissed the whole idea of duty, especially as it related to societal institutions like the family.

By the end of Victoria's reign the whole "family system" had begun to seem a crushing burden that offered no space for individual freedom. For women particularly, the large Victorian family created a formidable, exhausting set of obligations. A wife's duties were not limited to her husband and the numerous children she was likely to bear but extended through the whole kinship network down to the remotest collaterals. It is worth remembering that each leaf on the many-branched family tree that prefaces most Victorian biographies represented actual or potential required labor: the ceaseless round of visits and family entertainments; the obligatory correspondence that involved remembering birthdays and anniversaries as well as keeping in touch with distant relations; the weddings, the christenings, the funerals; the nursing and convalescence calls that came with frequent illness and the absence of homes for the elderly; and the management of servants whose work had to be constantly supervised if this complicated machine was to be kept running smoothly. Most of these duties would not be delegated to men, who had their own professional obligations and were often working uninterruptedly in order to supply the funds such an enterprise required. Woolf analyzes the compulsive labor of professional men in *Three Guineas* and concludes: "Money making becomes so important that they must work by night as well as by day" (*TG*, 131).

Is it any wonder that by 1900 the machine was grinding to a halt or that the next generation would come to think of the Victorian family as life-destroying, an institution that took more than it gave? Slowly but inexorably the ideological underpinnings that had secured the loyalty of the participants began to give way—the ideals of selflessness, of filial obligation, of reverence for the old; the treatment of frequent child-bearing as a blessing; the acceptance of time-consuming rituals like dressing for dinner or paying ceremonial calls. By the twentieth century such practices had assumed the character of intolerable obligations. The family network had become merely a net, increasingly seen as a trap for the free spirit. Joyce's Stephen Dedalus includes the family when he wills himself to "fly by those nets," and the idealization of escape from externally imposed bondage his metaphor implies becomes authoritative for a whole culture. To Wells's Ann Veronica, "her aunt and father, neighbors, customs, traditions, forces" all seemed "armed with nets and prepared to throw them over her directly her movements became in any manner truly free."[19] Staying behind, staying put, is identified with self-betrayal. The imperative impulse is toward flight.

But ideals are not actuality. In practice such impulses of liberation are often forgotten or betrayed. Virginia Woolf was interested in the situation of people whose desire for independence was eroded by their own residual conventionality. Particularly in *The Years*, the historical novel of family life that covers the period 1880–1935, she writes sympathetically of a generation caught between conflicting codes, whose longing for freedom is consistently unrealized. She focuses on the brothers and sisters of the Pargiter family, who come to maturity toward the end of the nineteenth century and survive well into the twentieth. Her superficially conventional heroine, Eleanor, stays on to run her father's house after her mother's death, since she is the eldest daughter and is needed. Without questioning the system, she automatically accepts the categorical obligation imposed by such writers as Frances Power

Cobbe in her *The Duties of Women* (1881): "If either parent *wants* the daughter, she ought not to leave him or her, *either* to marry or to go into a nunnery, or for any other purpose."[20]

It is only after her father's death (in 1910, Woolf's watershed year) that Eleanor can acknowledge the buried wish for freedom she had forced herself to deny all along. When her new friend Nicholas speaks about a future in which the soul has learned "to expand; to adventure; to form—new combinations," she responds eagerly: "When, she wanted to ask him, when will this new world come? When shall we be free? When shall we live adventurously, wholly, not like cripples in a cave? He seemed to have released something in her; she felt not only a new space of time, but new powers, something unknown within her" (*Y*, 319–20). But though she gives up the cavernous old family house and takes a modern efficiency flat, though she travels to Greece and India, has many friends, and manages to retain her vitality into old age, she knows that her liberation has come too late. In her fifties she meets the idiosyncratic, passionate, contradictory young man who has married one of her cousins, and experiences a new sensation: "That is the man, she said to herself, with a sudden rush of conviction, as she came out into the frosty air, that I should like to have married. She recognised a feeling which she had never felt. But he's twenty years younger than I am, she thought, and married to my cousin. For a moment she resented the passage of time and the accidents of life which had swept her away—from all that, she said to herself" (*Y*, 323).

Most of the other characters of Eleanor's generation have led similarly divided lives and feel something like her sense of historical betrayal. Kitty Malone makes the socially brilliant marriage her mother has encouraged and becomes Lady Lasswade, but though she fulfills the duties of her station flawlessly, it is alienated labor. In her old age she can allow herself to confess "I'd have given anything to be a farmer! . . . But in my youth . . . that wasn't allowed" (*Y*, 432). Her cousin Martin is similarly outraged by the choices that family tradition had forced upon him. His wish to be an architect was frowned on by his military father, so "they sent me into the

Army instead, which I loathed" (*Y*, 247). And his brother Edward, the distinguished classicist, seems to confess that his own vocational choice had been made under duress: "No, if I'd had my way . . . I should have been. . . . " But his sentence is never finished, and not even his sister Eleanor can imagine how it would have ended (*Y*, 461).

In all these passages the Pargiters look back on a wasted existence in a moment of recognition that comes too late. Rather than choosing for themselves in love, in work, they had followed the path dictated by family and convention. When they wake out of their long trance of duty they are middle-aged or old, and the system that has sustained and rewarded but at the same time deeply betrayed them seems at last only a set of meaningless rituals that serves no one's deepest needs. As Eleanor bends to give an elderly relation the customary kiss, she reflects, "She knew the whole procedure by heart. They, the middle-aged, deferred to the very old; the very old were courteous to them; and then came the usual pause. They had nothing to say to her; she had nothing to say to them" (*Y*, 225). In denying their own youthful resistance to duty and convention, the acquiescent late Victorian children had turned themselves into robots.

II

If it was no longer possible for Eleanor's generation to find the new world for which they had secretly longed, perhaps there was hope for the future. Most of the turn-of-the-century writers on the family thought the institution could be reformed, and their idealism was channeled into the project of reconstructing it. Their attacks were directed not only against the systemic nature of family life but also against certain of its defining characteristics that might be altered—specifically, its patriarchal and hierarchical structure, it large size, its lack of privacy, and its sexual hypocrisy. The task of the reformers was to assure the continuity of the "essential" family by transforming its most onerous "accidental" characteristics—its Victorian aberrations.

The first and most important target of attack was patriarchal power. Evangelicalism conceived of the Deity as a constant masculine presence in the house, and this vision of the
paterfamilias invested with spiritual authority could easily be
translated into purely secular terms. The whole system of law
supported his claim to obedience. In Blackstone's compact
and startling legal formula, "the husband and wife are one,
and the husband is that one."[21] Jeremy Bentham's *Theory of
Legislation*, a standard work of jurisprudence used throughout
the nineteenth century, described the first two conditions of
marriage in these terms: "*The wife shall be subject to the will of
the husband, reserving an appeal to the courts*," and "*The control of
the affairs of the family shall rest with the man alone*."[22] Virginia
Woolf's uncle, the eminent jurist Sir James Fitzjames Stephen,
in his ironically titled *Liberty, Equality, Fraternity* (1873), defended this patriarchal system in the most uncompromising
terms: men are naturally superior to women in every way;
marriage is not a relationship of equals but "a contract between a stronger and a weaker person involving subordination"; in all major decisions the wife "ought to obey her husband, and carry out the view at which he deliberately arrives"
just as the lieutenant obeys the captain of the ship.[23] Although
Leslie Stephen, Fitzjames's younger brother, stressed recipro-
cal duties rather than the chain of command, these patriarchal
conceptions defined the basic power structure of his own
family. His daughter Virginia grew up under this dispensation and came to think of patriarchy as the most common
form of family tyranny.

The domineering male becomes the focus of attention in
some of Woolf's most important works on the family. Her
most complex treatment is in *To the Lighthouse*, as we will see
in the next chapter. But from her earliest works, one can trace
a consistent attack on the middle-class paterfamilias lording
it over others. In *The Voyage Out* Terence Hewet reflects on
"what a bully the ordinary man is . . . the ordinary hard-
working, rather ambitious solicitor or man of business with a
family to bring up and a certain position to maintain" (*VO*,
252). Sometimes such behavior goes against the grain of the
particular man who finds himself in the role of authority, yet

convention compels him to act out the part. Mr. Hilbery, in
Night and Day, is rather remote and indifferent to his family,
but when faced with the temporary insurrection of his daughter he reverts to type: "He had an excuse for laying down laws
for the conduct of those who lived in his house, and this excuse, though profoundly inadequate, he found useful during
the interregnum of civilization with which he now found
himself faced" (*ND*, 506). In *The Years* Colonel Pargiter is presented as the quintessential patriarch, dominating his children merely by the power of his presence. In the Pargiter family there is no maternal buffer between father and children,
and the force of his authority seems for this reason more terrifying and uncontained to the younger generation:

> "It's Papa!" Milly exclaimed warningly.
> Instantly Martin wriggled out of his father's armchair; Delia
> sat upright. Milly at once moved forward a very large rose-
> sprinkled cup that did not match the rest. The Colonel stood at
> the door and surveyed the group rather fiercely. His small blue
> eyes looked round them as if to find fault.
>
> (*Y*, 11)

The concept of patriarchy places the blame for the un-
democratic nature of the Victorian family squarely on the paterfamilias. But its hierarchical structure meant that from the
children's point of view the home contained another potential
tyrant: the materfamilias. Bernard Shaw's *Mrs. Warren's Profession* (1894) shows that a mother too could issue directives,
wield financial power, and stir her daughter to rebellion.
When Vivie Warren decides to refuse her mother's money and
earn her own living, she does so because she can no longer
stand being subject to the maternal will, its wheedling, its
commands, its sentimental appeals. Woolf too was intensely
conscious of the potential abuse of a mother's power, less in
her own family than in her husband's. A visit from the elder
Mrs. Woolf produced a violently explosive entry in her diary.
She says of her mother-in-law's presence:

> I felt the horror of family life, & the terrible threat to one's lib-
> erty that I used to feel with father, Aunt Mary or George. . . .
> To be attached to her as daughter would be so cruel a fate that

> I can think of nothing worse; & thousands of women might be dying of it in England today: this tyranny of mother over daughter, or father; their right to the due being as powerful as anything in the world.
>
> (*D*, III, 194–95)

The Victorian family was hierarchically organized and coercively disciplined in part because of its large size: it was obviously more difficult to accommodate the impulses of a dozen individual wills than four or five, and the simplest solution to the problem was firm autocratic rule from above. The larger the army, the greater the need for regimentation. Mealtimes, for example, were undeviatingly set and unpunctual stragglers sharply reproved. The most trivial aspects of behavior had to be ritualized. "It is generally established as a rule," Mrs. Beeton writes in her classic *Book of Household Management* (1861), "not to ask for soup or fish twice, as, in so doing, part of the company may be kept waiting too long for the second course, when, perhaps, a little revenge is taken by looking at the awkward consumer of a second portion."[24] So we see Mr. Ramsay "scowling and frowning, and flushing with anger" in *To the Lighthouse* only because "poor old Augustus had asked for another plate of soup" (*TL*, 148) and made the whole table wait for him.

The family meant not just the relatively small circle of the same household but all one's living relations, who could be expected to visit frequently and congregate at regular intervals. Each of these individuals required attention and took up time; one's obligation to them, no matter how slight, was not a matter of choice. The little hooks of attachment seemed to pull in a dozen directions at once. When three generations of Pargiters congregate in the climactic scene of *The Years*, they have to hire a suite of offices to accommodate the party: no private house is large enough. And to the younger generation some of the elder presences seem like the tentacles of an octopus, dangerous, difficult to avoid (*Y*, 407).

A long-range solution to this problem was the deliberate shrinking of family size. The demographic statistics here are dramatic. The mid-Victorian family had an average of six children; by the 1920s the figure had dropped to two and two-tenths. This is perhaps the most significant change in the entire history of the family, and it occurred very quickly—in a period of fifty years. The historian J. A. Banks attributes it to "a radical change in the attitude towards parenthood. People no longer wish to have the large families which were customary in the days of their grandparents." [25] This fundamental alteration in the ideal of family life owes much to the work of the anti-Victorian rebels. John Stuart Mill was one of the first to see the issue in ethical and psychological terms, rather than in the economic ones used earlier by Malthus. "Little advance can be expected in morality," he wrote in his *Principles of Political Economy* (1848), "until the producing of large families is looked upon in the same light as drunkenness or any other physical excess." [26] In later generations this cause was taken over by the champions of birth control, who argued that the real victim of the large family was the exhausted mother. As Mona Caird wrote in the nineties, "If the new movement had no other effect than to rouse women to rebellion against the madness of large families, it would confer a priceless benefit on humanity." [27]

The new attitude certainly influenced the children of Leslie Stephen, as a glance at the family tree that prefaces Quentin Bell's biography of Virginia Woolf will confirm. The Stephen family at Hyde Park Gate consisted of eight siblings. The other marriages in the parents' generation produced five, seven, and eleven children. But the sons and daughters of Leslie and Julia Stephen did not carry on this tradition: when they came to marry, they had two or three children—or none at all. The facts concerning Leonard Woolf's family are even more striking. He was one of ten children; though he and his siblings entered into eleven marriages, they managed to produce among them a grand total of six children. [28] A letter Vanessa Bell wrote to her sister during Vanessa's first pregnancy makes it clear that the matter of family size was carefully considered in relation to the evils of Victorian domestic life: "I'm beginning to think 2 will be enough. Do you think we shall gradually fall into all the old abuses & that I shant have any idea what my children are like or what they want to do? . . . I'm not sure it doesn't mean hanging the most terrific millstone round one's neck."[29] And though Virginia Woolf was persuaded by others to remain childless, she was quite divided in her feelings about this fact, at times lamenting the absence of the modern family of two ("we might have had a boy of 12, a girl of 10"—*D*, III, 107), at times relieved that her childlessness made it unnecessary to divide her energy as a mother must (see *D*, III, 167). It is significant that the two mothers of large families in her fiction—Mrs. Ramsay and Mrs. Pargiter—die before their time, as her own mother did. There were many reasons, then, why the family had to be kept small if it was to protect its individual members.

The modern habit of thinking of the members of a family as individuals rather than as parts of a single organism was not easily acquired. Victorian domestic life offered little hope of privacy and encouraged what the rebels came to think of as herding. Family prayers, reading aloud, group excursions, meals taken together, frequent visitors to be entertained—all these common practices encouraged the family to think of itself as a unit and cut off the lines of retreat. If one takes a longer historical view of these customs, it appears that this closing in of the nuclear family was once thought of as an increase in privacy, since the individual family had loosened its ties to the surrounding community and withdrawn to ground it could call its own. Family historians like Philippe Ariès and Edward Shorter point to the relatively sequestered nature of modern family life in comparison with its medieval or Renaissance equivalent. The very architecture of the dwelling place changed significantly, with rooms that now opened off corridors rather than into each other and with doors that could be shut.[30] But by the late nineteenth century this separation of families into individual units was widely felt to have compromised rather than fostered the need for privacy. Once the family had needed protection from the constant scrutiny of the community; now the individual needed shelter from the eyes of the family.

This demand for private time and space within or outside the home became one of the most persistent demands of the reformers. The sense of outrage so powerfully expressed by the American writer Charlotte Perkins Gilman in her attack on domestic life, *The Home* (1903), would have found an echo in the minds of many English readers: "In the home who has privacy?" Gilman asks. "Privacy means the decent seclusion of the individual, the right to do what one likes unwatched, uncriticised, unhindered. Neither father, mother, nor child has this right at home."[31] By the end of the nineteenth century, the sealed-off family life that had once seemed liberating had built up the explosive potential of a pressure cooker. In the words of one modern commentator, the "excessive intimacy and interdependence that the family imposed upon its members" had created an atmosphere so oppressive that "both parents and children began to seek refuge from the forces that held it together with such overbearing intensity."[32]

It is all very well to live in a house with corridors and doors that shut if the family agrees to honor the retreat rights this architecture implies. But too often in the Victorian family the "room of one's own" was not safe from intruders. In *Night and Day* Ralph Denham takes to putting a sign marked OUT on the handle of his door when he wants to be alone, but he is obviously not playing the game by the rules: "What his family most resented, he reflected, was his wish for privacy. To dine alone, or to sit alone after dinner, was flat rebellion, to be fought with every weapon of underhand stealth or of open appeal" (*ND*, 21, 20). This rebellious sentiment was clearly rooted in Woolf's earliest sense of her own needs. She protests in a diary entry written when she was only fifteen that her father refuses to treat her room as her refuge (Berg Diary, 3 August 1897). The title of her first feminist book, *A Room of One's Own*, was a slogan that expressed a long-standing and urgent necessity.

Although this need for a private retreat was felt by both men and women in the late Victorian family, it was far less frequently honored with regard to women. Men's professional obligations provided a handy alibi for a withdrawal from family life, but since a woman's profession was taken to *be* family life, what comparable excuse could she offer? In the words of John Stuart Mill, "She must always be at the beck and call of somebody, generally of everybody."³³ The most uncompromising attack on Victorian family practices as they affected women's lives is to be found in Florence Nightingale's essay "Cassandra," written in 1852 but not published until the twentieth century. Nightingale's demand is for uninterruptible time and freedom from the endless, meaningless, trivial rituals of family life. The villain of her essay is not man but the family itself, which seems to take on a powerful life of its own:

> The family uses people, *not* for what they are, nor for what they are intended to be, but for what it wants them for—its own uses. It thinks of them not as what God has made them, but as the something which it has arranged that they shall be. If it wants someone to sit in the drawing-room, *that* someone is supplied by the family, though that member may be destined for science, or for education, or for active superintendence by God, *i.e.* by the gifts within. . . . And family boasts that it has performed its mission well, in as far as it has enabled the individual to say, "I have *no* peculiar work, nothing but what the moment brings me, nothing that I cannot throw up at once at anybody's claim"; in as far, that is, as it has *destroyed* the individual life.³⁴

As this passage suggests, the rituals of family life are at war both with individual need and with the sense of vocation. That Nightingale's subversive words, written in the middle of the nineteenth century, were not published until 1928 says much about the striking shift in values the twentieth century brought.

Given the pressures and duties of Victorian domesticity, a room of one's own was not only a necessity for those anxious to do serious work but also a retreat from the group mental life that produced the family's characteristic hypocrisy. The generations and the sexes were alienated from each other; young women were to be kept pure; the servants were not supposed to overhear family conflicts; casual acquaintances and unimportant relations were likely to invade the drawing room or be seated next to one at dinner at any time. This set of conditions made honest talk nearly impossible and established hypocrisy as the Esperanto of family life—an artificial language that was meant to be universally used even though it was no one's native tongue. In addition to attacking the Victorian family's hierarchical structure, large size, and absence of privacy, the reformers focused their critical attention on familial dishonesty. Ibsen and Butler, as we have seen, were honored for their exposure of sham. *The Way of All Flesh*, in Shaw's eyes, was important not only because it uncovered the self-serving impulses that masqueraded as moral righteousness but also because it depicted with honesty such unacceptable feelings as the hatred of one's parents: "It was his genius, always breaking through to the truth," Shaw says of Butler, "that revealed to him, whilst he was still a boy, that this devoted father to whom he could never be too grateful, and this pious angel mother in whose watchful care he was so fortunate, were at best a pair of pitiably perverted and intimidated nobodies, and that he hated them, feared them, and despised them with all his soul."[35] Such brutal unmaskings were felt to be necessary to individual survival.

For Woolf and the other modern reformers, absolute candor became the first rule of friendship and marriage, and this new mental habit was seen as an essential break with the past. In *The Years* the Victorian family's habitual dishonesty is shown to be pervasive and destructive. Everyone is playing a part; real emotions are seldom expressed; conversation is reduced to trivia; "home truths" are in fact rarely found there. The persistent attempts by various characters in the novel to speak frankly to each other are regularly interrupted or suppressed at the critical moment. The promise of honest talk is perpetually unfulfilled, betrayed by reticence, conventionality, and misunderstanding, until Martin Pargiter comes to see the lie as the basis of family life: "Everybody lies, he thought. His father had lied—after his death they had found letters from a woman called Mira tied up in his table-drawer. . . . Why had his father lied? What was the harm of keeping a mistress? . . . It was an abominable system, he thought; family life; Abercorn Terrace. . . . There all those different people had lived, boxed up together, telling lies" (*Y*, 239).

As this passage suggests, the most important lie in the Victorian family was sexual. Colonel Pargiter, whose wife had for years been an invalid, kept a mistress. Long after his wife's death he wants to tell his daughter about this woman to whom he is attached, but he cannot bring himself to do so. In fact no member of his family knows about her while he is alive. When Rose Pargiter is still a young child, she has a traumatic encounter with an exhibitionist, but the experience terrifies her so much that she cannot bring herself to confide it to anyone, ever, though it has probably had a permanent effect on her life. As a result of this characteristic reticence, the hidden aspects of Victorian sexual life have come to light only in the twentieth century. Modern commentators like Peter Cominos and Steven Marcus have revealed the existence of a sexual counterculture that thrived behind the facade of respectable family life but was never publicly acknowledged.

In *The Other Victorians* Marcus brilliantly analyzed the secret underworld of Victorian sexuality as the mirror image of the official code, one that denied all its assumptions and created such an urgent antithetical set of values that it could only lead to the collapse of the whole bicameral structure by the beginning of the modern period:

> The view of human sexuality as it was represented in the subculture of pornography and the view of sexuality held by the official culture were reversals, mirror images, negative analogues of one another. . . . It is essential for us to notice the similarities even more than the differences between these two groups of attitudes or cultures. In both the same set of anxieties are at work; in both the same obsessive ideas can be made out; and in both sexuality is conceived of at precisely the same degree of consciousness. It was a situation of unbearable contradiction. And it was at this point that the breaking through began.[36]

The "breaking through" in England is associated with the same insurrectionary movement around the turn of the century that we have been tracing throughout. Freud, who was of course the great international figure associated with the modern conception of sexuality, eventually found his English translators and publishers in the Bloomsbury group. But long before this a number of British writers had examined the Victorian code of sexuality in a critical spirit. In the work of Havelock Ellis, Edward Carpenter, Marie Stopes, Patrick Geddes, and others, many of the tenets of that code were exposed as crippling fictions. Even earlier, in the eighties and nineties, a literature of "free love" that included such notorious novels as Olive Schreiner's *The Story of an African Farm* (1883) and Grant Allen's *The Woman Who Did* (1895) had attracted public attention and upset the more conventional spirits. Leslie Stephen met Olive Schreiner during one of his Alpine holidays and explained in a letter to his wife that she "disapproves of marriage & thinks that everybody should be free to drop everybody else"; he quickly added: "I should drop *her* like a hot potato." [37] In both the Schreiner and Allen novels the heroine goes off with a lover she does not marry, has a child, is disgraced, and dies a sad and lonely death. The first rebels against the system are conceived as virtuous martyrs. By 1908, when Shaw published *Getting Married*, such unions had become fashionable and were beginning to be advertised by the "guilty parties": "Because our marriage law is inhuman and unreasonable to the point of downright abomination," Shaw wrote in the preface to the play, "the bolder and more rebellious spirits form illicit unions, defiantly sending cards round to their friends announcing what they have done." [38]

Bloomsbury was directly involved in this transvaluation of values, though this may not have been evident from the works its writers chose to publish in their own lifetimes. This anomaly requires some explanation. There is no doubt that in both speech and action the group was astonishingly liberated. Quentin Bell wonders "whether any group had ever been so radical in its rejection of sexual taboos."[39] What began as a revolution of the word was soon transformed into one of deed. By 1910 Vanessa Bell was proposing "the creation of a libertarian society with sexual freedom for all" (QB, I, 170). She embarked on an adulterous affair with Roger Fry and eventually had a child by Duncan Grant, though this fact is not recorded on the official family tree (QB, I, xv). When their conventional cousin Dorothea Stephen, the youngest daughter of that impassioned defender of patriarchy Uncle Fitzjames, objected to receiving Vanessa at her home because of what the servants might think, Virginia Woolf wrote her a blistering letter warning her that "I could not let you come here without saying first that I entirely sympathise with Vanessa's views and conduct" (L, II, 489).

The sexual permissiveness of the group really was extraordinary: homosexuality and lesbianism not only practiced but openly discussed; adulterous liaisons becoming an accepted part of the family circle; *ménages à trois, à quatre, à cinq*; and all of this happening shortly after the death of Queen Victoria, among people raised by the old rules. The most striking quality of these sexual experiments is the way in which the ideal of community seems to control and contain them. Former lovers become lifelong friends; marriage stretches without breaking; jealousy and sexual competition yield to an empathetic understanding and tolerance. Perhaps all of this was possible precisely because it was kept within the circle of intimates and was thus not subject to public scrutiny. Bloomsbury's sexual heterodoxy made at most an oblique appearance in their published work and has come to light only in the letters, diaries, and frank biographies that have appeared since their deaths, and in works like Forster's homosexual novel *Maurice*, which could not be published in 1914, when it was finished. In criticizing Victorian sexual mores, the Bloomsbury writers originally worked by mockery and innuendo (as in Woolf's *Orlando* or Strachey's *Elizabeth and Essex*) rather than by direct statement.

This deliberate inhibition of free expression seems odd until one remembers the fate of bolder experiments. In 1915 an English court found Lawrence's *The Rainbow* to be an obscene publication, and the remaining copies were seized and burned. This incident contributed significantly to Lawrence's decision to spend the rest of his life in exile. The case of *Ulysses* is well known and illustrates similar forces at work. As late as 1928, Radclyffe Hall's *The Well of Loneliness* was seized by the police and banned by the court. In such a climate of repression Bloomsbury chose to remain reticent about its break with Victorian sexual mores, and its published works were largely decorous. When Woolf was writing her biography of Roger Fry in 1940, she asked Keynes whether she could discuss Fry's sexual life frankly: "Can I mention erection?" she asks him. "No you cant," Keynes tells her. "I should mind your saying it. Such revelations have to be in key with their time. The time not come yet." Woolf wonders, "Is he right, or only public school?" but in the end she produced a reticent biography that Keynes patronizingly called "The official life," asking her, "Why not write the real life for the Memoir Club?" (*D*, V, 256, 314).

Such internal censorship made Woolf intensely uneasy, though it expressed a powerful inhibition of her own. In her essay "Professions for Women" she describes with some pride her conquest of the "Angel in the House"—that phantom encouraging women to flatter and be sympathetic—as it threatened to undermine the critical spirit of her own work. But despite this victory, Woolf goes on to say, there was one subject that remained off-limits to the young writer she had once been as she sat at her desk trying to describe her feelings: "She had thought of something, something about the body, about the passions which it was unfitting for her as a woman to say. Men, her reason told her, would be shocked. The consciousness of what men will say of a woman who speaks the truth about her passions had roused her from her artist's state of unconsciousness. She could write no more" (*CE*, II, 288). As a result, the chance of writing honestly, and for print, about her own sexual feelings had eluded her, and she could only hope that other women writers would take up the unfinished business.

And yet, despite these disclaimers, and despite the inhibition of response that at times made Woolf declare herself altogether indifferent to sexual passion, her fiction does deal with sexuality in new ways. In the first place, she writes with obvious involvement about women's fear of male aggression. In *The Voyage Out* the virginal Rachel Vinrace is suddenly seized by Richard Dalloway. His embrace unsettles her, and her dreams turn into nightmares of being trapped in a tunnel, a vault, "alone with a little deformed man [with] the face of an animal" (*VO*, 86). Of men's sexual desire she can at first only feel, "It *is* terrifying—it *is* disgusting" (*VO*, 91). And though she eventually falls in love with the less threatening Terence Hewet, her fear of violation persists, as her fantasies during her final illness reveal. Rachel first feels that she is ill as Terence reads the "Sabrina fair" passage from Milton's *Comus* to her. As a number of critics have pointed out, the Miltonic parallel suggests a fear of defloration.[40]

This revulsion from heterosexuality is expressed in a different way in *Mrs. Dalloway*, when Clarissa retreats from the conjugal bed: "So the room was an attic; the bed narrow; and lying there reading, for she slept badly, she could not dispel a virginity preserved through childbirth which clung to her like a sheet" (*MD*, 35–36). Such passages would not have been found in Victorian fiction, and it is a mistake to think that because they register an impulse toward sexual withdrawal rather than fulfillment they are any less candid. It was, Woolf felt, men's persistent attempts to shape female sexuality according to their own needs that made modern sexual "liberators" like Lawrence assume all could be set right by the phallic magic wand. In a sarcastic passage from *Orlando* that obviously refers to *Lady Chatterley's Lover* and must have been added to the manuscript at the last minute (both books were published in 1928) Woolf invents a little fable of a gamekeeper who has only to whistle under a woman's window to make her slip off her petticoat without delay (*O*, 242).

In addition, Woolf's fiction frequently depicts homosexual and lesbian attachments with sympathy and yet without special pleading. *Jacob's Room*, *The Waves*, *The Years*, and *Between the Acts* all include important characters who are attracted to their own sex; their feelings are taken seriously and treated with the same basic dignity as those of the more sexually conventional characters. Presenting such people as in some sense ordinary meant challenging both Victorian and post-Victorian sexual prejudices, and Woolf tries to show that the more generous spirits are capable of casting off those destructive proprieties. Here is Eleanor's reaction in *The Years* when she first hears of Nicholas's homosexuality:

> For a second a sharp shiver of repugnance passed over Eleanor's skin as if a knife had sliced it. Then she realised that it touched nothing of importance. The sharp shiver passed. Underneath was—what? She looked at Nicholas. He was watching her.
> "Does that," he said, hesitating a little, "make you dislike me, Eleanor?"
> "Not in the least! Not in the least!" she exclaimed spontaneously.
>
> (Y, 321)

Despite her reticence and her impatience with the more programmatic liberators, Woolf's work expresses sexual attitudes and feelings that were not common on either side of the great divide. In *Mrs. Dalloway*, for example, she could give a sense of Clarissa's intense romantic attraction to Sally Seton without identifying it as a strictly sexual passion or treating it as an attachment that could last. But she does not hesitate to give the moment its due: "Sally stopped; picked a flower; kissed her on the lips. The whole world might have turned upside down! The others disappeared; there she was alone with Sally" (*MD*, 40). Later in the novel Sally can reappear as a middle-aged matron, bursting with pride about her five sons. By comparison, the work of the more propagandistic anti-Victorians tended to simplify experience. Even E. M. Forster, in *Maurice*, is forced to turn his male lovers into lifelong companions and to assure us that their union would last unto death, like the proper Victorian marriage it was designed to challenge and displace. Unlike such writers, Woolf can show sexuality as both impure and unstable, and as perhaps not necessarily the searing, central human experience that *both* Victorian repression *and* the more strident forms of emancipation took it to be. Hers is not the language of modern liberation. But it is scarcely the language of Victorian sexual convention either. In its own quiet manner Woolf's treatment of the subject was helping her readers to think in new ways.[41]

III

Woolf's freshness is linked to her fundamental distrust of the whole concept of liberation, and it is here that she parts company with many of her contemporaries. As we have seen, most of the anti-Victorian writers used their work as an instrument of reform to discredit the hierarchical structure, unmanageable size, lack of privacy, and pervasive hypocrisy of the nineteenth-century family and to replace it with a smaller, more democratic, honest, and individualistic institution. The characteristic plot of such works stressed the steady movement toward independence. Freeing oneself from the bonds of family life or the prison of marriage became one of the exemplary resolutions in early modern literature and provided a new form of narrative closure. In such diverse works as Ibsen's *A Doll's House*, Shaw's *Mrs. Warren's Profession*, Butler's *The Way of All Flesh*, Gissing's *The Odd Women*, Gosse's *Father and Son*, Forster's *Maurice*, Joyce's *Portrait of the Artist as a Young Man*, and Lawrence's *The Rainbow* or *Lady Chatterley's Lover*, the movement toward liberation by rejecting family or marriage ties is turned into one of the dominant myths of modern consciousness. In the words of William Carlos Williams, "Divorce is / the sign of knowledge in our time, / divorce! divorce!"[42]

Woolf was clearly attracted to this vision but unable to believe in it. Some of her novels seem at first to be constructed according to the new formula. As we have seen, Katharine and Ralph in *Night and Day* intensely resent the familial pressures that abridge their freedom. By the end of the novel they are in open conflict with Katharine's father, who sees his formerly tractable daughter looking "like a wild animal caged in a civilized dwelling-place" (*ND*, 505). But the revolution is short-lived, and the rebels are quickly reintegrated into family and society. It is of course possible to treat this ending as a fraudulent conventional resolution that betrays the emotional logic of the novel. But Woolf's conservative ending expresses certain tendencies in her major characters that should have been evident all along. Her sense of the dividedness of human motives will not allow her to simplify feelings along the lines dictated by new ideological imperatives. Though Ralph rages against the pressures of his home, Katharine's visit to it releases a very different but equally genuine feeling: "All that brotherhood and sisterhood, and a common childhood in a common past mean, all the stability, the unambitious comradeship, and tacit understanding of family life at its best, came to his mind" (*ND*, 402).

Such conflicting feelings make for awkward resolutions in fiction, in which neither the conventional marriage plot (with its integrative force) nor the modern liberation plot (with its triumph of the independent self) presents an adequate model, and the resolution of *Night and Day* clearly gave Woolf a great deal of trouble. *The Years* presented similar difficulties. Here, more than anywhere else in her fiction, was an opportunity to record the triumph of modern liberation from the restraints of Victorian family life. There are indications that Woolf had this plot pattern in mind when she first started working on the novel. Some of the alternate titles she considered but later abandoned are revealing: *Sons and Daughters* (or *Daughters and Sons*), *Here and Now*, and *Dawn*, the last rejected out of the fear that it seemed "too emphatic, sentimental" (*D*, IV, 241). The concluding section of *The Years*, "Present Day," was to be the most important part of the book, longer than the others, and possibly designed to illustrate the new freedoms the post-Victorian "dawn" had brought. But though there are vestiges of such a conception in the finished work, they are constantly undercut by a more skeptical one. And the large party that brings all the Pargiters together at the end of the novel expresses a more complex vision than the liberation plot permits. Woolf's residual conservatism finally makes her present this family reunion as a moving event. At the end of the book the Pargiter brothers and sisters standing by the window, "the men in their black-and-white evening dress, the women in their crimsons, golds and silvers, wore a statuesque air for a moment, as if they were carved in stone" (*Y*, 467). And the force of family life that had once seemed merely oppressive gradually grows to something of great constancy. For despite all the domestic conflict and frustration and misery the novel records, Woolf also makes it clear that these are the ties that bind.

A remarkable letter to Vita Sackville-West suggests that Woolf felt a powerful longing for such familial bonds. She describes a family party at which she is more an outside spectator than a participant—a party that superficially resembles the one at the end of *The Years*: "The passion and joy of sons and daughters in their own society struck me almost to tears with self-pity and amazement. Nothing of that sort do we any of us know—profound emotions, which are yet natural and taken for granted, so that nothing inhibits or restrains—How deep these are, and unself conscious." And in the same letter she voices a comparably conservative sentiment about sexuality. The power of *Anna Karenina* to move us, she says, is entirely dependent on the reader's bedrock belief in marital fidelity: "Tolstoy hoists all his book on that support. Take it away, say, no it doesn't offend me that AK. should copulate with Vronsky, and what remains?" (*L*, III, 254–55). Such sentiments reveal a powerful longing for the whole system of family life that Woolf's generation had worked so hard to discredit, and they suggest why her own fiction cannot be identified with the most openly rebellious works of her contemporaries. For there was a part of her that mourned the passing of the old order and identified the new freedom with the trivialization of our deepest feelings.

Woolf's contained rebellion is the product of an inner divided loyalty. When Isa in *Between the Acts* thinks of her husband as "the father of my children, whom I love and hate"

(*BA*, 252), she is expressing in her own way her creator's complex sense of family life. On the one hand, Woolf felt a deep nostalgia for the security and emotional intensity the nuclear family had provided; on the other, she was implacably hostile to the fundamental assumptions and practices of nineteenth-century domestic life. The split runs right through all the members of the Bloomsbury group and must have been one of the things that drew them to each other. Forster could use a quotation from Shelley's hostile description of marriage as the title for *The Longest Journey*; he could write an unpublishable novel about a love affair that would never produce children; yet he lived for most of his adult life with his morally conventional mother even though he knew she "froze the depths" in him.[43] Roger Fry could say, "I've always hated families and patriarchalism of all kinds," yet in his sixties still dream about his father and be anxious to make his mother proud (*RF*, 281, 260–61). The persistent need for familial bonds made these anti-Victorian rebels form a group that in many ways mirrored family life. The deliberately chosen proximity of their Bloomsbury residences encouraged shared meals and constant visits, produced lifelong loyalties despite serious disagreements, and created a sense of group identity: the Bloomsberries, as they called themselves—a comic variant of a family name like the Pargiters.

A real revolution has no use for such conservative tendencies. Their presence in Woolf and in the other members of Bloomsbury undercut their wholehearted dedication to the cause. The movement that reevaluated the Victorian family around the turn of the century was aggressively critical, as we have seen. It assumed that there was virtually nothing worth rescuing in the particular traditions of nineteenth-century family life and that the modern family would have to be built on an entirely new foundation. The nostalgic element in Woolf's makeup as well as her skepticism about the possibility of rapid human change made her unable to work with complete devotion for the goals of the reformers. At the same time, and quite paradoxically, she felt an impatience with those goals because they were not radical *enough*. In this she was responding to a dissident strain within the movement that seemed bent on rejecting family life altogether rather than making it tolerable. Its most striking manifestation was a revolt against marriage—and not merely in its legal aspect.

This rejection of marriage was most strongly voiced by radical feminists. Sophia Jex-Blake, for example, wrote to her friend Dr. Lucy Sewall in 1869, "I quite agree with you. 'Never marry if you can help it'!" [44] Christabel Pankhurst warned her readers in 1913 that "marriage is intensely dangerous," and she paints a picture of the single state that directly challenges the traditional image of the pathetic spinster: "In the old days when marriage was the only career open to women, those who did not marry regarded themselves, and were regarded, as failures. . . . But nowadays the unmarried women have a life full of joy and interest. They are not mothers of children of their flesh, but they can serve humanity, they can do work that is useful and beautiful. Therefore their life is complete." [45]

These "new women" who treasured their independence and were determined not to lose it appeared in many works of fiction and drama written around the turn of the century because they had appeared in real life. Shaw's plays are filled with them: Vivie Warren, Lesbia Grantham (in *Getting Married*), Lina Szczepanowska (in *Misalliance*) are examples. But the most interesting literary treatment of the subject is probably George Gissing's *The Odd Women* (1893). Gissing's heroine, Rhoda Nunn, dedicates herself to training young women in work that would make them financially independent and therefore able to reject marriage altogether. For her, the institution is irredeemably corrupt, and she expresses her contempt for it in the strongest possible terms: "I would have girls taught that marriage is a thing to be avoided rather than hoped for. I would teach them that for the majority of women marriage means disgrace." [46] Gissing tests her seriousness by providing her with a suitor who deeply interests her—who is an intellectual equal, sexually attractive, and seemingly sympathetic to her cause. But he also shows that their union could never flourish, because the tendency toward domination and submission in the relation between the sexes is stronger, finally, than the wish for equality. The only solution for a woman of independent spirit is to reject marriage and family life unequivocally. Though she is deeply tempted, Rhoda will not surrender her maiden name—Nunn. And Gissing's novel ends not with the marriage of the central characters but with a general separation of the sexes.

There are many indications in Virginia Woolf's life and work that she found this radical solution attractive, if not finally compelling. She resisted her own suitors and did not marry until she was thirty, despite great pressure to do so. Shortly before she finally accepted Leonard's persistent suit, she wrote him, paradoxically, "The obvious advantages of marriage stand in my way. I say to myself. Anyhow, you'll be quite happy with him; and he will give you companionship, children, and a busy life—then I say By God, I will not look upon marriage as a profession" (*L*, I, 496). Many of her fictional characters echo these sentiments: Clarissa Dalloway and Sally Seton in their youth "spoke of marriage always as a catastrophe" (*MD*, 39); Lily Briscoe resists Mrs. Ramsay's coercive matrimonial idealism when she realizes "she need not marry, thank Heaven; she need not undergo that degradation. She was saved from that dilution" (*TL*, 159).

This urgent wish and need to be alone, this deep attraction to a state in which all permanent bonds to others are cut, is expressed in the climax of Woolf's first novel. Rachel's illness and death in *The Voyage Out* is a deliberate and shocking betrayal of the conventions of the marriage plot the book seemed to accept. Yet there are many indications in the earlier sections that the expected outcome, marriage, would be an entirely inadequate resolution. Even Terence, who loves Rachel deeply, imagines proposing to her in what is, to say the least, a rather unorthodox fashion: "I worship you," he plans to tell her, "but I loathe marriage, I hate its smugness, its safety, its compromise, and the thought of you interfering in my work, hindering me; what would you answer?" (*VO*, 298).

The entire novel reflects in its details Woolf's sense of the in-adequacy of marriage—its failure to cure human loneliness, its sexual threat, its impediment to individual growth. An es-cape from it must be found, and the solution she hits on is Rachel's fatal illness. As Phyllis Rose has suggested, the final scenes of the novel subvert its more conventional attitudes: "It endorses marriage, intimacy, but its emotional message, its hidden message, is the primacy of the self." [47]

In Woolf's mind illness is always associated with a retreat into oneself and often linked to creative power. "Six weeks in bed now would make a masterpiece" of *The Waves*, she writes in her diary as she is trying to work on that book through the countless interruptions of domestic life: "Every time I get into my current of thought I am jerked out of it" (*D*, III, 254, 253). And in her essay "On Being Ill" she identifies illness with the solitary realm in which we can taste solitude: "Human beings do not go hand in hand the whole stretch of the way. There is a virgin forest in each; a snow field where even the print of birds' feet is unknown. Here we go alone, and like it better so. Always to have sympathy, always to be accompanied, always to be understood would be intolerable" (*CE*, IV, 196). Rachel's illness, and the feverish fantasy life it releases in her, is also an intensely private realm no one else can enter. Its under-water images connect it with primal feelings and the deepest core of the self—terrifying, perhaps, but blessedly cut off from the banalities of the daylight world of courtship and marriage to which she had earlier been transported. Even her fiancé's presence in the room upsets her, because "She did not wish to remember; it troubled her when people tried to disturb her loneliness; she wished to be alone" (*VO*, 424).

Against such a deeply rooted resistance to union with others there can be no argument. It has nothing to do with the reform of existing institutions and the critique of particular domestic patterns. It seems to treat all familial bonds as mere fetters. But as we have seen, Woolf could also think nostal-gically of those bonds as vital links of affection that release some of our deepest feelings. Her difficulty lay in finding a fictional vehicle that would permit her to express these antithetical attitudes toward marriage and family life in a single work without simplifying the conflict. Neither the traditional marriage plot nor the modern liberation plot was adequate to her purposes. She would have to invent her own form—and in *To the Lighthouse* she did.

7

The Domestic Politics of
To the Lighthouse

Virginia Woolf was reluctant to call *To the Lighthouse* a novel, but what generic category suited it better, she asked herself in her diary—"elegy," perhaps (*D*, III, 34)? Her uneasiness is understandable, since the book she was writing rejected the conventional fictional structures she had inherited and came closer to recording the facts of her own life history than did any of her other novels. Her comments on *To the Lighthouse* express a peculiar uneasiness, not so much about the quality of what she was writing as about the book's structure, possible sentimentality, and fidelity to its real-life models. In trying to explore her deepest feelings about familial bonds, she had chosen to draw on her earliest memories and to use her parents as protagonists. The book was "to have father's character done complete in it; & mothers; & St Ives; & childhood" (*D*, III, 18)—an audacious undertaking filled with serious hazards for a novelist. Was it possible to tell the truth about one's parents? How did one avoid sentimentalizing them or turning them into caricatures in order to settle old scores? Above all, how could a novelist with such a strong sense of design keep hold of her right to shape every element of her fictional world if she felt an equal obligation to biographical truth? It is no wonder she waited so anxiously for her sister's verdict on the finished product and was so relieved when it was favorable. For Vanessa not only praised the novel as a powerful work of art but confirmed the uncanny fidelity of Virginia's vision: the picture of Leslie Stephen, Vanessa wrote, "seems to me to be the only thing about him which ever gave a true idea," and the "portrait of mother . . . is more like her to me than anything I could ever have conceived of as possible. It is almost painful to have her so raised from the dead" (*L*, III, 572).

And yet, for all Woolf's apprehension about distorting biographical truth, she grew to resent the common assumption that the major characters of *To the Lighthouse* simply *were* her parents. She wrote one correspondent that she disliked "being exposed as a novelist and told my people are my mother and father, when, being in a novel, they're not." And she assured another reader that "I did not mean to paint an exact portrait of my father in Mr Ramsay. A book makes everything into itself, and the portrait became changed to fit it as I wrote" (*L*, VI, 464, 517). She deliberately refused to reread the "documentary evidence" about her parents—their letters to each other, her father's memoir of his wife (*The Mausoleum Book*)—at the time she was writing *To the Lighthouse*, though she had access to these materials and might well have chosen to go back to them (*L*, III, 379). Stronger than her impulse to recapture the world of her parents was her need to shape her characters according to her own vision. "I have had my vision" are the last words of the novel, and perhaps the emphasis should fall on the word "my."

In *To the Lighthouse* Woolf tried not only to recover the memories of her childhood but also to record her tangled feelings about Victorian marriage and family life as well as about the substitutes for them that some rebellious modern spirits had proposed. Her book was concerned with her sense of institutional and ideological change and continuity, not just with the idiosyncrasies of her private history. And so it became necessary to shape the raw material, to rewrite the past in order to let the book make "everything into itself." She did not hesitate to schematize, to fabricate, to alter—in short, to exercise the prerogatives of the artist—in order to serve that need.

The differences between *To the Lighthouse* and the surviving records of Woolf's family are instructive. In subtle but nevertheless decisive ways she changed the characters of her parents to suit the requirements of her vision. In his autobiography Leonard Woolf records his sense of the disparity between Leslie Stephen and his fictional counterpart. There are, he says, "traces of unfairness" in the portrait of Ramsay: "Leslie Stephen must have been in many ways an exasperating man within the family and he exasperated his daughters, particularly Vanessa. But I think that they exaggerated his exactingness and sentimentality and, in memory, were habitually unfair to him owing to a complicated variety of the Oedipus complex."[1] Virginia Woolf expresses her own awareness of a semideliberate distortion of her father's memory when she reflects on the matter in her memoirs: "We were bitter, harsh, and to a great extent, unjust," she writes, though "there was some truth in our complaint." In trying to dissociate themselves from their father's view of the world, she and Vanessa had "made him the type of all that we hated in our lives" (*MB*, 56). In other words, they had turned Leslie Stephen into a symbol of his age and made him stand for all the conventions of Victorian domestic life they most detested. The conflict between individuals was turned into a conflict between rival codes. A good deal of this schematization invented in Woolf's youth survives in *To the Lighthouse*. The major characters are sometimes given stark symbolic identities. As Lily Briscoe sees the Ramsays standing together, for instance, she turns them into emblematic figures:

> So that is marriage, Lily thought, a man and a woman looking at a girl throwing a ball. . . . And suddenly the meaning which, for no reason at all, as perhaps they are stepping out of the Tube or ringing a doorbell, descends on people, making them symbolical, making them representative, came upon them, and made them in the dusk standing, looking, the symbols of marriage, husband and wife.
>
> (114–15)

Such passages underline the novel's thematic concerns by shifting the reader's attention away from the particular details of character and action to the general issues that concerned Woolf in writing *To the Lighthouse*. But in turning Leslie Stephen, for example, into a representative Victorian patriarch, she had to ignore a good deal about her model. For there is considerable evidence that her father was far from being a typical paterfamilias and did not consistently resemble his fictional counterpart.[2] It is true that like Mr. Ramsay he idolized his wife, was often impatient and short-tempered, was intensely uneasy about his professional success, and constantly demanded reassurance and sympathy from women. But the differences are equally striking and important to understand. For instance, in the novel Mr. Ramsay is barely on speaking terms with his children, has no respect for their feelings, and seems to communicate with them mainly through the intermediary of his wife. This is why the monosyllabic "Well done!" (316) he addresses to his son James at the end of the book is almost an epochal event in the boy's life.

The biographical facts were very different. Stephen's letters are full of tender passages about his children, whom he calls the "ragamice," and show an acute awareness of their individual gifts and needs. "I hope my little ones are tolerably jolly," he writes on one occasion; "I can always call up their little faces, specially Virginias. I see her eyes flash & her sweet little teeth gleam."[3] And the short memoir the young Virginia wrote for her father's first biographer stresses his willingness to play with the children for hours when they were very young, to read their favorite books aloud—*Tom Brown's School Days*, *Treasure Island*, Sir Walter Scott. Woolf recalls that he managed to get through *all* the *Waverley* novels and that "when we had finished the last he was ready to begin the first over again."[4] Though Mr. Ramsay also loves Scott, he reads *The Antiquary* to himself, after the children are in bed. And in the boat on the way to the lighthouse, James interprets his father's solitary reading as an aggressive act: "James felt that each page was turned with a peculiar gesture aimed at him: now assertively, now commandingly," and he dreads the moment when his father would look up from the page "and speak to him sharply about something or other" (282).

In *To the Lighthouse* Mr. Ramsay is presented as an advocate of absolute sexual polarization, the Victorian assumption that each sex is assigned its sphere and must remain in it. Although he is above such crude pronouncements as Tansley's

"women can't write, women can't paint" (134), he does ideal-
ize the traditional divisions. "He liked that men should labour
and sweat on the windy beach at night, pitting muscle and
brain against the waves and the wind; he liked men to work
like that, and women to keep house, and sit beside sleeping
children indoors, while men were drowned, out there in a
storm" (254). Such thoughts, as well as the masculine professional camaraderie of his relationship with Tansley and
Bankes, prefigure the patriarchal hostility to women's work
outside the home that Virginia Woolf would later attack in her
feminist books. But once again, the disparity between Mr.
Ramsay and Leslie Stephen is striking. He knew early on, for
instance, that his daughter was destined to be a writer, and he
gave her every encouragement. "Yesterday I discussed George
II with 'Ginia," he writes in 1893, when Virginia was eleven
years old. "She takes in a great deal & will really be an author
in time."[5]

Although Woolf resented all her life not having been sent
to the university like her brothers, it is not at all clear whose
decision this was or whether, given her determination to be
an imaginative writer, it was such a foolish one. In any case,
Leslie Stephen was very far from believing that women should
be decorative objects trained only in the usual feminine "accomplishments" while preparing themselves for matrimony.
His thoughts on the subject were quite uncompromisingly
radical for his time and are spelled out in a letter to Julia written before their marriage:

> What I chiefly hold is that women ought to be as well educated
> as men, indeed a great deal better than men are now. . . . [A
> woman] ought to learn something thoroughly when she grows
> up, thoroughly enough to be able to make her living by it, if it
> is of the paying kind, or to be an authority upon it, if it is not.
> What the something should be must of course depend upon
> her tastes, whether literary, scientific or artistic or whatever
> they may be. But I hate to see so many women's lives wasted
> simply because they have not been trained well enough to take
> an independent interest in any studies or to be able to work
> effectively at any profession.[6]

Such examples of heterodox thinking are entirely eliminated from the portrait of Mr. Ramsay, though Woolf could hardly have been ignorant of her father's views on the subject. But she wanted to stress the sexual polarization of Victorian family life and the effect of the cult of domesticity on women, and in order to be true to her sense of these matters, she had to sacrifice the elements in Stephen's identity that contradicted it.

The most striking example of this fictional transformation of Leslie Stephen, however, concerns not so much women's work as his own. In *To the Lighthouse* Mr. Ramsay is presented as unreasonably gloomy about his career and intolerably coercive in demanding reassurance from others. He is a failure, he insists; he has missed his chance of immortality; others have passed him by; the demands of marriage and family life have compromised the quality of his work; he will never reach R. All this is made to seem excessive and distasteful, even though Tansley and Bankes also treat Ramsay's later career as something of a decline. Nevertheless, he is recognized as one of the greatest metaphysicians of his time; he is surrounded by disciples, swamped by "the tributes that reached him from Swansea, Cardiff, Exeter, Southampton, Kidderminster, Oxford, Cambridge" (73); he uses "the energies of his splendid mind" (56) to produce a steady stream of lectures and books. For someone with such credentials to persist in calling himself a failure and demanding reassurance seems self-indulgent, and the reader is given little opportunity to respond sympathetically or even to understand what Mr. Ramsay may be talking about. We never really see the issue through his eyes.

Leslie Stephen also thought of himself as a failure, and there is evidence that he incessantly pressured his wife to reassure him about the quality of his work. "Success" and "failure" are subjective states as well as objective judgments, however; despite the public recognition that came his way, it is possible to see why Stephen felt as he did. He differs from Mr. Ramsay in never having chosen a field and may be said to have had four distinct careers—as a philosopher, as a literary critic, as an editor and journalist, and finally as the "inventor" of the *Dictionary of National Biography*. This may seem like a formidable achievement, but for Stephen much of it was simply hackwork or alienated labor. He cannot really be said to have had a sense of vocation, and he drifted into his various writing projects out of both financial necessity and despair at his achievement in any given enterprise. His feeling of professional failure, which he describes in *The Mausoleum Book*, is based on his recognition that he had spread himself too thin: "I think that I had it in me to make something like a real contribution to philosophical or ethical thought. Unluckily, what with journalism and dictionary making, I have been a jack of all trades; and instead of striking home have only done enough to persuade friendly judges that I could have struck."[7]

Someone familiar with the pattern of Stephen's career could see that there is a good deal of truth in this harsh self-assessment. Noel Annan, his most searching biographer, comes to a similar conclusion. Stephen, he says, was not one of the great minds of his generation: "He swam strongly with the stream instead of turning it to irrigate new country. Partly because he lacked supreme originality and partly because he was too anxious to teach the tenets of the faith, he remained an incomparable *vulgarisateur* unable to revise the premises on which he based his teaching. And Stephen knew his own measure."[8] Perhaps this sense of his intellectual limitations made Stephen accept the editorship of the *Dictionary of National Biography*, which has come to be seen as his greatest achievement. But that is scarcely the way he felt about it himself. For in supervising such a gigantic editorial project he was providing himself with a permanent alibi to stop doing original thinking, and his comments on the task are full of a deep despair and frustration. He refers to his editorial labor as his "treadmill," "the damned dictionary," or simply the "d.d.," and as "my revolting task."[9] He sticks to it nevertheless both out of financial necessity and out of the grim conviction "that work of this kind is the best that I am fit for." And in a letter written toward the end of his life to a close friend, he says with self-lacerating bitterness, "I have lost any illusions I may have had about the value of my work, and am content to take a modest price."[10]

Such a career—with its increasing disparity between public recognition and the inner conviction of failure—could provide the material for a complex and poignant picture of vocational ambition and frustration, of the sort George Eliot painted in her portrait of Lydgate, for instance. But for us to see the fictional counterpart of Leslie Stephen in an equally sympathetic way, we would have to be given continuous and relatively direct access to his mind. Although Mr. Ramsay is obviously of central importance in *To the Lighthouse*, the record of his thoughts is constantly interrupted by the thoughts of characters who are quite critical of him and who in most cases do not understand his work. Mrs. Ramsay hardly ever reads a book and finds men's professional lives alien territory; Lily Briscoe needs Andrew Ramsay to explain his father's ideas to her in the simplest possible terms because she has no notion what "subject and object and the nature of reality" might mean (40). In such ways, Mr. Ramsay's sense of failure is made incomprehensible, merely a threat to others. Woolf's diary reveals that she herself battled constantly with some of the same demons—the worries about her reputation, the fear that she was taking too much time from her fiction for journalism, the frequent conviction that what she was writing was simply bad. She did not finally think of herself as a failure, because unlike her father she had both a firm sense of vocation and a profoundly original mind; but she knew enough about his kind of professional despair to have produced a more empathetic fictional version of it if she had wanted to. It was, however, essential for her purposes to show how men's professional lives were both a threat to their families and hopelessly entangled in their worries about power and impotence, and the major male characters she invented had to be seen in this light.

We know less about Julia Stephen than about her husband, but what we do know suggests that the portrait of her as Mrs.

Ramsay, uncannily accurate though it was in many ways, was quite skewed in others. Like Mrs. Ramsay, Julia Stephen was home- and family-centered, astonishingly beautiful, and self-less almost to a fault. She admired her husband deeply; her feeling for him nearly matched his uxoriousness. And she had a kind of genius for resolving conflicts by bringing people together, a talent that sometimes took the form of matchmaking. Nevertheless, there was another side to her character that the portrait of Mrs. Ramsay ignores: she had a sense of vocation and professional commitment. Mrs. Ramsay relegates work to the "admirable fabric of the masculine intelligence" (164), and she feels herself unsuited even to the traditional philanthropy that ladies of her station took up, because of her "untrained mind" (20). Julia Stephen's mind may have been "untrained," but it was vigorous and in some ways surprisingly professional. Her one published book, *Notes from Sick Rooms* (1883), and her recently discovered but thus far unpublished stories for children and essays on public issues show her to have been quite different from Mrs. Ramsay in important ways.

She thought of nursing as a vocation and regularly idealized it in what she wrote. In one of her unpublished essays she describes the new career of hospital nurse in a way that tries to account for its powerful appeal to the many young women who were choosing it: "The wages are not the temptation—the freedom is not for there is none—the strictest observance of rules is one of the first duties of the Hospital Nurse and while her work is both manual & mental she is not treated as a heroine nor as a slave—she has chosen her lot of enforced work & rigid rule, because she has found that to serve was the highest expression of her nature & that to her it was easier to live under strict rule with clearly defined duties." [11] To the modern reader, this description calls up the image of the Lady with the Lamp and seems to confirm the familiar idea that women's work in Victorian England was simply a form of self-sacrifice. But as Lytton Strachey had shown in *Eminent Victorians*, the popular image of Florence Nightingale as a selfless angel of mercy is a sentimental distortion. Her reformation of the nursing profession was brought about not by "gentle sweetness and womanly self-abnegation" but "by strict method, by stern discipline, by rigid attention to detail, by ceaseless labour, by the fixed determination of an indomitable will." [12]

Julia Stephen's commitment to nursing was by no means as single-minded as Florence Nightingale's, in part at least because her first loyalty was to her own family, who resented her frequent departures to nurse the sick. But there is no doubt that some of the same vocational impulses were at work in her. *Notes from Sick Rooms* is a remarkable document. Written with a kind of no-nonsense professional seriousness, it shows the weight of an extensive and varied experience with illness as well as a detailed awareness of the psychological and physical needs of the patient. Her recommended practices require rigid self-discipline and hard-headedness on the part of the nurse. The book is full of detailed advice about ventilation, nourishment, sanitation, the preparation and administration of medicine, and so on. It reveals an ambition to do necessary work competently and efficiently. It also suggests that a nurse who has mastered her craft has a skill and sense of usefulness that is probably more like what the professional men of her circle would have felt about *their* work than it is like the modern vision of the pathetic, self-sacrificing Victorian female "condemned" to perpetual servitude in the sick room. Julia Stephen was convinced in any case that "service is the condition of our being," [13] and she meant this motto to apply to men as well as to women. Perhaps she had merely found a way of idealizing women's bondage, but that is certainly not the way she thought about the matter, and there is something arrogant and patronizing in the modern habit of treating such forms of idealism as self-delusion.

Julia Stephen's professional seriousness is also revealed in some of her other writings, though they have remained unpublished. The collection of her papers now in the Washington State University Library includes drafts of three essays—on the domestic arrangements of the English home, on the servant question, and on agnostic women—as well as a group of ten stories for children, most of them quite long and essentially complete. The most interesting of the essays is a spirited defense of the intellectual independence of women in matters of faith. It was written as a protest against an article published in *The Nineteenth Century* which claimed that women surrender their religious belief only "because they have subjugated themselves to the intellect of some [agnostic] man." In challenging this condescending assumption, Julia Stephen refuses to delegate women's mental life to "the admirable fabric of the masculine intelligence": "We will not concede that where a man chooses or rejects a faith from conviction a woman does so from a desire to please. . . . In the acceptance or rejection of a creed let the woman be judged as the man." [14] Such confident assertions bear little resemblance to the hesitant accents of Mrs. Ramsay, who in *To the Lighthouse* thinks "We are in the hands of the Lord," then reproves her wandering mind for drifting into such banalities (101).

The stories for children reveal a different kind of professionalism. Most of them are fully formed and carefully constructed fictions of considerable length, between twenty and fifty manuscript pages each. They survive in easily readable fair copies, sometimes in more than one version, which suggests careful revision and a determination to preserve and perhaps circulate them. There are indications that they were intended for publication, with drawings by Leslie Stephen, although it is not clear just how seriously this project was pursued. [15] In any case, they are not the work of an amateur storyteller but of someone who has thought about characterization, suspense, and narrative shape rather carefully and who writes with delightful inventiveness and considerable wit. I do not mean to make extravagant claims for these stories. They lack the authentic imaginative power of the classics of children's literature, and they run to formula. Many of them are cautionary tales about the disappointment in store for restless children who try to escape from the world of the routine and familiar: the young rebels soon weary of their freedom and long to return to hearth and home. They are functional parables written by someone with an unshakable faith in middle-class domestic life—the products of a sensibility that is finally rational, moralistic, and firmly conventional. But within those limits they are the work of a real writer with a flair for language and a shrewdly observant eye. In *To the*

Lighthouse Mrs. Ramsay reads James the Grimms' tale "The Fisherman and His Wife." It is an astute choice, since the story reinforces Mrs. Ramsay's belief that wives must be subordinate to their husbands. But her real-life counterpart did not have to depend on the traditional tales when she required a moral fable. She wrote her own.

All of these transformations of biographical fact into fiction have a common purpose: to suggest that work and family life are antithetical or rival commitments that simply cannot be combined. No one in *To the Lighthouse* can be said to have an equal loyalty to a vocation and to domestic life, and the book is filled with warnings and examples of the need to choose. Mr. Ramsay's sense of professional failure is associated in his mind and in the minds of others with his large family: "he would have written better books if he had not married" (110) is apparently one of his obsessive ideas. Charles Tansley dismisses Mr. Ramsay's later career in characteristically brutal fashion: "Of course Ramsay had dished himself by marrying a beautiful woman and having eight children" (141). And Mr. Bankes associates the end of Mr. Ramsay's promise with the assumption of the bonds of matrimony: "He had seen him divest himself of all those glories of isolation and austerity which crowned him in youth to cumber himself definitely with fluttering wings and clucking domesticities" (39–40).

The conflict between work and family life seems unresolvable in *To the Lighthouse*. Each character is forced to choose between these rival loyalties and to defend his or her choice by attacking the alternative. Even Lily Briscoe, who comes closest to understanding the appeal of both camps, sees the issue in either/or terms. She had felt the pressure of Mrs. Ramsay's will, pitying her and William Bankes for not being married, trying to push them toward each other. But Lily resists this coercion, and both she and Bankes—though they become close friends—choose their work over matrimony. Bankes's powers of resistance are stronger, no doubt, since he finds little to attract him in family rituals. Even at the dinner party, he is silently protesting the waste of time: "How trifling it all is, how boring it all is, he thought, compared with the other thing—work" (138). Lily Briscoe too chose work over

domesticity in a moment of vocational commitment associated with the solution to the design of the painting she is
working on. She had realized simultaneously that she "need
never marry anybody, and she had felt an enormous exulta-
tion" (271).

The sense that work and family life cannot be successfully
integrated is part of Woolf's vision of an era—the Victorian
world of her parents' generation that seemed to offer no encouragement to combine those commitments. The fault lies
neither in Mr. Ramsay nor in Mrs. Ramsay but in the institution they both support, in the gestalt of nineteenth-century
marriage. The segregation of the sexes, the paired idealization
of domestic angels and male careerists so prevalent in that era,
had divided people from each other and exaggerated their
differences. So Auguste Comte had written about women,
"Effectually to perform their Mission, they must abstain altogether from the practical pursuits of the stronger sex." [16]

This sense of the incompatibility of work and domestic rituals was carried forward into the twentieth century. Although
the extraordinary pressures of Victorian family life had exacerbated the problem, it could not be relegated entirely to the
past. There is scarcely a character in Woolf's fiction, and certainly no female character, who may be said to combine work
and family life successfully. Her women artists feel that they
have given up something vital. Lily Briscoe thinks of herself as
"a skimpy old maid, holding a paint-brush on the lawn" (278).
Miss La Trobe in *Between the Acts* reflects that "she was an outcast. Nature had somehow set her apart from her kind" (*BA*,
247). And in her essay "Women and Fiction," Woolf records
the "significant" fact that "of the four great women novelists—
Jane Austen, Emily Brontë, Charlotte Brontë, and George
Eliot—not one had a child, and two were unmarried" (*CE*, II,
143). She must have known that her own name would one day
be added to this list.

Woolf's decision to stress the conflict between vocation and
domestic life, then, was only in part an attempt to reproduce
the conditions of Victorian marriage. The issue was obviously
of deep personal concern to her. She regularly thinks about
the contrast between her childless state and Vanessa Bell's

fruitfulness. But Vanessa had written her, a year after her first child was born, that "I cant do a stroke of painting as long as I have Julian—such is maternity." [17] Woolf was determined that her own marriage would leave her free to work, and she agreed to marry Leonard in part because he firmly supported her sense of vocation. Shortly after her engagement she writes to assure her friend Violet Dickinson that in Leonard she has found the right man: "L. wants me to say that if I cease to write when married, I shall be divorced" (*L*, I, 502). Her choice of a man who respected her mind, who took her writing seriously, who would not insist on a large family or perhaps even on "conjugal rights," must have been founded on a conscious or unconscious conviction that in her own case at any rate the choice between work and a full domestic life could not be avoided. It was a version of the polarity she was to stress again and again in *To the Lighthouse*.

This does not mean, however, that nothing had altered since her parents' generation. In fact, the highly original discontinuous structure of Woolf's novel is largely determined by her wish to highlight historical and ideological shifts. In her preliminary notes for the book, she describes it as "two blocks joined by a corridor," [18] a design she sketches in this way:

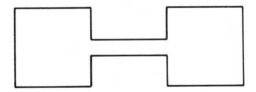

The narrative blocks are the first and third sections of the novel, and the corridor is "Time Passes," the lyric meditation that records the ten-year gap between them. Although no dates are given, the two major sections are set before and after the Great War. And the world described in the first part clearly associates it with the style of life prevalent before December 1910, when, as Woolf tells us, "human character changed" (*CE*, I, 320). She invented a fictional structure that would allow her to contrast the settled order of the traditional nuclear family with the freer but more chaotic relationships of modern life, and the narrow corridor of "Time Passes" serves to emphasize the tenuous connection between old and new. Part I presents a picture of Victorian family life, though strictly speaking the chronology of the book requires that it take place in the reign of King Edward. But in one passage Mrs. Ramsay is seen "quite motionless for a moment against a picture of Queen Victoria" (27)—as though the two images were merging—and Woolf herself was worried that the book would be dismissed by reviewers as "sentimental" and "Victorian" (*D*, III, 107).

To the Lighthouse has many of the characteristics of the turn-of-the-century attempts in fiction and drama to challenge the assumptions of Victorian family life, although it is a far more complex book than most of the militant reformers were capable of conceiving. Woolf's critical vision of traditional domestic life finds expression not only in the last or post-Victorian part of her novel, but even in the powerfully nostalgic first part, which already records the uneasiness or downright hostility of many of the characters. The whole way of life embodied in the Ramsays' marriage is silently challenged by those around them. It exerts a kind of coercive pressure that stiffens the resistance of others. Mrs. Ramsay has to use all her charm to bring the reluctant worshippers of domesticity into line. One of her children runs off to the attic "to escape the horror of family life" (116). Her daughters, she knows, are silently sporting "with infidel ideas which they had brewed for themselves of a life different from hers; in Paris, perhaps; a wilder life; not always taking care of some man or other" (16). Even the loyal Lily Briscoe is a very unreliable disciple: "There was something frightening about her," Lily reflects, as she imagines Mrs. Ramsay laughing, leading "her victims . . . to the altar" (157) of marriage—or of sacrifice to her household gods.

This critical spirit grows more powerful in Part III, after Mrs. Ramsay's death. Victorian family life has been displaced by a different order: an order in which women can be as absorbed in work as men, in which love and marriage are not necessarily linked, in which the isolated individual can survive and prosper. The marriage of Paul Rayley and Minta Doyle, which Mrs. Ramsay had worked so hard to bring about, has been a failure. Lily had never married Mr. Bankes, though "his friendship had been one of the pleasures of her life. She loved William Bankes" (272). And she addresses the departed spirit of Mrs. Ramsay to tell her of these new conditions: "It has all gone against your wishes. . . . Life has changed completely" (269). Part III of *To the Lighthouse* reflects the post-Victorian world Bloomsbury successfully created for itself after the death of Leslie Stephen. "And now we are free women!" Woolf had written exultantly to a friend in 1906 (*L*, I, 228). Without entirely severing their ties with the past, she and her sister, their brothers, and the young men they had met at Cambridge had fashioned a highly novel code of love and friendship, of family life and work. The characters in the last part of Woolf's novel live under the new dispensation. Although the Rayleys are still married in Part III, Minta's casual infidelity has made Paul take up with another woman. But the results are unexpected: "Far from breaking up the marriage, that alliance had righted it. They [Minta and Paul] were excellent friends" (268).

Such unorthodox relationships were familiar in Bloomsbury and were treated as a form of liberation from ancient superstition. Woolf recalls in her memoirs that around 1910 "the old sentimental views of marriage in which we were brought up were revolutionized. . . . I saw that there is nothing shocking in a man's having a mistress, or in a woman's being one. Perhaps the fidelity of our parents was not the only or inevitably the highest form of married life" (*MB*, 174). Around the same time, Vanessa Bell was writing her sister that "families are wicked institutions" and that even in the best ones "many vices seem inevitable, at any rate in the commanding members of the family."[19] This highly critical perspective on the abuses of domestic authority dominates the last part of *To the Lighthouse*, in which the power of the resistance has been greatly strengthened. Lily's reaction to Mr. Ramsay is much more hostile and unyielding than before: "That man, she thought, her anger rising in her, never gave; that man took" (231–32). And James's childhood rage against his domineering father has broadened into a general and principled war against the abuses of power: "Whatever he did . . . *that* he would fight, *that* he would track down and stamp out—tyranny, despotism, he called it—making people do what they did not want to do, cutting off their right to speak" (283; emphasis added).

The exposure of and partial liberation from Victorian domestic hierarchy and coercion affects not only the last part of Woolf's novel but the entire book. For example, it determines who in *To the Lighthouse* is permitted to think. As we have seen, Woolf's description of the change in human character "in or about December, 1910" stressed the transformation of traditional hierarchies, the shift in the relations "between masters and servants, husbands and wives, parents and children" (*CE*, I, 321). This sense of a revolution in the domestic order, in which formerly silent underlings (wives, children, servants) are suddenly given a voice, directly affects the narrative strategy of *To the Lighthouse*. Woolf makes certain that we will see the world she depicts largely through the eyes of women, children, and servants. Mrs. McNab, the housekeeper charged with keeping the Ramsays' summer retreat in decent repair, takes over Part II of the novel almost entirely. And Parts I and III, as Mitchell Leaska's interesting statistical study of whose consciousness we follow in the novel makes clear, are both dominated by women and children:[20]

	Narrator	*Percentage*
Part I	Mrs. Ramsay	42
	Omniscient	17
	Lily Briscoe	13
	Mr. Ramsay	8
	Others	20
Part III	Lily Briscoe	61
	Cam Ramsay	11
	Omniscient	10
	James Ramsay	8
	Mr. Ramsay	5
	Others	5

These figures reveal that something like a palace revolution has taken place and that in Woolf's novel at any rate the underlings have seized control of the instruments of communication. One recalls with astonishment that when she began *To the Lighthouse* she wrote in her diary that it would "have father's character done complete in it" and that "the centre is father's character" (*D*, III, 18). It was another center in modern literature that could not hold. In managing such a hierarchical revolution in fiction, Woolf's use of internal monologue proved indispensable. For though the record of spoken dialogue and observable action might suggest that the traditional hierarchy has been preserved and that the whole deferential system is intact, the evidence from psychic life confirms the power of the opposition. Mr. Ramsay barely gets a word in edgewise. "The energies of his splendid mind" are eclipsed by the thoughts of his dependents. He is often the focus of their attention and therefore remains of central importance, but their frequently hostile judgments of him erode his authority in the novel.

Woolf was acutely aware that even in literature the historical record was the product of the victors rather than the vanquished. She often voices her uneasiness about how little we know concerning the lives of the powerless. There had been a conspiracy of silence about them that Woolf set out to expose, at least insofar as her own experience could guide her. Marriage itself seemed to obliterate the independent identity of the wife, as even the title of her previous novel, *Mrs. Dalloway*, suggests. Woolf's dissatisfaction with novels for failing to provide a detailed record of a day in the life of a woman whose energy is spent in the home is righted in *Mrs. Dalloway* and *To the Lighthouse* and justified in her essay "Women and Fiction":

> Often nothing tangible remains of a woman's day. The food that has been cooked is eaten; the children that have been nursed have gone out into the world. Where does the accent fall? What is the salient point for the novelist to seize upon? It is difficult to say. Her life has an anonymous character which is baffling and puzzling in the extreme. For the first time, this dark country is beginning to be explored in fiction.
>
> (*CE*, II, 146)

But it was not only in her presentation of the powerless that Woolf's post-Victorian revisionism found expression. Her picture of those Vanessa Bell had called "the commanding members of the family" was equally affected. The portraits of both the Ramsays may be said to demystify authority, since Woolf allows us to go behind the surface impression each conveys of forceful character and irresistible sway to the turmoil of their mental state. The psychological novelist has techniques of exposure that not even a hero's valet could match. So Woolf shows us that far from being self-confident, principled, secure, the rulers of the family are often deeply unsure of themselves, as subject to panic and self-doubt as those whose lives they control. The habit of command is purchased at a high psychic price. Mrs. Ramsay cross-examines herself in trying to counter the charges against her—"wishing to dominate, wishing to interfere, making people do what she wished"— and she worries about her tendency to pressure people into marriage (92, 96–97). And Mr. Ramsay, of course, is simply a bundle of nerves in his perpetual anxiety about his work, his reputation, even about whether his wife loves him. Woolf, like Lytton Strachey and the other members of Bloomsbury, knew that Victorian domestic power relationships were buttressed by the myth of confident authority. If it could be shown, as Woolf tried to show, that behind this external confidence lay insecurity, frustration, even desperation, the spell that exacted obedience might be broken. Her psychological stripping of her major characters—like Strachey's in *Eminent Victorians*—is a version of "The Emperor's New Clothes."

Perhaps the strongest argument for seeing *To the Lighthouse* as an example of the liberation fable so prevalent in early modern literature is the prominence of Lily Briscoe. In a number of recent feminist readings of the novel, *To the Lighthouse* becomes a kind of *Bildungsroman* with Lily as the central character and the gradual growth of her independent vision as its teleological design. In one such interpretation, for instance, Lily's progress is triumphant: "By the end of her journey to the lighthouse, Lily has resolved many dilemmas for herself. She accepts her singleness, her need to paint. She accepts and acknowledges her hostility to Mrs. Ramsay's beliefs and machinations. Recognizing her love for Mrs. Ramsay, Lily moved beyond it to a love and respect for herself dependent on and integrated with her mature assessment of Mrs. Ramsay." [21] It is true that Lily grows in stature and assurance in the course of the novel, though whether she feels so confident that she has made the right choices is I think open to question. Nevertheless, she *has* changed in Part III. The very sentence "I have had my vision" has a ring of authority that would have been beyond her ten years earlier. Before, she had abandoned her painting; now she completes it. Before, she had played the role of succoring female at Mrs. Ramsay's direction; now she more or less successfully resists Mr. Ramsay's pressure for sympathy and simply goes on with her work. Middle age has given her a more detached perspective on the turbulent and contradictory impulses of her youth that allows her to live with the choices she has made, though with considerable regret for the road not taken.

There is also some evidence that Lily Briscoe's importance grew in Woolf's mind as she was writing the novel. Her preliminary notes and outlines do not suggest that such a person will figure in it prominently, even at the stage where she has already assigned roles to relatively minor characters like Paul and Minta, Charles Tansley, and Mr. Carmichael. [22] And when Lily does appear in the first draft, she is a much more timid soul, at least in Part I. Here, for example, is a passage from the earlier version that has no equivalent in the printed text:

> [Lily] said to Mr. Tansley, whom she supposed she would continue to reverence, for she had no militancy in her, & could not bear to be called, as she might have been called had she come out with her views a feminist, for it was safer, easier, less agitating to accept things & after all, one always did accept things. [23]

This is hardly the spirit of rebellion. Woolf must have felt the need, as she went on with her novel, to invent a more powerful antagonist to her commanding protagonists, a center of consciousness more closely attuned to her own.

Gradually, as the novel took shape, Lily became its most reliable witness, a voice the reader could trust. But in turning Lily into her own surrogate, Woolf could not simply make her an uncompromising rebel against authority. She had to strengthen her freedom and her bondage simultaneously, to make her a character permanently divided against herself, because only in that way could she be said to reflect Woolf's own feelings. So Lily's gestures of resistance are always accompanied by an internal backlash of guilt. She does not surrender to Mr. Ramsay's emotional blackmail, but her refusal makes her judge herself harshly: "There issued from him such a groan that any other woman in the whole world would have done something, said something—all except myself, thought Lily, girding at herself bitterly, who am not a woman, but a peevish, ill-tempered, dried-up old maid presumably" (234). The last word of the sentence suggests that Lily is not entirely convinced by this hostile assessment of herself but cannot challenge it either.

The continuous presence in Part III of such compromised rebellious gestures finally makes it impossible to see Woolf's novel as a liberation fable. As Avrom Fleishman has argued, the novel comes close to following the ancient comic formula in which an older dispensation is successfully usurped by a younger one but finally "lacks the revolutionary movement that overthrows the established, usually elder, generation and reorders the world."[24] Because Lily is still deeply attached to Mrs. Ramsay and so unsteady in her resistance to the old order, because Cam is similarly ambivalent and James anxious for praise from the father he claims to despise, the whole last section of the novel simply does not have the independent authority of Part I. Rather than completing her original symmetrical design of the novel (page 193), Woolf produced a book that might more accurately be pictured like this:

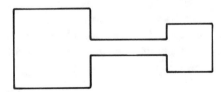

This may be a structural flaw in the novel, a failure of balance that Woolf had not anticipated. But it was the product of her need to record her conflicting feelings about Victorian family life and its alternatives accurately. Her distrust of marriage and the family had never been as uncompromising as her sister's; and she retained, through all her rebellious phases, a deep love for both her parents and the institution they had come to represent in her mind. At the time she was writing *To the Lighthouse*, Woolf noted in her diary her permanent need for "maternal protection which, for some reason, is what I have always most wished from everyone" (*D*, III, 52). Her memories of the mother she lost when she was thirteen are intensely nostalgic. But her feelings about her father—despite her hostility to what he had come to represent—remained positive in a different way. Vanessa Bell recalled that when she and Virginia as children discussed which parent each preferred, her own vote went to her mother, Virginia's to her father.[25] But it scarcely mattered which parent Woolf chose. She had a strongly positive feeling about their intense relationship, though she knew it was not untroubled. She carried the memory of that tie through all of her adult life. As late as 1940, when she does go back to the family documents she had refused to reread when she was working on *To the Lighthouse*, her impressions convey a sense of longing: "How serene & gay even their life reads to me: no mud; no whirlpools. And so human—with the children & the little hum & song of the nursery" (*D*, V, 345).

It is no wonder that with such charged memories Woolf worried constantly that *To the Lighthouse* would be dismissed as sentimental: "I go in dread of 'sentimentality'. Is the whole theme open to that charge?" (*D*, III, 110). This fear is voiced repeatedly as she is writing the book or worrying about its reception. She had after all been trained by her Bloomsbury colleagues to think of sentimentality—especially for the Victorian past—as a bacillus, likely to bring back those dangerous nineteenth-century illnesses known as reverence and filial piety. But perhaps she need not have worried, because by 1927, when *To the Lighthouse* was published, the revolutionary impulse of 1910 had largely spent itself, and more and more of the rebels were looking back with a sense of loss to the way of life that had disappeared. In part this was the product of World War I, the horror of which heightened, retrospectively, the positive qualities of what came before. In Part II of *To the Lighthouse* Mrs. McNab reflects on the death of Andrew Ramsay in battle, on the decay of the house when help is impossible to obtain during the war, and concludes "Things were better then than now" (212).

More sophisticated observers were reaching the same conclusion in the 1920 and 1930s. Woolf's Bloomsbury friend Mary (Molly) MacCarthy published a memoir called *A Nineteenth-Century Childhood* shortly before Woolf herself began working on *To the Lighthouse*. MacCarthy's book is full of longing for the past and suggests that the programmatic anti-Victorianism of the turn of the century had perhaps ended by destroying too much. In those years, she recalls, one could hear "the strong, rose-coloured glass of the nineteenth century conservatories cracking up. Now the wrecking is over. There is a great mass everywhere about, and something perhaps of the early morning misgiving after the spree."[26] And other writers were becoming aware of how much the successful attack on the nuclear family had cost. In 1929 Bertrand Russell, in a book that can hardly be called reactionary, nevertheless felt called upon to warn his readers that "the break-up of the family, if it comes about, will not be, to my mind, a matter for rejoicing" and to remind them that "the affection of parents is important to children."[27] It was a sign of the times that such rudimentary lessons needed to be taught by great philosophers.

The successes of the feminist movement had, paradoxically, also contributed to this nostalgia and helped to make a book like *To the Lighthouse* of deep interest to the young. On the one hand, a whole generation of women had grown up in an atmosphere (especially during the war years) so different from a nineteenth-century childhood that the old pattern had to be recreated for them like any other moment in the distant past. When in 1927 the biographer of Emily Davies described Davies's successful attempt to found the first women's college, she had to devote her first chapter to explaining the Victorian ideal of the female helpmeet and the nature of the opposition to women's education because she could not rely on her younger readers' knowledge of such matters.[28] On the other hand, when the young "liberated" women learned about the world of their grandparents, they often responded in ways that did not please the middle generation of reformers. As one such reformer complained, the new pressures emancipation had brought made some women "sigh, some softly, others loudly, for the old 'shelter.'"[29]

In such an intellectual climate of reconsidered revolution, yearning for the past, and doubt about progress, *To the Lighthouse* was likely to express the divided feelings not only of its author but of a wide audience. The modernist attack on the Victorian family had begun as a rejection of what seemed a life-destroying system. By the 1920s the propagandistic rhetoric common in the work of the first post-Victorian critics had begun to seem as simplistic as the Victorian idealizations of domestic life by writers like Ruskin or Coventry Patmore. And besides, the rebels had won. As they contemplated the fruits of their victory, some of them became aware that they had been attacking a part of themselves and that the brave new world which had displaced the old was not, in all ways, an improvement upon it. Such belated recognitions could produce a deeper vision of their experience, one that acknowledged loss as well as gain.

Out of such conflicting impulses Woolf constructed her novel: rebellion, residual love and loyalty, the whiff of freedom, the undertow of nostalgia. She was interested both in finding a vehicle to express this inner turmoil and in looking closely at the effect such conflicts have on those who feel them. There is an analytic as well as an expressive impulse at work in the novel, which allows her to look at divided characters like Lily Briscoe and Cam Ramsay with a certain detachment. Their conflicts make them more reliable surrogates for the author than some of the simpler beings in the book. But Woolf also shows us the cost of such exhausting emotional conflict. Lily is not a confident or successful artist, perhaps because so much of her energy goes into justifying her choice of vocation. She continues to ask herself why she bothers trying, even as she stands before her canvas: "Why then did she do it? . . . It would be hung in the servants' bedrooms. It would be rolled up and stuffed under a sofa. What was the good of doing it then, and she heard some voice saying she couldn't paint, saying she couldn't create" (245–46).

The firm ideology of Victorian family life often ended by producing such fundamental uncertainty in those who could neither believe in it nor reject it entirely. Woolf's interest in the type is illustrated in her essay on Edmund Gosse, whose rebellion against his fundamentalist upbringing had, she says, a debilitating effect on him as a writer: "He hints, he qualifies, he insinuates, he suggests, but he never speaks out, for all the world as if some austere Plymouth Brother were lying in wait to make him do penance for his audacity. . . . Fear seems always to dog his footsteps" (*CE*, IV, 83–84). And in her biography of Roger Fry, Woolf shows a similar conflict exerting an inhibiting force. For Fry's father had entirely disapproved of his son's artistic vocation. The son had gone on painting anyway, but with increasing despair as it became clear to him that some essential imaginative energy had been blocked by his continuing need to please his conventional parent: "'I will never show again,' he wrote to a friend after an unsuccessful exhibition of his paintings; 'I will go on painting, and when the canvases are dry, I will roll them up'" (quoted in *RF*, 236). Lily Briscoe would have recognized the mixture of defiance and defeat in such an announcement—the product of continued emotional dependence on a discarded model of conduct.

But if such ambivalence could not finally be resolved, it could be exploited. Woolf's most important decision in planning her novel was to make her own divided loyalty its structural principle. In *The Voyage Out* she had cut off the possibility of marriage by having her heroine contract a fatal illness immediately after her engagement; in *Night and Day* she had allowed her young lovers to take the conventional route to the promised land. Both endings may be said to simplify Woolf's feelings about marriage and family. In *To the Lighthouse*, by contrast, she constructed a fictional world in which domestic life could be powerfully described without finally being judged.

Everything about *To the Lighthouse* is invented to do away with the necessity of exclusive choice, from the individual sentence to the book's overarching structure. The sentence and the paragraph are turned into instruments for recording opposing responses. The words "but" and "yet," with their corrective force, become a mannerism of the novel's style—for example, as Mrs. Ramsay tries to sort out her feelings about Charles Tansley: "Yet he looked so desolate; yet she would feel relieved when he went; yet she would see that he was better treated to-morrow; yet he was admirable with her husband; yet his manners certainly wanted improving; yet she liked his laugh" (179).[30] Such indecisiveness in judging both others and oneself is the standard evaluative mode of *To the Lighthouse* and accounts for a good deal of its complexity. The characters who interest Woolf most in the book think in this way and show themselves self-consciously aware of the difficulty of judging others. Of these Lily Briscoe is paradoxically the most authoritative, because she treats the problem as insoluble: "One wanted fifty pairs of eyes to see with," she reflects, and "Half one's notions of other people were, after all, grotesque. They served private purposes of one's own" (303).

Woolf's techniques of rendering consciousness, already perfected in *Mrs. Dalloway*, could here be used more pointedly as a way of suggesting the impossibility of reaching a conclusion. The narrator describes Lily Briscoe's mental processes as too complex to transcribe: "To follow her thought was like following a voice which speaks too quickly to be taken down by one's pencil, and the voice was her own voice saying without prompting undeniable, everlasting, contradictory things," a state so volatile that Woolf compares it to a company of gnats dancing up and down in Lily's mind (43). By comparison with this vital, chaotic mental life, conversation seems a childish instrument, a primitive exercise in communication. "The tongue is but a clapper," as Woolf says dismissively in one of her short stories ("The String Quartet," *HH*, 30), and she wastes little space in recording its products in her novel. Typically, she will quote a trivial or telegraphically brief sentence or phrase spoken by someone, then return to the dancing gnats in the mind of one of the characters. Furthermore, the perspective shifts constantly, so that no single consciousness, no matter how open to contradictory impressions, is permitted to dominate the novel. In the first sixty pages, for example, we move from James Ramsay to Mrs. Ramsay to Charles Tansley to Lily Briscoe to Mr. Bankes to Mr. Ramsay. In such ways the novel comes close to providing the "fifty pairs of eyes to see with" that Lily finds necessary for accurate sight.

This is not merely a clever technique designed to show up the characters' distortions of vision, as so many fictional exercises in limited perspective have done. The "omniscient narrator," when she does appear, is scarcely more authoritative than her characters and seems to share their confusion. This is why it is so notoriously difficult to determine, in reading a given passage from *To the Lighthouse*, whether and exactly when the character's thoughts give way to the narrator's. The best comment on this difficult method of narration remains that of Erich Auerbach, who wrote of one typical section from the book:

> Who is speaking in this paragraph? . . . Perhaps it is the author. However, if that be so the author certainly does not speak like one who has a knowledge of his characters—in this case, of Mrs. Ramsay—and who, out of his knowledge, can describe their personality and momentary state of mind objectively and with certainty.[31]

Woolf must have felt that the obvious problems her chameleon method of narration created for the reader were both necessary and fruitful. She was dubious about the utility of the firmer means at her disposal.

The same impatience with authoritative interpretation affects her use of symbolism. She noted in her diary that she was using symbols more frequently in this novel, and of course the voyage to the lighthouse, the lighthouse itself, the sea, the window, the *boeuf en daube*, Minta's lost brooch are all meant to resonate with significance. And yet despite Woolf's occasional identifications (as in the passage describing the Ramsays as "symbols of marriage, husband and wife"), she is anxious to keep her emblems suggestive rather than easily interpretable. Like the characters themselves, they mean different things to different people, and Woolf is adamant in her insistence that the reader not try to translate them into abstractions. She defends this essentially Coleridgean use of symbolism as the only kind she can tolerate, because "directly I'm told what a thing means, it becomes hateful to me" (*L*, III, 385).

Woolf's ambivalent attitude is evident, as we have seen, in the novel's style, symbolism, and narrative method. It also affects its larger design. That she responded in such antithetical ways to traditional family life made it impossible for her to use either the nineteenth-century marriage plot or the modern liberation plot to structure her novel, though there are vestiges of each in *To the Lighthouse*. Part I ends with an engagement and a reaffirmation of the Ramsays' conjugal love, Part III with Lily's triumphant but solitary vision. But the book as a whole is conceived as an *inclusive fiction*, a structure that allows rival codes to coexist rather than forcing the reader to choose between them. It prompts Woolf finally to deny some of the divergences she has been tracing throughout the novel and to suggest that her principal characters have been following different paths to the same goal. Confrontations are avoided. Radical breaks become unnecessary. Reconciliation is in the air. So Mr. Ramsay and his hostile son are united when he praises James for having "steered them like a born sailor" (316). So Lily Briscoe finishes her painting and Mr. Ramsay reaches the lighthouse at the same moment, in separate actions Woolf wanted to narrate nonsequentially. The temporal rather than spatial order of words made this impossible, but she hoped to create the effect of simultaneity, "so that one had the sense of reading the two things at the same time" (*D*, III, 106).

A different kind of fusion shapes Lily's last descriptions of Mrs. Ramsay, in which she sees the older woman no longer as a threat or a coercive force but as a fellow artist merely working in a different medium: "Mrs. Ramsay bringing them together; Mrs. Ramsay saying 'Life stand still here'; Mrs. Ramsay making of the moment something permanent (as in another sphere Lily herself tried to make of the moment something permanent)—this was of the nature of a revelation" (249). The parenthesis reads like an afterthought, which is exactly what it was, since in the manuscript version of the novel the direct comparison does not occur.[32] As Phyllis Rose has shown, Woolf "dramatizes the working out of a way in which she can see herself as her mother's heir while still rejecting the model of womanhood she presents. She does this by conceptualizing Mrs. Ramsay as an artist, transforming the angel in the house, who had been for the Victorians an ethical ideal, into a portrait of the artist."[33] It is a very modern bit of legerdemain. The traditional praise for Mrs. Ramsay's domestic gifts, whether it stressed spirituality like Coventry Patmore or practical efficiency like Mrs. Beeton, did not generally use the language of art. In the scornful words of the classical archaeologist Jane Harrison, "Some people speak of a cook as an 'artist,' and a pudding as a 'perfect poem,' but a healthy instinct rebels."[34]

The final pages of the novel, then, strive to create the effect of harmony and reconciliation and try to echo the last moments of the dinner party scene. Woolf moves her novel with a firm hand from dissonance to consonance, and she certainly thought that in writing the book she had resolved her most painful feelings about her family and family life in general. On Leslie Stephen's birthday a year after the novel was published she wrote in her diary that "I used to think of him & mother daily; but writing The Lighthouse, laid them in my mind" (*D*, III, 208). This statement has been used to argue that Woolf succeeded in performing a kind of autopsycho-analysis a little like Freud's own. She has "worked through" her conflicts as the successful patient is said to do. But there are indications that the resolution (in both fictional and personal terms) is more willed and formulaic than emotionally convincing. Can we really imagine that Mr. Ramsay's praise of his son will significantly alter their tense relationship? Or that

Lily Briscoe's completion of her painting will make her less prone to the self-lacerating doubts that had undermined her confidence as an artist? Or that there aren't still exclusive choices to be made?

To the Lighthouse is a great achievement not because of its successful resolution but because of its intense dramatization of the deep conflict in its author's mind. This conflict would not be laid to rest, despite what Woolf said about the matter in 1928.[35] That year in fact begins a decade in which she wrote with concentrated energy about women's lives under patriarchal power, a decade that produced *A Room of One's Own*, *The Years*, and *Three Guineas*, all of which indicate that the subject matter of *To the Lighthouse* returned to haunt her. And toward the end of her life, in 1939–40, she goes back directly to the facts concerning the Stephen family in writing her memoirs and sees some of the same characters and events in a startlingly different way.[36] The apparent poise and decisive finality suggested by the ending of *To the Lighthouse* turned out, in her own career at least, to be only a ceasefire. As we will see in analyzing the feminist books that followed it, the fragile accord would often be broken. It was a psychic civil war in which both opponents had ancient territorial rights. In such conflicts—so expensive for the spirit, so fruitful for art—there can be no victor and no vanquished.

8

Woolf's Feminism in Historical Perspective

No other element in Woolf's work has created so much confusion and disagreement among her serious readers as her relation to the women's movement. She was a feminist, though she did not like the term. And many of her works, both fictional and discursive, are shaped by her desire to contribute to the liberation of women from the constraints of their lives. She deals with this issue directly in *A Room of One's Own* and *Three Guineas*, two books I want to look at in detail in the next chapter. But the general problems facing women—their restricted vocational opportunities, their relation to power and money, their rights and duties, their connections with men and with their own sex—are important in almost all her writings and are usually looked at from a feminist perspective. E. M. Forster—not a very sympathetic witness on this issue—wrote of her feminism: "There are spots of it all over her work."[1]

Forster's phrase treats Woolf's commitment as a disease, as Jane Marcus has pointed out.[2] It is a typically partisan statement, of the sort her feminism has aroused from the start. When *Three Guineas* was published, the prominent feminist Philippa Strachey wrote her an ecstatic letter saying, according to Woolf, that "its the very thing for which they have panted" (*D*, V, 147). "Thing," "they"—the words turn the book into an object designed for group use. In later decades, Woolf's feminism was attacked or championed according to the political exigencies of the moment. In the 1950s Monique Nathan dismissed it as "a quaint relic of the Victorian era, as misfitting and unbecoming as a last year's dress."[3] Fashion, however, is cyclical rather than progressive, and by the late 1960s Woolf's writings had established themselves as basic texts of the new women's movement. Margaret Drabble describes her discovery of *A Room of One's Own* as a turning point in her life: "I read it with mounting excitement and enthusiasm. . . . A more militant, firm, concerned attack on women's subjection would be hard to find. I could hardly believe that a woman from her background . . . could speak so relevantly to my own condition."[4] Such ecstatic awakenings now have their own period flavor. In more recent assessments Woolf's feminist commitment (particularly in *Three Guineas*) has been treated as *the* interpretive key to her work and as a model for the contemporary women's movement.

Such disagreement is a tribute to the continuing vitality of Woolf's feminist books, which have clearly not yet arrived at the taxidermist's shop. Yet the treatment of them as tools or threats by readers with their own political agendas tends to distort Woolf's vision. What is missing in these debates is a historical sense of her place in and particular contribution to the women's movement. She was conscious of writing in a tradition that had begun over a century before with Mary Wollstonecraft's *A Vindication of the Rights of Woman* and had continued well into her youth and adulthood. She had read the major texts of that movement with deep interest and engagement. But as we will see, her attitude toward the feminist legacy was essentially revisionist. She was by no means an uncritical partisan of the movement, and her alternating loyalty to and deviation from its familiar positions often produced contradictions in her thought. Until we see her work as a response to some of the received ideas of her time about women and "the cause," we will not fully understand it.

Woolf's interest in the women's movement begins early. A diary entry written when she was twenty-two reveals that she was already thinking about women's rights in historical terms. She reflects on the changing legal status of women since the eighteenth century and lists some of the major works and events associated with that history: Mill's *The Subjection of*

Women, Tennyson's *The Princess*, the founding of Newnham College, Cambridge, and so on (Berg Diary, Christmas 1904–May 27, 1905, 170). The list suggests a program of reading that Woolf certainly completed in the following decades. Her own direct involvement in the suffrage agitation can be precisely dated. On January 1, 1910, she wrote her friend and Greek tutor, Janet Case:

> Would it be any use if I spent an afternoon or two weekly in addressing envelopes for the Adult Suffragists?
> I dont know anything about the question. Perhaps you could send me a pamphlet, or give me the address of the office. I could neither do sums or argue, or speak, but I could do the humbler work if that is any good. You impressed me so much the other night with the wrongness of the present state of affairs that I feel that action is necessary. Your position seemed to me intolerable. The only way to better it is to do something I suppose. How melancholy it is that conversation isn't enough!
> (*L*, I, 421)

These are the words of a naive and reluctant political participant who nevertheless feels outraged enough by "the present state of affairs" to become an active suffragist. "Suffragist," it should be noted, not "Suffragette." The distinction between the constitutional methods of the former and the extralegal tactics of the latter had by this time been clearly established, and Woolf's decision to join the nonviolent section of the movement is characteristic and important.

The six months before January 1910 had seen the emergence of women's militant agitation for the vote, and the events of that half year must surely have been significant for Woolf. In July 1909, after years of more peaceful attempts at political persuasion had failed, the Suffragettes first advocated and used violence. The window-breakers and disrupters of the peace were arrested and for the first time chose to adopt the method of the hunger strike. This decision, as well as the government's retaliation by forcibly feeding the women prisoners, created a sensation and was fully reported in the *Times* and other newspapers that fall. Stories of women brutalized and assaulted, washed out of their cells with hoses, starving themselves into exhaustion and serious illness, held down by warders while doctors forced feeding tubes into their nostrils, all helped to create an image of the Suffragettes as victims and martyrs that brought many formerly apolitical women into the movement.[5] Woolf was among them. She responded not to the demand for votes but to the picture of coercive men imposing their will on the helpless.

Such responses are often primal in their power, but they have little connection with the day-to-day exigencies of a political movement. Woolf's career as an activist was short-lived. Though she attended meetings and addressed envelopes for the cause, her letters in 1910 reveal that she did so with increasing reluctance and detachment. The work seemed mechanical, the speeches perfectly predictable. By the end of the year she is asking Janet Case plaintively, "Do you ever take that side of politics into account—the inhuman side, and how all the best feelings are shrivelled?" (*L*, I, 441). She became contemptuous not only of political activism but of the goal of women's suffrage. The picture of dedicated workers for that cause in *Night and Day* is essentially satiric. When a parliamentary maneuver temporarily sets the cause back, the violent reaction of one of the dedicated suffragists is described with mock-epic irony: "Mrs. Seal was in a condition bordering upon frenzy. The duplicity of Ministers, the treachery of mankind, the insult to womanhood, the setback to civilization, the ruin of her life's work, the feelings of her father's daughter—all these topics were discussed in turn, and the office was littered with newspaper cuttings branded with the blue, if ambiguous, marks of her displeasure" (*ND*, 268). And when women finally win the vote in 1918, Woolf greets the moment of triumph with cool indifference: "Its like a knighthood; might be useful to impress people one despises" (*D*, I, 104). By 1924 she no longer considers herself a politically involved feminist at all: "I have travelled on," she says with dismissive brevity (*D*, II, 318).

It is, however, a mistake to take such passages as Woolf's declarations of independence from the women's movement. Rather, they seem to me to make a distinction between the narrowly political focus the Suffragette agitation had created and the wide range of issues the movement had raised from its beginnings. The concentration on female suffrage during Woolf's young adulthood (1903–14) was unprecedented in feminist history. What had begun as a comprehensive movement of thought about women's nature and status—legal, educational, psychological, economic, professional, marital, and political—had been turned into a much narrower cause deliberately centered on a single issue: the vote. This decision was conscious and strategic. As Mrs. Pankhurst wrote in summing up the militant agitation of the Women's Social and Political Union, "Our members are absolutely single minded; they concentrate all their forces on one object, political equality with men. No member of the W.S.P.U. divides her attention between suffrage and other social reforms."[6] The rationale for this single-mindedness was that political power would guarantee every other desirable reform. As one of the earliest workers for female franchise wrote in the 1880s, "It has been repeated till it has become a commonplace, that 'the Suffrage is the key of woman's position.' Obtaining it, every privilege she can reasonably desire must follow."[7] But in the view of a recent historian of the movement, what began as a reasonable tactical choice became, during the militant campaign, "an end in itself and practically an obsession."[8] By 1913 Mrs. Pankhurst's daughter Christabel was confidently predicting that votes for women would end prostitution and venereal disease.[9]

Woolf was acutely conscious of the naiveté of this faith. The franchise does not, after all, necessarily bring real power. And certain forces in life—psychological, economic, attitudinal, institutional—are not clearly subject to the influence of a political first cause. Her skepticism about the power of the vote was based on a conviction that human relationships and institutions are dismayingly conservative and likely to preserve the substance of the old in the form of the new. The psyche was much more resistant to change than the law. One of the very few female members of the new Parliament, Eleanor Rathbone, was also among the first to see that the exaggerated predictions of the power of the vote had not come true: "Progress has been rapid when it depended on political action and slow when it depended on changes in heart and habits. *What else could you expect when the instrument was the vote?*" [10]

Woolf's writing career roughly coincided with this post-franchise awakening to the difficulty of changing "heart and habits." The twenty years after the vote was won was a period of retrenchment in the women's movement. The immense expenditure of energy that the agitation for the vote had required inevitably produced a kind of exhaustion when the goal was finally reached. It also created a conservative backlash. The militant Suffragettes had come close to unleashing a war between the sexes. The rhetoric and policies of the W.S.P.U. evoked a good deal of open hostility toward women in men who might previously have hidden their contempt behind a screen of chivalric courtesy. One of the antisuffrage writers of the time even explicitly warned women that men's respect for them was part of a bargain, and that "the contract is infringed when woman breaks out into violence." [11] And another such polemicist concludes that "nowadays we are in presence of a powerful female sex-solidarity indicating the beginnings of a strong sex-league of women against men." [12] The Sex War or the Sex Discord, as it was called, became a significant issue of the time and reverberated for years after the vote was won.

A deep fissure had opened between the territories of women and men. In Forster's *Howards End*, written at the height of the militant movement, Margaret Schlegel despairingly wonders, "Are the sexes really races, each with its own code of morality, and their mutual love a mere device of Nature's to keep things going?" [13] Woolf's earliest fiction also depicts this acute conflict between the sexes and frequently links it to the suffrage movement. *The Voyage Out*, published in 1915 but finished early in 1913, is filled with men railing against women. Richard Dalloway condemns "the utter folly and futility" of female militancy and concludes his diatribe on the subject with the cry, "Well! may I be in my grave before a woman has the right to vote in England!" Mr. Pepper says "no" to women on principle and explains that he had never married "for the sufficient reason that he had never met a woman who commanded his respect." And St. John Hirst simply dismisses the whole sex: "They're so stupid." No wonder Woolf's heroine concludes that men and women "should live separate: we cannot understand each other; we only bring out what's worst" (*VO*, 44–45, 21, 122, 182). The uneasy male who feels the need to express his contempt for women, especially for independent women, reappears often in Woolf's fiction: William Rodney in *Night and Day*, Charles Tansley in *To the Lighthouse*, Giles Oliver in *Between the Acts*. By the 1920s it was widely felt that there really was a sex war, as women abandoned or tried to abandon the familiar roles assigned to them and move into preserves traditionally held by men. So in 1920 Arnold Bennett could publish a book called *Our Women* with the subtitle "Chapters on the Sex-Discord." And Dora Russell's work on the subject begins with a chapter entitled "Is There a Sex War?"—a question she answers in the affirmative.[14]

Clearly the vote was no guarantee of steady progress toward women's freedom and equality with men. The conflict between the sexes was merely one instance of certain psychological patterns that resisted political or institutional reform, that could in fact even be exacerbated by such change. Woolf saw these patterns as the chief impediments to continued progress and was convinced that it was the responsibility of writers like herself to shed light on them rather than proceeding strictly along the road of visible change. She was writing at a moment in history when most of the external battles in the women's movement had been won—the franchise, entry into the universities and professions, the right to divorce, and the right of married women to own property. Yet the war was far from over. Woolf was interested in the underlying psychological and economic causes of masculine dominance and feminine repressed anger or acquiescence, and she used her powers of observation and divination to probe depths the earlier feminist writers had left largely unplumbed.

II

Woolf's particular contribution to the women's movement was to restore a sense of the complexity of the issues after the radical simplification that had seemed necessary for political action. Why did women so often lack self-confidence? Why does Mrs. Ramsay dislike, "even for a second, to feel finer than her husband" (*TL*, 65)? And why is men's anger against women at times so violent, at others so "disguised and complex" rather than "simple and open" (*AROO*, 49)? These were the sorts of problems Woolf would try to illuminate in her work; they were the unfinished business of the women's movement of her time. As some critical sympathizers were beginning to feel in the decades after the major political and institutional issues were settled, too little had changed at the deepest level. In the retrospective anthology of essays *Our Freedom and Its Results* (1936), Mary Agnes Hamilton writes:

> Old, habitual ways of thinking and feeling live on, beneath the views that men and women put forward and believe that they believe in: automatically, and without any conscious irrationality, they revert to these older mental habits, and act in their sense. Tax them with harbouring any doubt as to female capacity and equality, and they will, indignantly, deny it; yet again and again the old, unconscious tissues betray the newer conscious opinion.[15]

Freud would have called such patterns of behavior "the return of the repressed," and Woolf's own treatment of them is very close to the insights and methods of depth psychology. Considerable portions of both *A Room of One's Own* and *Three Guineas* are devoted to the analysis of misunderstood or unacknowledged motives and impulses in the relations between the sexes. The contemptuous statements about women's native capacity she quotes in *A Room of One's Own* are treated as evidence for the conclusion that such masculine hostility to women is rooted in a "deep-seated desire, not so much that *she* shall be inferior as that *he* shall be superior" (*AROO*, 83). The argument is more fully developed in the later *Three Guineas*, particularly in the section on the "infantile fixation"

of Victorian fathers in conflict with their gifted daughters—
Mr. Brontë of Haworth, Mr. Barrett of Wimpole Street, Mr.
Jex-Blake, the father of one of the pioneers of women's medical
education. The method Woolf uses is consciously Freudian;
her hope for reform is based on the psychoanalytic strategy of
making the unconscious conscious. The "psychology of the
sexes," she says, cannot be left "to the charge of specialists"
but must be examined by the man she is addressing in the
book and the women she speaks for:

> Let us then grope our way amateurishly enough among these
> very ancient and obscure emotions which we have known ever
> since the time of Antigone and Ismene and Creon at least;
> which St. Paul himself seems to have felt; but which the Pro-
> fessors have only lately brought to the surface and named "in-
> fantile fixation," "Œdipus complex," and the rest.
>
> (*TG*, 235)

She was not the first feminist writer to expose the psychological imperatives at work in the relation between the sexes.
Some of her nineteenth-century predecessors occasionally examined the position of women from a similar perspective. In
The Subjection of Women (1869) John Stuart Mill attacks the familiar theory of women's "submissive nature" by treating it
simply as a form of brainwashing initiated by men: "All women
are brought up from the very earliest years in the belief that
their ideal of character is the very opposite to that of men; not
self-will, and government by self-control, but submission,
and yielding to the control of others." Mill's method is that of
psychological probing; for example, in explaining why a man's
absolute power over "his" women unleashes his hidden tyrannical impulses. Such legitimized power "seeks out and
evokes the latent germs of selfishness in the remotest corners
of his nature—fans its faintest sparks and smouldering em-
bers—offers to him a license for the indulgence of those
points of his original character which in all other relations he
would have found it necessary to repress and conceal."[16]

Mill scrutinized men's tyranny from a psychological perspective. Women writing in the nineteenth century seldom

permitted themselves to look at men so critically in print, but they occasionally examined the behavior of women in similar psychological terms. Emily Davies, for example, describes the effect of the pervasive sense of limited expectation on women's lives: "Probably only women who have laboured under it can understand the weight of discouragement produced by being perpetually told that, as women, nothing much is ever to be expected of them, and it is not worth their while to exert themselves. . . . Women who have lived in the atmosphere produced by such teaching know how it stifles and chills; how hard it is to work courageously through it."[17] And Florence Nightingale strikingly anticipated Woolf's critical vision of the "Angel in the House":

> In every dream of the life of intelligence or that of activity, women are accompanied by a phantom—the phantom of sympathy guiding, lighting the way. . . . A woman dedicates herself to the vocation of her husband; she fills up and performs the subordinate parts in it. . . . A man gains everything by marriage: he gains a "helpmate," but a woman does not.[18]

It should be clear then that Woolf was not initiating but continuing a line of inquiry concerning the behavior of men and women as it is determined by forces outside their conscious control. Yet these psychological compulsions had largely been forgotten in the feminist writings of Woolf's own time precisely because they seemed so ungovernable; a movement concentrating for the moment on legal and institutional reform was almost forced to ignore them. And so they were pushed into the background until the more immediate goals were achieved. When Woolf started writing, the movement was ready for the resurrection of these buried issues, and her audience was perhaps willing to attend to them seriously for the first time.

The most powerful vehicle for such probing was not the polemical tract but the novel, with its far more vivid sense of how people actually live. Woolf did not limit her investigation of the contest between the sexes to her discursive prose. We have already seen that in *The Voyage Out, Jacob's Room, To the*

Lighthouse, and *The Years,* the uneasy alliances of men and women are of major concern. And in *Between the Acts,* Woolf's final work, a marital conflict becomes a paradigm for war itself. Even her early, more conventional fiction illuminates the buried hostility in gender relations. Woolf's *Night and Day,* for example, is often dismissed as a traditional novel with a predictable romantic plot (roughly, boy meets, loses, and gets girl). But behind its familiar narrative formulas, there are some very disturbing forces at work. Katharine Hilbery and Ralph Denham meet, fall in love, and eventually marry. That they have a rough passage to this goal, however, is due not so much to the class difference between them (the surface impediment) as to a conflict about power and independence that the book never fully resolves.

Ralph is presented from the first as a brilliant and attractive but powerfully aggressive man. Because he is relatively poor and unknown, his ambition is a violent passion: he is "consumed with a desire to get on in the world" (*ND,* 130). He is interested not only in money and position but in making the world acknowledge the power of his mere presence. His reaction to Katharine's distinguished ancestry is curious. Though he envies her the privileges of her aristocratic world, he is appalled by the thought of such accomplished ancestors "cutting her out"—that is, preempting her possible achievements by their prior distinction: "I couldn't bear my grandfather to cut me out," he says to her brutally; "You're cut out all the way round" (10). He is a striving young man who cannot control the pugnacity in his voice and who thinks of the seasons, "spring and summer, autumn and winter, as so many stages in a prolonged campaign" (20).

The conquest of Katharine becomes the decisive battle of his private war. He is drawn to her precisely because she seems unattainable, and his erotic attraction is fueled by his ambitious drive. Metaphors of triumph dominate his feelings about her. "Could one have stripped off his mask of flesh," Woolf writes in a passage that reveals her interest in the hidden impulses behind such conventional notions as "love," "one would have seen that his will-power was rigidly set upon a single object—that Miss Hilbery should obey him. He wished her to stay there until, by some measures not yet apparent to him, he had conquered her interest" (57). And toward the end of the book, as he imagines her "slipping farther and farther from him into one of those states of mind in which he was unrepresented," his need is simply "to dominate her, to possess her" (518). Such passages, when taken out of context, might suggest that Ralph Denham is a conventional villain. But he is not. His violence is born of frustration, the fear that Katharine will spurn him and that his talents will go unrewarded in the world. When it becomes clear that his ambition will be satisfied, he becomes more vulnerable, gentle, and loving. His devotion to Katharine is genuine; furthermore, we soon realize that she needs him as much as he needs her.

For Ralph legitimizes Katharine's buried anger against her family. When we first meet her, she has no belief in herself and no way of articulating her despair. Forced to live in the shadow of her family heritage—a heritage she neither respects nor really understands—she seems to go underground. Like Ralph, she feels herself blocked and is likely to respond violently (in feeling, if not in words). Her anger is briefly acknowledged and then instantly withdrawn, as in this response to seeing a crowd of ambitious, career-minded young people at her friend Mary's house. Katharine says to her: "'Don't you see how many different things these people care about? And I want to beat them down—I only mean,' she corrected herself, 'that I want to assert myself, and it's difficult, if one hasn't a profession'" (54). Work and power are regularly connected in the book, but Katharine is not strong enough to take this route to self-assertion. She is a resentful but dutiful daughter and wastes her days doing her mother's will. She lives in a state of perpetual silent rage as her mother rattles on about the glories of the family's past: "She felt all the unfairness of the claim which her mother tacitly made to her time and sympathy, and what Mrs. Hilbery took, Katharine thought bitterly, she wasted" (117).

Katharine's way out of this paralyzed condition is through

Ralph, for he gives her the courage to rebel against her family's wishes, a courage she cannot command on her own. She uses his force as a prop because she instinctively knows that she will not be able to make her escape without its aid. She embarks on a secret relationship with him, though she is engaged to another man. This duplicity almost leads to a permanent break with her family, until her father reluctantly agrees to support the match. Katharine and Ralph are married and presumably live happily ever after in a world that gives Ralph his rightful place and Katharine her freedom. Yet the conventional ending of the novel short-circuits its most powerful current. Woolf had used her fictive situation to expose some of the inchoate elements at work in the courtship ritual—aggressiveness, frustration, the love of power, and the wish to attach oneself to it. The novel suggests that all these forces can now be laid to rest. This neat resolution marks the book as an early experiment in Woolf's career rather than a mature vision. Her later works, both fictional and discursive, would explore the ways in which established rituals and institutions failed to defuse such dangerous impulses in the relation between men and women. None of her other novels ends in a marriage, and the last page of *Between the Acts* describes the preparations for a major marital fight.

Woolf's interest in the psychological forces that shaped women's lives extended beyond those at work in love and marriage. She would probably have said that women's greater opportunities in the twentieth century—their improved legal and political status, their new financial independence, and their access to educational institutions and professions— were all undermined by the way they had been taught to think about their own capacities. It was all very well to reform laws and institutions, but if those scheduled to benefit from the changes continued to feel they were not worthy to receive those benefits, they would simply continue in the same grooves. Woolf tried to lay bare the forces contributing to the psychological discouragement of women—the process of socialization that eroded the sense of their independent powers. The condescending attitude, the sarcastic remark, the warning shake of the head from a powerful mentor were not subject to legislation; yet their net effect could be as devastating to women's achievements as any legal or institutional impediment.

Woolf was particularly interested in how girls and young women were systematically discouraged from taking their work seriously—if indeed they were even permitted to think they had a vocation other than that of ministering to men. We have seen in the picture of Ralph Denham that Woolf was more than a little repelled by the extreme form of ambition that dominated such a man. But in one of her diary entries, she speculates on why it is men rather than women who are encouraged to make their way in the world: "All young men do it. No young women; or in women it is trounced; in men forgiven. Its these reflections I want to enmesh in writing" (*D*, II, 326). Nor is it only early inhibition or discouragement that works against women's professional achievement. A woman who decides despite all impediments to follow a vocation soon encounters her share of active resistance from her male rivals. In the original version of "Professions for Women" Woolf tries to warn her female audience not only about men's hostility but about the debilitating effects of women's own angry response to it: "If you are always comparing your lot with the lot of men, if you are always thinking how much easier it is for them to earn a living than for you—you will have an enemy within who is always sapping your strength and poisoning your happiness" (*P*, xxxi).

Women might meet such vocational discouragement anywhere—in the family, in the professional circle they tried to enter, from women who had made more conventional choices, even from so-called liberated men who purported to encourage them. Arnold Bennett, for example, called himself "a convinced feminist" and opined that a serious career makes a woman more interesting than the "purely domestic woman." The book in which Bennett voiced these encouraging sentiments also contains the following passage: "Nearly every woman who adopts a professional career . . . abandons herself to the career, which becomes her religion, her god, her tyrant, her unique infatuation. She is changed into a fanatic. She will splendidly sacrifice on the altar, health, beauty, leisure, love, family ties—all. She exists for the career." [19]

What is the effect of such a passage on a young woman reader contemplating a vocational commitment? And why were such warnings never issued to men, who were presumably equally liable to become deeply absorbed in their work? Woolf was interested in these questions on the most general level, but she was particularly concerned to answer them as they affected women trying to think of themselves as artists. As she puts it in *A Room of One's Own*, "It is time that the effect of discouragement upon the mind of the artist should be measured, as I have seen a dairy company measure the effect of ordinary milk and Grade A milk upon the body of the rat" (*AROO*, 79–80). Woolf's concentration on the problem of women artists is neither obsessive nor unrealistic. The sort of discouragement she describes was pervasive in her culture. Thus Bennett, for example, could say with confidence that "intellectually and creatively man is the superior of woman" and justify his conclusion by insisting that "no woman at all has achieved either painting or sculpture that is better than second-rate, or music that is better than second-rate," and that "the literature of the world can show at least fifty male poets greater than any woman poet." [20]

There was nothing idiosyncratic in Bennett's views. Even the greatest of all male champions of women's freedom, John Stuart Mill, could write in *The Subjection of Women* that "all women who write are pupils of the great male writers." [21] And in Woolf's own time, a sympathetic woman writer, Clemence Dane, suggests that the absence of great female artists ("There has never been a woman Shakespeare! There has never been a woman Michael Angelo!") has become *the* trump card in the argument against women's equality. [22] The question of women's artistic achievement was thus seen in Woolf's time as a sort of last frontier in the exploration of their powers. As though she were writing in direct response to Dane's quotations, as well as to the taunts of a Bennett or the doubts of a Mill, Woolf devotes a considerable portion of *A Room of One's Own* to an explanation of why there has never been a woman Shakespeare. The long section of the book that constitutes an imaginary biography of Shakespeare's sister tries to answer the question of why the same imaginative capacity that flourished in him would have produced nothing but silence in a female member of the same line.

Essentially Woolf's thesis is that a woman artist of Shakespeare's time lacked not only money and freedom and breadth of experience but also the fundamental approval of her society that might have sanctioned her vocation. And so Shakespeare's sister writes nothing: "For it needs little skill in psychology to be sure that a highly gifted girl who had tried to use her gift for poetry would have been so thwarted and hindered by other people, so tortured and pulled asunder by her own contrary instincts, that she must have lost her health and sanity to a certainty" (*AROO*, 74–75). This kind of discouragement continued to the present day, Woolf felt, and she often described its effect in her own work. In *To the Lighthouse*, Lily Briscoe can hardly summon up the energy to go on with her painting because she regards herself as second-rate. This sense of herself as a failure is *learned*, deliberately inculcated and sex-based: her painting, she reflects, "would never be seen; never be hung even, and there was Mr. Tansley whispering in her ear, 'Women can't paint, women can't write . . .'" (*TL*, 78).

Woolf thought about such psychological pressures carefully when she contemplated marriage. She did not marry until she was thirty, though there had been no scarcity of suitors and proposals. It seems likely that the major reason for the success of her marriage to Leonard Woolf despite the powerful forces that threatened it—their sexual incompatibility, Leonard's coercive rationalism, and Virginia's precarious mental health—was his fundamental respect for her work and her gratitude for his support. This was uncompromising and included reading and commenting on all her works, acting as her literary agent, and making sure that her regular writing time was free from trivial interruptions and distractions. Virginia Woolf knew that the Leonards of this world are rare birds, and that it was common for women artists to encounter a much more ambivalent response at best. Furthermore, her Victorian upbringing had left its mark, and she was less successful in killing the feminine ideal of the "Angel in the House" than her essay on that subject, "Professions for Women," allows. The essay records her triumphant murder of that phantom of selflessness: "It was she who bothered me and wasted my time and so tormented me that at last I killed her" (*CE*, II, 285). But the mock-heroic tone of this assertion reveals its exaggeration. In fact, Woolf was quite conscious of the ways in which her adult professional life continued to be compromised by a loyalty to the supposedly discarded ideals of femininity. And if this was true for her, with a room of her own, an independent income, and a supportive husband, how much more true was it for women who had to work without these advantages—that is, for almost every other woman who had ever tried to create?

Woolf's sensitivity to such psychological impediments in the lives of women artists encouraged her to write about them from what was at the time a new perspective. It is remarkable how many of her literary essays deal with women, and though it was not unusual for a critic to write seriously about Jane Austen, the Brontës, and George Eliot, the unprecedented element in Woolf's approach was to see these major writers in relation not to the major male writers of their own time but rather in relation to their less successful sisters. Woolf essentially established the currently fashionable way of thinking about women's writing as an independent tradition. She also tried to assess women's achievements not against some absolute standard of greatness (though she was perfectly aware of what those standards were) but against the psychological and material forces at work in their lives. She wrote about this subject at length in *A Room of One's Own* but also in many shorter pieces that have a common thread. These include general discussions of the issue like "Women and Fiction," "Professions for Women," and "Women Novelists"; essays on important writers like Austen, the Brontës, George Eliot, Christina Rossetti, Elizabeth Barrett Browning, Katherine Mansfield, and Dorothy Richardson; a series on minor or failed writers—the Duchess of Newcastle, Dorothy Osborne, Mary Russell Mitford, Eliza Haywood, Laetitia Pilkington; and finally a group on women who resembled "Shakespeare's sister"—the wives, daughters, sisters, or confidantes of major male writers—including Dorothy Wordsworth, Sara Coleridge, Jane Welsh Carlyle, Anne Thackeray Ritchie, Mrs. Thrale.[23] Woolf's essays on these writers collectively attempt to describe the forces that encourage or inhibit a woman's literary vocation.

She never compromised her very high standards of quality in judging women's writing, despite the almost irresistible temptation to summon up an endless procession of mute inglorious Sapphos wasting their sweetness on the desert air. I think she was aware of the element of special pleading implicit in the whole argument and took care to be humanely sympathetic but intellectually tough-minded. For example, she dismisses one critic's claim that Eliza Haywood's romances "prepared the way" for Jane Austen as absurd. In the history of serious literature, Woolf says, "Mrs Haywood plays no perceptible part, save that of swelling the chorus of sound" (*BP*, 128). The essay on the Duchess of Newcastle is just as critical. But finally what interested Woolf in such careers is not the works they produced but the whole tragicomic history of women's attempts to write without a classical education, without encouragement, without a real belief in their own vocations or the leisure to pursue them.

She was as interested in the failed woman writer as in the success because she wanted to solve the problem of how to account for women's success and failure. Her essays on the subject are heavily anecdotal and biographical. In "Dr. Burney's Evening Party," for example, she deals with the ways in which literary talent in women like Mrs. Thrale and Fanny Burney was often dribbled away in diaries and letters, in the work of running a salon or coping with a difficult male genius like Dr. Johnson. She tries to anatomize the whole complex of inner and outer pressures working against artistic success for women. By now these forces have been so much discussed that they have become clichés. As Woolf said about the works of Mary Wollstonecraft, "their originality has become our commonplace" (*CE*, III, 195). But in Woolf's time such explanations certainly did not have wide currency. All it took to write Shakespeare's plays or Tolstoy's novels, after all, was pen, paper, and that magical quality "genius"—indefinable, perhaps, but for some reason much more likely to descend upon males than upon females. Woolf tried to show that genius is made as well as given, or at any rate, that its presence requires a kind of nurture more readily available to men than to women.

III

Woolf substitutes for the free-floating notions of genius or native talent something like a dialectical-materialist theory of artistic creation, particularly in this crucial passage in the essay "Women and Fiction":

> It is only when we know what were the conditions of the average woman's life—the number of her children, whether she had money of her own, if she had a room to herself, whether she had help in bringing up her family, if she had servants, whether part of the housework was her task—it is only when we can measure the way of life and the experience of life made possible to the ordinary woman that we can account for the success or failure of the extraordinary woman as a writer.
>
> (*CE*, II, 142)

The passage brings us to the other major theme in Woolf's feminism: money. I have suggested that she translated the predominantly political, legal, and institutional terms of the debate on women's rights and talents current in her own time into psychological and economic ones. She was, after all, writing in the century whose major social theorists were Freud and Marx. The most influential economist of the age was one of her closest friends. And her husband was a socialist who wrote about economic and class questions all his life. I am not suggesting that she could have held her own in the shoptalk of professional economists. But as we have seen, issues of money and class dominated her social thought, so that the presence of an economic perspective in her thinking about women should come as no surprise.

Financial issues are at the heart of her feminist writings. After discarding a number of other titles, she finally settled on *Three Guineas* as a way of emphasizing the power of the purse in the issues she discusses in that book. And *A Room of One's Own* could almost as plausibly have been called *Five Hundred Pounds a Year*, since the problem of women's incomes is as heavily stressed as the issue of inviolable space. Her advice to women is reminiscent of Iago's reiterated command to Roderigo, "Get money in thy purse. Fill thy purse with money." As she warns them, their "intellectual freedom depends on material things"; the conclusion, then, for any woman trying to shape her own life is to "earn five hundred a year by your wits" (*AROO*, 162–63, 99). There is something almost deliberately simple-minded in this message, as though Woolf were responding to centuries of deliberate mystification. She is interested not only in the obvious things money can buy— physical comfort, space, leisure, domestic help, education, a broader range of experience—but also in its magical and symbolic properties. Women novelists were first taken seriously when it was understood that they "could make money by writing. Money dignifies what is frivolous if unpaid for" (*AROO*, 97). In *Three Guineas* Woolf treats women's new right to earn their own livings as a change so important "that almost every word in the dictionary has been changed by it, including the word 'influence'" (*TG*, 29). Influence, of course, was what a woman was supposed to have in place of power; it involved the use of a whole range of seductive strategies designed to make those with real power—the males in her world—turn some of it over to her. But with financial independence, the calculated use of flattery and charm was no longer necessary. The result is an intellectual liberation, for the woman who has the power to earn her own living "need not acquiesce; she can criticize" (*TG*, 32). This is why Woolf argues that mothers should be supported by the state rather than by their husbands, to make sure they "have a mind and will of their own" (*TG*, 201).

The connection between financial independence and women's power of choice grew out of Woolf's reading and observation, despite the fact that she never knew want or had to work for a living. Yet the absence of necessity did not produce an absence of imagination. She knew that a number of writers before her had stressed the economic issue, and that in writing about women she could hardly ignore it even if it did not entirely accord with her own experience.[24] In her essay on Mary Wollstonecraft she emphasized that "the staple of her doctrine was that nothing mattered save independence," which Wollstonecraft treated as "the first necessity for a woman" (*CE*, III, 194). This sense of priorities might have been confirmed in a reading of some of the antisuffrage tracts of Woolf's own time—in, for example, Sir Almroth Wright's clinching argument for the legitimacy of masculine domination: "For no upright mind can fail to see that the woman who lives in a condition of financial dependence upon man has no moral claim to unrestricted liberty."[25] And Friedrich Engels had earlier examined the way in which women's financial dependence creates a peculiar kind of class distinction: "Within the family [the husband] is the bourgeois and the wife represents the proletariat." He concludes, "The supremacy of the man in marriage is the simple consequence of his economic supremacy, and with the abolition of the latter will disappear of itself."[26]

Woolf would have been just as skeptical of such rigidly logical economic determinism as she was of the political determinism of the suffrage writers. But what Engels was saying would probably have struck a responsive chord. Quentin Bell has shown how Leslie Stephen used his own financial power to legitimize his tyrannical impulses in his relations with his wife and daughters. When Vanessa took over the household accounts, the weekly cross-examinations in her father's study turned into classic scenes of Victorian patriarchal power, with the daughter forced to wait patiently until her father's accusations of extravagance, his threats and taunts and tears had at last spent themselves and he signed the check. During such scenes, Bell writes, Virginia "was consumed with silent indignation. How could her father behave with such brutality and why was it that he reserved these bellowings and screamings for his women?" (QB, I, 63). The climate of fear this financial power creates among the female dependents of such men often becomes the subject of Woolf's fiction. Mrs. Ramsay, for instance, is "not able to tell [Mr. Ramsay] the truth, being afraid, for instance, about the greenhouse roof and the expense it would be, fifty pounds perhaps, to mend it" (*TL*, 65). And in *The Years* Eleanor Pargiter enters her father's study to go over the household accounts rather like a clerk approaching her superior. The power of the purse confirms a position of authority that seems to radiate from every object in his room. When Woolf analyzes the character of the colonel in the essay portion of *The Pargiters*, she treats his financial control as the cornerstone of his absolute authority, for "the fact that the money was entirely his, that none of his sons and daughters could take up a profession or marry without asking his consent, had its effect on him—gave him a position of great power and responsibility" (*P*, 31).

Woolf's sense of the psychological meaning of money seems to have grown as she was finishing *To the Lighthouse* and beginning to think about *A Room of One's Own*. In 1927, after fifteen years of marriage, she and Leonard apparently decided at her insistence to have separate checking accounts for the first time, though they had always had what Leonard called a small "personal 'hoard'" after their joint expenses were met, to be spent as each saw fit without consulting the other.[27] Virginia calls her checkbook, perhaps with tongue in cheek, "this great advance in dignity," and she talks about earning "the first money of my own since I married," adding, "I never felt the need of it till lately" (*D*, III, 175, 140). From the year 1928 on, Woolf's income from her writing increased dramatically, and she must have been pleased to think that her *earned* income alone could now easily have covered all their joint expenses. For the first time in her life, she was not dependent on money inherited from her father or earned by her husband. She was financially her own mistress, and the sharp pleasure this fact gave her must have made her more conscious than ever that a woman's financial independence had an importance out of all proportion to the things money could buy.

I have tried to suggest the significance of Woolf's attitude toward money in her redefinition of the goals of the women's movement. But it should be clear that the group solidarity she was working for was not entirely that of her own sex. There was an important conflict of loyalty here—on the one hand, to other women; on the other, to male and female members of her own class—and Woolf was perfectly aware of it. It was in part this divided loyalty that made her hesitate to call herself a feminist at all, for she was honest enough to know that she was not equally concerned about the welfare of *all* women but rather working primarily for those she called the daughters and sisters of educated men. It is notable how often the word "own" occurs in her discussion of the problem: a room of one's own, an income of one's own, a mind and will of one's own, one's own work. The word appears with the regularity of a leitmotif. Its connection with ownership, with property and possession, is clear: it is much more likely to be used in bourgeois than in working-class discourse. And in that class the connection between possession and independence is revealed in the phrase "to be one's own man," which the *OED* defines as "to be master of oneself . . . to have the full control or use of one's faculties." There is no comparable phrase for women: "to be one's own woman" would have sounded absurd, precisely because of its political naiveté. Woolf was working for a future society in which this distinction between members of a single class would no longer exist.

Though she was clear-sighted enough to recognize this conflict of loyalties, there are indications that it made her distinctly uncomfortable. We have already seen that her firm middle-class identity undermined her feeling of kinship with working-class women. She was a lady; she had female servants who helped give her the freedom to write; and she was simply unwilling or unable to treat their needs with the sympathy she reserved for women of her own class. When, for example, her servants Lottie and Nelly complained about their quarters and warned her that "you won't get two girls to sleep in one room as we do," the ideal of a room of one's own was conveniently forgotten. Nelly's ultimatum that they "must" have various improvements in the kitchen made Woolf aware of her own class markings. "Must?" she says in her diary: "Is must a word to be used to Princes?" The tone is self-mocking, but the anger was real, and the requests were denied (*D*, II, 281).

At the same time, it is clear that Woolf wanted to think of herself not as privileged but as deprived. In an early draft of "Professions for Women" she addresses her audience conspiratorially: "As a failure, then, I speak to you who are also failures."[28] She regularly writes about women as "outlaws" and "outsiders" rather than as members of an establishment, and she stresses the powerlessness of middle-class women, who she says in *Three Guineas* "are weaker than the women of the working-class" because they do not even have the weapon of the strike at their disposal (*TG*, 24). Even the most sympathetic reader of Woolf's feminist works would I think have some difficulty in accepting her vision of this issue, if indeed one can dignify this self-contradictory bundle of attitudes with a word like "vision" at all. In her contemptuous review of *Three Guineas* in *Scrutiny*, Q. D. Leavis bases her attack on the assumption that Woolf "is quite insulated by class."[29] But perhaps the real reason for the sense of intellectual incoherence was rather that Woolf was not insulated *enough*.

This may become clear if we look briefly at the history of the women's movement from a class perspective and try to see how it was changing in Woolf's time. The nineteenth-century roots of the movement were solidly upper-middle-class. One of the first suffrage workers in England insisted that it was essential to distinguish "between proposals to admit the dregs of a population to the franchise, and those to admit the mothers, daughters and sisters of the men who already exercise it."[30] The same class perspective characterized the movement for women's higher education. As Emily Davies wrote in 1866, there was ample time for middle-class women to devote themselves to study, since "an educated woman, of active, methodical habits, blessed with good servants, as good mistresses generally are, finds an hour a day amply sufficient for her housekeeping." [31] Such passages reveal that the women's movement began as a theory of the leisure class, though of course its image of a disenfranchised and dispossessed sex might be and eventually was extended beyond its original class boundaries. This is exactly what was happening in Woolf's own time. The Suffragette agitation too began as an essentially middle-class movement masquerading as a movement for the liberation of a sex. But its slogan "Votes for Women!" was soon translated by more democratic voices into the mocking "Votes for Ladies!" [32] Between 1911 and 1914 the movement gradually split in two, with Christabel Pankhurst taking control of the middle-class W.S.P.U. and her sister Sylvia organizing the working women of London's East End in a rival organization. [33]

The conflict in the women's movement that these opposing tendencies reveal is also reflected in Woolf's work. She was, as she knew, ineradicably middle-class, but at the same time she voted Labour and was married to a socialist. As we have seen, she was writing in an age when the privileges of her class were increasingly under attack. All of these forces acting simultaneously produced a real confusion of loyalties and deprived her commitment to the women's movement of some of its authority. The demands of "educated men's daughters" could no longer convincingly be presented as the needs of women. Between the ideal of sisterhood and the requirements of the leisure class there was a fundamental conflict of interest, and Woolf never succeeded in finding her way out of this maze.

IV

Woolf's loyalties were further complicated by her strong feeling that the men of her own class were not worth imitating.

The whole arena of men's work seemed to be dominated by a competitive ethic that Woolf found repugnant. Men's careers consisted of an endless series of contests which they were trained to win. The pattern began in school and ended only in the grave, when the successful professional man, loaded with honors, decorations, offices, and cash, was at last permitted to rest. Woolf's picture of this *cursus honorum* was savagely satiric. She treats the competitive element in men's careers as a serious deflection from the more worthy aspects of their calling. The famous passage in *To the Lighthouse* in which Mr. Ramsay's attempt to think through a difficult philosophical problem is presented as an agonizing attempt to get from the letter Q to the letter R is especially revealing. He imagines the whole enterprise of thinking in competitive terms, as an attempt to get through the alphabet to Z. Mr. Ramsay is stuck at Q: "He reached Q. Very few people in the whole of England ever reach Q. . . . Z is only reached once by one man in a generation. Still, if he could reach R it would be something. . . . He braced himself. He clenched himself. . . . A shutter, like the leathern eyelid of a lizard, flickered over the intensity of his gaze and obscured the letter R. In that flash of darkness he heard people saying—he was a failure—that R was beyond him. He would never reach R" (*TL*, 56–57).

This passage deliberately ignores the intellectual *content* of Mr. Ramsay's thought to suggest its relative insignificance for him. What matters more than solving the problem is getting ahead of the competition. The heroic qualities he calls upon in his strenuous effort are compromised by his false goals. Woolf's comparison of his mental struggle to an attempt to master the alphabet deflates the whole enterprise, even though the letters P, Q, and R were commonly used (by Bertrand Russell, for example) in philosophical discourse. These letters were the conventional symbols for a series of distinct propositions in an argument, but they were essentially arbitrary and not used in the competitive or evaluative fashion Mr. Ramsay employs. The target of Woolf's satire is not philosophical thinking, of course, but the way in which a noble vocation could degenerate into a mere contest among men obsessed by images of personal triumph and failure. For Woolf was convinced not only that the prizes professional men pursued were worthless but that the pursuit itself nurtured a number of impulses certain to do harm: aggression, envy, pride. She was seriously worried that women who entered the professions would soon be indistinguishable from the driving and driven men they would join.

This prospect filled Woolf with alarm. Insisting that women must try to create their own models rather than follow the existing ones, she encouraged them to reject the glittering prizes men pursued—honors, awards, decorations: "We can refuse all such distinctions and all such uniforms for ourselves" (*TG*, 40). The first edition of *Three Guineas* was illustrated with photographs of distinguished men all but smothered in the robes of office, weighed down by their academic or official gowns, wigs, medals, maces, and other paraphernalia of triumph. The photographs were intended to change women's reaction to such symbols from awe to contemptuous indifference. And in her own life Woolf routinely refused all such offers; an honorary doctorate from the University of Manchester, for example, is rejected with relief: "No, thank Heaven, I need not emerge from my fiction in July to have a tuft of fur put on my head" (*D*, IV, 148).

What appalled Woolf was the fear that the professional sensibility is not fitted with brakes. Was it inevitable that women embarking on a career would be unable to stop themselves from desiring and acquiring more and more once they had begun to taste money and power? There seemed every reason to think so. In *The Voyage Out* Terence Hewet attacks the ambitious professional man as a "bully." When Rachel responds that at any rate he, Terence, did not act the part, he replies. "Oh, I'm different. . . . I've got between six and seven hundred a year of my own" (*VO*, 252–53). The passage connects financial necessity and professional brutality and also reveals that Woolf's rather detached perspective can be seen as a byproduct of her independent income. Were women without such means likely to become as aggressively competitive as the men Terence was describing? In *Three Guineas* Woolf argues that women must try to prevent themselves from taking this route. The Society of Outsiders she envisions consists of professional women who "would bind themselves not to continue to make money in any profession, but to cease all competition and to practise their profession experimentally, in the interests of research and for love of the work itself, when they had earned enough to live upon'" (*TG*, 204).

This is an example of the separatist strain in Woolf's feminism, which became more marked in her later career. She was searching for a form of professional commitment not based on the existing male models. As she put it in an important passage from an essay published in 1920:

> "I have the feelings of a woman," says Bathsheba in "Far from the Madding Crowd," "but I have only the language of men." From that dilemma arise infinite confusions and complications. Energy has been liberated, but into what forms is it to flow? To try the accepted forms, to discard the unfit, to create others which are more fitting, is a task that must be accomplished before there is freedom or achievement.
>
> ("Men and Women," *BP*, 30)

This separatist thinking was a radical departure from the assumptions of the women's movement. It was true that the W.S.P.U. had limited its membership to women and that the Pankhursts (particularly Christabel) had a good deal of contempt for women's organizations overtly or covertly dominated by men. Yet the fundamental goals of the Suffragettes and other organizations working for women's equality in the nineteenth and early twentieth centuries were not readily distinguishable from those of men. The very quest for equality easily shades into the ideal of identical values and lives. Woolf must have been particularly conscious of this when the First World War ended the opposition to the government of almost all the suffrage organizations and revealed the former rebels as loyal subjects of the Crown. As the historian George Dangerfield puts it, the Suffragettes "turned patriot to a woman."[34] Mrs. Pankhurst and Christabel dropped all suffrage activities and turned their militant organization into a frankly militaristic one. They made recruiting speeches,

handed the white feather to men in civilian clothes, and peti-
tioned the government "to open the munition factories to
women."[35]

Woolf would have treated such behavior as a categorical betrayal of the women's movement and all it stood for in her
mind. But the W.S.P.U.'s support of the war could have been
predicted from the tone and methods of the organization. It
was openly based from the first on male models of political
coercion. Mrs. Pankhurst was convinced that women would
never get the vote "until we employed the same violence that
men had used in their agitation for suffrage."[36] Her organization was conceived and run on the model of an army, with
unquestioned power vested in the supreme commander, flags,
colors, marches, strategy conferences, headquarters, assaults,
sabotage. The only inhibition was that its soldiers were not
permitted to kill. In all other ways they were to behave like the
members of a military force. As Christabel is supposed to
have said to Sylvia when she refused to obey orders, "We
want all our women to take their instructions and walk in step
like an army!"[37]

The whole cast of mind suggested by such martial methods
would have revolted Woolf, as we will see when we try to
understand her lifelong pacifism. But her misgivings about
some of the tactics of the women's movement were not merely
the product of her dislike of militancy. In a sense, the W.S.P.U.'s
enthusiastic support of the war only revealed a flaw in the
whole conception of "women's rights" that had disturbed
Woolf from the first. The movement had not sufficiently
divorced itself from the world created by men; it had been
largely uncritical of the existing institutions of society and
anxious merely to enter them. The whole competitive ethic
that dominated masculine culture had been incorporated into
its own ideals. There is a kind of social Darwinism in the earliest texts of the movement, as though the writers fully accepted the appropriateness of "survival of the fittest" as a goal
of women's liberation. To refuse women entry into parliament
or the professions, says John Stuart Mill, is to deprive those
institutions "of the stimulating effect of greater competition

on the exertions of the competitors," since many men in those professions "would be beaten by women in any fair field of competition." [38] The word "fit" constantly recurs in his book.

In the movement for women's higher education, too, the principle of admitting women to the same competitive examinations men take was treated as essential. Rival theorists suggested that entirely separate institutions, courses of instruction, and examinations ought to be established for women. But the most influential writer on the subject, Emily Davies, insisted "that the question of women's fitness for the higher education, represented by the university course, could be fairly solved only by submitting the women students to precisely the same course, under precisely the same tests, as the men." [39] Here too the issue is one of "fitness." The early feminists pressed for what they called "the common standard" because they felt that only in this way could women conclusively demonstrate their intellectual parity with men. Any separate institution or examination specifically designed for women was likely to be dismissed as inferior, and this was a chance the first workers for the equality of the sexes could not take. Yet the effect of this policy was to make such women unwittingly internalize and accept the whole system of masculine competitive rituals. When the suffragist leader Millicent Fawcett records the fact that her daughter became the first woman in Cambridge history to take first place in the highly competitive mathematical tripos examination, she writes about the event as though it were the culminating triumph of her life: "I should have been overjoyed if any girl, even the daughter of my dearest enemy, had gained a similar distinction. But that this great honour should come to our own child was a joy that could hardly be expressed." [40]

Woolf's revisionist attitude toward the feminist legacy is nowhere more apparent than in her hostility to such ways of thought. Perhaps it had been necessary at a certain historical stage to demonstrate that women were the equals of men and could compete successfully in their various arenas. But the point having been made and the franchise, as well as entry into the professions, obtained, the goals of the movement had to change. Woolf was in the vanguard of what one of her contemporaries, the M.P. Eleanor Rathbone, called "the new feminists" of the postfranchise era. Rathbone's contrast is enlightening. To the new school of feminists, she writes,

> the habit of continually measuring women's wants by men's achievements seems out of date, ignominious, and intolerably boring. "Here we have a world," we say, "which has been shaped by men to fit their own needs. It is, on the whole, a poor sort of world. . . . Now that we have secured possession of the tools of citizenship, we intend to use them not to copy men's models but to produce our own." [41]

This passage, which Woolf certainly read—the book was published by the Hogarth Press and edited by her friend Ray Strachey—was written while she was working on *Three Guineas* and is a useful condensation of her own separatist attitudes in that book. She was a "new feminist," in Rathbone's terms. She had read the works of her predecessors in the movement with care and learned a great deal from them. But she was not anxious to accept their goals or to follow their prescriptions for the future. On the one hand, her feminist books are acts of homage to the founders and pioneers of the movement, as their historical framework and heavy use of quotations demonstrates. Such homage was perhaps necessary at a moment when the movement seemed played out, its goals supposedly achieved, and the victors honored with the familiar badges of triumph: even that notorious rebel Christabel Pankhurst had become Dame Christabel in 1936. On the other hand, the vision of triumphant accomplishment seemed false to her. Though women's lives had changed, they had not changed radically enough, and Woolf felt that in some ways they had even changed for the worse.

She tried to redirect the movement along lines that might have seemed strange and even frightening to its founders. So many of the earliest feminist writers were anxious to assure their readers that when women's goals were achieved, nothing drastic would be altered in the society as a whole. The relations between men and women would be improved but not fundamentally transformed; women would still be loyal to the ideals of family life despite their new professional opportunities; and the other ideals and practices of English society would remain untouched. Woolf knew that this blandly reassuring vision of social stasis was unrealistic. Any revolution as fundamental as the one the feminists proposed was likely to change the whole existing familial and societal structure in fundamental ways, and she was far from dreading this outcome. The politics of family life, the competitive rituals of the professions, the ideals of patriotism, military triumph, and imperial power were to her mind very much in need of rethinking; and she was glad that the women's movement was forcing such revaluation, even if it was purchased at the price of comfortable relations between the sexes. By the end of her career, her feminist writings were seriously offending many of her male readers, and she learned to accept this as inevitable and even necessary.

But as we have seen, such radical tendencies in Woolf's thinking are always in conflict with a persistent traditionalism. We see this at work, for instance, in her residual doubts about her own competence to judge men's works at all. When she was twenty-one she asked herself in her diary if she even had a right to read and evaluate men's writings, and she voiced her fear of their ridicule (Berg Diary, 30 June–1 Oct. 1903, 39). This feeling of feminine incapacity and presumption never entirely left her. It is embodied in her portrait of Mrs. Ramsay, who is convinced it is right and proper that men should govern the world and empedestal their women. As we have seen in looking at *To the Lighthouse*, Woolf never managed to repudiate the ideals of Mrs. Ramsay entirely and could not escape a nostalgic feeling for that whole way of life. It was this pull toward nineteenth-century values that made her react with condescension or outright hostility to some of the more uncompromising feminists. The writer Olive Schreiner, for instance, seems to her one of the pathetic martyrs the cause demands, whose obsession with the relations between the sexes makes them "sacrifice their sense of proportion; lose their artistic power, their width & humour," who are "cramped & distorted by the intensity & narrowness of their convictions."[42] And in this description of Jane Carlyle's friend Geraldine Jewsbury, Woolf's sarcastic contempt is unmistakable:

> Meanwhile Geraldine lay on the floor and generalized and speculated and tried to formulate some theory of life from her own tumultuous experience. 'How loathsome' (her language was always apt to be strong—she knew that she 'sinned against Jane's notions of good taste' very often), how loathsome the position of women was in many ways! How she herself had been crippled and stunted! How her blood boiled in her at the power that men had over women! She would like to kick certain gentlemen. . . .

> (*CE*, IV, 37)

No wonder Woolf's feminist writings have proved to be such unreliable tracts for the movement, that Elaine Showalter, for example, could call her the contemporary equivalent of the "Angel in the House," "that phantom of female perfection who stands in the way of freedom."[43] There is no denying the power of these works or their importance in the history of the cause. But the quicksilver mind of the author, with its opposing tendencies, its anger, its charm, its dangerous wit that could be turned in any direction, did not easily slip into the harness of political hackwork, as we will see when we look more closely at *A Room of One's Own* and *Three Guineas*. Woolf wrote for women while she addressed an audience of men. She was not sure the change in women's lives could be interpreted as progress, though she would certainly not have traded the present for the past. The "Angel in the House" was a corpse at her feet while still hovering over her shoulder. The richness of texture as well as the internal contradictions evident in all her writings about women finally have their roots in her ideological impurity: she was her own woman.

9

Anger and Conciliation in *A Room of One's Own* and *Three Guineas*

Woolf's two discursive books about women's lives—*A Room of One's Own* (1929) and *Three Guineas* (1938)—are both attempts to find a vehicle to accommodate her twin needs in writing those works: to vent her anger about the subjection of women and to conciliate the male audience she could never entirely ignore. These needs are clearly antithetical and seem to call for entirely different forms of expression: the first, direct, passionate, personal, and rough; the second, charming, ironic, detached, and controlled. One has a sense in reading these works that impulse is at war with strategy and that this conflict accounts for a certain complexity of tone present in both books, but especially in the later *Three Guineas*.

That it was exceptionally hard for her to translate impulse into strategy is shown by a long, revealing entry in her diary at the time she was writing *Three Guineas*. She records meeting E. M. Forster at the London Library, that splendid private institution of which her father had once been president. Forster, who is on the governing committee of the library, tells her that her name had been proposed for membership on that board, only to encounter violent group resistance: "They were all quite determined," Forster says. "No no no, ladies are quite impossible. They wouldnt hear of it." Woolf's reaction (as recorded in her diary) is explosive:

> See how my hand trembles. I was so angry (also very tired)
> standing. And I saw the whole slate smeared. I thought how
> perhaps M[organ] had mentioned my name, & they had said
> no no no: ladies are impossible. And so I quieted down & said
> nothing & this morning in my bath I made up a phrase in my

book on Being Despised [the working title for what became *Three Guineas*] which is to run—a friend of mine, who was offered . . . one of those prizes—for her sake the great exception was to be made . . . said, And they actually thought I would take it. They were, on my honour, surprised, even at my very modified & humble rejection. You didnt tell them what you thought of them for daring to suggest that you should rub your nose in that pail of offal? I remarked. Not for a hundred years, she observed. . . . Yes, these flares up are very good for my book: for they simmer & become transparent: & I see how I can transmute them into beautiful clear reasonable ironical prose. God damn Morgan for thinking I'd have taken that. . . . For 2,000 years we have done things without being paid for doing them. You can't bribe me now. Pail of offal? No; I said while very deeply appreciating the hon. . . . In short one must tell lies, & apply every emollient in our power to the swollen skin of our brothers so terribly inflamed vanity.

(*D*, IV, 297–98)

This passage perfectly illustrates, in their raw state, the contradictory impulses at work in Woolf's feminism. On the one hand, there is her blind rage at these men's contempt for her sex. Her hand trembles, her sentence structure wobbles, she damns even her friend Morgan Forster. Her mind rapidly constructs and rejects various killing retorts. At the same time, her imagination is instantly put to work to transmute this anger into "beautiful clear reasonable ironical prose"— that is, into something very different from the barely coherent style of this entry. In part the impulse is literary, in part concessive. The proffered honor is to be rejected in a "very modified and humble" way. The sense of outrage cannot be expressed "for a hundred years." In the meantime, one dissembles and applies emollients to men's vanity.

In the original entry these two reactions are at war and seem almost to displace each other in alternate sentences. Woolf consciously used her diary to record turbulent feelings before she had mastered them. Three days later her detachment has decisively triumphed over her anger. She looks over the earlier passage and comments drily, "This little piece of rant wont be very intelligible in a years time. Yet there are some useful facts & phrases in it. I rather itch to be at that book" (*D*, IV, 298). The later reaction dismisses the earlier one. Anger is treated as embarrassing and childish; at best it only provides some interesting raw material for the artist to refine and contain.

This deliberate inhibition of anger in Woolf's work has become the focus of attention in recent commentary on her writings, particularly among feminist critics. Adrienne Rich writes that in re-reading *A Room of One's Own* she "was astonished at the sense of effort, of pains taken, of dogged tentativeness" in the tone of that book. "And I recognized that tone. I had heard it often enough, in myself and in other women. It is the tone of a woman almost in touch with her anger, who is determined not to appear angry, who is *willing* herself to be calm, detached, and even charming in a roomful of men where things have been said which are attacks on her very integrity." [1] And Elaine Showalter writes of both Virginia Woolf and Dorothy Richardson, "How much better it would have been if they could have forgiven themselves, if they could have faced the anger instead of denying it, could have translated the consciousness of their own darkness into confrontation instead of struggling to transcend it." [2] By refusing to express the anger she felt, according to Showalter, Woolf succeeded only in turning it against herself.

Behind these judgments lies the assumption that the inhibition of anger compromises the quality of art and that a more direct expression of Woolf's resentment might well have made her a greater writer. This idea is most forcefully argued by Jane Marcus in her essay "Art and Anger," which uses *A Room of One's Own* and *Three Guineas* as primary examples. Marcus prefers the angry first drafts to the more conciliatory published versions of Woolf's work and argues for the superiority of uncompromising feminist militancy in women's writing. She sees no conflict between art and anger and treats the whole issue as essentially unproblematic once the decision to speak out has been made. In her words, "Anger is *not* anathema in art; it is a primary source of creative energy. Rage and savage indignation sear the hearts of female poets and female critics. Why not spit it out as Woolf said, blow the blessed horn as [Elizabeth] Robins said. Why wait until old age as they did, waiting long to let out their full quota of anger. Out with it. No more burying our wrath, turning it against ourselves."[3] I hope to explain just why Woolf herself would have found it impossible (and during most of her career undesirable) to follow this straightforward advice.

For such critics Woolf's calculated strategy is a form of self-betrayal, her attempt to sound cool and Olympian seriously misguided. They see her neoclassical esthetic theory as an elaborate superstructure based on the unacknowledged repression of her own feelings. And they use her refusal to vent her anger to explain certain crucial elements in her life and work—her madness and suicide on the one hand, her playfulness and persistent use of fantasy on the other. In the former, anger is turned inward; in the latter, it is evaded. This approach to Woolf's feminism, despite its obvious impatience with her reluctant commitment to the cause, has I think succeeded for the first time in illuminating a central opposition in her work, and one worth tracing in detail. The conflict between angry and conciliatory impulses was a constant of her life, and she was steadily conscious of it *as* a conflict. But the resolutions and accommodations she devised changed over the years—in part as a response to her own shifts of feeling, in part as a reaction to transformations in her culture—and some of the answers that satisfied her near the beginning of her career no longer served her by the end. To understand the evolution of Woolf's feminism, we will have to trace the changes not only in her psyche but also in some of the esthetic and political forces of her time.

We have already seen that the neoclassical assumptions behind Woolf's choices were the staple of avant-garde literary practice in the first decades of the twentieth century. T. E. Hulme's influential attack on the romantic sensibility was written about the time Woolf was working on her first novel. In that essay he defends the deliberate inhibition of emotion, idealizes an art in which "there is always a holding back, a reservation" and attacks the whole notion that a poem is not a poem "unless it is moaning or whining about something or other."[4] A similar ideal is celebrated in T. S. Eliot's well-known formula (from the 1917 essay "Tradition and the Individual Talent") that poetry "is not the expression of personality, but an escape from personality," that "the more perfect the artist, the more completely separate in him will be the man who suffers and the mind which creates."[5] Fiction was to follow the same rules, and women writers voiced this belief as regularly as men. "I sympathise more than I can say with your desire to escape from autobiography," Katherine Mansfield wrote Hugh Walpole in 1927; "I think there is a very profound distinction between any kind of *confession* and creative work."[6] The whole literary climate of Woolf's time fostered the kind of detached, controlled, impersonal esthetic theory she adopted. It was a standard by which she regularly judged her fellow writers, male as well as female. Woolf would have had little sympathy with anyone who recommended that she get in closer touch with her own anger. She *was* in close touch with it; to have put those feelings on more prominent display would not, to her way of thinking, have produced better art; on the contrary.

But the decision to inhibit her anger in the feminist books was not only literary; it was also political, and rooted in the tradition of nineteenth-century feminist writing. Woolf was highly conscious of contributing to a movement that had, over a long period, worked out certain strategies of persuasion. *A Room of One's Own* and *Three Guineas* refer to or quote from such important figures in the nineteenth-century women's movement as Emily Davies, Anna Jemima Clough, Josephine Butler, Octavia Hill, Sophia Jex-Blake, and others. In addition, Woolf knew the arguments of prominent people in the suffrage agitation like Millicent Fawcett and the Pankhursts. The whole history of the women's movement was highly instructive for someone thinking about the uses of anger in political protest.

One can see the split between the concessive and the rebellious wings of the movement in the opposition between the constitutional suffragists and the militant Suffragettes. The issue dividing them was precisely the political utility of anger.

From the first, the militant campaign was an attempt to substitute angry political confrontation for the conciliatory, refined tactics of the earlier suffragists. The Pankhursts tested the effectiveness of expressed, public outrage and were convinced it produced results. In Christabel Pankhurst's words, "Where peaceful means had failed, one act of militancy succeeded and never again was the cause ignored."[7] The methods of Mrs. Fawcett's constitutional group were entirely different—low-key, patient, eschewing any kind of confrontation with men in power—and this too constituted a political strategy. Their tactics were based on winning general support from men as well as women, and they knew that such a goal could be achieved only by cool calculation. Whatever one may think of the relative merits of these two strategies, it is clear that Woolf worked with the constitutional rather than the militant group and that she supported the goal of uniting rather than dividing the society on such an issue.[8] Unity, harmony, merging are consistently idealized in her work, and her political books are no exception.

She could have found support for this impulse in the nineteenth-century history of the women's movement. From the first, the pioneers of feminism considered it politically essential to win support from men. Their writings are often deliberately shaped to avoid annoying the male reader. One of the most extraordinary examples comes from a letter Emily Davies wrote to a friend who had sent her a draft of an article on women's suffrage:

> In your paper there are two or three expressions I should like to have altered, e.g. I don't think it quite does to call the arguments on the other side 'foolish.' Of course they *are*, but it does not seem quite polite to say so. I should like to omit the paragraph about outlawry. You see, the enemy [i.e., antifeminist men] always maintains that the disabilities imposed upon women are not penal, but solely intended for their good, and I find nothing irritates men so much as to attribute tyranny to them. . . . Men cannot stand indignation, and tho' of course I think it is just, it seems to me better to suppress the manifestation of it.[9]

Davies's strategic silence was a carefully considered tactic. As one of her co-workers wrote to her, "Half our mischief comes from *screaming* American advocates." [10]

Nineteenth-century England, however, had its own supply of "screaming advocates," most notably Sophia Jex-Blake, the pioneer of medical education for women, whose case Woolf discusses at some length in *Three Guineas* (117–20). Unlike the more conciliatory feminists, Jex-Blake was constitutionally unable to contain her outrage: she had a very short fuse. When, after years of tireless effort, women medical students were finally admitted to Edinburgh University in 1869, the male students protested and tried to keep them out. There was a riot, threats, insults, accusations and counteraccusations, a hearing in which Jex-Blake vented her anger by directly attacking a number of individuals including the assistant to one of the professors, whose outrageous behavior could only be explained, she said, by the possibility that he was drunk at the time. The accusation not surprisingly resulted in a libel suit, which the young man won and which cost Jex-Blake nearly £1000 in legal fees. Her lack of circumspection led not only to this expensive defeat but also to the far more disastrous decision by the university authorities that the whole scheme of admitting women to the medical school had been a mistake: in the following year they were expelled without obtaining their degrees. It took nearly a decade for another British university to try the experiment again. Jex-Blake's biographer concludes that her insistence on confronting rather than mollifying her male opponents was probably counterproductive: "She might have shortened the battle if she had adopted a more conciliatory attitude." [11] She became an object lesson in the dangers of militant anger. As Ray Strachey puts it in her history of the women's movement, "She committed the error of allowing her indignation to be seen." [12]

In contrast to Sophia Jex-Blake and the Pankhursts, most of the first feminists decided early that it was as important to reassure men as to awaken women. It was men, after all, who made the laws, controlled the universities and professions, and owned the property. Their cooperation was seen as absolutely essential, at least until the basic privileges of political power and financial independence were won. The writings of the first feminists were filled with conciliatory gestures designed to convince men that "their" women would not be terrifyingly different after emancipation. Even Mary Wollstonecraft, with her fierce sense of women's need for independence, could paint the standard picture of the model wife anxious to "prepare herself and children, with only the luxury of cleanliness, to receive her husband, who returning weary home in the evening found smiling babes and a clean hearth."[13] And over a century later Millicent Fawcett was still telling her male readers that "the free woman makes the best wife and the most careful mother."[14] All such assurances were designed to speak directly to men's fear that the feminist movement would produce an alarming new kind of woman: indifferent to domestic duty, competitive with men, "unsexed," "unfeminine," masterful rather than submissive. Not so, the first feminists assure us: the liberated woman's primary loyalty would continue to be to her family, her new skills and powers would make her competent rather than combative, she would merely learn to become a better mistress in her own domain. Even the militant Sophia Jex-Blake assumed as a matter of course that domestic duties must take precedence over professional ones, that "women are women before they are doctors," as she says, and that "if a woman becomes a mother, I certainly think nothing outside her home can have, or ought to have, so much claim upon her as her children."[15]

That last statement—which comes from a letter to a woman friend rather than from a public document—should make us aware that this whole conciliatory way of thinking was not merely or consistently tactical: it also represented a vein of genuine conservative feeling in the first feminists, so that it becomes impossible to separate conviction from political calculation. Hindsight now makes us aware of how many dangerous cracks in the relations between the sexes were being papered over in the early writings of the movement. The stance is radically concessive, and the concessions are seldom treated as significant. It never seems to occur to such writers that a woman might have trouble choosing between vocation and family responsibility, might feel thwarted by the need to give up a profession after training herself to practice it. It makes us aware that every stage in a movement of social change combines tradition and innovation. The first audience will be aware of the new departures but oblivious to the continuities. Later observers will be conscious of the residual conservatism of the reformers—of how much they seemed to concede.

This split between rebellious and conciliatory methods illuminates some of the tensions in Woolf's own work. If one looks at these issues carefully, it soon becomes evident that there is a complex tangle of forces at work that does not support the theory of her unconscious repression of anger. For one thing, anger is not consistently denied either in Woolf's feminist books or in her novels: it is frequently given its due. Some of the most vivid passages in her fiction express rather than bury such intense emotion. The direct attack in *Mrs. Dalloway* on Dr. Bradshaw's coercive methods does not stand alone. In *The Voyage Out* Rachel responds to Terence's kiss with a flash of aggressive fantasy. In her mind "she only saw an old woman slicing a man's head off with a knife" (*VO*, 413). And in a famous passage in *To the Lighthouse* Mr. Ramsay's domination of his wife is described in a metaphor of extraordinary violence: the young James Ramsay feels his mother's "strength flaring up to be drunk and quenched by the beak of brass, the arid scimitar of the male, which smote mercilessly, again and again, demanding sympathy" (*TL*, 63). Such passages are designed to give space and prominence to the anger against men who attempt to crush women's wills. And they do not mince words.

We also find such explosions in Woolf's essays and in the two feminist books, the vehicles for a more unmediated expression of her own feelings. She says in her diary that in preparing to write *Three Guineas* she had "collected enough powder to blow up St. Pauls" (*D*, IV, 77). This hostile impulse is reflected in passages like the description of men in public life, the arena in which the humane private man turns into "a monstrous male, loud of voice, hard of fist, childishly intent upon scoring the floor of the earth with chalk marks, within whose mystic boundaries human beings are penned, rigidly, separately, artificially" (*TG*, 191). Such anger against tyrannical men is also voiced in the more steadily ironic *A Room of One's Own*, always as a response to male condescension toward women or to men's attempts to control women's lives. The target is the persistent coercive male voice, "now grumbling, now patronising, now domineering, now grieved, now shocked, now angry, now avuncular, that voice which cannot let women alone" (*AROO*, 112).

Yet such direct attacks on what Woolf called "masculinity" are admittedly rare in her fiction and discursive prose. She felt that they were too unguarded, too artless. Anger could be the root but must not be the flower. Far more typical of Woolf's method of expressing outrage is the following passage from *A Room of One's Own*:

> I thought of that old gentleman, who is dead now, but was a bishop, I think, who declared that it was impossible for any woman, past, present, or to come, to have the genius of Shakespeare. He wrote to the papers about it. He also told a lady who applied to him for information that cats do not as a matter of fact go to heaven, though they have, he added, souls of a sort. How much thinking those old gentlemen used to save one! How the borders of ignorance shrank back at their approach! Cats do not go to heaven. Women cannot write the plays of Shakespeare.
>
> (*AROO*, 69–70)

Here Woolf transmutes her anger into the "clear reasonable ironical prose" she speaks of in the London Library passage. She steadily maintains her detachment and control in her mock appreciation of the old gentleman's insight. Her techniques of persuasion are the familiar devices of such satire— the perspective of wide-eyed innocence, the ironic praise, the *reductio ad absurdum*. The passage succeeds in destroying the opposition without seeming to lift a finger. Yet the combative impulse that fuels the whole argument is a felt presence that lies not so far beneath the surface.

Woolf certainly distrusted her own anger. She regularly connects violent emotion of any kind with distortion and self-deception, again and again insisting that the direct expression of anger is fatal to art. The works of Lady Winchilsea and the Duchess of Newcastle "are disfigured and deformed by the same causes"—their bitterness at being excluded from the literary world (*AROO*, 92). And even Charlotte Brontë's books are spoiled by her indignation, "deformed and twisted" because "she will write in a rage where she should write calmly" (*AROO*, 104). The metaphors used in such passages reveal the conviction that art produced under the stress of anger is somehow monstrous and unnatural—a misshapen, premature birth rather than a perfectly formed child. But it is worth noting that though Woolf openly criticizes these writers, she also quotes them at length, thus simultaneously denying the "soundness" of their approach and incorporating their angry voices into her own text.

Anger terrified Woolf because it was so close to the state of madness she herself had known more than once. Her mad phases involved the expression of hostility toward those she loved most—her husband, her sister—the explosion of all those sentiments regularly censored in civilized life. Vanessa Bell's description of the 1915 breakdown emphasizes this aggressive anger: "She says the most malicious & cutting things she can think of to everyone & they are so clever that they always hurt" (QB, II, 26). No wonder Woolf feared the direct expression of rage in her work. Yet she was equally conscious of how indispensable these explosions had been to her art. Woolf's madness was an intensified form of her imaginative life, and she knew it generated or released images, narratives, and words that would eventually find their way into her books. She writes to Ethel Smyth many years later that when she was mad she had made up "poems, stories, profound and to me inspired phrases all day long as I lay in bed, and thus sketched, I think, all that I now, by the light of reason, try to put into prose" (*L*, IV, 231). And she has no doubts about the *teaching* power of insanity: "As an experience, madness is terrific I can assure you, and not to be sniffed at; and in its lava I still find most of the things I write about. It shoots out of one everything shaped, final, not in mere driblets, as sanity does" (*L*, IV, 180). These passages suggest Woolf's divided feelings about such heightened states of awareness: they are fascinating but frightening, indispensable to art yet at war with art's control. The imagination recollects emotion in tranquillity; the tranquillity is as essential as the emotion. One senses Woolf's perilous balance in a diary entry about the composition of *Three Guineas*: "I must very nearly verge on insanity I think. I get so deep in this book I dont know what I'm doing. Find myself walking along the Strand talking aloud" (*D*, V, 20).

Woolf's feminist books may finally give the impression of composure and ironic detachment, but they were conceived and written in a much more turbulent state. Her diary and early drafts show how great a distance she traveled between original impulse and finished product. The process of composition is consistently a search for greater control over intense feeling. Its necessary stages are described with insight by Woolf herself in a diary entry written in 1924: "I think writing must be formal. The art must be respected. This struck me reading some of my notes here, for, if one lets the mind run loose, it becomes egotistic: personal, which I detest; like Robert Graves. At the same time the irregular fire must be there; & perhaps to loose it, one must begin by being chaotic, but not appear in public like that" (*D*, II, 321). This was an esthetic theory that served Woolf's purposes for the greater part of her career. But as we shall see, by the end of her life her faith in it had begun to crumble.

The sharp distinction between what was permissible in private writing and what was fit for public scrutiny is essential to an understanding of Woolf's work. A knowledge of these two languages makes the elements of conciliation more glaringly apparent than they could have been to her first readers, who of course did not have access to her diary, letters, and early drafts. The distinction affects the technique of her feminist books down to the minutest details. Take, for example, the studied impersonality of *A Room of One's Own* and *Three Guineas*. The first is written in the persona of a character she calls "Mary Beton, Mary Seton, Mary Carmichael . . . any name you please (*AROO*, 8). The second consistently uses the pronoun "we" rather than "I." The effect is to play down the sense of personal grievance and to increase the feeling of detachment. These decisions were conscious, as we know from an important letter Woolf wrote to Ethel Smyth, whose own feminist polemics she found politically naive precisely because they were so personal. Woolf urges her to "escape the individual" and try to make her protest more general and objective. And she uses *A Room of One's Own* as an example:

> I didn't write 'A room' without considerable feeling even you will admit; I'm not cool on the subject. And I forced myself to keep my own figure fictitious; legendary. If I said, Look here am I uneducated, because my brothers used all the family funds which is the fact—Well theyd have said; she has an axe to grind; and no one would have taken me seriously, though I agree I should have had many more of the wrong kind of reader; who will read you and go away and rejoice in the personalities, not because they are lively and easy reading; but because they prove once more how vain, how personal, so they will say, rubbing their hands with glee, women always are; I can hear them as I write.
>
> (*L*, V, 194–95)

This heightened awareness of a possibly hostile audience strongly affects the *tone* of *A Room of One's Own*. In place of anger we have irony; in place of sarcasm, charm. The choices are designed not only to win over the opposition but also to reinforce the image of the author's cool self-possession. Her technique is both concessive and seductive. It affects the tentative way in which the speaker presents herself. She begins by assuring us that her vision of the controversial issues under discussion is not to be taken as authoritative: "One can only give one's audience the chance of drawing their own conclusions as they observe the limitations, the prejudices, the idiosyncracies of the speaker" (*AROO*, 7). But the idiosyncracies of Woolf's speaker are more calculated than beyond her control. Take, for example, the passage about how contemporary female novelists depict the relationship between women. Woolf notes that in recent fiction women are often presented as more involved with other women than with men. Yet her way of introducing this controversial subject is arch, playful, deliberately comic. It seems to address the women at Cambridge for whom the original lectures were written, but it is acutely conscious of the later audience of men standing behind them. She is reading, she says, a new novel by a woman:

> I turned the page and read . . . I am sorry to break off so abruptly. Are there no men present? . . . We are all women you assure me? Then I may tell you that the very next words I read were these—"Chloe liked Olivia. . . . " Do not start. Do not blush. Let us admit in the privacy of our own society that these things sometimes happen. Sometimes women do like women.
> (*AROO*, 123)

The comic technique of this passage makes what might have been disturbing to men more tolerable. "Chloe liked Olivia": the name Chloe recalls the innocence of pastoral, and the word "liked" hints at the possibility of a romantic attachment between women without insisting on it. Woolf has managed to say that contemporary women novelists are turning to an important human tie neglected in previous fiction—the intimate friendship possible between women. Yet she has said it without proclaiming it and by playing down its more controversial aspects. Whether one regards such passages as delightfully witty or offensively coy, it is clear that they represent Woolf's rhetorical strategy at its most strenuously ironic.

Though the irony of *Three Guineas* is more pointed and less genial, it is nevertheless consistently there. In the later book Woolf allows men to incriminate themselves by quoting them at length. The work is full of unintentionally revealing passages from the writings of benighted men that illustrate men's coerciveness, smugness, or condescension in their attitudes toward women. Woolf lets them go on, juxtaposes passages from different sources to suggest a kind of masculine conspiracy, and then deflates with an ironic sentence or two. The technique is extremely economical. For example, she quotes at length from a document produced by the Church of England that argues the unsuitability of women for the ministry on the grounds that "it would be impossible for the male members of the average Anglican congregation to be present at a service at which a woman ministered without becoming unduly conscious of her sex." Woolf's one-sentence comment on the Church's elaborate argument for this position is a little classic of irony: "In the opinion of the Commissioners, therefore, Christian women are more spiritually minded than Christian men—a remarkable, but no doubt adequate, reason for excluding them from the priesthood" (*TG*, 288–89).

Irony is aggression that pulls its punches. It can be a vigorous form of persuasion, but it deliberately refuses to attack the real adversary. As often as not, its origin is the power of the opposition. Woolf's acute sense of her audience's potential hostility also encouraged her to adopt the elaborate scholarly apparatus of *Three Guineas*—its reliance on facts and figures, on recognized authorities, on argument by citation and footnote. She begins the section on the discrimination against women in the professions by recourse to Whitaker's Almanack—that "impersonal and impartial authority" who can hardly be accused of having an axe to grind. The question of women's failure to rise to the highest professional positions is so important, she says, that it must be examined "by the white light of facts, not by the coloured light of biography" (*TG*, 83). The lid of the pressure cooker must be clamped down tight over the fiercely bubbling feelings. Behind the impersonal technique lies the fear of letting her book demonstrate any of the characteristics men have traditionally claimed to find in women: that they are illogical, hysterical, ignorant, and subjective, rather than clearsighted. In writing *Three Guineas* Woolf gritted her teeth, determined to beat the enemy at his own game. She was delighted that the *Times Literary Supplement* reviewer called her "the most brilliant pamphleteer in England" and that another critic commended her for being scrupulously fair and puritanically self-denying (*D*, V, 148). This was precisely the effect she was trying for; it must have pleased her to think she had mastered this alien discourse.

"Virginia Woolf is addressing an audience of women," Adrienne Rich writes of *A Room of One's Own*, "but she is acutely conscious—as she always was—of being overheard by men; by Morgan and Lytton and Maynard Keynes and for that matter by her father, Leslie Stephen."[16] Yet though it is true Woolf was consistently aware of her male readers, her attitude toward them changed significantly in the course of her career. She begins by feeling helpless and anxious about their possible contempt. One of the reasons it took her so long to finish her first novel was that she had to contend with the spectre of her father's disapproval. At work on *The Voyage Out*, she has a disturbing dream: "I dreamt last night that I was showing father the manuscript of my novel; and he snorted, and dropped it on to a table, and I was very melancholy, and read it this morning, and thought it bad" (*L*, I, 325). The dream reveals an involuntary incorporation of the alien standard by which her work is to be judged. At about the same time, she asks her brother-in-law Clive Bell, when she sends him a draft of the first hundred pages of the novel, "whether you have anything to say about that unfortunate work? I have a feeling at this moment that it is all a mistake, and I believe you could tell me. At any rate I put myself in your hands with great confidence" (*L*, I, 371). The self-deprecating humility of this plea makes pathetic reading, especially since the man she was addressing was her intellectual inferior. But it is worth noting that even at this very early stage she defends herself against the specifically masculine criticism her work arouses. Bell's comments on *The Voyage Out* are on the whole accepted with gratitude, but on one point she refuses to give way. He protests against the "prejudice against men" the work reveals to him, and Woolf abruptly turns the tables: "For psychological reasons which seem to me very interesting, a man, in the present state of the world, is not a very good judge of his sex" (*L*, I, 383).

Woolf never stops being sensitive to masculine criticism of her feminist writings. At the same time, however, she becomes increasingly conscious of men's hostility and steadily more willing to engage it. In writing *Three Guineas*, she faces the fact that she will need real courage to attack the entrenched positions that are the book's targets. When the men in her circle discuss the futility of pacifism, the inevitability of war, she becomes firmly convinced of the need to examine their attitudes from her own point of view: "I sat there splitting off my own position from theirs, testing what they said, convincing myself of my own integrity & justice" (*D*, V, 79). What had begun as a helpless fear of male authority had gradually turned into a skeptical and highly critical perspective on it. The result, as we will see in the next chapter, was an increasing alienation from some of her former allies. But of course she could not afford to ignore masculine culture, the realities of power being what they were. If men were determined to fight, her own life would inevitably be affected. There seemed to her no alternative to addressing men in their own language and to taking their assumptions as her own starting point. The strategy of *A Room of One's Own*—that of speaking to an audience of women while remaining conscious of the male readers behind them—seemed finally too coy and indirect.

The result was *Three Guineas*, in which Woolf considers her male audience more carefully, more calculatedly, than in any other work. An obsessive strategic thinking went into its composition and accounts for the striking absence of expressive freedom in its style and tone. Her perspective on masculine culture is thoroughly critical. But her rhetorical choices are determined by the need to avoid offending the males in her audience so seriously that they will stop reading the book. So she invents the well-meaning male correspondent who writes asking her how war might be prevented—a symbolic figure designed to represent the confused, liberal, established men with feminist sympathies who are the audience she most needs to reach. The working titles for the book—"On Being Despised," "Men Are Like That"—are rejected in favor of some-

thing less instantly offensive to such readers, the more neutral "Three Guineas."

Woolf's wish to avoid alienating the men in her audience
was not entirely a matter of strategy, however. As in the first
feminists, there is a residual conservative element in her identity that makes her reluctant, even in her most radical phases,
to abandon altogether the ideal of women and men working in
harmony for the same goals. Her bottled-up anger, her persistent concessiveness, are also expressions of her wish and
need to look at "the aggressor" as simply another human
being, educated from childhood to pursue destructive (and
self-destructive) goals. She is usually careful to separate the
learned qualities of "masculinity" from the biological fact of
maleness. And she consistently idealizes a future world in
which the sexes are no longer at cross-purposes.

This goal accounts for several important passages in her
feminist books, most notably the often-discussed section on
androgyny in *A Room of One's Own* and the attack on the term
"feminism" in *Three Guineas*. The discussion of androgyny begins with Woolf's vision of a man and a woman approaching a
taxicab from opposite sides of the street and driving off together. This deliberately trivial incident is raised to symbolic
significance to suggest the restored unity of the sexes. The
image—and the androgynous ideal it crystallizes—is so important to Woolf that she uses a variant of it as the final incident in *The Years*. In both books it is intended as a truce in the
sex war that is tearing the race apart. At the same time, the
ideal had a therapeutic purpose for Woolf herself. As Elaine
Showalter has suggested, "Androgyny was the myth that
helped her evade confrontation with her own painful female-
ness and enabled her to choke and repress her anger and ambition." [17] A similar motive is at work in Woolf's attack on the
word "feminism" in *Three Guineas*. The word, with its supposed insistence on "the rights of women," has done much
harm, she says, by pitting the sexes against each other. Once
the word is destroyed, "the air is cleared; and in that clearer
air what do we see? Men and women working together for the
same cause." But this idealistic conclusion follows a descrip-

tion of the burning of the word "feminism" which reveals that Woolf's anger is not repressed without a trace: "Let us therefore celebrate this occasion by cremating the corpse. Let us write that word in large black letters on a sheet of foolscap; then solemnly apply a match to the paper. Look, how it burns! What a light dances over the world!" (*TG*, 184–85). The buried comparison here is surely with the burning of witches, and Woolf's sarcastic tone suggests that her cooperative myth is indeed being used to choke her own anger. *Three Guineas* frequently manifests such contradictions between public assurances and a more ironic subterranean protest.

The assurances work not only to conciliate male readers but to soothe Woolf's own resentment. The cooperative ideal is based on the belief that men's aggression is as much a product of false training as is women's submission. In the original version of "Professions for Women" Woolf assures her audience of women "that there are men who have triumphed over all the difficulties of their very lopsided education, of their very specialised and arduous careers, men of civilisation, not only of education, men with whom a woman can live in perfect freedom, without any fear. Men too can be emancipated." [18] Such sentiments characterize Woolf at her most optimistic. Although it is very tempting (especially to a male critic) to present them as conclusive, they do not seem to me to have succeeded in convincing Woolf herself. The contrary vision— that "Men Are Like That" and not willing or able to change— is at least as powerful in her later career and dominates her last works. When she compares the nineteenth-century conflicts in the women's movement with contemporary ones, she sees little significant change: "There is the same waste of strength, waste of temper, waste of time, and waste of money. Almost the same daughters ask almost the same brothers for almost the same privileges. Almost the same gentlemen intone almost the same refusals for almost the same reasons" (*TG*, 120).

Despite Woolf's frequently reiterated hope for a revolution in the relation between the sexes, she was more deeply convinced of the unlikeliness of such a transformation. This pessimism is perhaps the deepest reason for the quite extraordinary concessions she is sometimes willing to make. For example, in *A Room of One's Own* she bases her whole theory of what women's novels will be like in the future on the assumption that women will never have long stretches of time free to work: "One would say that women's books should be shorter, more concentrated, than those of men, and framed so that they do not need long hours of study and uninterrupted work. *For interruptions there will always be*" (*AROO*, 117; emphasis added). The passage presents a particular domestic arrangement as a form of destiny. And it is at war with the more sanguine vision of liberated women who "have the habit of freedom and the courage to write exactly what [they] think" (*AROO*, 171) with which the book concludes.[19]

The disparity between visionary ideal and felt reality only exacerbated Woolf's bitterness. That her anger could not be publicly acknowledged, was strategically unwise as well as offensive to the idealist in herself, made it more internally pressing. And as we will see, the public events of the 1930s—the triumph of Fascism and the growing sense of the inevitability of war—struck Woolf as proof that the forces of aggressive masculinity were waxing rather than waning. As she brooded about them, the book on women's professions she was writing changed shape. Eventually it became *Three Guineas*, a meditation on the causal link between masculine domination and war. Its mood is far more bitter than *A Room of One's Own*. By the late 1930s the makeup of her geniality was washing off. She can no longer keep the anger out of her voice, even though she tries to quarantine it in the lengthy and extraordinary notes to *Three Guineas*. In these notes the indignation she has largely forced herself to keep out of the text bursts forth in a kind of mock-scholarly form—for example, in the attack on that patron saint of male supremacists, Paul: "He was of the virile or dominant type, so familiar at present in Germany, for whose gratification a subject race or sex is essential" (*TG*, 298).

Such expressions of anger in the notes to *Three Guineas* are mild compared with some of the passages Woolf originally intended to include in the book, such as this attack on the egotism of the masculine man, from an earlier draft:

> He has become an egomaniac; always writing about I; an egotist on such a scale that to assuage the pangs of his egotism he must keep a whole sex devoted to his service. The recreation of heroes. Women's place is in the home. She must devote herself to the recreation of heroes. What is that but the cry of a goose's swollen liver? the demand of the inflamed 'I' for pity, sympathy in its sufferings caused by a red and swollen egotism?[20]

The elimination of this passage is an example of Woolf revising anger out and is perhaps based on her realization that the imagery of the "goose's swollen liver," of men's "red and swollen egotism"—with its suggestion of tumescence—comes too close to an attack on biological maleness itself.

Though such passages do not find their way into the published work, Woolf's diary in the thirties and early forties reveals that she did not successfully censor these sentiments in her own thoughts. The first target is Hitler and the Nazis, about whom she writes in 1934, immediately after the carnage of the "Night of the Long Knives," "these brutal bullies go about in hoods & masks, like little boys dressed up, acting this idiotic, meaningless, brutal, bloody, pandemonium" (*D*, IV, 223). But soon her awareness of autocratic impulses shifts from the public to the private sphere, and we find her, in 1935, attacking even Leonard Woolf in a passage that has no precedents in the earlier diary. The cook enters in tears because of the way Leonard has treated her. And Woolf reflects that he is "very hard on people; especially on the servant class. No sympathy with them; exacting; despotic. . . . His extreme rigidity of mind surprises me. . . . His desire, I suppose, to dominate. Love of power. And then he writes against it" (*D*, IV, 326).

It is the stress, in *Three Guineas*, on the connection between Fascist brutality and ordinary, garden-variety impulses of authority in the men of her own country that offended so many of Woolf's first readers. She was pointing to a temperamental link between men who thought of each other as irreconcilable enemies—hardly an idea calculated to win male converts to the women's cause. By the time she came to write *Three Guineas*, her expressive needs were at odds with the tactical requirements of such a book, and this helps to account for its wide palette of tones—from good humor to rage, from enforced objectivity to biting subjective response. In the mid-1930s the form of the feminist book designed in part for an audience of men had become an inadequate vehicle for her needs as a writer.

Although this change represents an internal, psychological evolution, it was deeply influenced by the political and esthetic developments of the 1930s. The triumph of Fascism in Italy and Germany spelled the end of the "clever hopes . . . / Of a low dishonest decade," as Auden puts it in "September 1, 1939." Those hopes for progress, for world peace, for "men and women working together for the same cause" had sustained Woolf and the Bloomsbury group for nearly twenty years. But as the coming war became first thinkable, then perhaps necessary, and finally inevitable, the whole conciliatory habit of mind grew to seem unacceptable, because the slow march of progress it was designed to serve was exposed as a fiction. For the worlds Mussolini and Hitler created were consciously primitivist and regressive. They appealed not to modern notions of gradual reform but to ancient models of heroic greatness—in the Teutonic myths, in the image of Imperial Rome. And an essential part of the atavistic program of both Fascist regimes was a return to absolute sexual divisions. Woolf's outraged quotations in the cancelled *Three Guineas* passage—"The recreation of heroes. Women's place is the home. She must devote herself to the recreation of heroes"— were not exaggerated. The militarist ethos was firmly established in both Italy and Germany by the middle of the decade, as Woolf saw for herself in her 1935 journey to those countries. In the previous year Mussolini had declared that "war is the phenomenon which accompanies the development of humanity" and that "war is to man as maternity is to woman."[21]

Hitler's version of this separation of sexual spheres was more extreme but not different in kind. His twin cults of the army and motherhood revived the ancient division of labor and virtually eliminated the common ground that a century of feminism had won. Woman's world, as Hitler defined it in a 1934 speech, "is her husband, her family, her children, and her house." For it is not true, he goes on, that men's and women's spheres can overlap; the sexes' mutual respect "demands that neither sex should try to do that which belongs to the other's sphere."[22] The compensation women were offered for this loss of power was a new breed of men—virile, bold, hard as steel—to make possible and then to honor their sacred maternal mission. And to produce this new kind of man, the spirit of the armed forces was indispensable. Military training became the instrument of national regeneration—psychological as well as political. That is why Hitler could say in *Mein Kampf*: "What the German people owes to the army may be simply summed up in one single word, namely: everything."[23]

This martial myth was contagious, and Woolf was horrified to see how easily the disease could cross the English Channel. She noted the emergence of a comparable militarism in men whose minds and spirits she respected. Perhaps the most striking example was her own nephew Julian Bell. Julian was her sister's firstborn, a gifted young writer who had been brought up in a pacifist household and conditioned to think of war as an unmitigated disaster. In 1935 he edited an anthology of essays called *We Did Not Fight: 1914–18 Experiences of War Resisters* designed to make the case for conscientious objection vivid in the minds of the young men who might well have to decide whether to fight in the next war. Bell's introduction to this volume praises the "magnificent tradition of personal integrity and intellectual courage" shown by those in his parents' generation who resisted the call to arms. But there was an ominous undercurrent in his essay that suggested a new direction in "pacifism." His own generation will not be satisfied simply to say no, Bell argues. It will "hit back as hard and shrewdly as possible, to bring down, by hook or by crook, any government and any governing class that dares to make war." In other words, the antidote to war would be revolution. In Bell's paradoxical formula, "The war-resistance movements of my generation will in the end succeed in putting down war—by force if necessary." [24] There is pride in this statement rather than tragic resignation. Its author had caught the bacillus.

By 1937 Bell had become a participant in the Spanish civil war, where he was killed at the age of twenty-nine. Before he left England, he wrote a long open letter to E. M. Forster justifying not only his personal decision but war itself. He wanted to explain why he and others of his generation were no longer pacifists. It was not merely that resistance to Fascism must inevitably evoke a military response to military provocation. There was something attractive in the soldier's life, some vital current that only war's savage power could release. And Bell ends up acknowledging in himself a "barbaric lust for action of which war is the type. It is this that makes me feel . . . that the soldier is admirable." [25] In Woolf's memoir of Julian Bell, written a few days after his death, she tries to grasp his point of view but finally throws up her hands: "What made him do it? I suppose its a fever in the blood of the younger generation which we can't possibly understand. I have never known anyone of my generation have that feeling about a war" (QB, II, 258).

Bell's was by no means a unique reaction, and it was not strictly limited to his own generation. Auden could write of "the conscious acceptance of guilt in the necessary murder" in the original version of his poem "Spain 1937." [26] And Yeats argued in his prose work *A Vision* (1937) that war was necessary to revitalize an effete civilization: "Love war because of its horror, that belief may be changed, civilisation renewed." [27] His testamentary poem "Under Ben Bulben," written in 1938, addressed to the next generation and deliberately designed to be the final statement in his *Collected Poems*, includes the lines

You that Mitchel's prayer have heard,
'Send war in our time, O Lord!'
Know that when all words are said
And a man is fighting mad,
Something drops from eyes long blind,
He completes his partial mind,

For an instant stands at ease,
Laughs aloud, his heart at peace.[28]

Such passages were the immediate products of contemporary politics, but they were also made possible by a transformation of the esthetic principles of early modern literature. The impersonal and putatively apolitical methods of the first great writers of the century were gradually discredited in the atmosphere of crisis preceding the Second World War. In 1934 a baffled T. S. Eliot could record the disparity between his own working assumptions and those of the new age in these words: "I suffer, like most of my generation, in not having been brought up to think about politics and economics. . . . It seemed that politics could be left to an inferior class of people, actuated by vanity and love of power, who liked politics."[29] For the younger generation, such attitudes were naive, even troglodytic. Artists could no longer afford to play the role of Joyce's God of the creation—"invisible, refined out of existence, indifferent, paring his fingernails." They became participants in an increasingly politicized, polarized, and acrimonious literary culture. The steady growth of this engagement is traced in Samuel Hynes's history of the thirties, *The Auden Generation*. In the last years of the decade, Hynes shows, literary works typically record a polarization of society into Far Left and Far Right, with the mediating values of more neutral observers "cast out by both sides, tossed into the middle of the conflict, to be trampled down because they are irrelevant."[30]

In short, the contemplative neutrality of the observer-artist came to be seen as a luxury of another era, no longer honorable in a world on the brink of disaster. This new esthetic dispensation directly affected the public evaluation of Woolf's work. The receptive or respectful or enthusiastic response that generally greeted her new works in the 1920s gradually gave way to what Woolf called a series of "severe swingeings": "Bloomsbury is ridiculed; & I am dismissed with it" (*D*, IV, 288–89). These attacks—in influential journals like *Scrutiny* and in books like Wyndham Lewis's *Men Without Art* (1934)— were essentially political in nature. They accused Woolf and

Bloomsbury of practicing an etiolated estheticism, based in Walter Pater and made possible by their parasitic leisure-class status. Q. D. Leavis gave her hostile review of *Three Guineas* the sarcastic title "Caterpillars of the Commonwealth Unite!"[31] And Wyndham Lewis's attack on Woolf was rooted in masculine *ressentiment* against Bloomsbury's "feminizing" of culture: "It has been with a considerable shaking in my shoes, and a feeling of treading upon a carpet of eggs, that I have taken the cow by the horns in this chapter, and broached the subject of the part that the feminine mind has played—and minds as well, deeply feminized, not technically on the distaff side—in the erection of our present criteria. For fifteen years I have subsisted in this to me suffocating atmosphere."[32] By the mid-thirties the atmosphere had changed, and a new esthetic-political style—activist, partisan, and aggressive—had taken its place.

Woolf's response to this new intellectual climate was complex. We have already seen that the conciliatory habits of mind she had perfected over many years came to seem suspect and were replaced by a greater willingness to attack. But though she could imitate the new style she did not really want to adopt it. The old inhibitions had been weakened but were not dissolved. She struggled to find a form that would allow her to express her feelings without turning her into a self-righteous polemicist. And she had already begun some years earlier to question the whole esthetic tradition that dictated authorial reticence. In the late 1920s she first entertained the notion that a less shaped and controlled vehicle might be qualitatively superior to the more finished works of art she had idealized. This radical idea never became a settled conviction, but one finds her increasingly willing to consider it. Her own diary becomes not merely useful as a quarry but intrinsically interesting to her. In an entry written in 1926 she envisions a work that might properly be called "the greatest book in the world. This is what the book would be that was made entirely solely & with integrity of one's thoughts. Suppose one could catch them before they became 'works of art'? Catch them hot & sudden as they rise in the mind" (*D*, III, 102). The passage suggests that something important is left out of works of art—especially the most perfected ones.

These new standards of judgment, so different in their assumptions and values from the ideal of anonymity Woolf had espoused, served to legitimize a more directly expressive kind of writing than the sort she had so carefully mastered. She showed a new and unapologetic interest in the diary, the letter to an intimate friend, the autobiographical memoir intended for the drawer. She worked in all these genres in her last years, and as they have been published they have come to seem as important as some of her more familiar works. By 1939, for instance, she was writing her autobiography. The long section of this unfinished book published in *Moments of Being* is distinctly private and was written for her old friends in the Memoir Club. And so she allows herself to write about her childhood more personally than she had ever done, without pretending that "I" could easily be translated into "we." She also finds herself criticizing "the Victorian game of manners . . . founded upon restraint, sympathy, unselfishness" that she and her sister had learned at the family tea-table. Such civilized qualities are "helpful in making something seemly and human out of raw odds and ends. But the Victorian manner is perhaps—I am not sure—a disadvantage in writing. When I re-read my old *Common Reader* articles I detect it there. I lay the blame for their suavity, their politeness, their sidelong approach, to my tea-table training" (*MB*, 129).

This final statement on art and restraint is very different from Woolf's earliest esthetic convictions. Though it is still guarded, it suggests that she has over the years become increasingly aware of the concessions her writing involved and increasingly unwilling to make them. For anger, as Kent says in *King Lear*, "hath a privilege." In the 1939 memoir she allows herself for the first time to voice her deep resentment about her father's autocratic behavior: "Never have I felt such rage and frustration. For not a word of my feeling could be expressed." But after forty years the silence can finally be broken, and Woolf lets him have it:

> Even now I can find nothing to say of his behaviour save that it was brutal. If, instead of words, he had used a whip the brutality would have been no greater. . . . He had so ignored, or refused to face, or disguised his own feelings, that not only had he no conception of what he himself did and said; he had no idea what other people felt. Hence the horror and the terror of these violent displays of rage. These were sinister, blind, animal, savage.
>
> (*MB*, 125–26)

Certainly there is not much "suavity" or "politeness," not much evidence of the "sidelong approach" here. It is powerful writing, designed to satisfy an inner need for Woolf at a certain moment in her life. But unlike her more controlled public works, the passage releases intense emotions over which she has not achieved mastery. There seemed, finally, no satisfactory way for her to reconcile the needs of art and self-expression, of conciliation and anger, at least not in a single work. For someone with a sensibility as complex as hers, the only solution seemed to be to write simultaneously in different forms—the political tract, the diary, the novel of fact and of fantasy, the essay, the memoir—and in different tones: charm, detachment, wit, anger, defiance. Her work in the 1930s seems significantly more fragmented, more divided against itself, than the work of the previous decade. An essential confidence in herself as a center of gravity and in her individual books as adequate expressive vehicles for her vision had gradually been eroded, so that even a late masterpiece like *Between the Acts* seemed unsatisfactory to her: she wrote it, she says, "with my brain half asleep" (*L*, VI, 486). The image is telling. She had come to feel that in order to write at all she had to anesthetize one part of her brain or another. The problem of bringing the warring parts of herself together in a single work had come to seem insoluble. In this impasse, her psyche was recording the fact that "war" had once more in her lifetime become not just a metaphor for inner conflict but a brutal fact of life.

10

Pacifism Without Hope

I

The first public expression of Virginia Woolf's lifelong contempt for war took the form of a prank. In February 1910 she and her brother Adrian, Duncan Grant, and three of their friends dressed up as the emperor of Abyssinia and his entourage for an official inspection of H.M.S. *Dreadnought*, the pride of the British fleet. The hoax was brilliantly successful. They were given a full tour of the vessel; a Guard of Honour was produced for their inspection; they were even offered a twenty-one-gun salute. In due course the story of this breach of military security reached the newspapers. The First Lord of the Admiralty was sharply questioned in the House of Commons. His Majesty's Navy had become a satiric butt, and various patriotic spirits were decidedly not amused. Adrian recalls their pompous cousin Harry Stephen informing him that "His Majesty's ships are not suitable objects for practical jokes."[1] For the *Dreadnought* was widely regarded as a symbol of British military superiority in the armaments race that led up to the First World War. In 1908 the so-called *Dreadnought* panic produced the slogan "We want Eight." One of the more impassioned defenders of military preparedness wrote at the time: "When the German army is looting the cellars of the Bank of England, and carrying off the foundations of our whole national fortune, perhaps the twaddlers who are now screaming about the wastefulness of building four more *Dreadnoughts* will understand why sane men are regarding this opposition as treasonable nonsense."[2] The violence of such statements suggests that the *Dreadnought* hoax, undertaken in youthful high spirits rather than as a principled protest, had nevertheless an undercurrent of seriousness that would surface only a few years later when these prize vessels and toy sailors began to spill real blood. Virginia Woolf entered into the masquerade as a lark, but Quentin Bell is surely right in concluding that it would "reinforce political sentiments which had for some time been taking shape in her mind" (QB, I, 161).

Woolf's hatred of war dated from her earliest training and continued to her death. It was immeasurably strengthened by her experience of the First World War and by her increasing despair as it became clear that it was not to be the last. Her Bloomsbury intimates constantly reinforced this feeling, as we will see. But it also reflects the attitude of her father, whose uncompromising contempt for war was all the more striking because it preceded the *fashion* of pacifism by half a century. Leslie Stephen wrote to Julia in 1877, "I hate all patriotic sentiments; they invariably mean vulgar bray."[3] His first biographer noted that "few people loathe war as he loathed it. . . . When a war was raging, he would walk out of his way to escape the sight of newspaper posters with their 'killed' and 'wounded' or he would lie awake at night thinking of the revolting horrors of a battlefield."[4] Woolf recalled that he was willing to let his sons enter any profession "with the exception of the Army and Navy" (*CE*, IV, 79). It is significant that when Mr. Ramsay in *To the Lighthouse* quotes "The Charge of the Light Brigade," he repeats not the more reassuring passages of Tennyson's celebratory poem but the line "Someone had blundered" (*TL*, 33, 44). It was a view of war Stephen's daughter would affirm and deepen.

We have already seen that in *Jacob's Room*, *Mrs. Dalloway*, and *Three Guineas* war and its consequences are of major concern. As Joan Bennett noted many years ago, war is a form of human misery that haunts Woolf's books.[5] She was an instinctive pacifist who found it impossible to imagine a situation that justified the use of force. While others were carefully distinguishing between "just" and "unjust" wars, war and revolution, combatant and noncombatant service, all she could feel was an involuntary revulsion for the whole business.

Woolf was acutely conscious of *costs* and unable to justify them by any system of accounting. She understood that certain causes were worth defending with commitment, but her idea of legitimate defense did not include killing; for "the moment force is used, it becomes meaningless & unreal to me" (QB, II, 259). And so her prescription in *Three Guineas* for any woman who finds her country preparing for war is absolute withdrawal: "to take no share in patriotic demonstrations; to assent to no form of national self-praise; to make no part of any claque or audience that encourages war; to absent herself from military displays, tournaments, tattoos, prize-givings and all such ceremonies as encourage the desire to impose 'our' civilization or 'our' dominion upon other people" (*TG*, 198). Even when her pacifist faith is tested by her nephew's death in the Spanish civil war, she refuses to accept the standard anodynes for the death of heroes: "I can't feel, when Janet and Portia Holman talk of the encouragement Julian gave by his death, that they are right. They seem to me fire-eaters; emotional, distorted in the way patriots are distorted by the emotional excitement of death, glory, etc. all of which I detest, and think one should discount at all costs."[6]

Whether the cause was social justice or the power and prestige of nations, Woolf could feel no sympathy for those who contemplated violence. Here she differed from other left-wing intellectuals of the time, including her husband. During the General Strike in 1926 Britain seemed to many people on the brink of civil war, and the Woolfs were on the side of the strikers. But the means she and Leonard were willing to tolerate differed sharply: "She wanted peace, he wanted victory" (QB, II, 122). By the mid-1930s, when many English observers of the international situation reluctantly acknowledged the need for armed resistance to Italian and German Fascism, Woolf could not go along. At the 1935 Labour Party conference where these issues were hotly debated, she did not agree with those who demanded intervention: "My sympathies were with Salter who preached non-resistance. He's quite right. That should be our view" (*D*, IV, 345). The events in Europe in the four decades of her adult life would stretch this pacifist commitment to the limit and increasingly bring her into conflict with those on her own side. To her, nonviolence was an article of faith rather than a discretionary tactic—the closest thing to a religion her secular skepticism permitted.

Woolf's name does not appear among the sponsors of the many organizations engaged in war resistance between 1914 and 1941, the year of her death. One does not find her mentioned in the histories of the Peace Pledge Union or the No-Conscription Fellowship or the League of Nations Society or the Women's International League for Peace and Freedom. She was a novelist rather than a political activist, and her qualities did not shine on public platforms or committees. But she was intimate with many people whose primary energies were given to such work, most especially Leonard, and she was in deep sympathy with their aims. "We were all C.O.'s in the Great War," she wrote in her memoir of Julian Bell (QB, II, 258), making no distinction in that word "we" between the men who faced military service and the woman who was in any case exempt. Hers was a writer's resistance. She used her pen to undermine what she took to be the foundations of war: militarism and nationalism.

Her critical mode was satire, as we have seen. By exposing patriotic sentiment and martial ardor as forms of absurdity, she tried to counter the cradle-to-grave conditioning that treated them with reverence. In Woolf's work militant patriots always seem ridiculous. The stiff Tory gentlemen in *Mrs. Dalloway* gazing with reverence through the famous bow window of White's at the passing royal limousine are like marionettes as they "stood even straighter, and removed their hands, and seemed ready to attend their Sovereign, if need be, to the cannon's mouth, as their ancestors had done before them. The white busts and the little tables in the background covered with copies of the *Tatler* and bottles of soda water seemed to approve" (*MD*, 21–22). And we have seen how Lady Bruton's patriotic sentiments in the same novel are turned into comic opera. Heroic ardor is treated as so much bunkum. When North Pargiter in *The Years* calls on his mordant cousin Sara in 1917 with the melodramatic announcement "I leave for the

Front tonight," she can only picture him as a lieutenant in the "Royal Regiment of Rat-catchers" (*Y*, 307), perhaps a more accurate image of life in the trenches than one was likely to find in the official or unofficial propaganda.

When the war began, the young men at Oxford were being trained by such armchair patriots as the Professor of English Literature, Walter Raleigh, a man who thought of the Boer War as "a breath of fresh air" and greeted the guns of August with rapture. In Woolf's sarcastic essay on him the coming of the Great War is the fulfillment of his life: "He did what a man of his age could do. He drilled. He marched. He wrote pamphlets. He lectured more frequently than ever; he practically ceased to read. At length he was made historian of the Air Force. To his infinite satisfaction he consorted with soldiers. . . . The Professor of English Literature had lived at last" (*CE*, I, 317–18). Among the young men such patriotic fervor might have inspired is the gifted Andrew Ramsay in *To the Lighthouse*. But Woolf's picture of his end is very far from a heroic consummation and is relegated to a parenthesis: "[A shell exploded. Twenty or thirty young men were blown up in France, among them Andrew Ramsay, whose death, mercifully, was instantaneous]" (*TL*, 207). The anonymity, the parenthetic dismissal, the futility of this death are all intended to act as antidotes to the poison of the martial myth.

Woolf's contempt for patriotism and militarism was a constant of her life, but she felt it most strongly when her country supposedly required her absolute devotion, during the two world wars. The sight of her fellow Britons aflame with jingoistic passion revolted her. "I think patriotism is a base emotion," she wrote in her diary in 1915, after noting "the entire absence of emotion" in herself when the national anthem was played at a concert (*D*, I, 5). And July 1940, when the Battle of Britain is about to begin in earnest, finds her reading her account of the *Dreadnought* hoax to a public audience (QB, II, 251) and noting in her diary that patriotism and the other feelings bred by war are "all sentimental & emotional parodies of our real feelings" (*D*, V, 302). The distinction is important, since Woolf's love of England was real and went deep. In a letter to Ethel Smyth, she tried to differentiate her own feeling for her country from that of her more conventional friend: "Of course I'm 'patriotic': that is English, the language, farms, dogs, people: only we must enlarge the imagination, and take stock of the emotion" (*L*, VI, 235).[7]

Such swimming against the current reinforced Woolf's sense that she was an outsider in her society. But though she was certainly filing a minority report, she was not without allies. She had mentors and colleagues in the women's movement, in Bloomsbury, and among other antiwar writers in modern Britain, and she did not at first feel entirely isolated in her protest. She would have remembered that Mary Wollstonecraft attacked the military profession as "injurious to morality": "A standing army, for instance, is incompatible with freedom; because subordination and rigour are the very sinews of military discipline."[8] Clive Bell insisted in his *Civilization* that "a highly civilized person can never unquestioningly accept the ethics of patriotism."[9] And as late as 1939, E. M. Forster had written a sentence that became notorious but that Woolf probably admired: "I hate the idea of causes, and if I had to choose between betraying my country and betraying my friend, I hope I should have the guts to betray my country."[10]

Many pacifist writers of the period echoed or helped to shape Woolf's satiric attacks on militarism and nationalism. During the First World War Fenner Brockway wrote in the journal of the No-Conscription Fellowship, "Our opponents may say that it is better to live under home-made militarism than German. We reply that to us, militarism is the enemy, not a particular brand of it."[11] Beverley Nichols noted in his influential antiwar polemic *Cry Havoc!* (1933) that "the generic name for all these poisonous germs which cause war is . . . Patriotism."[12] And in 1934 Francis Meynell, who had been a conscientious objector in World War I, defined the writer's task in a passage that anticipated Woolf's attack on militarist conditioning in *Three Guineas*: "The martial music, the medals, the religious blessing of banners, the uniforms to catch the eye of the child as well as that of its nurse, the picture of the soldier always as a saviour, not as a destroyer—it is by ruses and disguises such as these that the adult mind is rendered childish, and the horror and pain and frustration and crippling of war are made a schoolboy's holiday."[13]

Woolf's cultural loyalties were European rather than British. She thought Proust the greatest novelist of the century, taught herself some Russian so she could collaborate on translations of Tolstoy and Dostoevsky, wrote essays on French and Russian literature. The Hogarth Press brought out works by Gorky, Chekhov, Tolstoy, Dostoevsky, Andreyev, Bunin, Svevo, Rilke, and Freud.[14] Bloomsbury cosmopolitanism was both cultural and experiential. Roger Fry introduced French Postimpressionist painting to a reluctant British public. Fry, Vanessa Bell, and Duncan Grant spent a significant portion of their lives in France; Leonard Woolf lived for seven years in Ceylon; Forster took two long journeys to India, lived in Egypt, fell in love with Italy, and these rival commitments are reflected in his work. It is understandable that patriotism found no quarter here. Woolf often writes about the refusal to think in narrow national terms. Miss Kilman in *Mrs. Dalloway* is fired from her teaching post during the war, even though her brother is killed fighting on the Allied side, "because she would not pretend that the Germans were all villains" (*MD*, 136). The air raid scene in *The Years* takes place as a motley group of friends—English, French, Polish—strengthen the ties that bind them. At the end of the scene Renny reflects, "I have spent the evening sitting in a coal cellar while other people try to kill each other above my head" (*Y*, 318). This sense of meaningless conflict is echoed in a letter Woolf wrote on the second day of World War II: "Yes, I sit in a dumb rage, being fought for by these children whom one wants to see making love to each other" (*L*, VI, 355). There is in all of these passages an angry refusal to contain one's sympathies within the borders of one's own country. This internationalism was the Bloomsbury code, a faith modern history made increasingly difficult to put into practice.

The ideal of harmony and fellow feeling across artificial human boundaries is reflected in Woolf's literary techniques. The attack on war and nationalism brought out her satiric streak, but the more positive aspect of her pacifist vision shaped her work in a different way. It pressed the disparate elements toward fusion. As one authority on pacifism has suggested, "The thought of a general peace presupposes a change of consciousness that would make the concept of unitary humanity possible."[15] This ideal is expressed in Woolf's novels as a series of opportunities for breaking down the barriers that separate people. In *To the Lighthouse* Mrs. Ramsay, so conscious of the "strife, divisions, difference of opinion, prejudices twisted into the very fibre of being," takes upon herself "the whole of the effort of merging and flowing and creating" (*TL*, 19, 131). Thus begins the movement toward harmony in the dinner party scene. But the party in *To the Lighthouse* was neither the first nor the last such event in Woolf's fiction. The social occasion in which a group of separate individuals come to feel—however temporarily—a sense of communion is an important incident in virtually every novel she wrote: *The Voyage Out* brings the English tourists together on a river journey and at a dance; *Mrs. Dalloway* culminates in a grand party; the six friends in *The Waves* hold a farewell dinner for Percival, "drawn into this communion by some deep, some common emotion" (*W*, 90–91); *The Years* ends with a family reunion, and *Between the Acts* with a village pageant. Such events are the set pieces of Woolf's novels, and they always serve to test the characters' capacities for identifying emotionally with others toward whom they initially feel indifference or hostility. Their triumphs are temporary and become increasingly difficult to achieve in the course of Woolf's career. But these efforts are always worth making and are the private basis of the more public virtues she celebrates: the feeling of comradeship across artificial barriers, the sense of human unity.

Woolf tries to put the petty divisions between people in perspective by viewing them from a great distance of time or space. *Orlando* skips through four centuries; *The Years* was originally supposed to carry us from the nineteenth into the twenty-first century; the pageant in *Between the Acts* moves from the Middle Ages to the present day. We recall the startling change of perspective in *Jacob's Room* that makes us see the events and characters as through the wrong end of a telescope. And Woolf often shifts the time scheme of her novels from human to natural, as in the interludes that separate the parts of *The Waves*, or the "Time Passes" section of *To the Lighthouse*, or the descriptions of the changing seasons that introduce the chapters of *The Years*. All these extensions of time and space show us how trivial the fierce contests that often dominate human life appear from a distance. Though Woolf had neither church nor scripture, she did experience an emotion that Freud called "the oceanic feeling" and saw as the basis of all religious faiths—a sense of oneness with her kind and with nature.[16]

Like all faiths, it made little sense in strictly rational terms. There is an uncanny quality in Woolf's characters that enables them to communicate telepathically. In *Mrs. Dalloway* Septimus and Clarissa think the same thoughts in almost the same words without having met. Clarissa accurately imagines his state of mind at the moment of his suicide and feels instinctively that "somehow it was her disaster—her disgrace" (*MD*, 203). Septimus, Woolf wrote, was intended to be Clarissa's "double";[17] he "was invented to complete the character of Mrs Dalloway" (*L*, V, 36). When one thinks of the difference of sex, of class, of age, of experience between the two characters, the assertion becomes more startling. And yet the novel manages to make the wordless communication between the two emotionally convincing. In *The Waves* the six characters do not speak to one another; they soliloquize. Yet they always know what the others are thinking, and their thoughts and feelings overlap and echo like the voices of a fugue. The result is a composite portrait, in Ralph Freedman's words, of "six figures not as a social group but as a single organism—one symbol of a common humanity."[18] In these experimental works Woolf deliberately smudges the outline of the individual and creates a world in which the borders that separate us become permeable and sometimes disappear altogether. The isolated, particular person comes to seem a social fiction; the individual identity is extended and diffused until it melts into the identity of others and of the world around it.[19] In Woolf's novels it is Mrs. Ramsay who best describes this "community of feeling with other people which emotion gives as if the walls of partition had become so thin that practically (the feeling was one of relief and happiness) it was all one stream, and chairs, tables, maps, were hers, were theirs, it did not matter whose" (*TL*, 175–76).

This vision of the possibility of human unity affects not only the larger elements of Woolf's fiction (plot, time scheme, characterization) but also the sentence and the paragraph. A passage from *Mrs. Dalloway* (which records Clarissa's thoughts as she walks through the West End to order flowers for her party) gives us a sense of how Woolf's prose embodies this ideal:

> Her only gift was knowing people almost by instinct, she thought, walking on. If you put her in a room with some one, up went her back like a cat's; or she purred. Devonshire House, Bath House, the house with the china cockatoo, she had seen them all lit up once; and remembered Sylvia, Fred, Sally Seton—such hosts of people; and dancing all night; and the waggons plodding past to market; and driving home across the Park. She remembered once throwing a shilling into the Serpentine. But every one remembered; what she loved was this, here, now, in front of her; the fat lady in the cab. Did it matter, then, she asked herself, walking towards Bond Street, did it matter that she must inevitably cease completely; all this must go on without her; did she resent it; or did it not become consoling to believe that death ended absolutely? but that somehow in the streets of London, on the ebb and flow of things, here, there, she survived, Peter survived, lived in each other, she being part, she was positive, of the trees at home; of the house there, ugly, rambling all to bits and pieces as it was; part of people she had never met; being laid out like a mist between the people she knew best, who lifted her on their branches as she has seen the trees lift the mist, but it spread ever so far, her life, herself. But what was she dreaming as she looked into Hatchards' shop window?
>
> (*MD*, 11–12)

The passage is capacious and inclusive rather than selective or narrowly focused. It moves seamlessly from the past of Clarissa's youth ("dancing all night") to this moment in middle age when she first feels her mortality, from herself to other people, from poetic reverie to prosaic observation of "the fat lady in the cab." At one moment the setting is transcendent, timeless and unlocalized; at others it is very precisely given. The Serpentine in Hyde Park, Bond Street, Hatchards' bookshop in Piccadilly: all are familiar London sights. It would be easy to trace the route of Clarissa's morning walk quite precisely on a map. But this does not prevent her mind from ranging far and wide. People melt into each other, into the buildings, into the trees, into the air itself, and yet we do not lose the feeling of Clarissa Dalloway thinking. The sentence expands to hold more than it seems possible for one sentence to carry, as in the remarkable 136-word example ("Did it matter, then, she asked herself . . ."), with its cascading phrases that cannot bear to make an end. The style is an instrument of coherence that refuses to compartmentalize or exclude, a verbal expression of the ideal of human unity. It represents only one strand in Woolf's thinking about human relationships, and we have seen how intensely aware she was of the threats to this ideal—in the estrangement, isolation, and conflict that pervade not only *Mrs. Dalloway* but all of her fiction. Nevertheless, the vision of community was an equally inalienable part of her identity and seems to me to have been the emotional basis of Woolf's pacifism. Its roots lay in her earliest childhood memories, when she saw her world as "globular; semi-transparent . . . not giving a clear outline" (*MB*, 66), and this fact helps to explain its persistence throughout her adult life and its embodiment in so many of her works.

It was an ideal that was to be severely tested by experience, however, and particularly by her experience of the First World War. Woolf says in her biography of Roger Fry that "a break must be made in every life when August 1914 is reached" (*RF*, 200), and her own is no exception. She and her associates in Bloomsbury were unusual in never for a moment feeling that this was a justified or necessary war. The more familiar pattern among her countrymen was a period of patriotic enthusiasm, with the young men rushing to volunteer for military service, followed by a gradual disillusionment as the horrendous slaughter in the trenches continued. For Woolf the war was an unmitigated disaster from first to last. The sight of her compatriots filled with enthusiasm to "Smash the Hun" and "Hang the Kaiser" appalled her: "Now that they have been roused," she wrote to Duncan Grant in 1915, "they seem full of the most violent and filthy passions" (*L*, II, 71). As the casualties mounted into the millions, her sense of the nightmare quality of it all grew: two of her cousins dead in one week, a single shell killing one of Leonard's brothers and seriously wounding another (*L*, II, 100, 171).

Those closest to her felt the same revulsion. Leonard Woolf called these years "the most horrible period of my life," in which nothing seemed to happen "except the pitiless, useless slaughter in France."[20] Clive Bell wrote in his 1915 pamphlet *Peace at Once* (which was quickly seized and destroyed by the police) that "war is mere destruction and butchery," that "victors and vanquished are almost meaningless terms. Everyone loses; sorrow, suffering, and death are the only winners."[21] And on Armistice Day Vanessa Bell could feel neither triumph nor joy: "The waste of the whole thing strikes me as more idiotic than ever."[22] The dominant images in Bloomsbury were of futility, useless sacrifice, and ruinous waste. These sentiments were not widely shared during the war, though they came to be accepted after the event by millions of people who would have found them anathema in 1914–18. Bloomsbury was part of a small dissident minority. Vanessa Bell wrote to her sister in 1915, "I see more & more that we are completely isolated from our kind."[23] It is not quite true that all the Bloomsbury males were conscientious objectors during the war, as Woolf claims. Some received medical exemptions; some never even came before a tribunal. But they were all antiwar and sympathetic to the C.O.'s. There were five million British soldiers who served in the war and only 16,500 conscientious objectors, a statistic that reveals how tiny the band of protestors actually was.[24]

As the war finally came to an end, there was a moment of hope. Surely now it would be possible to acknowledge its futility and to make certain that it had after all been a war to end war, as some of the leaders had promised. The world would be rebuilt on new foundations. The characters in *The Years* who have survived the air raid drink to this vision of the future: "'Here's to the New World!' they all cried, raising their glasses, and clinking them together" (*Y*, 315). As the end of the war approaches, Woolf records feeling "this extraordinary back ground of hope; a tremendously enlarged version of the feeling I can remember as a child as Christmas approached" (*D*, I, 200). Perhaps out of this tragic carnage a greater international understanding could emerge. Bloomsbury might help bring it to birth. In 1919 Keynes published his blistering and far-sighted attack on the Versailles Treaty, *The Economic Consequences of the Peace*, "a book that influences the world," Woolf notes in her diary (*D*, II, 33). Leonard Woolf had been working for the creation of "an international authority to prevent war" and published "the first detailed study of a League of Nations" in the middle of the war itself.[25] His commitment to the League was to consume a major part of his time and energy for the next twenty years.

But despite such hopes for peace, some alarming symptoms were already beginning to appear. The most disturbing to Woolf was the general eagerness to forget the war entirely as soon as it was over—a response we have seen at the heart of *Mrs. Dalloway*. Could such an enormous disaster simply be expunged from memory? If so, it was only a matter of time before it was repeated. Woolf's insistence on recollecting the war in the decade after the Armistice is essential to an understanding of her work in the 1920s. The war not only helped to shape *Jacob's Room* and *Mrs. Dalloway* but is often recalled in her diary as well. In 1920 she can still write, "Our generation is daily scourged by the bloody war" (*D*, II, 51). A year later she describes the wounded veterans she sees constantly in London, with "stiff legs, single legs, sticks shod with rubber, & empty sleeves" as well as the "dreadful looking spiders propelling themselves along the platform—men all body—legs trimmed off close to the body" (*D*, II, 93). Winifred Holtby noticed as early as 1932 that Woolf introduced some reference to the war in nearly everything she wrote, "as though its memory were the scar of an old wound she could not hide." [26]

It took a decade and more for the survivors to be able to write about it not in the elevated form of "war poetry" but in prosaic detail. The most important literary and autobiographical accounts—Siegfried Sassoon's *Memoirs of a Fox-Hunting Man* and *Memoirs of an Infantry Officer*, Robert Graves's *Goodbye to All That*, Richard Aldington's *Death of a Hero*, Edmund Blunden's *Undertones of War*, Ernest Hemingway's *A Farewell to Arms*, R. C. Sherriff's *Journey's End*, Vera Brittain's *Testament of Youth*, as well as (on the other side) Erich Maria Remarque's *All Quiet on the Western Front*—were all published between 1928 and 1933, though Ford Madox Ford's Tietjens tetralogy (1924–28) anticipated the vogue by a few years. This interval was necessary before the veterans could detach the events from the heroic illusions the war had created. Sassoon insists that "all squalid, abject, and inglorious elements in war should be remembered." [27] Graves ends his book with the hope that after ten years of trying to record his memories of the war without distortion, he may finally have "learned to tell the truth—nearly." [28] His account is a detailed, realistic description of life in the trenches, with all signs of glamour or heroism expunged. The tone is deflationary, ironic; incidents that a more martial writer would have described tragically are often treated as absurdities. The impulse is to diminish rather than enlarge. Such books were impossible to write closer to the war itself. They imply that the enormous sacrifice had been meaningless and unnecessary. Only when the grief of the survivors had run its course could they bear to think that death in combat had been a mere "stupid waste." [29]

Out of this delayed revulsion a new and influential image of the war emerged: that of a fratricidal conflict in which the combatants had no real quarrel. This Bloomsbury had felt from the first, but it was only now that the idea became generally acceptable. In Sherriff's powerful play *Journey's End* the captured German soldier is merely a pathetic boy, and a young English officer concludes, "The Germans are really quite decent, aren't they? I mean, outside the newspapers?"[30] Vera Brittain's *Testament of Youth* pictures the English and German soldiers as men forced to fight who "bore no grudge against one another." She tells the story of a grave on the English side of the line "inscribed with the words: 'Here lie two gallant German officers.' The men who put up the cross congratulated themselves a little on their British magnanimity, but when, later, they pushed the enemy out of the trenches in front of the wood, they found another grave as carefully tended, and inscribed: 'Here lie five brave English officers.'"[31] Remarque's *All Quiet on the Western Front* is based on a similar vision, seen through the eyes of the disillusioned German combatants.

Such debunking of what Brittain calls "that voracious trio" God, King, and Country[32] fed directly into the strong pacifist movement of the 1930s. There is a clear connection between these delayed reconsiderations of the war and the "King and Country" debate staged at the Oxford Union in 1933, in which the Oxford students voted heavily in favor of the motion "that this House will in no circumstances fight for its King and Country." The historian Martin Ceadel calls this event, which shocked patriotic Englishmen, "a backward-looking protest at what had happened in August 1914."[33] It crystallized a belated revulsion against the First World War and ratified the promise that it would be the last.

Fifteen years after the Armistice, pacifism had suddenly become fashionable. In 1933 and 1934 it was transformed from a fringe into a popular movement, with its own propagandists, mass organizations, and public meetings. Canon Sheppard's Peace Pledge Union (which required its members to sign the statement "I renounce War and never again, directly or indirectly, will I support or sanction another") attracted 150,000 people, though many of them were not as uncompromisingly pacifist as the pledge they signed. Its populist politics were a frank bid for mass support, as in Sheppard's plan for a "Peace Circus" in which luminaries from Albert Einstein to Charlie Chaplin would preach pacifism to the converted.[34] It is striking that the two most influential antiwar books of these years, Beverley Nichols's *Cry Havoc!*

(1933) and A. A. Milne's *Peace with Honour* (1934), were produced by men now better known for writing children's books.
Their style is intellectually primitive. Milne begins by telling
us, "In short, I think that war is a Bad Thing."[35]

But the real problem with the pacifist fashion of the mid-
thirties was not that it was simplistic but that it had come too
late. The political realities of Europe had changed radically in
the previous five years, and the shift in popular sentiment
that might once have been strong enough to prevent another
war was by then powerless to stop it. There is an underlying
despair in the antiwar activities of Bloomsbury at this time.
When Forster asks Virginia Woolf in 1935 to attend an anti-
Fascist conference, he writes, "I have no doubt as to the
importance of people like ourselves *inside* the conference. We
do represent the last utterances of the civilised." But his letter
contains two extraordinary typographical errors: "impotence"
for "importance," "past" for "last."[36] Stephen Spender recalls
asking Leonard Woolf in 1934 if there would be another war;
"he replied: 'Yes, of course. Because when the nations enter
into an armaments race, as they are doing at present, no other
end is possible.'"[37] In the following year Virginia Woolf writes
in her diary the terse sentence "War seems inevitable" (*D*,
IV, 336).

II

What had changed everything, of course, was the emergence
of Hitler and Mussolini and the martial ardor they successfully revived in their countrymen. Most pacifists were still
working with the assumption that no country really wanted
war and that popular sentiment would not support another.
What then was one to make of the mass following the Fascist
dictators had attracted or of Mussolini's statement that Fascism "believes neither in the possibility nor the utility of perpetual peace. It thus repudiates the doctrine of Pacifism"?
The Woolfs certainly knew the passage, having published the
essay from which it comes.[38] The pacifist treatment of World
War I as a pointless conflict between nations that had no real

quarrel was no longer a useful paradigm for understanding contemporary events. The triumph of Hitler created a crisis for those in the antiwar movement. They might stick their heads in the sand, as A. A. Milne still did in 1934 (he called his chapter on Hitler "Fascist Interlude"); they could, like Bertrand Russell, lead an intellectual double life, continuing to write that a world war was worse than any foreign occupation while feeling that the Nazis were "utterly revolting—cruel, bigoted, and stupid morally and intellectually" and must therefore be resisted;[39] they could conclude, as Leonard Woolf reluctantly did in 1935, that war was virtually inevitable and "that Britain must make itself strong enough on land and sea and in the air to defeat Hitler."[40]

Most of them found it extremely difficult to accept the apparent bankruptcy of their movement and of the hopes on which it had rested. Pacifism became more and more indistinguishable from appeasement. Major territorial concessions to Hitler were defended in one pacifist journal as "an honest and sensible attempt to settle grievances instead of quarrelling and finally fighting about them."[41] It was perhaps a case of finding the right treatment after the disease had advanced too far to be cured. As Leonard Woolf concludes in his autobiography, "The perpetual tragedy of history is that things are perpetually being done ten or twenty years too late."[42] Keynes had warned in 1919 that the vindictive peace terms of Versailles would only produce a belligerent Germany eager for revenge, but at that point France and England were determined to "make Germany pay." By the mid-thirties the machine could no longer be put in reverse, and the middle ground between rival nations had once again become a no-man's land.

This polarization produced a hopeless dilemma for pacifists and war resisters. When the war broke out, the movement was close to collapse. Pacifist propagandists began to write patriotic tracts. In 1940 A. A. Milne brought out his pamphlet *War with Honour* as a kind of apology for his earlier *Peace with Honour*, though it is recognizably in the same style: this war, he says, is "not a war between nations, but a war between Good and Evil."[43] A few kept the faith: Vera Brittain, for example, published a book in 1942 called *Humiliation with Honour*, and Ralph and Frances Partridge (on the fringes of Bloomsbury) lived though the painful experiences recorded in Frances's book *A Pacifist's War*. They were distinctly in the minority. Antiwar writers like Bertrand Russell, Storm Jameson, and many others renounced their former convictions. As one cynical member of the Peace Pledge Union said at the time, "There is more rejoicing in the Ministry of Information over one repentant pacifist, than over ninety and nine good militarists which need no repentance." [44]

Bloomsbury certainly had its share of them. Leonard Woolf decided to join the Home Guard when the government appealed for help, despite his wife's disapproval of his decision. [45] In 1940 he published a book with the Orwellian title *War for Peace* justifying Britain's role in the conflict. David Garnett and Duncan Grant, both C.O.'s in the First World War, firmly supported the Second. Garnett "completely abandoned" his pacifism and accepted a commission in the R.A.F.; Grant wrote later that "the circumstances of the second war were so different to the first that I had no conscientious objection to joining the Home Guard." [46] By 1940 E. M. Forster was delivering "Three Anti-Nazi Broadcasts" and defending this war unequivocally: "In Hitler's war Germany is not a hostile country, she is a hostile principle. She stands for a new and bad way of life and, if she won, would be bound to destroy our ways." [47]

What effect did this new patriotic consensus among her previous allies have on Virginia Woolf? She could not see the issues in the required new way, and her spirit was lacerated in the last years of her life by an increasing sense of isolation. Though she was willing to acknowledge "that this war's better than last" (*L*, VI, 483), the similarities between these two orgies of killing seemed to her to outweigh the differences, and the erosion of the group support on which she could count in the First World War must have been devastating. The preparations for the new conflict merely struck her as "1914 but without even the illusion of 1914." She calls the 1939 declaration of war "the worst of all my life's experiences. . . . One

merely feels that the killing machine has to be set in action."
And as the war goes on, she records the feeling, two months
before her suicide, that "we live without a future. Thats whats
queer, with our noses pressed to a closed door" (*D*, V, 170,
234–35, 355). The Woolfs had been planning to take their own
lives in the event of a successful Nazi invasion of Britain, since
a prominent Jewish socialist like Leonard and an antifascist
writer like Virginia were virtually certain to be sent to a
concentration camp. In fact, both their names appear on a
Gestapo arrest list prepared for the planned German attack.[48]
But by 1941 the danger of invasion had passed, and Virginia
Woolf's despair cannot really be related to fears for her own
safety or Leonard's. Actually, she was quite fearless.

But Woolf had come to the end of her idealism and was
forced to recognize the barrenness of the faith she could not
bring herself to give up. Her "madness" reasserted itself; she
began to hear voices she had not heard since 1915, the date of
her last complete breakdown. The connection between these
periods of mental instability does not strike me as accidental.
Vera Brittain, in her obituary notice of Woolf, wrote, "Her end
was perhaps a kind of protest, the most terrible and effective
she could make, against the real hell which international
conflict creates."[49] And Octavia Wilberforce, the doctor and
friend who was treating Woolf in the week before her death,
concluded that "it was the association of the 1914 War & her
worst phase that had haunted her mind now." On the day
after Woolf's suicide Wilberforce wrote, "As long as war was
on I don't think it would have been possible to hold V's mind
& without War I'm sure I could have helped & completely
saved her. Tragic."[50]

Woolf's disorientation is evident in the style of her last
works. Gone are the long, swelling sentences that seem to
include everything and everyone in a single suspended gram-
matical unit. Her prose becomes nervous, atomistic, and dis-
junct. The diary entries written in time of war are jagged,
such as "Madrid not fallen. Chaos. Slaughter. War surrounding our island" (*D*, V, 32) and seldom written in complex sentences, as in this description of an air raid: "They came very

close. We lay down under the tree. The sound was like someone sawing in the air just above us. We lay flat on our faces,
hands behind head. Dont close yr teeth said L." (*D*, V, 311).
This is as near as Woolf comes to the style of Ernest Hemingway, and it affected her last novel, *Between the Acts*, as well as
her diary. Here is Miss La Trobe feeling she has lost the attention of her audience: "Every second they were slipping the
noose. Her little game had gone wrong. If only she'd a backcloth to hang between the trees—to shut out cows, swallows,
present time! But she had nothing. She had forbidden music.
Grating her fingers in the bark, she damned the audience.
Panic seized her. Blood seemed to pour from her shoes" (*BA*,
210). As James Naremore has noted, Woolf's art "is aimed
at creating or revealing a world where there are no discrete
events. . . . From the first her style was designed to affirm a
continuity between things, to show that life cannot be ar-
bitrarily divided."[51] But it was precisely this "affirmation" that
the failure of her pacifist ideals called into question. She had
come to distrust the mellifluous style of her earlier works.
"Parsimony" was to be the aim of *Between the Acts*, she writes,
grown out of "shame at my own verbosity" (*D*, V, 352). The
reassuring cadences of *Mrs. Dalloway* or *To the Lighthouse* or
The Waves would no longer flow. *Between the Acts*, as we shall
see in the next chapter, was the product of a different vision.

The underlying assumption of all the different antiwar and
pacifist movements of the century had been the possibility of
"a change of consciousness that would make the concept of
unitary humanity possible."[52] Woolf had worked for such a
transformation all her life. Her idealism was as indispensable
to her work as her critical satire and may be said to have
licensed it. If the idealism turned out to be mere illusion,
the secular faith in community that had sustained her would
seem no more reliable than the Christianity she could never
take seriously. This was a crisis of belief as devastating in its
way as the Victorian breakdown of confidence in a benevolent
deity.

Pacifism, nonviolence, and international cooperation had
all been profoundly moral commitments for those who be-

lieved in them, not mere political tactics. They were rooted in scripture—in the commandment "Thou shalt not kill," in Christ's injunction to turn the other cheek and to "love thy neighbor as thyself," in the warning that those "that take the sword shall perish with the sword." Probably the largest group of pacifists had based their conscientious objection on their Christian faith. Tolstoy was the first writer in modern times to link Christianity with an absolute refusal to fight, and his pacifist works were widely known in other countries.[53] Such English pacifists as Leyton Richards, H. R. L. Sheppard, G. H. C. Macgregor, Max Plowman, and Cecil John Cadoux all published influential books between the wars explaining the Christian basis of nonviolence. What strikes one in reading such works is their untroubled confidence in the triumph of their cause and the authority of their vision. Hindsight makes us aware of bland assurances that now have a hollow ring. Canon Sheppard writes in 1935, "The history of the Jews is the supreme epic of non-resistance; their survival the complete and conclusive proof of the futility of force."[54]

Having no Christian faith, Woolf was likely to be suspicious of such easy affirmations. But the more secular forms of pacifism were at first just as optimistic. The great spokesman for nonviolent resistance at this historical moment was, of course, Mahatma Gandhi. His writings and actions influenced many Western pacifists who were important to Woolf, such as George Lansbury, the leader of the Labour Party from 1931 to 1935 and a believer in unilateral disarmament (see *D*, IV, 345). Lansbury wrote in 1938 that "Gandhi has staked out a road which, if followed, would free mankind from the curse of war; but his policy must be accepted without compromise."[55] Gandhi's belief in nonviolent resistance as a way of preventing war was based on his conviction that its moral force would convert the enemy into a friend. He had a profoundly idealistic faith in the ultimate goodness of man. "If Englishmen were as a nation to become non-violent at heart," he writes during the Abyssinian crisis, "the moral force generated by such an act would stagger Italy into willing surrender of her designs." And he was certain that if the German

Jews "adopt active non-violence, i.e. fellow feeling, for the gentile Germans . . . the stoniest German heart will melt." [56] It was a faith Woolf very much wanted to share, but her realism made it impossible for her to do so. Increasingly she found herself linked to a band of idealists without a viable theory of tactics.

Those in the war resistance movement who had thought more seriously about tactics were not in the strict sense pacifists at all: they believed in collective security as embodied in the League of Nations and in mutual disarmament treaties. Bloomsbury was heavily involved in this movement—through Goldsworthy Lowes Dickinson at Cambridge, who may have invented the phrase "League of Nations" and was "the first person in this country to formulate the idea," according to Forster's biography of him;[57] through the influence of Keynes; and most significantly through Leonard Woolf, whose book *International Government* (1916) formulated "the first definite plans for shaping the League." [58] The League was established after the First World War with the highest hopes that here, finally, was an organization designed to prevent war that had a reasonable chance of success. Those who established it were not dreamy idealists but the political leaders of powerful nations. And the whole machinery of the League—including the controversial sanctions clause in its covenant, which proposed an international "military, naval or air force" [59] to stop the aggression of individual states—seemed rooted in the realities of world politics.

It was therefore particularly shocking that this instrument of *Realpolitik* was to be no more effective in preventing war than the Quakers or the Peace Pledge Union. From the perspective of pure pacifists this was the result of the League's inherent militarism, as ratified in the sanctions clause, which in effect licensed war so long as it was agreed to by the more powerful nations.[60] But even those, like Leonard Woolf, who had no such pacifist scruples and worked hard for the League saw early on that its chances for success were slim. The United States Congress would not commit the country to membership; the losing belligerents of the First World War were at first excluded; the organization quickly became an instrument of Anglo-French hegemony. Furthermore, the history of the thirties showed that the League's threats and sanctions were quite ineffectual in a real international emergency like the Japanese invasion of Manchuria or the Italian attack on Abyssinia. By the time Hitler began his series of incursions and annexations, most of its supporters knew it could be written off. Another Bloomsbury idealistic commitment had turned out to be based on illusion. As Leonard Woolf was later to admit, he had spent "between 150,000 and 200,000 hours" of his life "sitting on committees and writing books and memoranda," trying to make the world a better place, only to discover that none of his ideals had been brought nearer to realization and that he might just as well have spent his time playing Ping-Pong.[61] Virginia Woolf was exposed to his frustration day after day, year after year, and the knowledge that even this comparatively hardheaded approach to war prevention was doomed to fail could only have heightened her despair.

It was a despair that expressed not only the hatred of war she had always felt but a new sense of intellectual frustration. What could account for the failure of all these noble schemes? Why had the combined efforts of so many intelligent people of good will and high principle come to nothing? What was the flaw in the antiwar argument that they had failed to understand? Once it became clear that the logic of war was somehow stronger than the logic of peace, it was natural to ask such questions. They were to lead to a fundamental critique of the movement and the assumptions on which it was based. Chief among these in Bloomsbury was rationalism. The power of reason to make the world a better place was an unquestioned assumption in the Cambridge circle that nurtured the young men of the group. They were convinced that most human problems could eventually be solved by patient and scrupulous intellectual investigation. If Bloomsbury worshipped a god, it was the human brain. This rationalist faith is evident even in the title of Goldsworthy Lowes Dickinson's major pacifist work, *War: Its Nature, Cause and Cure* (1923), with its echo of medical treatises.

The same bedrock belief in the power of rational understanding can be seen in the work of Leonard Woolf. He writes
in *The Framework of a Lasting Peace* (1917) that he will be "dealing with men as pre-eminently noble in reason" and that his
"only means of locomotion are logic and reason."[62] It is as
though he had forgotten the rest of the speech from *Hamlet* to
which he alludes. When he recalls this phase of his life in his
autobiography, his faith in reason remains unquestioned. As
World War I drew to a close, he writes,

> the supreme political problem was to find means, if possible,
> for preventing war. That meant that one must find the chief
> causes of war and one must discover methods to destroy or
> counteract those causes. As in all cases of political action, to
> do this required the use of reason. To find the causes of social
> or political phenomena you have to use your reason to analyse
> a series of complicated situations or events; to find means of
> influencing or altering the series of events requires a con-
> structive use of reason.[63]

The whole passage, including the dryness and relentless logic
of the prose, suggests a kind of tunnel-vision rationalism. The
mind at work here—analytic, judicious, and plodding—was
probably incapable of grasping something Leonard Woolf's
wife understood instinctively: that even the best human beings are driven by forces not so amenable to rational control.
At bottom Virginia Woolf had much less faith in the triumph
of reason than most of her Bloomsbury colleagues, and this is
reflected both in the imaginative and emotional flights of her
prose (even her discursive prose) and in her distrust of the
syllogistic arguments and great rational structures men like
Leonard were busy building.

But she was not to be the only local renegade on this issue.
The most brilliant critique of Bloomsbury rationalism came
from within the group. It was the paper Keynes read to the
Memoir Club in September 1938, an analysis of the limitations
of their own vision that Woolf thought "very packed profound
& impressive" (*D*, V, 168) when she heard it. Written on the
eve of the Munich crisis, Keynes's essay is related to the sense
of bankruptcy the war resistance movement felt at this mo-

ment. His words have a valedictory air, as though he is saying farewell to a whole vision of human nature:

> We were among the last of the Utopians, or meliorists as they are sometimes called, who believe in a continuing moral progress by virtue of which the human race already consists of reliable, rational, decent people, influenced by truth and objective standards. . . . In short, we repudiated all versions of the doctrine of original sin, of there being insane and irrational springs of wickedness in most men. . . . As cause and consequence of our general state of mind we completely misunderstood human nature, including our own. The rationality which we attributed to it led to a superficiality, not only of judgment, but also of feeling. It was not only that intellectually we were pre-Freudian, but we had lost something which our predecessors had without replacing it.[64]

Keynes shifts the ground from logical analysis to psychology and religion. It is as though the whole rationalist basis of war prevention—the assumption that an intellectual understanding of causes would lead to cure—is under attack. Keynes seems to be calling for a new understanding of human nature.

What he sought had already been provided in the works of Freud, particularly in three essays that directly commented on the causes of war: "Thoughts for the Times on War and Death" (1915), *Civilization and Its Discontents* (1929), and *Why War?* (1933), the last an exchange of letters with Albert Einstein. All were published in English translations by the Hogarth Press, and in 1939 the Woolfs brought out a volume consisting of substantial selections from these three works under the title *Civilization, War and Death*.[65] Freud's gloomy conclusion is that "war cannot be abolished."[66] Violence satisfies an instinctual need in human beings that is in permanent conflict with the rational, civilizing code by which they are forced to live. The suppression of instinctual need that civilized behavior imposes cannot be indefinitely sustained and at intervals produces the volcanic explosion we call war. Human beings, as Freud puts it in *Civilization and Its Discontents*, are "creatures among whose instinctual endowments is to be reckoned a powerful share of aggressiveness. As a result, their neighbour is for them not only a potential helper or sexual object, but also someone who tempts them to satisfy their aggressiveness on him, to exploit his capacity for work without compensation, to use him sexually without his consent, to seize his possessions, to humiliate him, to cause him pain, to torture and to kill him." And as proof Freud offers the decisive event in modern history: "Anyone who calls to mind . . . the horrors of the recent World War—anyone who calls these things to mind will have to bow humbly before the truth of this view." [67]

Woolf's familiarity with Freud is a matter of some dispute. The firm she and Leonard had founded was Freud's British publisher. Her brother Adrian Stephen and his wife, Karen, were among the first English psychoanalysts, as was Lytton Strachey's brother James, who translated Freud and edited the Standard Edition. She was obviously familiar with psychoanalytic ideas, as her relatively early essay "Freudian Fiction" (1920) and a number of references throughout her work suggest. Yet she claimed as late as 1932 that she had never read anything by Freud or his disciples (*L*, V, 36).

In 1939, shortly after World War II began, she determined to read him in earnest: "to enlarge the circumference. to give my brain a wider scope: to make it objective; to get outside." Her impulse grows out of a new sense of the narrowness of her own vision and a determination to see beyond its familiar range. Her reading both impressed and depressed her, as a diary entry written a week later suggests: "Freud is upsetting: reducing one to whirlpool; & I daresay truly. If we're all instinct, the unconscious, whats all this about civilisation, the whole man, freedom, &c?" And she approves of Freud's honesty in insisting on "the falseness of loving one's neighbours," which may refer to the passage quoted above (*D*, V, 248, 250). Her reading notes on Freud link his insights to her own obsession with the causes of the two world wars.[68] His work had helped her to think about these issues in fresh ways and was to have a significant impact on the way she wrote about civilization and instinct in her last novel.

Freud's theory of war implied that believers in pacifism and nonviolence were intellectually naive because their faith was founded on a misunderstanding of human nature. Keynes had said that Bloomsbury made the mistake of rejecting "all versions of the doctrine of original sin." Freud might be said to have provided a psychological version for modern religious skeptics, and there is little doubt that Woolf found it of great interest. Finally, however, her way of looking at these issues differed from his. For he was a man and she was a woman, a distinction in "human nature" that from Woolf's point of view the psychoanalysts had not sufficiently taken into account.

Her own understanding of the subject—not just in *Three Guineas* but from the start of her career—is based on distinguishing a masculine from a feminine human nature. She called the First World War "this preposterous masculine fiction" even in the middle of it (*L*, II, 76). And when, in *A Room of One's Own*, she set out to describe men's consuming ambition, she anticipated Freud's passage on human aggression, quoted above, except that she intended it to apply only to men, whose possessive and acquisitive instinct "drives them to desire other people's fields and goods perpetually; to make frontiers and flags; battleships and poison gas; to offer up their own lives and their children's lives" (*AROO*, 58). The distinction becomes the basis of *Three Guineas*, and its most controversial idea. We recall that Woolf originally thought of calling the book *Men Are Like That* (*D*, IV, 77). She argues that at least one human instinct is not found equally in men and women: "For though many instincts are held more or less in common by both sexes, to fight has always been the man's habit, not the woman's" (*TG*, 13). So convinced is she of men's habitual combativeness that she cannot even bring herself to trust the pacifist organizations dominated by men. And so in *Three Guineas* she insists that women in the antiwar movement must work separately. Their aim must be to challenge the ethos of "masculinity" that makes war seem acceptable. As she puts it in her 1939 reading notes on Freud, "Thus the woman part is to achieve the emancipation of man [from 'the male attributes']. In that lies the only hope of permanent peace." [69]

Woolf's separatism may also have been influenced by her sense of the combativeness that underlay the words and actions of some of the men in the peace movement. Her reading of the belated "war books" that appeared around 1930 was surprisingly hostile, as a suppressed passage in the essay that became "Professions for Women" shows. "If I were reviewing [war] books now," she wrote in 1931, "I would say this was a stupid and violent and hateful and idiotic and trifling and ignoble and mean display. I would say I am bored to death by war books. I detest the masculine point of view. I am bored by his heroism, virtue, and honour" (*P*, 164). This outburst may at first seem incomprehensible, since the books she was attacking were usually seen as antiwar. What Woolf noticed in them, nevertheless, was a protest vitiated by a continuing romantic glorification of fighting. This was not, I think, a perverse reading of some of these works. For example, Sassoon's *Memoirs of an Infantry Officer* is often treated as a classic exposé of the war. Sassoon describes his growing sense of its futility, which culminates in the publication of his famous (or infamous) letter of protest. In it he wrote: "*I believe that this War, upon which I entered as a war of defence and liberation, has now become a war of aggression and conquest . . . for ends which I believe to be evil and unjust*." [70] The words are uncompromising and courageous, but Sassoon's subsequent actions cannot be said to have endorsed them. In the later *Sherston's Progress* he treats his protest letter as an unaccountable lapse, thinks of his psychiatrist at the military hospital as someone working "to cure me of my pacifist errors," and decides to go back to the front because it is "better to be in the trenches with those whose experience I had shared and understood than with this medley of civilians." [71] For a serious pacifist Sassoon's war trilogy makes very unsatisfactory reading. And his vacillation was not unique.

Even in the nonviolence movement inspired by Gandhi, Woolf might have noted a comparable impurity. Gandhi always described his tactics as a manly form of active resistance and resented any attempt to see them as "passive." "Nonviolence," he wrote in 1926, "presupposes ability to strike. It is a conscious deliberate restraint put upon one's desire for vengeance. But vengeance is any day superior to passive, effeminate and helpless submission."[72] This buried fear of lacking virility comes to the surface when Gandhi's ideas are translated for Western consumption. In Richard Gregg's *The Power of Non-Violence*, an influential summary by an American disciple, Gandhi's theory of nonviolent resistance is described as a superior martial weapon that uses "the very principles of military strategy." The "peaceful resister" is said to have the "will to conquer," along with "the important virtues of the violent fighter,—enterprise, courage, strenuous action, and endurance."[73] When such writers presented themselves as spokesmen for the cause of peace, was it any wonder that Woolf mistrusted the organizations they founded and the gospel they preached?

This may help us to understand Woolf's link between pacifism and feminism in *Three Guineas*. All during the 1930s, but especially as she was writing this book, she read the newspapers assiduously in order to compile evidence for her theory of the connections between "masculinity" and war. She pasted press cuttings, letters, and extracts from works she had read into three bound volumes, which she used as a quarry for the damning quotations in *Three Guineas*.[74] The items she collected reinforced her theory that the impulses that lead to war are rooted in the male psyche or in the way men are brought up.

Woolf's approach to the problem was both a product and a further cause of her growing sense of isolation. There were virtually no precedents for her views in the antiwar literature of the time—whether written by men or by women. Even Vera Brittain's *Testament of Youth*, which Woolf read "with extreme greed" when it first came out (*D*, IV, 177), did not blame the war on men, though Brittain was both a pacifist and a feminist. She wanted, as she recalls in a later book, to write "the epic of the women who went to the war,"[75] but the word "epic" suggests that she had not succeeded in avoiding the heroic vision of war any more than had her male counterparts. Other women from whom Woolf might have expected approval were quite critical. In an exchange of letters with Princess Bibesco, who wrote to ask for Woolf's help in an anti-

Fascist exhibition, Woolf asks why the "woman question" is being ignored and receives the snappish answer: "I am afraid that it had not occurred to me that in matters of ultimate importance even feminists cd. wish to segregate & label the sexes" (quoted in *D*, IV, 273). And Vita Sackville-West wrote to question the whole theory of sex differentiation proposed in *Three Guineas*: "Is it not true that many women are extremely bellicose and urge their men to fight? What about the white feather campaign in the last war? I am entirely in agreement with you that they ought not to be like that, but the fact remains that they frequently are."[76]

From the Bloomsbury males she could hardly have expected much support. Leonard "gravely approves" of *Three Guineas* when he reads it but withholds real praise (*D*, V, 127, 133); others had no hesitation in dismissing the book. As Quentin Bell recalls, "Maynard Keynes was both angry and contemptuous; it was, he declared, a silly argument and not very well written. What really seemed wrong with the book— and I am speaking here of my own reactions at the time—was the attempt to involve a discussion of women's rights with the far more agonising and immediate question of what we were to do in order to meet the ever-growing menace of Fascism and war. The connection between the two questions seemed tenuous and the positive suggestions wholly inadequate" (*QB*, II, 205).

The combined desertion, skepticism, and outright hostility of all these former allies must have caused Woolf acute pain. Her divergence from those on whom she had depended left her stranded. The minority report might have to be filed by a minority of one. But her anguish was not merely personal. Rather, it expressed the sense of hopelessness that the whole antiwar movement had come to by the late thirties. It was all very well to demand a solution to the problem of what to do "in order to meet the ever-growing menace of Fascism and war." But other writers on the subject, whether they had pinned their hopes on Christian principles or international class solidarity or collective security or nonviolent resistance, had been no more successful than Woolf in finding such solutions. Behind her last writings on the subject there is an unspoken acknowledgment that it was too late, that war could no longer be prevented, that another generation was to be wasted. In *Three Guineas* and *Between the Acts* she records the anxieties of the present moment and stretches the time scheme to the distant past and future. Her feminist belief in the possibility of remolding the sexes is clearly not conceived as the work of a single generation, since the traditional molds had themselves evolved over hundreds of years. The pacifist utopia of human unity would not come into being without new men and women. As she writes to Lady Simon in 1940, in a letter that raises questions to which she had no answers, "Can one change sex characteristics? How far is the women's movement a remarkable experiment in that transformation? Mustn't our next task be the emancipation of man? How can we alter the crest and the spur of the fighting cock?" The faith voiced in this letter that the "sexes can adapt themselves" (*L*, VI, 379–80) was a vision only—the last remnant of Woolf's idealism, which the events of her time had worn to a frayed thread. That hope was her lifeline. She would cling to it until the end.

11

Between the Acts and the Coming of War

In none of her other novels is Woolf as conscious of and responsive to contemporary events as in *Between the Acts*. Conceived early in 1938, finished in February 1941, and published only after her death in that year, the book reflects the impact on her of the extraordinary circumstances of the time—the Munich crisis, the declaration of war, the fall of Paris, the preparations for a German invasion, the Battle of Britain, the Blitz—moments in the history of her country and her civilization in which the threat of catastrophic ruin was constant. She was not a reporter and had no wish to record these incidents directly in her work or to write a "topical novel." But as her diary for those years shows, she was constantly responding to the decisive historical events taking place. This persistent intrusion of public life into her private diary was unprecedented in her career, so it comes as no surprise that the sense of crisis also affected her fiction in deep if indirect ways. What she wrote about Henry James's reaction to the coming of the First World War could be said of her own response to the Second: "It was Belgium, it was France, it was above all England and the English tradition, it was everything that he had ever cared for of civilization, beauty, and art threatened with destruction and arrayed before his imagination in one figure of tragic appeal" ("Henry James," *CE*, I, 267).

Images of calamity dominate the diary entries for the period: "The whole of Europe may be in flames—its on the cards"; war will mean "the complete ruin . . . of civilisation, in Europe"; "Now we are in the war. England is being attacked. I got this feeling for the first time completely yesterday. The feeling of pressure, danger horror. . . . Of course this may be the beginning of invasion" (*D*, V, 142, 162, 313–

14). Nor was this desperate mood idiosyncratic. As E. M. Forster wrote in 1939, in an essay appropriately called "Post-Munich" that captures the apocalyptic feeling of the time, "The pillars of the twenty-thousand-year-old house are crumbling, the human experiment totters, other forms of life watch."[1]

Between the Acts is deeply imbued with this sense of crisis. It takes place on the eve of the war, on a day in June 1939. The traditional village pageant, its major event, is juxtaposed against a very untraditional tension and nervous expectancy in many of its characters. It is strange that F. R. Leavis in his review of the novel criticized Woolf's lack of interest "in the world 'out there.'"[2] In fact, the novel refers constantly to events in the external world. As one of the book's more recent critics has seen, there is "an almost obsessive preoccupation with history on virtually every page."[3] There are frequent references to the imminence of war. Giles Oliver is in a state of suppressed rage because of his helplessness before the inevitable catastrophe. He compares Europe to an enraged hedgehog and sees his world "bristling with guns, poised with planes." As he looks at the pastoral landscape before him, he fears that "at any moment guns would rake that land into furrows; planes splinter Bolney Minster into smithereens" (66–67). The conversation of the audience stresses the same anxiety: "And what about the Jews? The refugees . . . the Jews" (145); "It all looks very black." "No one wants it— save those damned Germans" (177); "And what's the channel, come to think of it, if they mean to invade us?" (232).

The tension reflected in these passages affects the private lives of the major characters as well, creating feverish impatience in some and self-protective withdrawal in others. Lucy Swithin contentedly reads in her Outline of History about a time before human beings even existed in England, when rhododendron forests covered what is now Piccadilly. But Giles and his father are addicted to the newspaper; late on the day of the pageant they are already sharing the early edition: "The morning paper—the paper that obliterated the day before" (252). In the novel, journalism (and its implied obsession with the present moment) is the enemy of cultural continuity. Even the literary-minded Isa finds that she no longer has the patience to read the volumes in the family library because she is as "book-shy" as her contemporaries: "For her generation the newspaper was a book" (26). The pervasive feeling of contained violence in the personal relationships of the novel—the conflict between Isa and Giles, Giles's instinctive hatred of William Dodge, the perpetual disturbance generated by Mrs. Manresa, etc.—are not directly caused by contemporary public events but are meant to embody similar forces in a microcosmic setting. "War" for Woolf meant the conflict between individuals as well as between nations. What Lukács saw in Scott's historical novels is equally true of Woolf's characters in *Between the Acts*: "Certain crises in the personal destinies of a number of human beings coincide and interweave within the determining context of an historical crisis."[4]

History in *Between the Acts* stretches from primeval times through the various eras of English civilization presented in the pageant to the critical year 1939. But between this vast panorama and the present moment there is a smaller historical context evoked in the title of the novel and often of major importance in Woolf's work. As has frequently been pointed out, the book's title refers (among other things) to the two world wars. We have seen how profoundly Woolf was affected by the Great War and by her growing conviction that the peace "between the acts" was to be merely an interlude. In the last section of *The Years* she had already made it clear that history was about to repeat itself. The genteel Eleanor Pargiter explodes when she sees a newspaper photograph of one of the Fascist dictators, tears it across, flings it on the floor, shouts "damned bully!" And then, seeing the look of astonishment on her niece's face, she explains, "You see . . . it means the end of everything we cared for" (*Y*, 356–57).

The Years can be read as a critique of the idea of progress. The historical period it spans (1880 to the mid-1930s) sees the realization of the goals of its characters: the patriarchal Victorian family has been displaced by more honest and equal relationships; women's suffrage has been won; women are free to take up a profession or lead independent lives; Ireland has become a nation. Yet the sense of restlessness and dissatisfaction is as powerfully present in the younger, "liberated" generation as it had been in its elders. And in the final pages of the book a couple of cockney children who represent the future sing an utterly incomprehensible song that appalls the listening adults: "The rhythm seemed to rock and the unintelligible words ran themselves together almost into a shriek. . . . There was something horrible in the noise they made. It was so shrill, so discordant, and so meaningless" (*Y*, 464).

By the time Woolf wrote *Between the Acts*, the concept of a gradual improvement either in history or in human relationships had come to seem naive. As she says in *Three Guineas*, "It seems as if there were no progress in the human race, but only repetition" (*TG*, 120). To understand how disturbing such an idea must have been to her and to the whole liberal milieu from which she came, one has only to recall such books as *Howards End* or *A Room of One's Own*. Both end with an ecstatically hopeful vision of the future: "'The field's cut!' Helen cried excitedly—'The big meadow! We've seen to the very end, and it'll be such a crop of hay as never!'"[5] "For my belief is that if we live another century or so . . . then the opportunity will come and the dead poet who was Shakespeare's sister . . . will be born" (*AROO*, 171–72). The informing idea of such works is the possibility of progress, the tenuous but tenaciously held belief that human relationships are moving toward greater freedom, opportunity, and fulfillment. By the late thirties this precarious faith seemed bankrupt, and Woolf was beginning to think of history as retrogressive rather than progressive.

This dismaying conclusion shook her intellectual set to its foundations. Bloomsbury had believed in the gradual triumph of civilization, but, as Woolf said in her biography of Roger Fry, after the Great War "it was no longer possible to believe that the world generally was becoming more civilized" (*RF*, 213). In the memoirs of several members of the Bloomsbury group, this loss of confidence in the eventual eradication of barbarism is given great weight. Keynes looked back on the optimistic faith of his Cambridge friends before the war with a sense of the flimsiness of their fundamental assumptions: "We were not aware that civilisation was a thin and precarious crust erected by the personality and will of a very few. . . . And as the years wore on towards 1914, the thinness and superficiality, as well as the falsity, of our view of man's heart became, as it now seems to me, more obvious."[6] And Leonard Woolf treats World War I as the end of "light and hope" and the period from 1933 to 1939 as "the six years in which civilization was finally destroyed."[7] The book he published in 1939 was called *Barbarians at the Gate*. It should be obvious how far all of them had come from the faith of their intellectual forbears, the "intellectual aristocracy" whose work, in Noel Annan's words, was based on the doctrine "that the world could be improved by analysing the needs of society and calculating the possible course of its development."[8] For it seemed increasingly likely that the world could not be improved at all, that it was just as capable of slipping back to its most savage rituals as of moving forward to the Bloomsbury paradise of peace, freedom, and rationality.

Virginia Woolf too was deeply affected by the thought of a turn from civilized to primitive behavior, but until the late thirties she did not necessarily treat such regression as retrogression or degeneration. The issue is significant to her even in her first novel, *The Voyage Out*, in which the river journey the English tourists take into the South American hinterland is associated with some of man's deepest experiences— love, sexuality, disease, death. Its echoes of Conrad's *Heart of Darkness* are surely not accidental. As the English party wends its way into the interior of the country, Woolf says: "They seemed to be driving into the heart of the night" (*VO*, 325). That sentence is echoed on the last page of *Between the Acts*. Isa and Giles, it is said, "must fight, as the dog fox fights with the vixen, in the heart of darkness, in the fields of night" (256). But by the time Woolf came to write her last book, these images had become charged with sinister implications.

The idea of a return from civilization to barbarism is of crucial importance to an understanding of *Between the Acts*. In the book's most shocking passage Giles finds a snake "choked with a toad in its mouth. The snake was unable to swallow; the toad was unable to die. A spasm made the ribs contract; blood oozed. It was birth the wrong way round—a monstrous inversion" (119). The image suggests not only the return of predatory forces into the garden world of the Olivers' country house but also a perverse assault in which both antagonists are inevitably destroyed—a symbol with obvious relevance to the threat of a second global conflict. Giles is appalled, raises his foot, and stamps the life out of snake and toad. But his instinctive violence makes it clear that he too is a natural killer, a frustrated man of war, and serves to underline the continuity between the animal kingdom and the world of men. During the Munich Crisis, when air raids seemed imminent, Woolf heard an announcement on the radio that "all poisonous snakes at the Zoo would be killed, & dangerous animals shot" and recorded her phantasmagoric "Vision of London ravaged by cobras & tigers" (*D*, V, 178). And in a notebook she kept while she was working on *Between the Acts*, she described "London in War" in these terms: "Nature prevails. I suppose badgers & foxes wd. come back if this went on, & owls & nightingales. This is the prelude to barbarism."[9]

"Lupus est homo homini." This parallel is constantly drawn in *Between the Acts*, usually to underline human predatoriness. The images of hedgehog, dog fox and vixen, snake and toad have already been mentioned, but there are dozens of others. Mrs. Haines destroys her husband's romantic feeling for Isa "as a thrush pecks the wings off a butterfly" (10); in the Restoration playlet of the pageant characters named Sir Spaniel and Lady Harpy tear each other apart; and in the last scene of the novel Bartholomew, Giles, and Lucy are reduced in Isa's mind to "the grasshopper, the ant, and the beetle" (253). Mrs. Swithin reads in her Outline of History of a prehistoric age populated by "elephant-bodied, seal-necked, heaving, surging, slowly writhing, and, she supposed, barking monsters; the iguanodon, the mammoth, and the mastodon; from whom presumably, she thought . . . we descend" (13). But the word "presumably" in this passage merely records

Mrs. Swithin's civilized hesitation to recognize what is everywhere apparent around her: man's capacity for violence and
destruction.

The whole extraordinary last scene of the novel can be read
as an imaginary return to a precivilized world. The walls of
Pointz Hall suddenly seem to become transparent; the house
loses its shelter and lies open to sky and field; Isa and Giles
revert to "dwellers in caves" as they prepare for the inevitable
fight they have put off all day.[10] The connection with the coming war is patent. Giles's behavior is, despite his patriotic feeling for England, very close to the Fascist threat he fears. His
aggressive masculinity and Nordic looks remind one of the
Master Race; William Dodge sees him as "the muscular, the
hirsute, the virile" (127). He is filled with hatred and contempt: for "old fogies who sat and looked at views over cof-
fee and cream" (66); for the homosexual William, whom he
thinks of as "a toady; a lickspittle" (75); even for his wife. He
is a good indigenous example of the ethos Woolf had seen in
the first days of Italian Fascism and described in *A Room of
One's Own*: "I began to envisage an age to come of pure, of
self-assertive virility, such as . . . the rulers of Italy have already brought into being" (*AROO*, 154). In *Three Guineas* she
made it clear that this was no longer a vision of the future but
of the present.

It was not always thus. Woolf's novel is rooted in an acute
longing for an earlier, more civilized phase of English culture
as well as in her observation of the barbaric present. Its setting
is not the London of a powerful, sophisticated industrial
culture but a "remote village in the very heart of England"
(22). Time seems to have stood still in this spot; the guide-
book written over a century before scarcely requires revision,
for "1833 was true in 1939" (65). The village is a backwater,
characterized by a sense of historical continuity rather than
change. The delivery boy's surname can be found in Domes-
day Book; the Swithins "were there before the Conquest" (39);
even the swallows have come back for centuries to the ancient
barn where the pageant is held. Woolf's choice of this setting
suggests a strong feeling of nostalgia for an older English

culture—rural rather than industrial, feudal rather than democratic, simple rather than complex, and, above all, unified.
The village is an essentially stable community, steeped in tradition and seemingly impervious to the destructive forces of
the present. All the villagers are known and recognized, even
in the disguises they assume when playing their roles in the
pageant.

Woolf's first notes for the book stress the idea of community: "'I' rejected: 'We' substituted . . . we all life, all art, all
waifs & strays" (*D*, V, 135). The capacity to think and feel
"we" is essential to her vision. What is being tested is the
liberal-pacifist ideal of mankind's fundamental unity. The
most persistent point of view in the book, as one critic has
observed, "is that of a hypothetical group-consciousness,
aware of the crucial thoughts and feelings each member is
contributing to the shared experience of the moment."[11] But
not everyone in the community is still capable of using the
word "we." Mrs. Parker says to Giles:

> "Surely, Mr. Oliver, we're more civilized?"
> "*We*?" said Giles. "*We*?" He looked, once, at William. . . . It
> was a bit of luck—that he could despise him, not himself.
>
> (132–33)

The "we" Giles finds it impossible to say is the pronoun
characteristically used by the chorus of peasants in Miss La
Trobe's pageant, always there in the background through all
the eras it depicts:

> *Digging and delving* (they sang) *hedging and ditching, we pass.*
> *. . . Summer and winter, autumn and spring return . . . All passes*
> *but we, all changes . . . but we remain forever the same.*
>
> (164)

The peasants are the antithesis to Woolf's sense of historical
decay, serving to suggest the continual existence of an *essential* England that might survive even the present moment of
internal dividedness and international confrontation. They
embody such hope as the novel retains. Woolf found the same
quality in Hardy's peasants: "They drink by night and they

plough the fields by day. They are eternal. . . . They always have something typical about them, more of the character that marks a race than of the features which belong to an individual. . . . When they disappear, there is no hope for the race" ("The Novels of Thomas Hardy," *CE*, I, 259–60).

The idealization of this kind of world is a version of pastoral. Its connections with the image of the Golden Age (in both literature and history) are manifest in Woolf's essays "On Not Knowing Greek," in which she imagines just such a village as the setting for the great Greek tragedies and then finds an English equivalent in a place remarkably similar to the rural retreat of *Between the Acts*:

> . . . some village, in a remote part of the country, near the sea. Even nowadays such villages are to be found in the wilder parts of England, and as we enter them we can scarcely help feeling that here, in this cluster of cottages, cut off from rail or city, are all the elements of a perfect existence. Here is the Rectory; here the Manor house, the farm and the cottages; the church for worship, the club for meeting, the cricket field for play. Here life is simply sorted out into its main elements. Each man and woman has his work; each works for the health or happiness of others.
>
> (*CE*, I, 1–2)

The regular cadences of the passage emphasize Woolf's sense of the stability and order of this world where fellowship prevails and modern hostilities have not yet commenced.

It is presumably to such a place that Ralph Denham, in *Night and Day*, wants to escape in order to write his "history of the English village from Saxon days to the present time." But the very task he sets himself is an exercise in nostalgia; Woolf compares Ralph to a man "who has lost his chance of some beautiful inheritance" (*ND*, 236–37). And she herself was intensely conscious of how visionary this image of an English community untouched by the divisive forces of the present was. Though she idealized a world in which different classes, sexes, and nations exist in harmony, she was increasingly aware of the forces that impede this goal, that fragment society and divide it into opposing camps. She was at once deeply in need of communal harmony and perfectly aware of how easy it is to ignore reality in fabricating it. So, for example, the village in *Between the Acts* is only apparently a homogeneous domain untouched by the forces of modern life. In actuality, we find, it is full of interlopers: Miss La Trobe "wasn't presumably pure English" (72) and is treated like an outsider; the rich Ralph Manresa is a colonial adventurer now "got up to look the very spit and image of the landed gentry" (51); even Giles is only a weekend guest in his own house, spending his weekdays as a stockbroker in London. And the newspapers, with their ominous tidings, easily reach this remote spot, as do the "twelve aeroplanes in perfect formation" that interrupt the rector's words after the pageant: "The word was cut in two. A zoom severed it" (225).

The sense of such places threatened with destruction, of everything Woolf cared for in English culture perhaps coming to an end, affected her deeply as she was finishing the book. In one of her diary entries for January 1941 she asks, "What is the phrase I always remember—or forget. Look your last on all things lovely" (*D*, V, 351). And as she wanders through the "desolate ruins" of her old London haunts during the Blitz, she sees the houses "gashed; dismantled; the old red bricks all white powder . . . all that completeness ravished & demolished" (*D*, V, 353). Such fears for the survival of the country turned many an alienated British writer into an uneasy patriot in the late thirties and early forties. In 1940 E. M. Forster published a deeply nostalgic village pageant, *England's Pleasant Land*, which also invoked the ideal of community: "The two nations will form one nation, and within this nation both squire and villager will have a share in the soil; England's pleasant land has come into being." [12] In the same year George Orwell, that "international" socialist, found himself writing, "It is all very well to be 'advanced' and 'enlightened', to snigger at Colonel Blimp and proclaim your emancipation from all traditional loyalties, but a time comes when the sand of the desert is sodden red and what have I done for thee, England, my England?" [13]

Between the Acts is also an expression of a reawakened love for one's native land. But Woolf's deep if inchoate feeling is very different from the mindless patriotism then in vogue, such as the hope voiced by one member of the audience that the pageant would end—like all good pageants—"with a Grand Ensemble. Army; Navy; Union Jack" (209). Yet there is a different kind of feeling for one's country—a love for its history, its idiosyncratic culture and traditions, a passionate attachment to the land itself—and this the novel honors because it was Woolf's own. She felt it as she thought of London during the Blitz: "Odd how often I think with what is love I suppose of the City: of the walk to the Tower: that is my England; I mean, if a bomb destroyed one of those little alleys with the brass bound curtains & the river smell & the old woman reading I should feel—well, what the patriots feel" (*D*, V, 263). *Between the Acts* expresses this love of country and seems to affirm the continuity of English cultural tradition. The pageant, in its use of dozens of quotations from English literature as well as in its casting of the same villagers to play different parts in different eras, obviously suggests cultural continuity. The relative stability of village life confirms the idea. If there were to be a roll call of names common in the village a century ago, "half the ladies and gentlemen present would have said: '*Adsum*; I'm here, in place of my grandfather or great-grandfather'" (92). And if you were to look down on the countryside from a plane, "you could still see, plainly marked, the scars made by the Britons; by the Romans; by the Elizabethan manor house; and by the plough, when they ploughed the hill to grow wheat in the Napoleonic wars" (8).

Yet it is, I think, a distortion to read *Between the Acts* as an essentially celebratory work affirming unity and continuity, a book that moves, like *Mrs. Dalloway*, *To the Lighthouse*, and *The Waves*, toward the resolution of conflict. A number of critics have interpreted it in this way, and there are individual passages in the novel that support the theory.[14] But the reassuring words are almost all uttered by two characters who do not seem to me to speak for the author—the Rev. Streatfield and Lucy Swithin. The worthy clergyman concludes that Miss La Trobe's pageant shows us "we are members one of another.

Each is part of the whole. . . . We act different parts; but are the same" (224). Of course it is obligatory given his profession that he come to such a spiritually uplifting conclusion. But that his vision is selective and incomplete is suggested by his utter imperviousness to the interruption of his sermon by a formation of war planes overhead. An astute member of the audience, however, points to the disparity: "If one spirit animates the whole, what about the aeroplanes?" (230–31). And Woolf's introduction of Streatfield in this passage obviously emphasizes his limitations: "What an intolerable constriction, contraction, and reduction to simplified absurdity he was to be sure!" (221).

Lucy Swithin too treats the pageant as an affirmation of human unity. "What a small part I've had to play!" she says to Miss La Trobe in her enthusiasm. "But you've made me feel I could have played . . . Cleopatra!" (179). And she denies the difference between one historical epoch and another: " 'The Victorians,' Mrs. Swithin mused. 'I don't believe' she said with her odd little smile, 'that there ever were such people. Only you and me and William dressed differently.'" To which William drily replies, "You don't believe in history" (203). To treat these passages as though they had the author's full assent one must ignore the many indications in the novel that Woolf expects us to see Lucy Swithin as warm-hearted but dim-witted. Almost everyone treats her with affectionate condescension. The young people in the village know her as Old Flimsy. Her brother says dismissively that she "belongs to the unifiers" (140), as though that were a familiar category of the misled. He thinks her "imperceptive" and stresses her determined evasion of anything unpleasant: "Skimming the surface, she ignored the battle in the mud" (237). And in a highly ironic passage William and Isa effectively demolish her authority:

> She was off, they guessed, on a circular tour of the imagination—one-making. Sheep, cows, grass, trees, ourselves—all are one. If discordant, producing harmony—if not to us, to a gigantic ear attached to a gigantic head. And thus—she was smiling benignly—the agony of the particular sheep, cow,

or human being is necessary; and so—she was beaming seraphically at the gilt vane in the distance—we reach the conclusion that *all* is harmony, could we hear it. And we shall.

(204)

Such passages do not merely satirize the particular character, Lucy Swithin; they call into question the whole benevolent view of the world in which she believes and which Woolf herself once took rather more seriously. It is as if Mrs. Swithin were a character from *To the Lighthouse* or *The Waves* who is wandering about in the wrong book and cannot see that the world has changed profoundly. She is a visionary who fabricates a benevolent providence, who makes consoling fictions out of the cosmic emptiness. We might have been alerted by some of Woolf's previous works to see that when a character affirms such a kindly universal order, he or she is suppressing something unpleasant. For example, when Septimus Smith, in *Mrs. Dalloway*, is most anxious to forget the terrible memories of the war and the death in it of his friend Evans, he insists that "Heaven was divinely merciful, infinitely benignant" (*MD*, 76), a faith that immediately produces a vision of a resurrected Evans: "But no mud was on him; no wounds" (*MD*, 78). Such a providential view, like Lucy Swithin's, is here designed literally to ignore "the battle in the mud."

For all her irony about her aunt, Isa Oliver has a touch of the same disease. She is constantly writing poetry but cannot bear to show it to anyone because it could scarcely survive a daylight scrutiny. The lines she writes are a kind of geriatric pastoral, full of echoes from an older poetic dispensation and quite incapable of conveying the reality of her own experience. For example, she daydreams about flight (in both senses of the word) as she thinks about her attraction to Haines: "Where we know not, where we go not, neither know nor care. . . . Flying, rushing through the ambient, incandescent, summer silent . . . air" (21). But while she composes these "elevated" lines she is busy ordering fish on the tele-

phone, and the two worlds refuse to mesh. Rather, they alternate and displace each other—the poetic word and the prosaic fact. But since the prosaic facts in the novel include a great
deal of significance to Woolf, Isa's poetry must be seen simply
as an escape from the tensions and abrasions of the real world
in which she finds herself. Its aim is ascent, imaginative departure; in pursuing this goal it simplifies experience in a way
once described by Robert Penn Warren in his definition of
"pure poetry": "The pure poem tries to be pure by excluding,
more or less rigidly, certain elements which might qualify or
contradict its original impulse." [15] For Isa those elements include the real time and place in which she exists, the trivial,
the sordid, the earthbound.

Isa's poetry is only one of a number of attempts in the book
to purify or censor observation and the language in which it is
expressed. On the very first page Mrs. Haines insists that her
fellow guests should not be discussing a subject so vulgar as
the cesspool on a beautiful summer night. But the structure of
the novel's first sentence makes it clear that such antiromantic
deflation, the deliberate juxtaposition of beautiful and sordid,
is an integral part of Woolf's strategy: "It was a summer's night
and they were talking, in the big room with the windows
open to the garden, about the cesspool" (7). The technique is
an implicit criticism of all the purifiers in the novel—Isa, Lucy
Swithin, the Rev. Streatfield, and others. It is based on the assumption that an artist gains strength as Antaeus did, by
touching the earth—a myth Mrs. Swithin alludes to (32). And
it connects with Woolf's description of Miss La Trobe's artistic
imagination at work: "Words of one syllable sank down into
the mud. She drowsed; she nodded. The mud became fertile"
(247–48).

Woolf had regularly treated art as a force for unity and per-
manence in her previous fiction. The classic passage is Lily
Briscoe's meditation in *To the Lighthouse* on the parallel between Mrs. Ramsay's work and her own painting: "Mrs. Ramsay bringing them together; Mrs. Ramsay saying 'Life stand
still here'; Mrs. Ramsay making of the moment something

permanent (as in another sphere Lily herself tried to make of the moment something permanent)—this was of the nature of a revelation. In the midst of chaos there was shape" (*TL*, 249). But this confidence in the power of art to unify and immortalize is almost entirely lost by the time we come to *Between the Acts*.[16] It is not merely the vapidness of Isa's poetry but her lack of belief in it and in herself that tells us something has gone very wrong. In fact, the whole literary tradition has ceased to be meaningful to the characters in the novel. When they try to recall the words of the "to be or not to be" soliloquy, a passage from the "Ode to a Nightingale" is the only thing that comes to mind, and even that is mangled ("the weariness, the torture, and the fret"—68). The poetic tags in both this scene and the rest of the novel become mere cultural detritus, bits of flotsam and jetsam floating about in the characters' minds like fragments of a sunken vessel. Even the traditionalist Lucy Swithin, though she speaks grandly of "the poets from whom we descend by way of the mind," has no confidence in her hold on the past: "I ignore. I forget" (85).

The novel gives us the sense of a once vital cultural tradition that has lost its authority and connection with the present. Woolf's preliminary notes for *Between the Acts* suggest how unreliable this group consciousness had become: "The dispersal. The common mind broken up. What each thought, privately."[17] As Bart Oliver stands in his library, he can make no use of what is there: "Books: the treasured life blood of immortal spirits. Poets; the legislators of mankind. . . . A great harvest the mind had reaped; but for all this, compared with his son, he did not care one damn" (138). And when, in the last act of the pageant, the characters reappear, declaiming a fragment either from their parts or from a literary source, the effect is of absolute chaos:

> *I am not* (said one) *in my perfect mind.* . . . Another, *Reason am I.* . . . *And I? I'm the old top hat.* . . . *Home is the hunter, home from the hill.* . . . *Home? Where the miner sweats, and the maiden faith is rudely strumpeted.* . . . *Sweet and low; sweet and low, wind of the western sea.* . . . *Is that a dagger that I see before me?*
> (215–16, Woolf's ellipses)

And so on. It is as if Western culture had been dissected and then stuck together again in random order to form a freakish organism with no chance of life.[18]

This sense of cultural disintegration has sometimes been used to attack *Between the Acts* itself and more particularly to question the coherence of the pageant and its relevance to the rest of the book. W. H. Mellers, in an early essay on the novel, asks whether it does not "seem likely that the mysteriously ambiguous 'meaning' of the pageant which the vicar and audience in their stupidity cannot discover is equally illusory to its creator?"[19] And R. L. Chambers insists that the book has two distinct emotional centers, one in the present-day characters, the other in the pageant, and that there is no "inherent and necessary connection between the two."[20] It is easy enough to show that such connections do exist, but in some critical attempts to demonstrate the book's coherence the pageant has, I think, been mistakenly interpreted as a deliberate antithesis to the fragmented present-day world, a work of art that confirms the synthesizing power of the artist and triumphantly unites the audience.[21] It seems to me to be no such thing. Rather, it is an attempt by Miss La Trobe (and by her creator) to trace the pervasive sense of fragmentation and isolation in the modern world to its historical roots.

The pageant can be seen as providing us not so much with a comprehensive vision of the past as with a prehistory of the present. It follows English culture through its historical stages to emphasize the gradual but persistent decay of the sense of community. Its shifts in time suggest not the idea of progress but what intellectual historians have called "the theory of progressive degeneration."[22] In the earliest, medieval section England is personified first as a child, then as a young girl, and her people are not yet given names. They are in fact the chorus that naturally says "we": "'To the shrine of the Saint . . . to the tomb . . . lovers . . . believers . . . we come.' They grouped themselves together" (98). Like the Canterbury pilgrims to whom they are compared, what these Englishmen have in common is more significant than what divides them. Woolf describes this phase of English culture in a posthumously published fragment, "Anon." The earliest writers in the literary tradition did not impose their individual personalities on their work but wrote anonymously, she argues: "It gave the early writing an impersonality, a generality. It gave us the ballads; it gave us the songs. It allowed us to know nothing of the writer. . . . He can say what every one feels."[23]

This sense of national unity is gradually modified in the succeeding sections of the pageant. In Elizabeth's time it remains strong, and her lines suggest that her subjects, though they are now differentiated into types, still respond to the same things:

> *Then there was heard too*
> *On granite and cobble*
> *From Windsor to Oxford*
> *Loud laughter, low laughter*
> *Of warrior and lover,*
> *The fighter, the singer.*
> (102–3)

The first sign of the fragility of this sense of community, however, comes in the Renaissance playlet in this section. Although it ends happily with the union of the young couple, the world it evokes is, like that of Shakespeare's romances on which it is based, full of plotting and intrigue. And although in the final scene "dukes, priests, shepherds, pilgrims and serving men took hands and danced," Woolf calls the scene a "medley" (111–12). The word, with its overtones of conflict and heterogeneous combination, is precisely chosen.

The tension increases in the Restoration playlet, which ends not with a grand reconciliation of the principals but with a dispersal. In the final scene Lady Harpy Harraden is left to mourn her solitude: "*All gone. I'm alone then. Sans niece, sans lover; and sans maid*" (173). The plot of this piece turns entirely on the characters' attempts to get the better of each other. Even the young lovers are presented as cruel and calculating, worthy heirs to the greedy, self-obsessed culture they are about to enter. The title of the playlet, "Where There's a Will There's a Way," refers not only to the mercenary motives of the characters in pursuit of the fortune disposed of in the will but also to the power of the individual will to carve out a disproportionate share for itself.

This pursuit of power and wealth dominates Woolf's vision of Victorian England in the next act of the pageant. Its symbol is the truncheon that Budge, dressed as a constable, wields over the entire Empire. His rule is coercively moral, and he thinks of Victoria's subjects not as a community but as a network of potential rebels who must be kept under strict surveillance in the slums where they might congregate. All meetings of individuals are now treated as threats to the state:

> *The ruler of an Empire must keep his eye on the cot; spy too in the kitchen; drawing-room; library; wherever one or two, me and you, come together. Purity our watchword; prosperity and respectability. If not, why, let 'em fester in . . . Cripplegate; St. Giles's; Whitechapel; the Minories. Let 'em sweat at the mines; cough at the looms; rightly endure their lot. That's the price of Empire; that's the white man's burden.*

(190–91)

And the evangelical lovers in the Victorian playlet are not satisfied merely to assert their own wills; they are looking forward to a life of converting the heathen will into a semblance of their own.

It is inevitable that the pageant's concluding sketch, "Present Time. Ourselves," should stress the utter fragmentation of life in the modern period, in which the medieval sense of a human community has finally been shattered. The jazz rhythms Miss La Trobe uses in the scene seem to "shiver into splinters the old vision; smash to atoms what was whole" (214). And the little mirrors the players focus on the audience are unable to hold more than one person at a time and often not so much: "Now old Bart . . . he was caught. Now Manresa. Here a nose . . . there a skirt . . . Then trousers only . . . Now perhaps a face. . . . And only, too, in parts" (214). This vision of contemporary life as essentially discontinuous, a collection of "scraps, orts and fragments," has been prepared for by every previous section of the pageant, as Miss La Trobe traces the gradual triumph of individualism over communal identity. The theme obviously connects with and illuminates the situation of the present-day characters in the novel, whose lives we have been following simultaneously—each trapped in the prison of self, rarely if ever able to feel a sense of vital connection to another human being.

This is not the way the pageant ends, however. The scene is followed by the playing of a magnificent piece of classical music which serves to remind the audience that it was once possible to produce "from chaos and cacophony measure" (220); then comes the Rev. Streatfield's sermon-interpretation: "Scraps, orts and fragments! Surely, we should unite?" (225). Both seem to suggest a more hopeful vision of the future than we have been led to expect. But though the possibility of a return to community is never denied in the pageant, as the periodic reappearance of the chorus confirms, the forces of dispersal are shown to be steadily in the ascendant and moving with the power of historical inevitability. "We should unite," says the rector. "Can we unite?" asks the pageant. The answer is far from reassuring, for both pageant and novel have shown us the strength of the impulses in human nature and society that work against communal ideals—greed, sexual jealousy, the love of power, the privacy of fantasy and need—all of increasing importance as the code of individualism extends its hegemony.

Furthermore, the hope for a restoration of communal ideals among the members of the audience presupposes that they have understood Miss La Trobe's pageant and the degeneration of their culture that it depicts. But this is very far from true. Although "for one moment she held them together—the dispersing company" (117), her sense of triumph quickly gives way to a deeper feeling of failure as the members of the audience slip out of her grasp and back into their own familiar patterns. In reality, the pageant fails to unite the spectators, and their comments in the intervals and after the performance only confirm their separateness: "I thought it brilliantly clever. . . . O my dear, I thought it utter bosh" (230). And as the gramophone repeats its plaintive *"dispersed are we,"* the coherent vision of the pageant is dissipated in a long passage recording the trivial, unconnected chatter of the departing guests (230–35). There is no unity of response, no coherence of interpretation, no sense of minds moving toward a common goal. The audience is unchanged.

Stuart Hampshire calls Miss La Trobe an "unmagical, muttering Prospero, who in her art attempts the impossible."[24] Her failure can be attributed to the gulf between herself and her audience. She too is a victim of the cultural fragmentation she records: "She was an outcast. Nature had somehow set her apart from her kind" (247). And her feeling about her public is resentful: "I am the slave of my audience" (247); "O to write a play without an audience—*the* play" (210). This alienation is only another symptom of the artist's increasing insignificance in the world Woolf depicts. Just as it has jettisoned traditional culture, so it has no use for a new literary work. Far from being a powerful force for unity, art has become an evanescent event, at best merely a momentary stay against confusion. The "barbarians at the gate" who threatened England's culture from without had a set of unconscious allies in the philistines within.

The pageant in *Between the Acts*, then, is intended to show us a society and a cultural tradition breaking down into its component parts. To lay the blame on the artist or the audience, however, is misguided. Woolf's way of thinking about the problem is not at all moralistic. Many of her earlier books move toward a climactic moment of unification—the dinner party in *To the Lighthouse*, Clarissa's identification with Septimus in *Mrs. Dalloway*, Bernard's final monologue in *The Waves*. But though this has often been noticed (and celebrated), what has frequently been ignored is the strength of the opposing tendency in Woolf's work—her sense of the pervasiveness of human isolation. Until the last years of her life, it is probably right to say that this was the subsidiary theme, the minor key over which the major usually triumphed. Yet it has its moments of authority in her earlier work: Katharine in *Night and Day* is suddenly struck by "the infinite loneliness of human beings" (*ND*, 299); Mrs. Ramsay looks round at her guests and thinks "Nothing seemed to have merged. They all sat separate" (*TL*, 130); Rhoda in *The Waves* laments, "I am alone in a hostile world" (*W*, 113).

In *Between the Acts* this subsidiary theme becomes dominant. Its characters are divided against each other. Even when they do not quarrel, they live in different mental and emotional worlds. Bart and his sister Lucy are seen as polar opposites: "What she saw he didn't; what he saw she didn't—and so on, *ad infinitum*" (33). Others are treated similarly—Giles and William are antithetically conceived; Mrs. Swithin's nickname is "Flimsy," Miss La Trobe's "Bossy." The major characters in *Between the Acts* are substantially less complex than those in Woolf's previous novels. They contain fewer contradictory elements in their own natures because they are treated as component parts of a larger organism. The novel is not really interested in examining character in its complexity—the mysterious "Mrs. Brown" of Woolf's early essay on fiction—but in anatomizing society and exploring its internal conflicts. There is no character in the book whose vision emerges as authoritative, in the way that Bernard's does in *The Waves*, for example. Each is a specialist occupying his own bit of space: they are scraps, orts, and fragments.

In stressing this sense of atomization in Woolf's last novel, I do not want to simplify its complex tonality. There is in fact a carefully modulated balance, particularly in the final sections of the book, of mellifluous and discordant elements. And though the more sanguine or celebratory responses are often demolished by the more cynical ones, they are nevertheless permitted their moments of lyrical intensity, as in Lucy Swithin's vision of the fish in the pond, a metaphor for the pied beauty of human diversity:

> Then something moved in the water; her favourite fantail; the golden orfe followed. Then she had a glimpse of silver—the great carp himself, who came to the surface so very seldom. They slid on, in and out between the stalks, silver; pink; gold; splashed; streaked; pied.
> "Ourselves," she murmured.

(239)

Nor is the creative impulse dead. Even as Miss La Trobe acknowledges the failure of the pageant, her fertile mind is already inventing another play. What *has* changed in *Between the Acts* is the power of the opposition to these integrating forces. Negation regularly has the last word: "The gramophone gurgled *Unity—Dispersity*. It gurgled *Un . . dis . . .* And ceased" (235). "It was Yes, No. Yes, yes, yes, the tide rushed out embracing. No, no, no, it contracted. The old boot appeared on the shingle" (251). We have come a long way from the confident last words of *Ulysses*, written two decades earlier: "yes I said yes I will Yes."

"Once there was no sea," Lucy Swithin recalls reading in her *Outline of History*, "no sea at all between us and the continent" (38). But since that time the British Isles had been formed, separated from other nations by a body of water. This historical fact is given symbolic resonance in Woolf's novel. The world it examines has been further broken down into something like an archipelago, with each character marooned on a different island. The image recalls Matthew Arnold's picture of human beings isolated from their fellows by "the unplumbed, salt, estranging sea."[25] This sense of human solitude and alienation had always been a powerful undertow beneath Woolf's greatest affirmations. That it had come to dominate her final book is no doubt the product of many forces—the approach of old age and the death of friends, among others. But one of the most important causes was historical, the fact that the novel was conceived and written in perhaps the darkest moment of her country's history, when the faith in peace and progress, the belief in human brotherhood seemed no better than lost illusions. The possibility voiced on the last page that out of the quarrel between Isa and Giles "another life might be born" is only a desperate hope against hope. Perhaps it was the seed of another, a more confident novel to follow *Between the Acts*. If so, it was a work Woolf never lived to write.

Epilogue

I have suggested that there was a close connection between the crisis through which Europe was passing at the end of Woolf's life and her own increasing desperation. The moment seems in retrospect not merely a passing emergency but a fundamental turning point. It is no exaggeration to say, as many did say at the time, that European civilization was threatened with extinction. Europe weathered the historical crisis. But Woolf's powers of defense were too weak to sustain life. Behind her despair was a loss of faith in the feasibility of a project that had always engaged her—transforming the flawed institutions and repressive ideology of her youth. Woolf was no social engineer, and the reform of society and human relationships was in any case not her only passion. But she consistently felt that what she wrote contributed to a movement of change to which she was deeply and steadily committed.

When Leonard Woolf in his autobiography described his generation's successful "struggle for social and intellectual emancipation [from the] 'rules and conventions' of the last days of Victorian civilization,"[1] he was suggesting that the battle had been won. And it was perfectly true that many of the identifiable abuses against which the reformers had directed their criticism had been eliminated or modified in important ways. We have looked at several in this book: the hierarchical family, sexual hypocrisy, upper-class complacency, the belief in martial ideals and in Britain's imperial mission, the assumption that women are inferior to men. To identify such patterns as the rules and conventions of a particular era, however, is really a way of containing and dismissing them. Behind the whole project of reform with which both Leonard and Virginia Woolf were associated are a number of assumptions that would later be questioned. It is based first of all on clear notions of grievance and redress. The abuses could be identified and isolated; the remedies proposed, though by no means painless, were nevertheless available. Behind this faith lay a belief in the malleability of human beings and institutions. Reform was manageable because ideologies and social structures were seen as open to fundamental change.

Such confident meliorism was perhaps the greatest casualty of the two world wars, greater even than the horrendous loss of life, since its eclipse undermined the hope that human existence could ever be significantly improved. We have seen how often Woolf justified her critical scrutiny of society and its institutions by connecting it with the goal of reform. Her idealism may be said to have legitimized her satire, since she could feel that her irony and sarcasm were instruments of a higher cause. When she writes in her memoirs that she and Vanessa in their youth had thought of themselves as "explorers, revolutionists, reformers" (*MB*, 126–27), she reveals the link between her earliest sense of herself and the pervasive contemporary faith in improvement. This belief in her project managed to survive the First World War, perhaps because in the 1920s that disaster still seemed aberrant, unrepeatable. The works she wrote in the twenties convey a feeling of assurance, even of exuberance, that was not to carry her far into the next decade. The genial climate changed, and the satiric impulse in her final works had more the tone of bitter disappointment.

She felt increasingly that her old faith in human betterment had been facile and could not be sustained in the face of present realities. Some of her last letters suggest a kind of bafflement or frustration. A year after the new war began, she confessed to one correspondent that neither she nor Leonard could understand "what anyone . . . could have done, which would have made the slightest difference to what has happened." And a few months later she wrote to another, "The human race seems to repeat itself insufferably" (*L*, VI, 415, 464). Such a vision conflicts with the sanguine spirit of explorers, revolutionists, and reformers. It seemed conceivable to Woolf that the improvements for which she and her associates had worked—though many of them had come about—were merely superficial alterations, and that at a deeper level too little of consequence had changed. Perhaps the old abuses had not really disappeared but merely assumed a new shape. Perhaps a flawed society, like a neurotic individual, could manifest symptoms of what Freud had called the return of the repressed.

Her fear lay in the possibility that certain qualities in human beings could never be altered. Her hope crystallized in a vision of a radically changed world in the distant future. As we have seen, her social criticism in her final years had become more and more intransigent, and by the end of her life she could legitimately lay claim to an outsider status that had never been fully hers before. Her idealism at the last took the form of an attempt to change not merely social institutions, familial patterns, or ideological assumptions but "human nature" itself; and she was perfectly aware of the apparent self-contradiction implicit in this task. What eluded her was any understanding of how the present could conceivably lead to the future she imagined. The outline for *Reading at Random*, the cultural history she left unfinished at the time of her death, gives us a sense of this impasse. It is reasonably familiar and straightforward from the Middle Ages through the nineteenth century. But then comes the injunction "Skip present day. A Chapter on the future."[2] Woolf's longer historical sense, the farsightedness that thought in centuries rather than in decades, convinced her that even the radical transformations she had in mind—of feminine and masculine identity, of the aggressive "instinct"—might well come about. But in the short run she gave up hope.

By the end of her life the pressures of the immediate present had become so powerful that a writer as sensitive to her environment as Woolf was could not conceivably ignore them. She describes this atmosphere of crisis as early as 1936, in the essay "The Artist and Politics": "When society is in chaos," she writes, the artist's studio "is far from being a cloistered spot. . . . It is besieged by voices, all disturbing." The novelist who might in a more peaceful time have kept the public world at a distance "turns from the private lives of his characters to their social surroundings and their political opinions" (*CE*, II, 232, 230). Woolf's works in the last years of her career were clearly affected by the turbulent historical currents of that time. But we know that her awareness of the social and political pressures acting on individual lives was not suddenly created by the exigent forces of the moment. As I have tried to show, her work consistently reveals a consciousness of social movements, of historical events, of societal institutions, of shifts in power in both the public and the private sphere. At the same time, it demonstrates a capacity for individual resistance, a determination in herself and her stronger characters to shape their lives according to their needs.

What had changed in the final years was the balance of power: the society that had earlier seemed malleable had come to seem inexorable; the individual had apparently lost the capacity to resist. In her despair Woolf took her own life. But there is no reason to think that the feelings of this stage of her career have greater authority than the earlier ones or that the pessimism of *Between the Acts* is her last will and testament. The passage of time has provided a perspective on this historical moment that Woolf herself could not command. And the larger pattern of her life and thought can now be grasped in a way that proved impossible at the time. All her works have survived. New generations of readers have increasingly found in them a searching, non-utopian account of the relation between the individual life and the life of the community, and a belief in the possibility—even the inevitability—of society's eventual responsiveness to the criticism of the human beings who constitute it.

Notes

INTRODUCTION

1. Irma Rantavaara, *Virginia Woolf and Bloomsbury* (Helsinki: Annales Academiae Fennicae, 1953), 65.

2. Lyndall Gordon, *Virginia Woolf: A Writer's Life* (Oxford: Oxford Univ. Press, 1984), 176.

3. E. M. Forster, "India Again," *Two Cheers for Democracy* (New York: Harcourt, Brace, 1951), 321.

4. Woolf's sense of psychological reality has been examined in depth in books like Harvena Richter's *Virginia Woolf: The Inward Voyage* (Princeton: Princeton Univ. Press, 1970) and James Naremore's *The World Without a Self: Virginia Woolf and the Novel* (New Haven: Yale Univ. Press, 1970).

CHAPTER 1

1. E. M. Forster, *Virginia Woolf* (Cambridge: Cambridge Univ. Press, 1942), 13–14.

2. Jean Guiguet, *Virginia Woolf and Her Works*, trans. Jean Stewart (London: Hogarth, 1965), 297.

3. Virginia Woolf, Manuscript Diary, Hyde Park Gate, 30 June– 1 Oct. 1903, 34, Berg Collection, New York Public Library. The diaries Woolf kept at erratic intervals between 1897 and 1909 have not yet been published. Permission to quote from them remains restricted. They are in eight holograph notebooks and an additional typescript copy of an unlocated original in the Henry W. and Albert A. Berg Collection of English and American Literature (Astor, Lenox, and Tilden Foundations), New York Public Library. Subsequent references to these diaries use the title Berg Diary and are incorporated in the text.

4. Forster, 19.

5. Leonard Woolf, *Downhill All the Way: An Autobiography of the Years 1919–1939* (London: Hogarth, 1970), 27.

6. Samuel Hynes's valuable analysis of Woolf's quarrel with Bennett makes it clear that the issues are rather more complex than she allows. See his "The Whole Contention Between Mr Bennett and

Mrs Woolf" in his *Edwardian Occasions: Essays on English Writing in the Early Twentieth Century* (London: Routledge and Kegan Paul, 1972), 24–38.

7. Richard Ellmann, *James Joyce* (New York: Oxford Univ. Press, 1959), 88.

8. *Selected Letters of E. M. Forster*, ed. Mary Lago and P. N. Furbank (Cambridge: Harvard Univ. Press, 1985), II, 32.

9. Roman Jakobson, "On Realism in Art," trans. Karol Magassy, in *Readings in Russian Poetics: Formalist and Structuralist Views*, ed. Ladislav Matejka and Krystyna Pomorska (Cambridge: MIT Press, 1971), 45.

10. The best study, I think, remains Harvena Richter's *Virginia Woolf: The Inward Voyage* (Princeton: Princeton Univ. Press, 1970). The brilliant chapter on *To the Lighthouse* in Erich Auerbach's *Mimesis: The Representation of Reality in Western Literature*, trans. Willard R. Trask (Princeton: Princeton Univ. Press, 1953), is indispensable. See also the sections on Woolf in Dorrit Cohn's *Transparent Minds: Narrative Modes for Presenting Consciousness in Fiction* (Princeton: Princeton Univ. Press, 1978).

11. This polarity of "fact" and "vision" has been analyzed at length, though I believe much too schematically, in Alice van Buren Kelley's *The Novels of Virginia Woolf: Fact and Vision* (Chicago: Univ. of Chicago Press, 1973).

12. F. R. Leavis, "Keynes, Lawrence and Cambridge," *The Common Pursuit* (London: Chatto and Windus, 1952), 257.

13. R. H. Tawney, *Equality*, 4th ed. (London: George Allen and Unwin, 1952), 81. The book was originally published in 1931.

14. Robert Graves and Alan Hodge, *The Long Week-End: A Social History of Great Britain, 1918–1939* (London: Faber and Faber, 1940), 27.

15. *Report of the War Office Committee of Enquiry into "Shell-Shock,"* Parliamentary Papers, 1922 Session, Command Paper 1734, XII, 97.

16. Ibid., 128, 133. My attention to this report was drawn by Eric J. Leed's references to it in his fine analysis of the psychological effects of the Great War on its participants, *No Man's Land: Combat and Identity in World War I* (Cambridge: Cambridge Univ. Press, 1979).

17. Arnold Kettle, "Virginia Woolf: *To the Lighthouse*," in his *An Introduction to the English Novel*, 2d ed. (London: Hutchinson, 1967), II, 99.

18. Berenice A. Carroll, "'To Crush Him in Our Own Country': The Political Thought of Virginia Woolf," *Feminist Studies* 4 (1978): 99, 101, 116–17.

19. Jane Marcus, ed., *New Feminist Essays on Virginia Woolf* (Lincoln: Univ. of Nebraska Press, 1981) and *Virginia Woolf: A Feminist Slant* (Lincoln: Univ. of Nebraska Press, 1983).

20. Phyllis Rose, *Woman of Letters: A Life of Virginia Woolf* (New York: Oxford Univ. Press, 1978), xiii.

21. Margaret Drabble, *Virginia Woolf: A Personal Debt* ([New York]: Aloe Editions, 1973), 3.

22. Jane Marcus, "Thinking Back Through Our Mothers," in *New Feminist Essays on Virginia Woolf*, 4; "Tintinnabulations," *Marxist Perspectives* 2 (1979): 146.

23. Jane Marcus, "Art and Anger," *Feminist Studies* 4 (1978): 8.

CHAPTER 2

1. Vanessa Bell, *Notes on Virginia's Childhood: A Memoir*, ed. Richard J. Schaubeck, Jr. (New York: Frank Hallman, 1974), [2].

2. Charles Dickens, *Our Mutual Friend, The New Oxford Illustrated Dickens* (London: Oxford Univ. Press, 1952), 128 (ch. 11).

3. Quentin Bell, *Bloomsbury* (London: Weidenfeld and Nicolson, 1968), 78.

4. Leonard Woolf, *Sowing: An Autobiography of the Years 1880–1904* (London: Hogarth, 1970), 152–53.

5. *The Collected Letters of D. H. Lawrence*, ed. Harry T. Moore (New York: Viking, 1962), I, 332. In his autobiography, Leonard Woolf challenges Lawrence's dismissive judgment. See *Sowing*, 153.

6. Jean Guiguet, *Virginia Woolf and Her Works*, trans. Jean Stewart (London: Hogarth, 1965), 455.

7. Virginia Woolf and Lytton Strachey, *Letters*, ed. Leonard Woolf and James Strachey (London: Hogarth, 1969), 43.

8. John Maynard Keynes, "My Early Beliefs," in his *Two Memoirs* (London: Rupert Hart-Davis, 1949), 97.

9. John Holloway, *The Victorian Sage: Studies in Argument* (New York: Norton, 1965), 12.

10. Jane Marcus defends Woolf's use of propaganda in *Three Guineas* and other discursive works in her essay "'No More Horses': Virginia Woolf on Art and Propaganda," *Women's Studies* 4 (1977): 265–90. She makes no distinction, as I think Woolf would have, between using propagandistic methods in fiction and using them in discursive writing.

11. Matthew Arnold, "The Function of Criticism at the Present Time," in *The Complete Prose Works of Matthew Arnold*, Vol. III: *Lectures and Essays in Criticism*, ed. R. H. Super (Ann Arbor: Univ. of Michigan Press, 1973), 260. Percy Bysshe Shelley, "A Defense of Poetry," in *Shelley's Prose*, ed. David Lee Clark (Albuquerque: Univ. of New Mexico Press, 1954), 296.

12. Virginia Woolf, Holograph Reading Notes XIV, 27, Berg Collection, New York Public Library.

13. Percy Lubbock, *The Craft of Fiction* (New York: Jonathan Cape and Harrison Smith, 1931), 185.

14. *Joseph Conrad on Fiction*, ed. Walter F. Wright (Lincoln: Univ. of Nebraska Press, 1964), 202.

15. *Critical Writings of Ford Madox Ford*, ed. Frank MacShane (Lincoln: Univ. of Nebraska Press, 1964), 16, 86, 81.

16. Joan Bennett, *Virginia Woolf: Her Art as a Novelist*, 2d ed. (Cambridge: Cambridge Univ. Press, 1964), 27.

17. Grace Radin, in *Virginia Woolf's "The Years": The Evolution of a Novel* (Knoxville: Univ. of Tennessee Press, 1981), offers a detailed analysis of the conflict in Woolf's mind between stating and withholding her ideas. Her study of the successive drafts of the novel reveals "the extent to which feminist, pacifist, and sexual themes have been deleted, obscured, or attenuated" (148).

18. James Hafley, *The Glass Roof: Virginia Woolf as Novelist* (Berkeley: Univ. of California Press, 1954), 74. See also James Naremore's analysis of her method, which concludes: "It is characteristic of Virginia Woolf to interpret the mental life of a character rather than transcribe it" (*The World Without a Self: Virginia Woolf and the Novel* [New Haven: Yale Univ. Press, 1973], 78).

19. See the interesting analysis of free indirect speech, using examples from Woolf and other writers, in Ann Banfield's "Narrative Style and the Grammar of Direct and Indirect Speech," *Foundations of Language* 10 (1973): 1–39. Perhaps the most helpful analysis of the *kind* of narrative method Woolf perfected in these works is the chapter "Narrated Monologue" in Dorrit Cohn's *Transparent Minds: Narrative Modes of Presenting Consciousness in Fiction* (Princeton: Princeton Univ. Press, 1978), 99–140.

20. J. K. Johnstone, *The Bloomsbury Group: A Study of E. M. Forster, Lytton Strachey, Virginia Woolf, and Their Circle* (London: Secker and Warburg, 1954), 274.

21. *Journal of Katherine Mansfield*, ed. J. Middleton Murry (New York: Alfred A. Knopf, 1931), 13.

22. Leonard Woolf, "Lytton Strachey," *New Statesman and Nation* (January 30, 1932), as reprinted in *The Bloomsbury Group: A Collection of Memoirs, Commentary and Criticism*, ed. S. P. Rosenbaum (Toronto: Univ. of Toronto Press, 1975), 180.

23. E. M. Forster, "Bloomsbury, An Early Note (February 1929)," in *The Bloomsbury Group*, ed. Rosenbaum, 26.

24. P. N. Furbank, *E. M. Forster: A Life* (New York: Harcourt Brace Jovanovich, 1978), I, 218.

25. Michael Holroyd, *Lytton Strachey: A Critical Biography* (New York: Holt, Rinehart and Winston, 1968), I, 393; II, 100.

26. E. M. Forster, *Marianne Thornton: A Domestic Biography, 1797–1887* (New York: Harcourt, Brace, 1956), 324.

27. E. M. Forster, *Howards End, The Abinger Edition of E. M. Forster* (London: Edward Arnold, 1973), 172 (ch. 19).

28. *The Collected Essays, Journalism and Letters of George Orwell*, ed. Sonia Orwell and Ian Angus (London: Secker and Warburg, 1968), II, 314.

29. N. G. Annan, "The Intellectual Aristocracy," in *Studies in Social History: A Tribute to G. M. Trevelyan*, ed. J. H. Plumb (London: Longmans, Green, 1955), 285.

CHAPTER 3

1. David Daiches, *Virginia Woolf* (New York: New Directions, 1963), 61.

2. Virginia Woolf and Lytton Strachey, *Letters*, ed. Leonard Woolf and James Strachey (London: Hogarth, 1969), 103.

3. *Selected Letters of E. M. Forster*, ed. Mary Lago and P. N. Furbank (Cambridge: Harvard Univ. Press, 1985), II, 21.

4. Joan Bennett, *Virginia Woolf: Her Art as a Novelist*, 2d ed. (Cambridge: Cambridge Univ. Press, 1964), 95, 96.

5. J. K. Johnstone, *The Bloomsbury Group: A Study of E. M. Forster, Lytton Strachey, Virginia Woolf, and Their Circle* (London: Secker and Warburg, 1954), 332, 334.

6. Woolf's most interesting comment on her own experimental methods in fiction was a direct response to critics who treated her next novel, *Mrs. Dalloway*, as a conscious methodological experiment. Her insistence on the inaccuracy of this view is equally pertinent to an understanding of *Jacob's Room* and is worth quoting at some length: "The book, it was said, was the deliberate offspring of a method. The author, it was said, dissatisfied with the form of fiction then in vogue, was determined to beg, borrow, steal or even create another of her own. But, as far as it is possible to be honest about the mysterious process of the mind, the facts are otherwise. Dissatisfied the writer may have been; but her dissatisfaction was primarily with nature for giving an idea, without providing a house for it to live in. . . . The novel was the obvious lodging, but the novel it seemed was built on the wrong plan. Thus rebuked the idea started as the oyster starts or the snail to secrete a house for itself. And this it did without any conscious direction. . . . It was necessary to write the book first and to invent a theory afterwards" (Virginia Woolf, "Introduction" to *Mrs. Dalloway* [New York: Modern Library, 1928], vii–viii). It is evident from this description that Woolf begins with a subject rather than with a method and that the subject seems to have a will of its own rather than allowing the novelist to shape it according to a preconceived theory of narration or a preexisting form.

7. Paul Fussell, *The Great War and Modern Memory* (New York: Oxford Univ. Press, 1975), 248.

8. John McCrae, *In Flanders Fields and Other Poems* (New York: Putnam's, 1919), 3.

9. A. J. P. Taylor, *English History, 1914–1945* (Harmondsworth: Penguin, 1970), 126n, 165–66.

10. For a detailed chronology, see Avrom Fleishman, *Virginia Woolf: A Critical Reading* (Baltimore: Johns Hopkins Univ. Press, 1975), 49–50.

11. Winifred Holtby, *Virginia Woolf* (London: Wishart, 1932), 116. More recent critics who have commented on the significance of the war in the book include Josephine O'Brien Schaefer, *The Three-Fold Nature of Reality in the Novels of Virginia Woolf* (The Hague: Mouton, 1965), 70–71; Carolyn G. Heilbrun, *Towards Androgyny: Aspects of Male and Female in Literature* (London: Victor Gollancz, 1973), 164; Nancy Topping Bazin, *Virginia Woolf and the Androgynous Vision* (New Brunswick, N.J.: Rutgers Univ. Press, 1973), 92–93; and Fleishman, 54. See also the excellent essay on Woolf's critical depiction of prewar British culture by Carol Ohmann, "Culture and Anarchy in *Jacob's Room*," *Contemporary Literature* 18 (1977): 160–72.

12. Erik Erikson, *Identity: Youth and Crisis* (New York: Norton, 1968), 156.

13. Virginia Woolf, *Jacob's Room*, holograph dated April 15, 1920–March 12, 1922, pt. I, 123, Berg Collection, New York Public Library.

14. *The Poetical Works of Rupert Brooke*, ed. Geoffrey Keynes (London: Faber and Faber, 1946), 23; *The Collected Poems of Wilfred Owen*, ed. C. Day Lewis (Norfolk, Conn.: New Directions, 1964), 44; Siegfried Sassoon, *Collected Poems, 1908–1956* (London: Faber and Faber, 1961), 119; H. G. Wells, *Mr. Britling Sees It Through* (New York: Macmillan, 1916), 431–32.

15. Carol Ohmann's finely judged description of Woolf's tone in *Jacob's Room* is worth quoting: "Neither is the novel an angry one. It is elegiac, rather, in its treatment of Jacob, and serenely so, mourning in tranquillity its hero's death and the end of what appeared to be his promise" (Ohmann, 171).

16. *The Collected Poems of Dylan Thomas* (New York: New Directions, 1953), 112.

17. Lytton Strachey to Leonard Woolf, 17 September 1908, Berg Collection, New York Public Library.

18. See chapter 10 of the *Jacob's Room* holograph (pt. I, 85–91), Berg Collection, New York Public Library. The chapter was later revised for publication as a short story, "A Woman's College from Outside," in *Atalanta's Garland: Being the Book of the Edinburgh University Women's Union 1926* (Edinburgh: Edinburgh Univ. Press, 1926), 11–16, and is reprinted in *BP*, 6–9. On Woolf's irreverent attitude toward Cambridge, see Irma Rantavaara, *Virginia Woolf and Bloomsbury* (Helsinki: Annales Academiae Fennicae, 1953), 102.

19. Virginia Woolf, "Reflections upon beginning a work of fiction to be called, perhaps, Jacobs Room," *Jacob's Room* holograph, pt. I, 1, Berg Collection, New York Public Library.

20. James Joyce, *Ulysses* (New York: Random House, 1946), 683.

21. Virginia Woolf and Lytton Strachey, 103, 104.

22. Lytton Strachey to Leonard Woolf, 21 November 1906, Berg Collection, New York Public Library.

23. Frances Marshall, in *Recollections of Virginia Woolf*, ed. Joan Russell Noble (London: Peter Owen, 1972), 76.

CHAPTER 4

1. Virginia Woolf, "Introductory Letter to Margaret Llewelyn Davies," in *Life as We Have Known It*, by Co-operative Working Women, ed. Margaret Llewelyn Davies (London: Hogarth, 1931), xviii–xix. The phrase "not touch one hair of my comfortable capitalistic head" is a later revision of the blander "not matter to me a single jot." The earlier version was originally published in *The Yale Review* (1930) and has been reprinted under the title "Memories of a Working Women's Guild" in *The Captain's Death Bed* and in the *Collected Essays*. The differences between the two versions, including the one mentioned above, are analyzed by Jane Marcus in her "'No More Horses': Virginia Woolf on Art and Propaganda," *Women's Studies* 4 (1977): 280–82.

2. E. M. Forster, *Virginia Woolf* (Cambridge: Cambridge Univ. Press, 1942), 24.

3. Karl Mannheim, "The Problems of the Intelligentsia," in his *Essays on the Sociology of Culture*, ed. Ernest Manheim (London: Routledge and Kegan Paul, 1956), 117.

4. N. G. Annan, "The Intellectual Aristocracy," in *Studies in Social History: A Tribute to G. M. Trevelyan*, ed. J. H. Plumb (London: Longmans, Green, 1955), 253–54. Annan's argument is essentially a social evolutionist revision of the biological determinism found in earlier discussions of the subject, particularly in Francis Galton's influential *Hereditary Genius* (1869, often reprinted), a book Woolf mentions in *Night and Day* (30).

5. Gaetano Mosca, *The Ruling Class*, trans. Hannah D. Kahn, ed. Arthur Livingston (New York: McGraw-Hill, 1939), 419. Mosca's *Elementi de scienza politica*, of which this is a translation, was originally published in 1896.

6. T. S. Eliot, *Notes Towards the Definition of Culture* (London: Faber and Faber, 1962), 48.

7. Leonard Woolf, *Sowing: An Autobiography of the Years 1880–1904* (London: Hogarth, 1970), 186, 190.

8. Clive Bell, *"Civilization" and "Old Friends"* (two books pub-

lished as one volume) (Chicago: Univ. of Chicago Press, 1973), 122. *Civilization* was originally published in 1928.

9. R. F. Harrod, *The Life of John Maynard Keynes* (New York: Harcourt, Brace, 1951), 192–93.

10. For an interesting stylistic analysis of Woolf's unconvincing attempt to record the *language* of working-class speech and thought, see Jeremy Hawthorn, *Virginia Woolf's Mrs Dalloway: A Study in Alienation* (Sussex: The University Press, 1975), 102–4.

11. Julia Stephen, untitled manuscript beginning "A number of articles have appeared lately dealing with the life of domestic servants," 11. Julia Stephen Archive, Washington State Univ. Library, Pullman, Wash.

12. Henrietta O. Barnett, "Women as Philanthropists," in *The Woman Question in Europe: A Series of Original Essays*, ed. Theodore Stanton (New York: Source Book Press, 1970), 116. The book was originally published in London and New York in 1884.

13. *Life of Octavia Hill as Told in Her Letters*, ed. C. Edmund Maurice (London: Macmillan, 1913), 212.

14. Thorstein Veblen, *The Theory of the Leisure Class: An Economic Study in the Evolution of Institutions* (New York: Macmillan, 1899), 44.

15. R. H. Tawney, *Equality*, 4th ed. (London: George Allen and Unwin, 1952), 158.

16. Vilfredo Pareto, *The Mind and Society*, ed. Arthur Livingston, trans. Andrew Bongiorno and Arthur Livingston (London: Jonathan Cape, 1935), III, 1430, 1419. Pareto's book, entitled *Trattato di sociologia generale*, was originally published in 1916, revised in 1923.

17. Mosca, 50, 422, 447.

18. Bell, 178.

19. John Maynard Keynes, "A Short View of Russia," *Essays in Persuasion* (London: Macmillan, 1931), 300.

20. José Ortega y Gasset, *The Revolt of the Masses*, trans. anon. (London: George Allen and Unwin, 1932), 18–19, 89–90.

21. Karl Mannheim, *Man and Society in an Age of Reconstruction*, trans. Edward Shils (London: Kegan Paul, Trench, Trubner, 1940), 92, 95. The book was published in German in 1935.

22. Eliot, 108.

23. Leonard Woolf, *Downhill All the Way: An Autobiography of the Years 1919–1939* (London: Hogarth, 1970), 63, 17.

24. Leonard Woolf, *Downhill All the Way*, 68.

25. Leonard Woolf, *Beginning Again: An Autobiography of the Years 1911–1918* (London: Hogarth, 1968), 232.

26. Leslie Stephen to Julia Duckworth (Stephen), 18 July 1877, Berg Collection, New York Public Library.

27. Leonard Woolf, *Beginning Again*, 139, 133.

28. *The Letters of Ezra Pound, 1907–1941*, ed. D. D. Paige (London: Faber and Faber, 1951), 204, 297.

29. Leonard Woolf, *Beginning Again*, 94.

30. E. M. Forster, "Bloomsbury, An Early Note (February 1929)," in *The Bloomsbury Group: A Collection of Memoirs, Commentary and Criticism*, ed. S. P. Rosenbaum (Toronto: Univ. of Toronto Press, 1975), 26. Forster's manuscript in the King's College Library, Cambridge, reads "acquired," not "required" as in the Rosenbaum anthology. Raymond Williams's searching critique of the Bloomsbury group's class assumptions ratifies Forster's sense of them: "The Significance of 'Bloomsbury' as a Social and Cultural Group," in *Keynes and the Bloomsbury Group*, ed. Derek Crabtree and A. P. Thirlwall (New York: Holmes and Meier, 1980), 40–67.

31. *Recollections of Virginia Woolf*, ed. Joan Russell Noble (London: Peter Owen, 1972), 170.

32. *Recollections of Virginia Woolf*, 50, 146.

33. *Recollections of Virginia Woolf*, 18.

34. Quoted in Leonore Davidoff, *The Best Circles: Society Etiquette and the Season* (London: Croom Helm, 1973), 78.

35. Virginia Woolf, "Anon," Notebook 1938–39, 76, Berg Collection, New York Public Library. The notebook is filed as [Articles, essays, fiction and reviews] v. 8.

36. John Maynard Keynes to Vanessa Bell, 28 July 1917 and 31 January 1918, Garnett Collection, Northwestern Univ. Library, Evanston, Ill.

37. Virginia Woolf, "Introductory Letter to Margaret Llewelyn Davies," xxi.

38. Mannheim, *Essays on the Sociology of Culture*, 160.

CHAPTER 5

1. E. M. Forster, *Virginia Woolf* (Cambridge: Cambridge Univ. Press, 1942), 8; Jean Guiguet, *Virginia Woolf and Her Works*, trans. Jean Stewart (London: Hogarth, 1965), 71–72.

2. Bernard Blackstone, *Virginia Woolf: A Commentary* (London: Hogarth, 1949), 98.

3. Compare the assessment of the interwar governments in Charles Loch Mowat's *Britain Between the Wars, 1918–1940* (London: Methuen, 1962): "adequate discharge of routine duties, complacency, the failure of imagination and will" (144).

4. A. D. Moody, *Virginia Woolf* (Edinburgh: Oliver and Boyd, 1963), 21.

5. In Forster's *Howards End* Helen Schlegel attacks the Wilcox family in similar terms, as representatives of a new social force that

disguises its power hunger in impersonality: "There's a nightmare of a theory that says a special race is being born which will rule the rest of us in the future just because it lacks the little thing that says 'I'" (E. M. Forster, *Howards End*, *The Abinger Edition of E. M. Forster* [London: Edward Arnold, 1973], 231 [ch. 27]).

6. Jean O. Love, for example, writes that the party is an "indiscriminate mingling and, finally, fusion into a single whole of persons from different social strata" in her *Worlds in Consciousness: Mythopoetic Thought in the Novels of Virginia Woolf* (Berkeley and Los Angeles: Univ. of California Press, 1970), 158.

7. See A. J. P. Taylor, *English History, 1914–1945* (Harmondsworth: Penguin, 1970), 194–95.

8. Virginia Woolf, notebook dated Nov. 9, 1922–Aug. 2, 1923, 12, Berg Collection, New York Public Library.

9. Ibid., 4.

10. See, for example, J. K. Johnstone, *The Bloomsbury Group: A Study of E. M. Forster, Lytton Strachey, Virginia Woolf, and Their Circle* (London: Secker and Warburg, 1954), 340–41.

11. J. Hillis Miller, "Virginia Woolf's All Souls' Day: The Omniscient Narrator in *Mrs. Dalloway*," in *The Shaken Realist: Essays in Modern Literature in Honor of Frederick J. Hoffman*, ed. Melvin J. Friedman and John B. Vickery (Baton Rouge: Louisiana State Univ. Press, 1970), 113.

12. Quoted in Wallace Hildick, *Word for Word: A Study of Authors' Alterations with Exercises* (London: Faber and Faber, 1965), 185, from the British Museum MS of *Mrs. Dalloway*.

13. Woolf, notebook dated Nov. 9, 1922–Aug. 2, 1923, 2.

14. A. D. Moody, "The Unmasking of Clarissa Dalloway," *Review of English Literature* 3 (1962): 68–69.

15. Isabel Gamble, "The Secret Sharer in *Mrs. Dalloway*," *Accent* 16 (1956): 251.

16. Alice van Buren Kelley, *The Novels of Virginia Woolf: Fact and Vision* (Chicago: Univ. of Chicago Press, 1973), 104.

CHAPTER 6

1. G. M. Young, *Portrait of an Age: Victorian England*, 2d ed. (Oxford: Oxford Univ. Press, 1977), 131.

2. Walter E. Houghton, *The Victorian Frame of Mind, 1830–1870* (New Haven: Yale Univ. Press, 1957), 346.

3. John Ruskin, *Sesame and Lilies*, in *The Complete Works of John Ruskin*, ed. E. T. Cook and John Wedderburn (London: George Allen, 1903–10), XVIII, 122.

4. Leslie Stephen, *The Science of Ethics* (New York: G. P. Putnam's Sons, 1882), 134.

5. Leslie Stephen, *Social Rights and Duties: Addresses to Ethical Societies* (London: Swan Sonnenschein, 1892), II, 244.

6. Frederick Engels, *The Origin of the Family, Private Property and the State*, trans. Alick West and Dona Torr (London: Lawrence and Wishart, [1941]), 5.

7. George Dangerfield, *The Strange Death of Liberal England* (New York: Putnam's, 1961), 149. For a brief summary of the attacks around the turn of the century on the theory of the patriarchal family, see the entry "Family" in the eleventh edition of the *Encyclopaedia Britannica* (1910).

8. Samuel Butler, *The Way of All Flesh* (New York: Dutton, 1917), 439 (ch. 84).

9. Bernard Shaw, *Misalliance: A Debate in One Sitting*, in *Complete Plays with Prefaces* (New York: Dodd, Mead, 1962), IV, 85.

10. H. G. Wells, *Ann Veronica: A Modern Love Story* (New York: Harper and Brothers, 1909), 150.

11. Leonard Woolf, *Sowing: An Autobiography of the Years 1880–1904* (London: Hogarth, 1970), 151–52, 163.

12. Virginia Woolf and Lytton Strachey, *Letters*, ed. Leonard Woolf and James Strachey (London: Hogarth, 1969), 43.

13. Noel Gilroy Annan, *Leslie Stephen: His Thought and Character in Relation to His Time* (Cambridge: Harvard Univ. Press, 1952), 104.

14. Michael Holroyd, *Lytton Strachey: A Critical Biography* (New York: Holt, Rinehart and Winston, 1968), I, 75.

15. Shaw, *Misalliance*, IV, 143; *Getting Married*, in *Complete Plays with Prefaces*, IV, 362.

16. *Samuel Butler's Notebooks*, ed. Geoffrey Keynes and Brian Hill (London: Jonathan Cape, 1951), 100; Butler, *The Way of All Flesh*, 333 (ch. 67).

17. Virginia Woolf, *Freshwater: A Comedy*, ed. Lucio P. Ruotolo (New York: Harcourt Brace Jovanovich, 1976), 44.

18. George Edward Moore, *Principia Ethica* (Cambridge: Cambridge Univ. Press, 1956), 149; emphasis added.

19. Wells, 75.

20. Frances Power Cobbe, *The Duties of Women* (Boston: Geo. H. Ellis, 1882), 111.

21. Quoted in Lawrence Stone, *The Family, Sex and Marriage in England, 1500–1800* (New York: Harper and Row, 1977), 331. See also Stone's description of the Victorian paterfamilias, 667.

22. Jeremy Bentham, *The Theory of Legislation*, ed. C. K. Ogden (London: Kegan Paul, Trench, Trubner, 1931), 230–31.

23. James Fitzjames Stephen, *Liberty, Equality, Fraternity* (New York: Henry Holt, 1882), 212, 214, 217–18.

24. Isabella Beeton, *The Book of Household Management*, new edition (London: Ward, Lock, 1880), 12.

25. J. A. Banks, *Prosperity and Parenthood: A Study of Family Planning Among the Victorian Middle Classes* (London: Routledge and Kegan Paul, 1954), 3–4.

26. Quoted in C. V. Drysdale, *The Small Family System: Is It Injurious or Immoral?* (London: A. C. Fifield, 1913), 45.

27. Mona Caird, *The Morality of Marriage, and Other Essays on the Status and Destiny of Woman* (London: George Redway, 1897), 185. See also the attack on frequent conception in Marie Stopes's *Married Love, or Love in Marriage* (New York: Truth Publishing, 1921), 141, and the chapter called "The Wickedness of Creating Large Families" in Margaret Sanger's *The New Motherhood* (London: Jonathan Cape, 1922), 79–96.

28. See the Woolf family tree reproduced in *The Letters of Virginia Woolf*, ed. Nigel Nicolson and Joanne Trautmann (London: Hogarth, 1977), III, 522.

29. Vanessa Bell to Virginia Stephen, 3 August 1907, Berg Collection, New York Public Library.

30. See Philippe Ariès, *Centuries of Childhood: A Social History of Family Life*, trans. Robert Baldick (New York: Vintage, n.d.), 398–99; Edward Shorter, *The Making of the Modern Family* (New York: Basic Books, [1977]), 205, 218.

31. Charlotte Perkins Gilman, *The Home: Its Work and Influence* (Urbana: Univ. of Illinois Press, 1972), 39.

32. Stephen Kern, "Explosive Intimacy: Psychodynamics of the Victorian Family," *History of Childhood Quarterly* 1 (1974): 438.

33. John Stuart Mill, *The Subjection of Women* (New York: D. Appleton, 1870), 139.

34. Florence Nightingale, "Cassandra," in Ray Strachey, *Struggle: The Stirring Story of Woman's Advance in England* (New York: Duffield, 1930), 404–5. The original English edition of Strachey's book is called *"The Cause": A Short History of the Women's Movement in Great Britain* (London: G. Bell, 1928).

35. Bernard Shaw, *Pen Portraits and Reviews* (London: Constable, 1932), 53.

36. Steven Marcus, *The Other Victorians: A Study of Sexuality and Pornography in Mid-Nineteenth-Century England* (New York: Basic Books, 1966), 283–84. See also Peter T. Cominos, "Late Victorian Sexual Respectability and the Social System," *International Review of Social History* 8 (1963): 18–48, 216–50.

37. Leslie Stephen to Julia Duckworth Stephen, 4 February 1887, Berg Collection, New York Public Library.

38. Shaw, *Getting Married*, IV, 317.

39. Quentin Bell, *Bloomsbury* (London: Weidenfeld and Nicolson, 1973), 42.

40. See, for example, Nancy Topping Bazin, *Virginia Woolf and the*

Androgynous Vision (New Brunswick, N.J.: Rutgers Univ. Press, 1973), 54–56.

41. For a more detailed consideration of Woolf's revisionist treatment of sexual life, see Harold Fromm, "Virginia Woolf: Art and Sexuality," *Virginia Quarterly Review* 55 (1979): 441–59.

42. William Carlos Williams, *Paterson* (New York: New Directions, 1963), 28.

43. Quoted in P. N. Furbank, *E. M. Forster: A Life* (New York: Harcourt Brace Jovanovich, 1978), I, 218.

44. Margaret Todd, *The Life of Sophia Jex-Blake* (London: Macmillan, 1918), 216.

45. Christabel Pankhurst, *The Great Scourge and How to End It* (London: E. Pankhurst, 1913), 66, 131–32.

46. George Gissing, *The Odd Women* (New York: Norton, 1977), 99.

47. Phyllis Rose, *Woman of Letters: A Life of Virginia Woolf* (New York: Oxford Univ. Press, 1978), 73.

CHAPTER 7

1. Leonard Woolf, *Sowing: An Autobiography of the Years 1880–1904* (London: Hogarth, 1970), 182.

2. For a detailed analysis of the differences between Leslie Stephen and Mr. Ramsay, see John Bicknell, "Mr. Ramsay Was Young Once," in *Virginia Woolf and Bloomsbury: A Centenary Celebration*, ed. Jane Marcus (Bloomington: Indiana Univ. Press, 1986), 52–67.

3. Leslie Stephen to Julia Duckworth Stephen, 6 October 1886, Berg Collection, New York Public Library.

4. Frederic William Maitland, *The Life and Letters of Leslie Stephen* (London: Duckworth, 1906), 474.

5. Leslie Stephen to Julia Duckworth Stephen, 29–30 July 1893, Berg Collection, New York Public Library. For a detailed analysis of Leslie Stephen's intellectual influence on Woolf, see Katherine Hill's "Virginia Woolf and Leslie Stephen: History and Literary Revolution," *PMLA* 96 (1981): 351–62. Hill argues that Stephen was determined to make his daughter his intellectual heir and "trained her extensively in history and biography to give her the background fundamental to this achievement" (351).

6. Leslie Stephen to Julia Duckworth (Stephen), 18 July 1877, Berg Collection, New York Public Library. It is worth noting that this is not an argument for the higher education of women, a cause to which Stephen was largely indifferent. In fact, he had serious doubts about the general quality of university education, suggested in his phrase "a great deal better than men are now." Rather, he believed that individual vocation should determine the training provided. When it became clear that Vanessa wanted to be a painter, she

received the kind of formal instruction appropriate to that ambition. Virginia's equally precocious choice of a literary vocation was taken seriously from the start and fostered by her father. He would not have thought a university education particularly useful for a writer, male or female, and though Virginia Woolf was to see her lack of academic training as a deprivation, there is something to be said for Stephen's view. Her striking intellectual independence owes a good deal to her freedom from the constraints imposed by the standard university degree programs.

7. *Sir Leslie Stephen's Mausoleum Book*, ed. Alan Bell (Oxford: Clarendon, 1977), 93.

8. Noel Gilroy Annan, *Leslie Stephen: His Thought and Character in Relation to His Time* (Cambridge: Harvard Univ. Press, 1952), 279.

9. Leslie Stephen to Julia Duckworth Stephen, 23 October 1884, 5 February 1885, 8 February 1885, 3 February 1886, Berg Collection, New York Public Library.

10. Maitland, 387, 471. Lyndall Gordon has argued that it was Stephen's "disappointment" at the reception of his ambitious philosophical work *The Science of Ethics* in 1882 that made him accept the editorship of the *DNB* in that year (*Virginia Woolf: A Writer's Life* [Oxford: Oxford Univ. Press, 1984], 25). It was also the year of Virginia's birth.

11. Julia Stephen, essay beginning "Among all the changes & upheavals which late years have brought," 4–5, Julia Stephen Archive, Washington State Univ. Library, Pullman, Wash.

12. Lytton Strachey, *Eminent Victorians* (New York: Harcourt, Brace and World, n.d.), 156.

13. Julia Stephen, "Among all the changes," 3.

14. Julia Stephen, "Agnostic Women," 1, 14, Julia Stephen Archive, Washington State Univ. Library, Pullman, Wash.

15. In two of Leslie Stephen's letters to Julia (5 February and 18 July 1885) he refers to negotiations with Routledge—ultimately unsuccessful—for publishing "our little work." I am grateful to John Bicknell for calling these references to my attention.

16. Quoted by Frances Power Cobbe, in *Woman's Work and Woman's Culture: A Series of Essays*, ed. Josephine E. Butler (London: Macmillan, 1869), 18.

17. Vanessa Bell to Virginia Stephen, 27 August 1909, Berg Collection, New York Public Library. The conflict between creative work and childrearing is also obliquely suggested in *A Room of One's Own*, as Harvena Richter has demonstrated. Woolf's use of the traditional ballad "Mary Hamilton" in that book, Richter argues, intimates that "the creative woman . . . dare not have children of her own" ("Virginia Woolf and Mary Hamilton," *Virginia Woolf Miscellany*, no. 24 [Spring 1985], 1). The ballad is about a young woman who kills

her illegitimate child; the variant texts are reproduced in Bertrand H. Bronson, *The Singing Tradition of Child's Popular Ballads* (Princeton: Princeton Univ. Press, 1976), 320–22.

18. Virginia Woolf, *"To the Lighthouse": The Original Holograph Draft*, ed. Susan Dick (London: Hogarth, 1983), Appendix A, 11.

19. Vanessa Bell to Virginia Stephen, 26 December 1909, Berg Collection, New York Public Library.

20. Adapted from Mitchell A. Leaska, *Virginia Woolf's "Lighthouse": A Study in Critical Method* (London: Hogarth, 1970), 208.

21. Jane Lilienfeld, "'The Deceptiveness of Beauty': Mother Love and Mother Hate in *To the Lighthouse*," *Twentieth Century Literature* 23 (1977): 346–47; see also Sally Alexander Brett, "No, Mrs. Ramsay: Feminist Dilemma in *To the Lighthouse*," *Ball State University Forum* 19 (1978): 48–56, and the related attack on Mrs. Ramsay in Carolyn G. Heilbrun's *Toward a Recognition of Androgyny* (New York: Harper and Row, 1974): 155–60.

22. See the entry dated 6 August 1925 in Virginia Woolf, *"To the Lighthouse": The Original Holograph Draft*, 2.

23. Ibid., 138. To make this passage more readable, I have not transcribed all of Woolf's deletions and insertions.

24. Avrom Fleishman, *Virginia Woolf: A Critical Reading* (Baltimore: Johns Hopkins Univ. Press, 1975), 120–21.

25. Vanessa Bell, *Notes on Virginia's Childhood: A Memoir*, ed. Richard J. Schaubeck, Jr. (New York: F. Hallman, 1974), [9].

26. Mary MacCarthy, *A Nineteenth-Century Childhood* (London: Heinemann, 1924), 18. Woolf reviewed the book in *TLS*, 2 October 1924, 609 (*L*, III, 135n).

27. Bertrand Russell, *Marriage and Morals* (London: George Allen and Unwin, 1929), 240.

28. Barbara Stephen, *Emily Davies and Girton College* (London: Constable, 1927), 1–18.

29. Mary Agnes Hamilton, "Changes in Social Life," in *Our Freedom and Its Results*, ed. Ray Strachey (London: Leonard and Virginia Woolf at the Hogarth Press, 1936), 280.

30. Thomas G. Matro has analyzed Woolf's use of "yet" and "but" in *To the Lighthouse* at length in his valuable essay "Only Relations: Vision and Achievement in *To the Lighthouse*," *PMLA* 99 (1984): 212–24.

31. Erich Auerbach, *Mimesis: The Representation of Reality in Western Literature*, trans. Willard R. Trask (Princeton: Princeton Univ. Press, 1968), 531.

32. Virginia Woolf, *"To the Lighthouse": The Original Holograph Draft*, 261.

33. Phyllis Rose, *Woman of Letters: A Life of Virginia Woolf* (New York: Oxford Univ. Press, 1978), 169.

34. Jane Ellen Harrison, *Ancient Art and Ritual* (New York: Henry Holt, 1913), 132.

35. For a psychoanalytic explanation of Woolf's failure to "work through" her grief and anger about her parents in *To the Lighthouse*, see Mark Spilka, *Virginia Woolf's Quarrel with Grieving* (Lincoln: Univ. of Nebraska Press, 1980), 75–109.

36. Much of this material has been published as "A Sketch of the Past," *MB*, 61–137. But there is also a recently discovered, thus far unpublished, typescript composed in 1940 ("the Juggs typescript," British Library Add. MSS 61973) that includes Woolf's most detailed discussion of her feelings about her father. I am grateful to Noel Annan for calling it to my attention.

CHAPTER 8

1. E. M. Forster, *Virginia Woolf* (Cambridge: Cambridge Univ. Press, 1942), 23.

2. Jane Marcus, "Art and Anger," *Feminist Studies* 4 (1978): 93.

3. Monique Nathan, *Virginia Woolf*, trans. Herma Briffault (New York: Grove, 1961), 28. Original French edition published in 1956.

4. Margaret Drabble, *Virginia Woolf: A Personal Debt* ([New York]: Aloe Editions, 1973), 3.

5. For an account of this phase of the Suffragette movement, see Andrew Rosen, *Rise Up, Women!: The Militant Campaign of the Women's Social and Political Union, 1903–1914* (London: Routledge and Kegan Paul, 1974), 118–32.

6. Emmeline Pankhurst, *My Own Story* (1914; New York: Kraus Reprint, 1971), 57.

7. Frances Power Cobbe, "Introduction," *The Woman Question in Europe: A Series of Original Essays*, ed. Theodore Stanton (New York: Source Book, 1970), xiv.

8. Constance Rover, *Women's Suffrage and Party Politics in Britain, 1866–1914* (London: Routledge and Kegan Paul, 1967), 2.

9. See Christabel Pankhurst, *The Great Scourge and How to End It* (London: E. Pankhurst, 1913). H. G. Wells's thinly disguised portrait of Christabel Pankhurst in his novel *Ann Veronica* stresses this obsession: "Freedom! Citizenship! And the way to that—the way to everything—is the Vote." To the objection "that much of a woman's difficulties are economic" she can only respond with the refrain, "Everything will follow. . . . The Vote is the symbol of everything" ([New York: Harper and Brothers, 1909], 242–43).

10. Eleanor F. Rathbone, "Changes in Public Life," in *Our Freedom and Its Results*, ed. Ray Strachey (London: Leonard and Virginia Woolf at the Hogarth Press, 1936), 16. Emphasis added.

11. Sir Almroth E. Wright, *The Unexpurgated Case Against Woman Suffrage* (New York: Paul B. Hoeber, 1913), 57.

12. E. Belfort Bax, *The Fraud of Feminism* (London: Grant Richards, 1913), 143.

13. E. M. Forster, *Howards End, The Abinger Edition of E. M. Forster* (London: Edward Arnold, 1973), 237 (ch. 28).

14. Dora Russell, *Hypatia, or Women and Knowledge* (London: Kegan Paul, Trench, Trubner, [1925]), 1. By this time, another historical event had greatly exacerbated the relations between the sexes: the aftermath of World War I. Sandra Gilbert analyzes the war "as an apocalyptic turning point in the battle of the sexes" in her important essay "Soldier's Heart: Literary Men, Literary Women, and the Great War," *Signs: Journal of Women in Culture and Society* 8 (1983): 426.

15. Mary Agnes Hamilton, "Changes in Social Life," in *Our Freedom and Its Results*, 259.

16. John Stuart Mill, *The Subjection of Women* (New York: D. Appleton, 1870), 27, 67.

17. Emily Davies, *Thoughts on Some Questions Relating to Women, 1860–1908* (New York: AMS, 1973), 131.

18. Florence Nightingale, "Cassandra," in *"The Cause": A Short History of the Women's Movement in Great Britain*, ed. Ray Strachey (London: G. Bell, 1928), 407. Woolf knew the essay well: see *AROO*, 84n. A longer and exceptionally interesting analysis of it was apparently cut from *A Room of One's Own* at the last moment. It occurs in the typescript of the book originally sent to Harcourt Brace and now with the Monk's House Papers. Woolf advises her audience to read Nightingale's essay "if you want to know to what a pitch of hysteria, to what a shriek of nervous agony those conditions could bring a woman of fine nature, of high intellectual powers. . . . It was partly the thought of the frittered energies, of the great gifts ruined and run to seed, that haunted her and maddened her" (*A Room of One's Own*, typescript, 100, Monk's House Papers B 15:1, Univ. of Sussex Library).

19. Arnold Bennett, *Our Women: Chapters on the Sex-Discord* (New York: George H. Doran, 1920), 112, 108, 103–4. See also Woolf's comments on H. G. Wells's critical remarks about women's failure to use their new professional opportunities (*D*, IV, 75).

20. Bennett, 112–13.

21. Mill, 132.

22. Clemence Dane, *The Women's Side* (London: Herbert Jenkins, 1926), 131.

23. Many of these essays have now been collected in Virginia Woolf, *Women and Writing*, ed. Michèle Barrett (New York: Harcourt Brace Jovanovich, 1979).

24. Ellen Moers, in her *Literary Women* (Garden City, N.Y.: An-

chor Books, 1977), argues that "money and its making were characteristically female rather than male subjects in English fiction" (101).
Her chapter "Money, the Job, and Little Women: Female Realism" is
an extended discussion of the issue. Probably the most important
study of women's financial situation published before Woolf's own
work is Charlotte Perkins Gilman's *Women and Economics* (1898). I do
not know whether Woolf was familiar with the book, though it was
widely read in the United States and Britain and translated into several languages. Gilman's call for an end to women's financial dependence was largely forgotten during the suffrage phase of the
women's movement, however.

25. Wright, 26.

26. Frederick Engels, *The Origin of the Family, Private Property and
the State*, trans. Alick West and Dona Torr (London: Lawrence and
Wishart, [1941]), 79, 89.

27. Leonard Woolf, *Downhill All the Way: An Autobiography of the
Years 1919–1939* (London: Hogarth, 1967), 142. It is interesting that
around this time Virginia Woolf also started keeping a detailed record of her own income and expenses—a task she had previously en-
trusted to the methodical Leonard. See her unpublished account book
dated July 1928–July 1937 in the Washington State Univ. Library.

28. Virginia Woolf, "Professions for Women," notebook dated
8 April 1933, 125, Berg Collection, New York Public Library.

29. Q. D. Leavis, "Caterpillars of the Commonwealth Unite!,"
Scrutiny 7 (1938): 203.

30. Cobbe, xvi.

31. Emily Davies, *The Higher Education of Women* (New York: AMS,
1973), 109–10.

32. See E. Sylvia Pankhurst, *The Suffragette Movement: An Intimate
Account of Persons and Ideals* (London: Longmans, Green, 1931), 416.

33. See George Dangerfield, *The Strange Death of Liberal England*
(New York: Harrison Smith and Robert Haas, 1935), 212; and
Strachey, *"The Cause,"* 245.

34. Dangerfield, 387. The generalization is not quite accurate:
Sylvia Pankhurst, for example, opposed the war.

35. Christabel Pankhurst, *Unshackled: The Story of How We Won the
Vote*, ed. Lord Pethick-Lawrence (London: Hutchinson, 1959), 290.

36. Emmeline Pankhurst, 267.

37. E. Sylvia Pankhurst, 517.

38. Mill, 95, 94.

39. Maria G. Grey, "The Women's Educational Movement," in
Woman Question in Europe, 43.

40. Millicent Garrett Fawcett, *What I Remember* (London: T. Fisher
Unwin, 1924), 140.

41. Rathbone, 57–58. For a detailed analysis of the distinction

between these two kinds of feminism, see the interesting essay by Naomi Black, "Virginia Woolf and the Women's Movement," in *Virginia Woolf: A Feminist Slant*, ed. Jane Marcus (Lincoln: Univ. of Nebraska Press, 1983), 180–97, especially 182–83.

42. Virginia Woolf, draft of her review of *The Letters of Olive Schreiner*, in [Mrs. Dalloway. Fragments] Holograph pages in note-book dated Hogarth House, Richmond, 7 January 1924, 241, Berg Collection, New York Public Library. These critical sentiments are considerably toned down in the published version of the review. See Virginia Woolf, "Olive Schreiner," *New Republic* 42 (1925): 103.

43. Elaine Showalter, *A Literature of Their Own: British Women Novelists from Brontë to Lessing*, new rev. ed. (London: Virago, 1982), 265.

Chapter 9

1. Adrienne Rich, "When We Dead Awaken: Writing as Re-Vision," in her *On Lies, Secrets, and Silence: Selected Prose, 1966–1978* (New York: Norton, 1979), 37.

2. Elaine Showalter, *A Literature of Their Own: British Women Novelists from Brontë to Lessing* (Princeton: Princeton Univ. Press, 1977), 262.

3. Jane Marcus, "Art and Anger," *Feminist Studies* 4 (1978): 94.

4. T. E. Hulme, "Romanticism and Classicism," in his *Speculations: Essays on Humanism and the Philosopthy of Art*, ed. Herbert Read (London: Routledge and Kegan Paul, 1924), 120, 126.

5. T. S. Eliot, "Tradition and the Individual Talent," in his *Selected Essays, 1917–1932* (New York: Harcourt, Brace, 1932), 10, 7–8.

6. *The Letters of Katherine Mansfield*, ed. J. Middleton Murry (New York: Knopf, 1941), 338.

7. Christabel Pankhurst, *Unshackled: The Story of How We Won the Vote*. ed. Lord Pethick-Lawrence (London: Hutchinson, 1959), 55.

8. See her letter to Janet Case, 1 January 1910 (*L*, I, 421).

9. Barbara Stephen, *Emily Davies and Girton College* (London: Constable, 1972), 108.

10. Ibid., 145.

11. Margaret Todd, *The Life of Sophia Jex-Blake* (London: Macmillan, 1918), 283.

12. Ray Strachey, *"The Cause": A Short History of the Women's Movement in Great Britain* (London: G. Bell and Sons, 1928), 180–81.

13. Mary Wollstonecraft, *A Vindication of the Rights of Woman*, ed. Charles W. Hagelman, Jr. (New York: Norton, 1967), 215.

14. Millicent Garrett Fawcett, *Women's Suffrage: A Short History of a Great Movement* (London: T. C. and E. C. Jack, [1912]), 41.

15. Todd, 503.

16. Rich, 37.

17. Showalter, 264. Showalter's whole chapter on Woolf is an attack on the evasiveness of Woolf's androgynous ideal. See also Carolyn Heilbrun, *Towards Androgyny: Aspects of Male and Female in Literature* (London: Victor Gollancz, 1973), 115–67; and Marilyn Farwell, "Virginia Woolf and Androgyny," *Contemporary Literature* 16 (1975): 433–51.

18. Virginia Woolf, typescript of January 21, 1931, Speech before the London/National Society for Women's Service, Berg Collection, New York Public Library, 21. The passage is published in Virginia Woolf, *The Pargiters: The Novel-Essay Portion of "The Years,"* ed. Mitchell A. Leaska (New York: New York Public Library, 1977), xxxiv, with erroneous reading of "manipulated" for "emancipated."

19. For an interesting study of such internal contradictions in the argument of *A Room of One's Own*, see John Burt, "Irreconcilable Habits of Thought in *A Room of One's Own* and *To the Lighthouse*," *ELH* 49 (1982): 889–907. Burt sees the conflict between Woolf's optimistic and pessimistic impulses moving the book "into a thicket of self-refutation from which there appears to be no escape" (893).

20. Virginia Woolf, [*Three Guineas*] later typescript, Berg Collection, New York Public Library, 120–21. Such passages confirm Sandra Gilbert's interpretation of *Three Guineas* as a vehicle for Woolf's "violent antipatriarchal fantasies paradoxically embedded in an ostensibly nonviolent treatise on the subject of 'how to prevent war'" ("Soldier's Heart: Literary Men, Literary Women, and the Great War," *Signs: Journal of Women in Culture and Society* 8 [1983]: 445). But it is worth noting that Woolf excised the most intense expressions of her disgust in revising for publication.

21. Quoted in Herman Finer, *Mussolini's Italy* (London: Victor Gollancz, 1935), 175.

22. *The Speeches of Adolf Hitler*, trans. Norman H. Baynes (London: Oxford Univ. Press, 1942), I, 528–29.

23. Adolf Hitler, *Mein Kampf*, ed. John Chamberlain et al. (New York: Reynal and Hitchcock, 1939), 384.

24. Julian Bell, "Introduction," *We Did Not Fight: 1914–18 Experiences of War Resisters* (London: Cobden-Sanderson, 1935), xv, xix.

25. "War and Peace: A Letter to E. M. Forster," in *Julian Bell: Essays, Poems and Letters*, ed. Quentin Bell (London: Hogarth, 1938), 389.

26. W. H. Auden, *Spain* (London: Faber and Faber, 1937), 11. He later changed the line to "The conscious acceptance of guilt in the fact of murder" (*The English Auden: Poems, Essays and Dramatic Writings*, ed. Edward Mendelson [London: Faber and Faber, 1977], 212).

27. W. B. Yeats, *A Vision* (New York: Macmillan, 1956), 52–53.

28. W. B. Yeats, *Collected Poems* (New York: Macmillan, 1951), 342.

29. T. S. Eliot, "In Sincerity and Earnestness: New Britain As I See It," *New Britain* 3 (1934): 274.

30. Samuel Hynes, *The Auden Generation: Literature and Politics in England in the 1930s* (New York: Viking, 1977), 301.

31. Q. D. Leavis, "Caterpillars of the Commonwealth Unite!," *Scrutiny* 7 (1938): 203–14.

32. Wyndham Lewis, *Men Without Art* (London: Cassell, 1934), 170.

CHAPTER 10

1. Adrian Stephen, *The "Dreadnought" Hoax* (London: Hogarth, 1936), 43. See also QB, I, 157–61 and 213–16.

2. Quoted in Stephen Hobhouse, "Fourteen Months' Service with the Colours," *We Did Not Fight: 1914–18 Experiences of War Resisters*. ed. Julian Bell (London: Cobden-Sanderson, 1935), 159; and Norman Angell, *The Great Illusion: A Study of the Relation of Military Power in Nations to Their Economic and Social Advantage* (London: William Heinemann, 1910), 44.

3. Leslie Stephen to Julia Duckworth (Stephen), 5 August 1877, Berg Collection, New York Public Library.

4. Frederic William Maitland, *The Life and Letters of Leslie Stephen* (London: Duckworth, 1906), 436.

5. Joan Bennett, *Virginia Woolf: Her Art as a Novelist*, 2d ed. (Cambridge: Cambridge Univ. Press, 1964), 70.

6. Virginia Woolf, "Reminiscences of Julian," Monk's House Papers A 8:9, Univ. of Sussex Library.

7. The Nicholson-Trautmann edition of the letters gives "enlarge the imaginative," but I read the word in the Berg manuscript as "imagination."

8. Mary Wollstonecraft, *A Vindication of the Rights of Woman*, ed. Charles W. Hagelman, Jr. (New York: Norton, 1967), 45. Unlike some of the Continental powers, Britain had long opposed standing armies, a national tradition Wollstonecraft is here supporting.

9. Clive Bell, *"Civilization" and "Old Friends"* (two books published as one volume) (Chicago: Univ. of Chicago Press, 1973), 83.

10. E. M. Forster, "What I Believe," *Two Cheers for Democracy* (London: Edward Arnold, 1951), 78.

11. Quoted in F. L. Carsten, *War Against War: British and German Radical Movements in the First World War* (London: Batsford, 1982), 68.

12. Beverley Nichols, *Cry Havoc!* (London: Jonathan Cape, 1933), 209.

13. Francis Meynell, "What Shall I Do in the Next War?" in *Manifesto*, ed. C. E. M. Joad (London: George Allen and Unwin, 1934), 137.

14. For a list of Hogarth Press publications see J. Howard Woolmer, *A Checklist of the Hogarth Press, 1917–1938* (Andes, N.Y.: Woolmer-Brotherson, 1976).

15. Wilhelm Emil Mühlmann, "Pacifism and Nonviolent Movements," *Encyclopaedia Britannica*, 15th ed., *Macropaedia*, XIII, 847.

16. Sigmund Freud, *Civilization and Its Discontents*, in *The Standard Edition of the Complete Psychological Works*, trans. and ed. James Strachey (London: Hogarth, 1966–74), XXI, 64.

17. Virginia Woolf, "Introduction," *Mrs. Dalloway* (New York: Modern Library, 1928), vi.

18. Ralph Freedman, *The Lyrical Novel: Studies in Hermann Hesse, André Gide, and Virginia Woolf* (Princeton: Princeton Univ. Press, 1963), 252.

19. For a detailed study of such moments in Woolf's fiction, see James Naremore, *The World Without a Self: Virginia Woolf and the Novel* (New Haven and London: Yale Univ. Press, 1973).

20. Leonard Woolf, *Beginning Again: An Autobiography of the Years 1911–1918* (London: Hogarth, 1964), 197.

21. Clive Bell, *Peace at Once* (Manchester: National Labour Press [1915]), 38–39.

22. Vanessa Bell to Virginia Woolf, 11 November 1918, Berg Collection, New York Public Library.

23. Vanessa Bell to Virginia Woolf, 22 August 1915, Berg Collection, New York Public Library.

24. John Rae, *Conscience and Politics: The British Government and the Conscientious Objector to Military Service, 1916–1919* (London: Oxford Univ. Press, 1970), 71. For an authoritative account of Bloomsbury's response to the war, see Quentin Bell, "Bloomsbury and 'the Vulgar Passions,'" *Critical Inquiry* 6 (1979): 242–48.

25. Leonard Woolf, *Beginning Again*, 186.

26. Winifred Holtby, *Virginia Woolf* (London: Wishart, 1932), 82.

27. [Siegfried Sassoon], *Memoirs of a Fox-Hunting Man* (London: Faber and Gwyer, 1928), 335.

28. Robert Graves, *Good-bye to All That* (London: Jonathan Cape, 1929), 441.

29. Richard Aldington, *Death of a Hero: A Novel* (London: Chatto and Windus, 1929), 31.

30. R. C. Sherriff, *Journey's End* (London: Victor Gollancz, 1929), 52.

31. Vera Brittain, *Testament of Youth: An Autobiographical Study of the Years 1900–1925* (London: Victor Gollancz, 1933), 167, 144.

32. Ibid., 450.

33. Martin Ceadel, *Pacifism in Britain, 1914–1945: The Defining of a Faith* (Oxford: Clarendon, 1980), 127, 131.

34. H. R. L. Sheppard, *We Say "No": The Plain Man's Guide to Pacifism* (London: John Murray, 1935), 141, 153.

35. A. A. Milne, *Peace with Honour: An Enquiry into the War Convention* (London: Methuen, 1934), 8.

36. E. M. Forster to Virginia Woolf, 6 June 1935, Berg Collection, New York Public Library. Both errors are corrected by Forster, the first with an exclamation point that makes it clear he knew what he had done.

37. Stephen Spender, *World Within World* (London: Hamish Hamilton, 1951), 154.

38. Benito Mussolini, *The Political and Social Doctrine of Fascism*, trans. Jane Soames (London: Hogarth, 1933), 11.

39. Bertrand Russell, *Autobiography* (London: George Allen and Unwin, 1968), II, 191.

40. Leonard Woolf, *Downhill All the Way: An Autobiography of the Years 1919–1939* (London: Hogarth, 1967), 243.

41. Quoted in Ceadel, 277.

42. Leonard Woolf, *Downhill All the Way*, 225.

43. A. A. Milne, *War with Honour* (London: Macmillan, 1940), 16–17.

44. Quoted in Vera Brittain, *Testament of Experience: An Autobiographical Story of the Years 1925–1950* (London: Victor Gollancz, 1957), 217.

45. Leonard Woolf, *The Journey Not the Arrival Matters: An Autobiography of the Years 1939–1969* (London: Hogarth, 1969), 46. And see the 15 May 1940 entry in Virginia Woolf's diary (*D*, V, 284).

46. David Garnett, *The Flowers of the Forest, Being Volume Two of The Golden Echo* (London: Chatto and Windus, 1955), 104. Duncan Grant to John Rae, 20 March 1965, in Dr. Rae's possession.

47. Forster, "Three Anti-Nazi Broadcasts," *Two Cheers for Democracy*, 43.

48. *Die Sonderfahndungsliste G. B.*, 222, Hoover Institution Archives, Stanford University. The list was found after the war by Allied investigators. I am grateful to Peter Stansky for calling it to my attention. See also Leonard Woolf, *The Journey Not the Arrival Matters*, 46.

49. Brittain, *Testament of Experience*, 282. She also describes, with more solid evidence, the war-induced suicide in November 1939 of the "lifelong peace-worker" Helena Swanwick (226).

50. Octavia Wilberforce to Elizabeth Robins, 28 March 1941, 29 March 1941, Monk's House Papers, Univ. of Sussex Library.

51. Naremore, 236–37.

52. Mühlmann, XIII, 847.

53. Tolstoy's major pacifist works, *The Kingdom of God Is Within You* (1893) and *The Law of Love and the Law of Violence* (1909), are included in Leo Tolstoy, *The Kingdom of God and Peace Essays*, trans. Aylmer Maude (London: Oxford Univ. Press, 1935).

54. Sheppard, 54.

55. George Lansbury, *My Quest for Peace* (London: Michael Joseph, 1938), 13.

56. M. K. Gandhi, *Non-Violence in Peace and War* (Ahmedabad: Navajivan Publishing House, 1962), I, 120, 176–77.

57. E. M. Forster, *Goldsworthy Lowes Dickinson* (London: Edward Arnold, 1934), 163.

58. David A. Martin, *Pacifism: An Historical and Sociological Study* (London: Routledge and Kegan Paul, 1965), 98.

59. Quoted in *The Intelligent Man's Way to Prevent War*, ed. Leonard Woolf (London: Victor Gollancz, 1933), 558.

60. See, for example, Aldous Huxley, *Ends and Means: An Enquiry into the Nature of Ideals and into the Methods Employed for Their Realization* (London: Chatto and Windus, 1937), 109.

61. Leonard Woolf, *The Journey Not the Arrival Matters*, 158.

62. Leonard Woolf, "Introduction," *The Framework of a Lasting Peace* (London: George Allen and Unwin, 1917), 10.

63. Leonard Woolf, *Downhill All the Way*, 198. This approach to war prevention was influenced not only by Leonard Woolf's Cambridge mentors, Dickinson and G. E. Moore, but also by Norman Angell's important book *The Great Illusion*. The power that will eventually master the world, Angell predicts, will be "the force of intelligence, character, and rationalism" (212). Leonard Woolf acknowledges his debt to Angell in *Beginning Again*, 223.

64. John Maynard Keynes, "My Early Beliefs," *Two Memoirs* (London: Rupert Hart-Davis, 1949), 98–100. Keynes's essay is reprinted in *The Bloomsbury Group: A Collection of Memoirs, Commentary and Criticism*, ed. S. P. Rosenbaum (Toronto: Univ. of Toronto Press, 1975), 48–64.

65. The book was edited by John Rickman and designed for a more general audience than the editions of Freud's individual works the press had been publishing since 1922.

66. Freud, "Thoughts for the Times on War and Death," *Standard Edition*, XIV, 299.

67. Freud, *Civilization and Its Discontents*, XXI, 111–12.

68. See Virginia Woolf, Holograph Reading Notes, XXI, 4–6, Berg Collection, New York Public Library.

69. Ibid., XXI, 6.

70. [Siegfried Sassoon], *Memoirs of an Infantry Officer* (London: Faber and Faber, 1930), 308.

71. Siegfried Sassoon, *Sherston's Progress* (London: Faber and Faber, 1936), 58, 74.

72. Gandhi, I, 64.

73. Richard B. Gregg, *The Power of Non-Violence* (London: George Routledge and Sons, 1935), 94, 97, 93.

74. Monk's House Papers B 16:f, Univ. of Sussex Library. Brenda

Silver provides a detailed summary of the contents of these volumes in her *Virginia Woolf's Reading Notebooks* (Princeton: Princeton Univ. Press, 1983), 255–314. See also her comments in the introduction, 22–24.

75. Brittain, *Testament of Experience*, 77.

76. *The Letters of Vita Sackville-West to Virginia Woolf*, ed. Louise DeSalvo and Mitchell A. Leaska (New York: William Morrow, 1985), 415. One significant exception to such support for war among British women was the Women's Cooperative Guild, with which Woolf had long been associated. For a study of the W.C.G.'s "stubborn and consistent opposition to the use of force," see Naomi Black's "Virginia Woolf and the Women's Movement," in *Virginia Woolf: A Feminist Slant*, ed. Jane Marcus (Lincoln: Univ. of Nebraska Press, 1983), 180–97. There are indications, however, that Woolf could no longer take the optimism of the W.C.G. seriously by the 1930s. See the highly critical diary entry (20 June 1933) in which she describes the speeches at the W.C.G. Jubilee as "wind blown, gaseous": "they say things that arent true: they say we are on the brink of a new world" (*D*, IV, 165).

CHAPTER 11

1. E. M. Forster, *Two Cheers for Democracy* (New York: Harcourt, Brace, 1951), 21.

2. F. R. Leavis, "After 'To the Lighthouse,'" *Scrutiny* 10 (1942): 296.

3. Werner J. Deiman, "History, Pattern, and Continuity in Virginia Woolf," *Contemporary Literature* 15 (1974): 56. Leonard Woolf clearly saw the connection between the novel and the war: "The theme of it—perhaps one might say the hero of this novel—is England and the pageant of English history, and, though the war itself is not referred to except once obliquely in the roar of a flight of planes over the garden, it is, as it were, a background or backcloth to the history and the pageant" (Leonard Woolf, script for BBC broadcast on Virginia Woolf, 20 June 1945, Leonard Woolf Papers, I R, Univ. of Sussex Library).

4. Georg Lukács, *The Historical Novel*, trans. Hannah and Stanley Mitchell (Boston: Beacon, 1963), 41.

5. E. M. Forster, *Howards End, The Abinger Edition of E. M. Forster* (London: Edward Arnold, 1973), 340.

6. John Maynard Keynes, "My Early Beliefs," *Two Memoirs* (London: Rupert Hart-Davis, 1949), 99–101.

7. Leonard Woolf, *Downhill All the Way: An Autobiography of the Years 1919–1939* (London: Hogarth, 1970), 9, 48.

8. N. G. Annan, "The Intellectual Aristocracy," in *Studies in Social*

History: A Tribute to G. M. Trevelyan, ed. J. H. Plumb (London: Longmans, Green, 1955), 250.

9. Virginia Woolf, "London in War," Monk's House Papers A 20:5, Univ. of Sussex Library.

10. An earlier version of the ending emphasizes the aggressive anger even more strongly. Its last sentences read: "Then, the rage which they had suppressed all day burst out. It was their part—⟨to tear each other asunder,⟩—to fight" (Virginia Woolf, *Pointz Hall: The Earlier and Later Typescripts of "Between the Acts,"* ed. Mitchell A. Leaska [New York: University Publications, 1983], 188).

11. Renée Watkins, "Survival in Discontinuity: Virginia Woolf's *Between the Acts,*" *Massachusetts Review* 10 (1969): 358.

12. E. M. Forster, *England's Pleasant Land* (London: Hogarth, 1940), p. 18.

13. *The Collected Essays, Journalism and Letters of George Orwell,* ed. Sonia Orwell and Ian Angus (London: Secker and Warburg, 1968), I, 535.

14. For example, Avrom Fleishman sees the book as an expression of Woolf's "faith in the collective imagination of mankind to create a harmonious consciousness—which we may call a vital culture—out of its members' disparate private experience" (*The English Historical Novel: Walter Scott to Virginia Woolf* [Baltimore: Johns Hopkins Univ. Press, 1971], 251).

15. Robert Penn Warren, "Pure and Impure Poetry," *Selected Essays* (New York: Random House, 1958), 16.

16. This is also J. Hillis Miller's conclusion: "It seems as though Woolf may be putting in question, in this last work, the ability of art to create an other than factitious stay against fragmentation" (*Fiction and Repetition: Seven English Novels* [Cambridge: Harvard Univ. Press, 1982], 221).

17. Virginia Woolf, *Pointz Hall,* 470.

18. For a fuller discussion of the literary quotations in *Between the Acts,* see Nancy Topping Bazin, *Virginia Woolf and the Androgynous Vision* (New Brunswick: Rutgers Univ. Press, 1973), 210–21.

19. W. H. Mellers, "Virginia Woolf: The Last Phase," *Kenyon Review* 4 (1942): 386.

20. R. L. Chambers, *The Novels of Virginia Woolf* (Edinburgh: Oliver and Boyd, 1947), 50.

21. For example, Marilyn Zorn writes that "the Pageant acts for the novel as a truly ritualistic experience, as a vehicle for releasing the individual from the burden of his aloneness, his absorption in the ego and time, and his subjection to change" ("The Pageant in *Between the Acts,*" *Modern Fiction Studies* 2 [1956], 32).

22. Arthur O. Lovejoy and George Boas, *Primitivism and Related Ideas in Antiquity* (New York: Octagon, 1965), 3.

23. Virginia Woolf, "Anon," ed. Brenda Silver, *Twentieth Century Literature* 25 (1979): 397.

24. Stuart Hampshire, "Virginia Woolf," *Modern Writers and Other Essays* (London: Chatto and Windus, 1969), 46.

25. "To Marguerite—Continued," *The Poems of Matthew Arnold*, ed. Kenneth Allott (London: Longmans, Green, 1965), 125.

Epilogue

1. Leonard Woolf, *Sowing: An Autobiography of the Years 1880–1904* (London: Hogarth, 1970), 152.

2. "'Anon' and 'The Reader': Virginia Woolf's Last Essays," ed. Brenda Silver, *Twentieth Century Literature* 25 (1979): 375. As Silver points out in her introduction, "Woolf's inability to see a transition from present to future, connected as it is to the larger question of historical continuity, surfaces in her struggle to shape her work" (359).

Index

Compositor:	G&S Typesetters, Inc.
Text:	10/12 Palatino
Display:	Palatino
Printer:	Murray Printing Co.
Binder:	Murray Printing Co.